Luminos is the Open Access monograph publishing program from UC Press. Luminos provides a framework for preserving and reinvigorating monograph publishing for the future and increases the reach and visibility of important scholarly work. Titles published in the UC Press Luminos model are published with the same high standards for selection, peer review, production, and marketing as those in our traditional program. www.luminosoa.org

THE BERKELEY SERIES IN POSTCLASSICAL ISLAMIC SCHOLARSHIP

SERIES EDITORS
Asad Q. Ahmed, University of California, Berkeley
Margaret Larkin, University of California, Berkeley

1. *The Light of the World: Astronomy in al-Andalus,* by Joseph Ibn Naḥmias and edited, translated, and with a commentary by Robert G. Morrison

2. *Language between God and the Poets: Maʿnā in the Eleventh Century,* by Alexander Key

3. *Reason and Revelation in Byzantine Antioch: The Christian Translation Program of Abdallah ibn-al-Faḍl,* by Alexandre M. Roberts

4. *Avicenna's Theory of Science: Logic, Metaphysics, Epistemology,* by Riccardo Strobino

5. *Palimpsests of Themselves: Logic and Commentary in Postclassical Muslim South Asia,* by Asad Q. Ahmed

6. *Being Another Way: The Copula and Arabic Philosophy of Language, 900–1500,* by Dustin D. Klinger

Being Another Way

Being Another Way

The Copula and Arabic Philosophy of Language, 900–1500

Dustin D. Klinger

UNIVERSITY OF CALIFORNIA PRESS

University of California Press
Oakland, California

Suggested citation: Klinger, D. D. *Being Another Way: The Copula and Arabic Philosophy of Language, 900–1500*. Oakland: University of California Press, 2024. DOI: https://doi.org/10.1525/luminos.201

Cataloging-in-Publication Data is on file at the Library of Congress.

ISBN 978-0-520-40163-1 (pbk.)
ISBN 978-0-520-40164-8 (ebook)

32 31 30 29 28 27 26 25 24
10 9 8 7 6 5 4 3 2 1

For Noor and Irfaan

CONTENTS

MAP

FIGURES

ACKNOWLEDGMENTS

My research on the copula and the analysis of propositions in Arabic logic began in the context of a seminar on Aristotle's *De interpretatione* and its Greek and Arabic commentaries. Rusty Jones and Khaled El-Rouayheb jointly ran the seminar at Harvard in 2017, and Jacob Rosen participated. I thank all participants for this stimulating teaching event and the discussions inside and outside the classroom. Since then, I have incurred the debt of many people whom I cannot all mention here. I hope they will know that they are meant.

My special thanks are due to Khaled El-Rouayheb from the Harvard Department of Near Eastern Languages and Civilizations, Jacob Rosen from the Harvard Philosophy Department, Riccardo Strobino of Tufts, and Tony Street of Cambridge, for their support and valuable criticism. Without Tony's intellectual candor and indefatigable humor, turning the dissertation into a readable book would have been indefinitely harder. Rob Wisnovsky of McGill has been an inspiring interlocutor since my first year at Harvard, even before I had begun the project in earnest, and he has been extraordinarily helpful with aiding me to get access to manuscripts as travelling became restricted due to the pandemic. I also would like to thank Shady Nasser of Harvard, from whom I have learned much about early Arabic literary criticism and the Arabic grammatical tradition.

I warmly thank the editors of *Nazariyat: Journal for the History of Islamic Philosophy and Sciences* for granting me permission to reuse in slightly modified form, on pages 145–151, some of the material from an article titled "A New Take on Semantics, Syntax, and the Copula: Note on Quṭb al-Dīn al-Rāzī al-Taḥtānī's Analysis of Atomic Propositions in the *Lawāmiʿ al-asrār*" (DOI: https://dx.doi.org/10.12658 /Nazariyat.5.2.M0073en), which I had previously published in their journal (Klinger, 2019).

Research for this project was made possible by several grants and fellowships. In the summer of 2019, the Fondation Hardt pour l'étude de l'Antiquité classique in Switzerland kindly awarded me a research scholarship to use their library and stay on their wonderful premises in Vandœuvres, where I worked on the material now presented in chapter 1.

Most of the manuscript research for chapters 5–8 was made possible by a Dissertation Research Fellowship awarded by the Anadolu Medeniyetleri Araştırma Merkezi (ANAMED) of Koç University in Istanbul during the academic year 2019–2020. I am grateful for this opportunity, and thankful for everything I learned from conversations with other ANAMED fellows. I would like to especially thank the staff of Süleymaniye Yazma Eser Kütüphanesi and of Hacı Selimağa Yazma Eser Kütüphanesi for their kind and knowledgeable help with locating and retrieving manuscripts. Other research trips to Tunis, Tehran, and Cairo were made possible by grants from the Center for Middle Eastern Studies and the Department of Near Eastern Languages and Civilizations at Harvard.

The superb environment at Villa I Tatti, the Harvard University Center for Italian Renaissance Studies in Florence, where I held a fellowship during the fall semester of 2020, provided ideal conditions for the writing of a good part of the dissertation. Again in 2023–2024, as an Andrew W. Mellon Fellow, I greatly benefited from the calm and convivial atmosphere at the Villa to see this book through publication.

Last but not least, I thank my family and friends for their steady encouragement and support, and most of all you, Laura. Without you I don't know what I would be. Let us together dedicate this book to Noor and Irfaan.

For the transliteration of Arabic words and names I use the Arabic ALA-LC romanization system of the Library of Congress, except that ع is transliterated as ʿ, ء as ʾ, and the final ة is left untransliterated, unless the word is part of an *iḍāfa*, so that I have *mawḍūʿ*, *asmāʾ*, and *ḥikma* (but *ḥikmat al-ʿayn*). Persian names follow the Arabic system and Persian words the Persian ALA-LC system. For Greek I use the ALA-LC "Ancient and Medieval Greek" system, without diacritics.

Dates are given according to the Gregorian calendar throughout, BCE and CE. Unless they predate the Islamic calendar or are more recent than 1850 CE, they are given according to both calendars, as (Islamic lunar/Gregorian). Publications are all listed with Gregorian dates, giving the Islamic dates in square brackets if appropriate. Publications from Iran have Islamic solar dates in square brackets but are not otherwise marked.

I have tried to work with the most reliable editions of texts. But since philological research on post-classical Islamic intellectual history is still in its infancy, this was not always satisfactory. For unedited texts I have attempted to compare several manuscripts where possible. For the relevant sections from Kātibī's commentaries on the *Kashf al-asrār* and the *Mulakhkhaṣ*, as well as those from Ḥillī's *Muḥakamāt*, I compared two early manuscripts to establish the text. Readers who wish to consult the original texts with which I have worked (in Greek, Latin, Arabic, and Persian) are referred to Klinger, 2021.

Translations are all mine unless otherwise indicated. For the translations from Fārābī's *Commentary on the De Interpretatione* I have used the excellent English translation by Zimmermann, 1981, as a working template, but freely modified it. In many cases it will be unrecognizable. I have striven to render as best as I could the idiosyncrasies of the source language when they mattered in a given context. Inevitably, such policy is sometimes at the cost of legibility. In the interest of consistency, I use three key notions throughout: "statement-word" for Greek *rhema* and Arabic *kalima*, "nexus" for Arabic *nisba*, and "copula" for *rābiṭa*.

ABBREVIATIONS

AM	*al-Alfāẓ al-mustaʿmala fī l-manṭiq*, by Fārābī, Abū Naṣr
AP	atomic proposition
APo	*Analytica Posteriora*, by Aristotle
APr	*Analytica Priora*, by Aristotle
ca.	circa (around)
CAG	*Commentaria in Aristotelem Graeca*
Cat	*Categoriae*, by Aristotle
cop	copula
d.	died
DI	*De interpretatione*, by Aristotle
Easterners	*al-Ḥikma al-mashriqiyya*, by Ibn Sīnā, Abū ʿAlī
fl.	*floruit* (flourished)
IM	*ism mushtaqq* (derived name)
Isag	*Eisagoge*, by Porphyry
Ishārāt	*Kitāb al-Ishārāt wa l-tanbihāt*, by Ibn Sīnā, Abū ʿAlī
Kashf	*Kashf al-asrār ʿan ghawāmiḍ al-afkar*, by Khūnajī, Afḍal al-Dīn
KḤ	*Kitāb al-Ḥurūf*, by Fārābī, Abū Naṣr
Lawāmiʿ	*Lawāmiʿ al-asrār fī sharḥ Maṭāliʿ al-anwār*, by Taḥtānī, Quṭb al-Dīn al-Rāzī
Maṭāliʿ	*Maṭāliʿ al-anwār*, by Urmawī, Sirāj al-Dīn
NP	noun-phrase
NW	naming-word
Poet	*Poetica*, by Aristotle
reg.	*rexit* (reigned)
Rhet	*Rhetorica*, by Aristotle
Soph. El.	*Sophistici Elenchi*, by Aristotle

SW	statement-word
Top	*Topica*, by Aristotle
VP	verbal phrase
VP$_{op}$	verbal phrase-forming operator

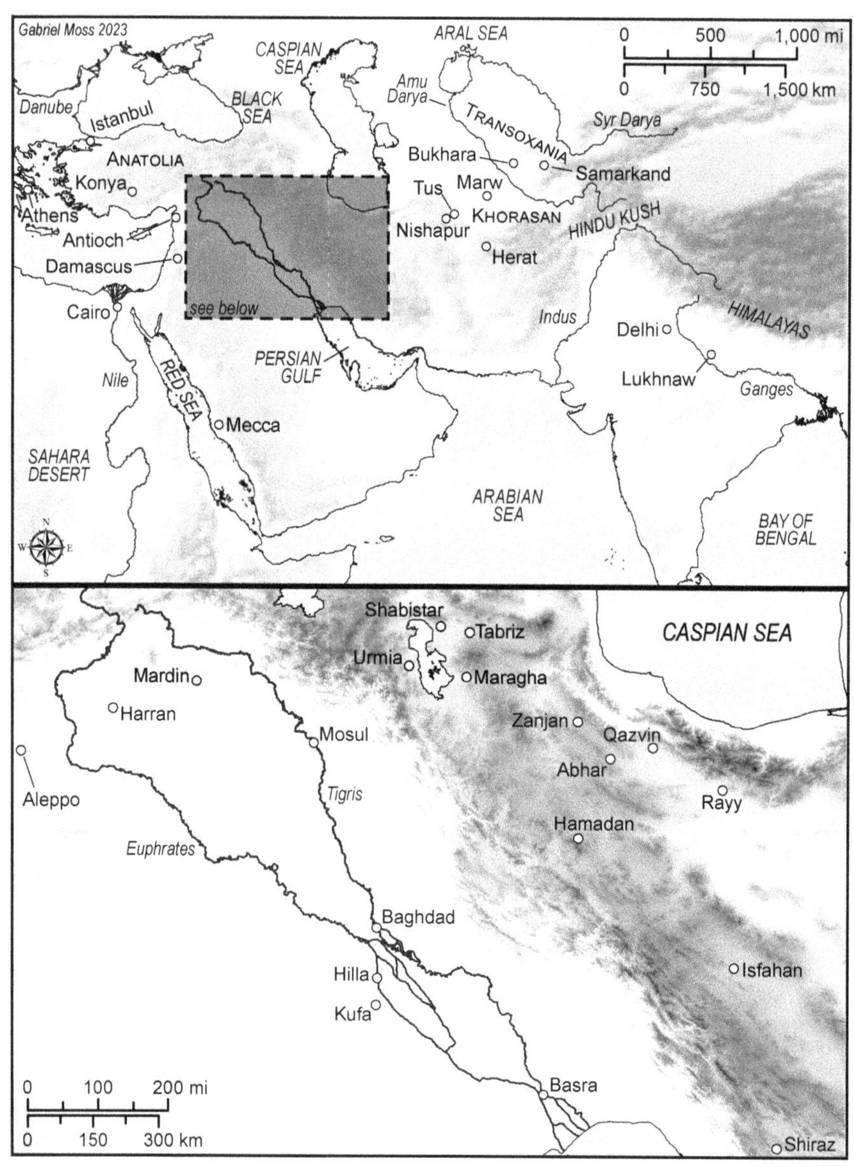

The Eastern Islamic World.

Introduction

This book is a diachronic study of discussions on a specific problem in Arabic philosophy—the problem of the semantic role of the copula—from their beginnings during the Graeco-Arabic translation movement to the early 10th/16th century in the Islamic East. The semantic role of the copula, or the problem of predication as it is sometimes called, is a fundamental issue in logic and the philosophy of language, in the philosophy of mind, and in metaphysics. (More on what the problem is about shortly.)

The fact that there is a continuous story to be told about such a fundamental philosophical problem in the Arabic tradition is itself a powerful argument against any lingering or recently revived ideas that in the post-classical period Arabic philosophy lost its intellectual vigor.[1] Following this story, the book argues that discussions about the copula contributed to a surge of interest in questions pertaining to what we today would call philosophy of language. Post-classical Arabic philosophers began to intensely discuss questions of meaning, reference, the analysis of propositions, and the relation of the problem of predication to the notions of judgment and truth.

Telling the story of the problem of predication in post-classical Arabic philosophy would have been inconceivable even two decades ago. The reasons for this have to do with three recalcitrant dogmas of Islamic studies that are entwined with the discipline's own colonialist history. The first dogma was that the "Golden Age" of Arabic philosophy ended with al-Ghazālī's (d. 505/1111) proscription of the philosophers as apostates. The second was that later Muslim clerics prohibited the study of logic. The third was that works written in the form of commentaries are unoriginal. And since most Arabic philosophical works written in the post-classical period are commentaries, this meant that most of post-classical Arabic philosophy was not worthy of being studied.

These dogmas were late modern articles of faith that conditioned the approach of orientalist Western scholars to post-Avicennan Arabic philosophy. Their role was to keep intact the idea of declining anti-rationalist and religiously oppressive Islamic societies against which the progress of an enlightened Western world would stand out in sharp-enough relief to justify its colonialist ideology. Since 2002, when Dimitri Gutas first critically assessed misguided approaches to the study of Arabic philosophy, these dogmas, too, have been exposed for what they are.[2] But the countless histories their believers have oppressed still need to be written. This book tells one such story, a small contribution to a postcolonial and more global history of philosophy.

Telling a detailed story of the problem of predication in the Arabic tradition would remain near impossible even now, were it not for the considerable work others have recently done in the study of post-classical Arabic logic. One simple reason is that the sheer amount of material, a great part of which remains unedited and housed in manuscript libraries around the globe, would be impossible to navigate for a single scholar.

But thanks to recent work especially by Asad Ahmed, Khaled El-Rouayheb, Tony Street, and Rob Wisnovsky, authors and texts that not long ago were hardly more than names in reference works or titles in manuscript catalogues have now acquired sharper contours and concrete relationships. More than anything else, this book is indebted to Khaled El-Rouayheb's *The Development of Arabic Logic*. Without the biobibliographical guide of *The Development* and its author, planning and undertaking the research trips to manuscript archives would have been impossible.

While the study of post-classical Arabic logic has advanced in great strides over the last decade, most approaches to the material have been based on specific texts or authors, or specific technical problems in syllogistic.[3] Building on this work, this book is an attempt to broaden the view and study not specific authors or texts, but a specific problem across authors, texts, time, and space: it is a *Problemgeschichte*.

In one sense, namely in the sense that there is a continuous *history* of the problem of predication to be told at all, this problem history forms the backbone of the book's overarching argument, which shows the continuity of original philosophical "research" in the Islamic East well into not only the Timurid period, but even the early Safavid period.

In another sense, namely in the sense that there is a history of this particular *problem* to be told, this problem history is not only of historical but also of philosophical interest. The Arabic philosophers surveyed in this study engaged with questions that speak to core issues in early analytic philosophy. Following their arguments allows us, so to speak, to observe *in vitro* how philosophers thought about the problem of predication from within a linguistic framework whose grammar is in some sense closer to modern logic than to Aristotelian syllogistic. To better understand what that means, it is necessary to properly introduce the copula as a philosophical problem.

THE COPULA AS A PHILOSOPHICAL PROBLEM

Donald Davidson (1917–2003), one of the most influential philosophers of the late 20th century, in his posthumously published monograph *Truth and Predication* (2005) described the problem of predication thus:

> Arabic is an economical language: a sentence can get along without an explicit verb. One can say, in effect, "Man mortal," or "Today rainy," or "John sad." This feature of Arabic recently led to a political tempest in Egypt. A book was banned because a review suggested that the author had written "The Koran bad." The words were spoken by a character in a novel by the Syrian author Haida [*sic*] Haidar, but the reviewer had omitted three little dots between the subject and the adjective. The original context had made clear that Haida [*sic*] had not intended what in English would have been supplied by the word "is." Confusion about predication can create problems; one of those problems concerns the copula or its absence.
>
> In English, "John mortal" is not a sentence. It becomes one if the word "is" is inserted between noun and adjective. This is a fact of syntax or grammar. But what is the semantic role of the copula? This question and related questions about the nature of predication have been evident since Plato. Yet despite the earnest regard which the semantics of natural languages has attracted over the years, no one who was aware of the problem has come up with a satisfactory account of predication. Or, to put the point more accurately, a satisfactory account exists, but apparently no one has noticed that this account solves the problem. [. . .]
>
> The topic should attract our attention. After all, if we do not understand predication, we do not understand how any sentence works, nor can we account for the structure of the simplest thought that is expressible in language. At one time there was much discussion of what was called the "unity of the proposition"; it is just this unity that a theory of predication must explain. The philosophy of language lacks its most important chapter without such a theory; the philosophy of mind is missing a crucial first step if it cannot describe the nature of judgment; and it is woeful if metaphysics cannot say how a substance is related to its attributes.[4]

Davidson was no Arabist, but his anecdotal observations on Arabic grammar are perhaps more apposite than he himself would have expected. The problem of predication has been in evidence since Plato. However, regarding the question of the semantic role of the copula, this is true not only for the Western philosophical tradition. It is also true, and perhaps in a far more interesting way, for the Arabic philosophical tradition. Davidson was right to point out that Arabic grammar does not require the use of a copula ("is"), and the problem of the copula or its absence has indeed created confusion. But I doubt that he imagined the severity of the confusion it caused and the extent to which it elicited philosophical discussions in the wake of the Graeco-Arabic translation movement. These discussions are the subject of the present book.

Davidson argued that there exists a solution to the problem of predication, and that it was proposed by the logician and mathematician Alfred Tarski (1901–1983). Or rather, Davidson thought that Tarski's account, when construed in the way done in *Truth and Predication*, shows that the problem as it has been conceived is a pseudo-problem rooted in an ancient mistake. But Davidson was not the first to think that the ancient problem of predication had been dissolved by a mathematician. He was the first to think that this mathematician was Tarski and not Frege, as many in the analytic tradition have thought before him. I think we do well not to see either Frege's or Davidson's proposal as the final answer to an ancient philosophical problem. And some more recent contributors would agree.[5]

I do not here intend to offer a solution. Rather, my aim is to plug a "vast historical hole" in Davidson's (or anyone's) account of the problem of predication, one that he himself acknowledged and encouraged others to fill (though he likely did not think of the medieval *Arabic* tradition).[6] Much in the optimistic spirit of *Truth and Predication*, I hope that this historical account, partial though it may be, will help to "recognize the pattern of errors into which people have been led and [to] find a reasonable position which retains much of what seemed attractive about the wrong paths while avoiding the pitfalls."[7]

The focus in this book is on chapters 2 and 3 of Aristotle's *De interpretatione* (*DI*) and their reception history. It is in these chapters that Aristotle most comprehensively discusses the simple categorical statement and its component parts, and it is primarily in their reception history—in both Greek and Arabic—that the question of the role of the copula is being raised. This choice of focus immediately brings to the fore a fundamental issue in modern scholarship on Aristotelian logic. Since the issue is so central to the history of the problem of predication, and to the history of logic itself, I better address it head-on. This will also allow me to provide a conceptual and terminological framework for the problem of predication that will be of use throughout the book.

The issue is this. The core of Aristotle's logical system, the syllogistic, is presented in the *Analytica Priora* (*APr*). What Aristotle presupposes there about how predication works seems to be different from what he states in the *DI*. To illustrate the difference, let me introduce two different proposals for the syntax of predicative sentences.

The first proposal, which I shall call the Forbidden Tree (figure 1), is the one usually associated with Aristotelian syllogistic as it developed in the Western philosophical tradition. The idea is that the most simple items that are truth-apt—which I shall call atomic propositions (AP) for short—consist of two terms (T,T*), namely a subject (S) and a predicate (P). The terms are connected (X) by a copula ("is" or "are" in English, here "cop"). The two constituent terms of a proposition belong to one and the same grammatical category. On this proposal, both terms are names, and they may switch around between subject- and predicate-position: they are homogenous and interchangeable. The syntactic role of the copula is here to take two terms and turn them into an AP. The analysis of "Socrates is wise" is represented by:

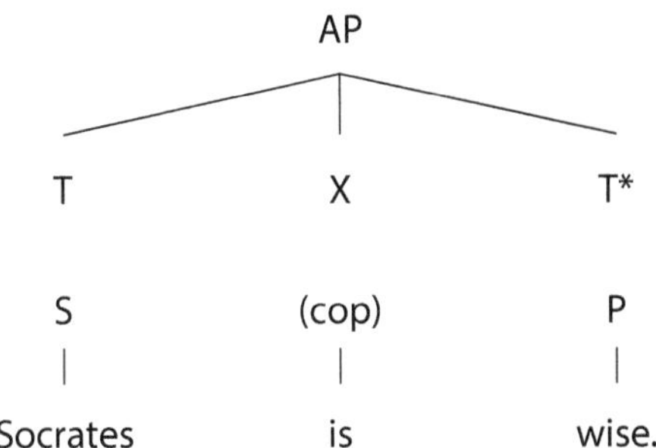

FIGURE 1. Syntactic Forbidden Tree.

The second proposal, to which I shall refer as the Tree of Life (figure 2), is the one largely embraced by modern linguists, and, notably, Fregean logic.[8] Here, an AP syntactically dissolves into a noun-phrase (NP) and a verbal phrase (VP). A VP may contain a full verb, or else it is the role of the copula to turn a NP into a VP. In fact, while the word "is" on the Forbidden Tree–proposal is an actual logical copula (syntactically taking two terms to make an AP, i.e., AP:T,T*), on this proposal there is no copula, or only what we may loosely call a grammatical copula. (I shall be using "copula" throughout to refer to a linguistic item, and generally in this loose sense, specifying in each case when I use it in a different sense.)

The word "is" here acts, syntactically, as a VP-forming operator (VP_{op}) on expressions that are NPs (VP:NP), and as such it is part of the predicate. The two constituents of a proposition belong to different grammatical categories, NP and VP, and hence they are heterogenous and not interchangeable. "Socrates is wise" is on this proposal represented by the following syntactic tree:

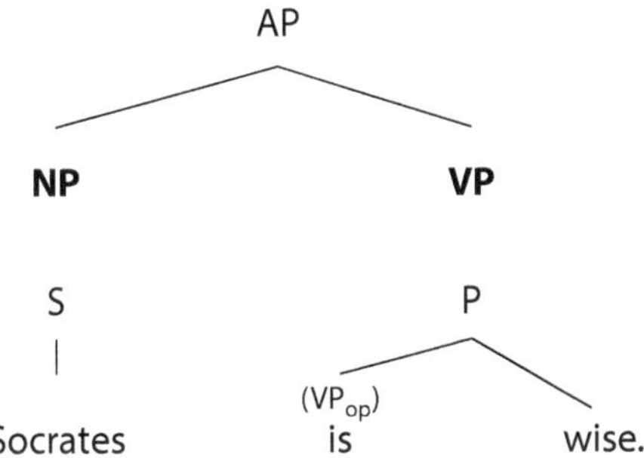

FIGURE 2. Syntactic Tree of Life.

The crucial difference between the two proposals is that on the first there is *homogeneity* between terms and hence a copula is needed to glue the terms together, whereas on the second *heterogeneity* ensures that the elements of APs stick together like the pieces of a jigsaw puzzle. There is no need for a logical copula.

The homogeneity-view of predication is presupposed by Aristotelian syllogistic, which crucially requires interchangeability. Predicate-terms need to be able to appear in the subject-position and vice versa. For example, any syllogism in the first figure requires the middle term to appear as the subject-term in the major premise and as the predicate-term in the minor premise. Take *Barbara:*

> All humans are mortal
> All Harvard professors are humans
> ∴ All Harvard professors are mortal

Were the terms not homogenous, they also would not be interchangeable, and "humans" could not appear now as a subject, now as a predicate.

It has been taken for granted not only that Aristotle's real view on predication was the one presupposed by the *APr*, but also that this was the view nearly everyone in the Aristotelian tradition adopted.[9] And it is generally assumed that *this* view was a logical blunder, ultimately defeating any "reasonable semantics of predicates."[10] The mistake, it has been maintained, was to disregard the fact that a predicate-term cannot appear in the subject-position without undergoing a change of sense.[11] This has been considered a basic syntactic mistake that ultimately explains, from a modern point of view, why Aristotelian syllogistic never got very far. It needed Frege's embracing the Tree of Life to create the possibility of introducing many-placed predicates and multiple quantification, and thus give us the far more powerful predicate calculus.[12] The homogeneity of terms was a long-lasting and fundamental, because syntactically basic, equivocation in the history of logic.

Chiefly responsible for disseminating the idea that Aristotle had made a fundamental mistake was the Oxford logician Peter Geach (1916–2013). He thought that Aristotle fatally changed his mind on the analysis of APs and that the severity of this mistake was such that it can only be compared to the original sin:

> Unfortunately, Aristotle abandoned at the same time other positions he had held in the *De interpretatione*. He lost the Platonic insight that any predicative proposition splits up into two logically heterogenous parts; instead, he treats predication as an attachment of one term (*horos*) to another term. Whereas the *rhema* was regarded as essentially predicative, "always a sign of what is said of something else," it is impossible on the new doctrine for any term to be essentially predicative; on the contrary, any term that occurs in a proposition predicatively may be made into the subject-term in another predication. I shall call this "Aristotle's thesis of interchangeability"; his adoption of it marks a transition from the original name-and-predicable theory

to a *two-term* theory. [. . .] Aristotle's going over to the two-term theory was a disaster, comparable only to the fall of Adam.[13]

Davidson agreed with Geach that the Aristotelian Forbidden Tree–view was hopelessly confused as an account of predication. And he concurred that it was not until Frege that a satisfactory solution to the problem of predication was even possible—he only denied that Frege had at the same time supplied that solution.[14] The crux of the matter is that Geach, in turn, had also pointed out that Aristotle in *DI* 1–4 presented predication in terms of the Tree of Life, clearly embracing heterogeneity. Geach assumed that Aristotle changed his mind and moved over to the homogeneity-view, which then became the prevalent view until Frege.

Yet—and the present study amply bears this out for Graeco-Arabic Aristotelianism, though it is also true for its Western counterpart[15]—the Aristotelian tradition never abandoned the *DI* as part of the *Organon* (as opposed to, e.g., the *Categories* or the *Posterior Analytics*, as was the case in later Arabic logic) and so the heterogeneity-view persisted. Anyone holding a version of Geach's view will have to explain that fact. More precisely, maintaining a version of that view would require showing how authors who clearly embrace heterogeneity in some of their writing thought (or failed to think) that this was reconcilable with the homogeneity presupposed by the syllogistic, *and* showing that they thought that the logical copula required by homogeneity ultimately superseded heterogeneity as the fundamental logical relation. This, I suppose, may be done, but it is a task that cannot be undertaken here.

Rather, the present study contributes to this issue in the scholarship on Aristotelian logic by documenting the persistence and evolution of the heterogeneity-view in the Graeco-Arabic tradition as it engaged with the first chapters of the *DI*. If seen this way, the discussions on the semantic role of the copula in the context of the *DI*—even if the homogeneity-view is rejected as a basic semantic mistake—may in principle hold in store insights relevant for the problem of predication.

"BEING" ANOTHER WAY: THE COPULA IN THE ARABIC PHILOSOPHICAL TRADITION

It might come as a surprise that a philosophical tradition whose primary language of expression does not require the use of a grammatical copula developed such an interest in the question of its semantic role. As Davidson remarked, the fact that the insertion of "is" or an equivalent between a noun and an adjective turns a succession of words into a sentence "is a fact of syntax or grammar."[16] More precisely, we should say, it is a fact of the syntax or grammar of *some* languages: for example, of Greek, Latin, Persian, German, English—but not of Arabic, or, let us say, Syriac, some Slavic languages, or some artificial languages like Frege's *Begriffsschrift*. A straightforward explanation of why discussions about the copula arose in the Arabic tradition is given by the Arabic renditions of the Greek equivalent of "is" during the Graeco-Arabic translation movement.

In Aristotle's works, and particularly in the *DI*, translators were confronted with passages in which that little word "is" (*esti*) mattered for philosophical argument or logical analysis. So they forged artificial expressions to have ready at hand a single word (rather than circumlocutions) to translate the Greek "*einai*" and its various grammatical forms. Would discussions about the role of the copula have arisen without these translations? That is of course a moot question—but I do not see why they *could not* have. The simple reason is this: there still is, in Arabic, a difference between saying "John, mortal," listing words as it were, and "John mortal," signifying what in English would be expressed by "John is mortal."

Of that difference Arabic scholars, including grammarians with no business in Aristotelian logic, were aware. And most philosophers agreed that the difference here is that in the second case but not in the first there is a relation (*nisba*, which I shall call "nexus," pl. nexūs, throughout) indicated between what "John" stands for and what "mortal" stands for. This nexus, most Arabic philosophers thought, is best signified by an artificial copula, though it may be left out as in Arabic it is implicitly understood.

So much was widely agreed. But this sounds as if Arabic philosophers took APs to be best represented by the Forbidden Tree. For saying that two terms are connected by a copula signifying the nexus between the things they stand for appears to be just another way of saying that the logical copula syntactically takes two terms to make an AP. This, however, was not the case.

From the very beginning, Arabic philosophers recognized a type of heterogeneity that was—even though purportedly Aristotelian—ultimately rooted in the grammatical structure of Semitic languages, and thus markedly different from anything in the Western tradition, as far as I can see. In Arabic, and in Semitic languages in general, most words consist of three radicals. From this trilateral root many vocables, including grammatical verbs, can be morphologically derived. Usually, the meanings of these vocables are derived from the basic semantic spectrum of the root vocable (though at times their meanings can be widely disparate). Such derived vocables were seen as *including* the signification of a nexus to a subject and as such were essentially distinct from proper names or non-derived vocables that did not include the signification of a nexus.

Much of the developments in conceptualizing the proposition and its parts in the classical period of Arabic philosophy (ca. 300–600/900–1200) was foreshadowed by the Greek commentators of late antiquity. To illustrate this continuity, we should acknowledge another syntactic tree as a third basic proposal. On this proposal "NW" is a naming-word, "SW" a statement-word, and the brackets are significant, so that there is, on a syntactic level, homogeneity between NWs and heterogeneity between NW and SW:

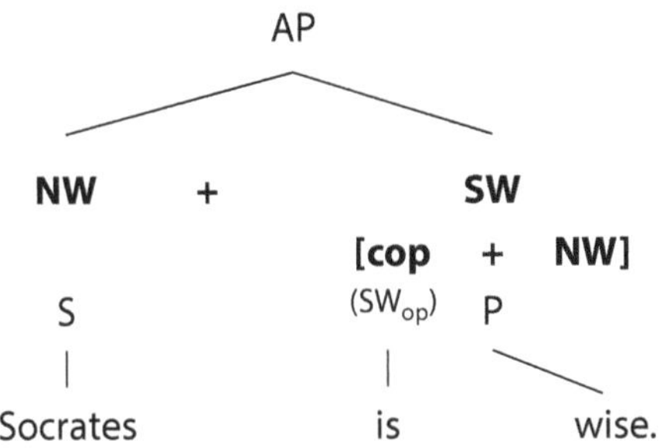

FIGURE 3. Syntactic Tree Three.

The role of "is" here is twofold. As a grammatical copula it acts as an operator taking a NW and turning it into a SW. But by signifying a relation that is irreducible in analysis, it still acts as a logical copula, taking two NWs to make an AP. This is because SWs, which can only occur in the predicate-place, are always analyzable as consisting of a copula and a NW. In other words: Only NWs can occur in the subject-place. If an NW appears in the predicate-place, it can only act as a predicate, if it is conjoined by a copula that signifies that what the NW signifies is related to what the subject signifies. The signification of this relation is always contained in SWs and may be contained in certain NWs, so that in some cases no grammatical copula needs to be expressed. Conceptually, however, the relation so signified is an irreducible element and is always part of the predicate. (Hence, it is important that the brackets are significant.) Tree Three is a hybrid of the two Trees of Paradise, and it raises various new problems—but it is, ultimately, closer to the Tree of Life, because on the syntactic deep level, the copula is part of the SW. Most of the contributions by the Greek and Arabic authors surveyed in this study, various though they are, can be made to fit this third proposal.

STRUCTURE OF THE BOOK

The book consists of two parts. The first part deals with the Graeco-Arabic transformation of the problem of predication and the subsequent Arabic appropriation of this heritage by Fārābī and Avicenna, spanning the so-called classical period (roughly 300/900–600/1200). The second part covers the post-classical period (roughly 600/1200–900/1500) and follows the tradition from Baghdād and Khurāsān to the Persian heartland, then to Samarqand, and eventually to Shīrāz, with a look ahead to the Indo-Muslim tradition in Mughal India.

This structure reflects the book's overall argument that Arabic philosophy, of which logic became an integral part, did not degenerate after the 6th/12th century. To the contrary, the evidence suggests that instead of being a mere coda to the great philosophers of the classical period, we should see the early post-classical period as an overture to a prolific 8th/14th century in which Arabic logic fully emancipated itself from its Greek roots. In the period leading up to the 10th/16th century, it came to include, in conversation with developments in adjacent scientific disciplines, rigorous research in what we would call philosophy of language.

Each part has a different character owing to the fact that there is plenty of scholarship on Aristotle and the classical Arabic philosophers treated in the first part, but very little on most of the post-classical authors treated in the second. While authors surveyed in the first part hardly need introduction, in the second part I have tried to give the reader a sense of the lives and works of the characters whose contributions I discuss. I have engaged more broadly with scholarship in the first part, whereas in the second part I have often found myself on new territory. Another difference is that the source texts in part 1 are all direct or indirect comments on the *DI*. In part 2 this was no longer possible. There, setting out from the commentaries on Avicenna's *Ishārāt* III.7, I follow a more labyrinthine path through the intertextual web of handbooks, philosophical summae, and their commentaries, glosses, and superglosses.

In both parts I have striven to contextualize the discussions on the problem of predication within larger developments. In the first part I highlight the importance of the historical circumstances (chapter 2) and cross-cultural translation (chapter 3) for the appropriation of Greek logic. The decisive role Avicenna played in the emancipation of Arabic logic from the Greek textual tradition is emphasized in chapter 4. In the second part, larger developments that are both reflected by and visibly shaped the discussions on the problem of predication are the critical attitude first toward Avicenna (chapter 5), and then toward Rāzī (chapter 6). Further, the need for logic handbooks to be used in madrasa teaching (chapters 6 and 7) and the emergence of formal disputation theory (chapter 7) decisively shaped new forms of philosophical argumentation within the genre of the commentary. Finally, developments in other linguistic disciplines, especially in rhetoric and semantics and in the new science of ʿilm al-waḍʿ, had a palpable impact on the reconceptualization of the problem of predication (chapter 8). While these developments are interwoven with the narrative of the individual chapters, the guiding thread has been the development of the discussions on the problem of predication.

In chapter 1 a close reading of Aristotle's *DI* 2–3 provides the Greek background to the Arabic appropriation of the problem of predication. Revisiting Geach's Myth of Adam's Fall, the chapter shows how the question of the semantic role of the copula first emerged when Aristotle's Greek commentators, who attempted a coherent interpretation of the *Organon*, were forced to make sense of apparently contradictory passages on the role of the word "is" in predication.

Chapter 2 supplies the historical background to the translation and appropriation of the Greek tradition by the first Arabic philosophers. Historical circumstances required Fārābī to make Greek logic understandable, and palatable, to a hyper-critical audience that insisted that the sole route to knowledge and understanding was Arabic grammar. Fārābī argued that language is historically constructed in such a way that it is inherently ambiguous. He conceived of his own philosophical project as being concerned with disambiguating language by studying utterances insofar as they signify meanings. Fārābī thinks that that is especially what the *DI* does.

Chapter 3 presents Fārābī's novel reading of the analysis of atomic propositions in his commentary on the *DI*. Applying the theory of etymological word formation from Arabic grammar to Aristotle's notion of paronymy, Fārābī stipulates syntactic rules based on a type of heterogeneity between nouns that are etymologically derived and nouns that are not. Further, he holds that categorical statements need a copula. For lack of an Arabic word, he advises to use "*mawjūd*" (literally, is found). Contrary to its grammatical form, Fārābī considered "*mawjūd*" a logical particle, signifying a second-order concept, namely that of a predicative function.

Chapter 4 discusses Avicenna's take on the linguistic section of the *DI* in the *Shifā'*, where he further develops Fārābī's theory of derived names by systematically integrating two different types of *maṣādir* (verbal nouns). Then two passages from his later works are briefly introduced: they appear to be contradictory and were to catch the attention of Fakhr al-Dīn al-Rāzī, with whose challenge to Avicenna part 2 begins.

Chapter 5 introduces, in the context of the early reception of Avicenna, two figures whom Ibn Khaldūn called the first of the "later logicians." Rāzī challenged Avicenna's position that the copula "*huwa*" is needed to signify the nexus of the meaning of the predicate to the meaning of the subject. According to Rāzī, the meaning of a derived name includes the nexus and the use of "*huwa*" would amount to a useless repetition. Khūnajī criticizes Rāzī, arguing that what is signified by "*huwa*" is not the same as what is included in the signification of a derived name.

Chapter 6 charts how Rāzī's and Khūnajī's critical attitude shaped a scholarly praxis among a group of logicians connected to the Marāgha observatory that led to a dramatic increase in the output of logical works. Ṭūsī criticized Rāzī's Repetition Argument, and Abharī, Kātibī, and Urmawī contributed to a deepening of the discussions on the copula, shifting the focus to questions about the right conception of the nexus in light of modality and conversion.

Chapter 7 looks at three scholars of the post-Marāgha generation: Samarqandī, Ḥillī, and Taḥtānī. Samarqandī is discussed as a paradigmatic case for the confluence of new dialectical theories and logical research. Ḥillī and Taḥtānī authored some of the most influential commentaries on the works of the Marāgha generation, paving the way for an intensification of logical research. Taḥtānī developed a universal notion of unsaturatedness, rejecting the copula.

Chapter 8 looks at how the debates further developed in Samarqand, Shīrāz, and later Mughal India. Characteristic of these discussions is the increasing influence of semantic theories from rhetoric (*balāgha*) and the new science of imposition (*ʿilm al-waḍʿ*). The rejection of doctrines on the copula, now seen as a superfluous remnant that originated with the Arabic translations of Aristotle's Greek, finds a full expression in Taftāzānī, who remarkably turns back to Fārābī to understand the origins of those doctrines. Jurjānī, who weaves together the threads of semantic theories from *balāgha* and *ʿilm al-waḍʿ*, replaces the old doctrines with a truly Arabic account of the semantic role of the copula. Mediated by Dawānī, the Mughal tradition partly reverted to Avicennan doctrines. However, Mughal authors tended to treat the problem in prominent places of logical works, discussing it in connection with the nature of judgment (*ḥukm*).

PART ONE

Revisiting the Myth of Adam's Fall

*The Graeco-Arabic Translation Movement
and the Transformation of the Copula (900–1200)*

1

Setting the Scene

The Copula, Aristotle, and the Ancients

A copula, like the little word "is," seems to be responsible for turning a mere list of words, like "Socrates, wise," into a sentence of which we can say that it is true or false. But when I say "Socrates is wise," the copula plays an additional role. For it not only says that Socrates is wise, but also shows—if uttered in earnest—that I believe that what I say is true. The copula appears to have yet another more basic function. It relates two things in such a way that they first unite as an item that can be judged true or false. The insertion of "is" into a mere list of words thus has at least a threefold function. It relates two things so that they become an item. It expresses that this item is true. And it shows that the speaker believes it is true.

How is it, then, that some languages like Arabic do not have a copula? Can speakers of those languages not relate things and express true sentences or judgments? Of course they can. If you tell me, in Arabic and without using a copula, that Socrates is wise, I understand the exact same thing as I do from the English sentence. But how can this be? This is one of the puzzles that exercised medieval Arabic philosophers.

The problem of the semantic role of the copula cuts deeper, however. Even in the basic relating function, the copula is ambiguous. It would seem that "is" means different things in "Octavian is Augustus," "Socrates is wise," "There is a God," and "A whale is a mammal." Octavian and Augustus are related insofar as they are the *same* person. Socrates and wisdom are related insofar as Socrates *has* wisdom. God is strictly speaking not related to anything: God is simply said to *exist*. And whales are related to mammals insofar as they share characteristics with other animals, like humans, that allow them to be *classified* together as mammals. This ambiguity is problematic, because what appear to be formally similar statements are in fact not. And often, what looks like a valid inference is in fact not.

Relating two things and affirming their relation are operations of our mind. Expressing that relation is a function of our language. In any sentence "A is B" that I utter, it would seem that the copula "is" plays this multifaceted role. Because the relating function that is absolutely basic to our thought and language use is so hopelessly ambiguous, logicians have been trying to hold the ambiguity of the copula in check. In doing so, they often have had to venture into fundamental discussions about the nature of our thought, of truth, and of judgment. To give an account of that relating function does not actually require that one's language customarily uses a copula. The same mental operation is required to affirm a sentence in Arabic.

The philosophical construal of this basic relation function has a long history. In fact, it has two histories: one in the Latinate-European tradition, the other in the Arabic tradition. Both histories share the same beginning in the logical writings of Aristotle. Both underwent a translation process from Greek. But while the Latinate tradition comprised only Indo-European languages with largely similar grammatical structures, the Arabic tradition had to translate Aristotle's Greek logic into a language with a radically different structure. Among other things, Arabic simply does not use a copula in present-tense statements.

It is virtually impossible to understand the medieval Arabic discussions on the copula without considering the—sometimes-haphazard—transmission of ideas in the Aristotelian tradition. The Arabic reception of Aristotle was to a large extent mediated by the Greek commentators. What the early translator-philosophers in 2nd/8th-century Baghdād understood from Aristotle's texts was however not only prefigured by the commentators' interpretations. It was also shaped by the process of translation and acculturation. Chapter 2 provides the historical context for this process of translation and acculturation. This chapter makes brief reference to the problem of the semantic role of the copula in the Western tradition, specifically Geach's myth of Aristotle's fall. The proposal is to revisit the shared Aristotelian beginning of the two histories and then tell, for the first time, the Arabic history.

THE MYTH OF ADAM'S FALL

Geach's myth of Aristotle's fall has remained an influential position among historians of logic.[1] Why was the step from the Tree of Life in the *DI* to the Forbidden Tree in the *APr* so calamitous? According to Geach, the investiture of the copula led medieval Latin logicians first to construe its semantic role as a sign of identity, and later as a sign now signifying class-membership, now class-inclusion.

On this view, the terms had to denote classes, which ultimately led to the doctrine of distribution, according to which "some men" refers to some part of the class of men.[2] Such views wreak havoc on any semantic theory, for you never know which part of a class is being meant. Consider:

> Some men are philosophers
> All philosophers can control their temper
> ∴ Some men can control their temper

And:

> Some men smoke hashish
> Some men study logic
> ∴ Some men who study logic smoke hashish[3]

If "some men" denotes a part of the class of men, in the first example you need to establish a rule that "some men" refers to the same individuals in both cases for it to be formally valid.[4] If you apply that rule to the second example, however, that will be formally valid, too, and this is better avoided.[5] Chiefly responsible for this malaise was, in Geach's view, the copula:

> For the newer books tell us that "is" means different things in "Socrates is a philoso-pher" and "Every logician is a philosopher"; that the first "is" is a copula of class-membership and the second a copula of class-inclusion. Of course, this ambiguity is mere illusion; the predicable expression "is a philosopher" means exactly the same in both propositions, just as "errs sometimes" means exactly the same in "Socrates errs sometimes" and in "Every logician errs sometimes"; and here there is no copula to pin the ambiguity upon. The whole problem comes about because of the successive corruptions of logic that I have been describing.[6]

However, according to Geach, "thanks to Russell and Frege, most of the logical insights that were lost by Aristotle's Fall have been recovered."[7] What Frege recovered was the insight that the simplest statements consist of two heterogenous parts with no need for a copula. Frege's revolutionary idea was that the form of a proposition is best captured by the mathematical notion of a function.

For Frege, "the fundamental logical relation [was] that of an object falling under a concept."[8] On that view, a proposition is a function of its constituents, which are of two types: objects and concepts. The sense of a proposition is the objective thought expressed by it. Its reference is its truth-value. APs are thus written as the function

$F(a)$

where "$F(\ )$" stands for an unsaturated concept-expression (*Begriffswort*) and "a" for a saturated object-expression (*Eigenname*) referring to an object. Its sense is that a is F, and its reference is the True, iff a falls under the concept F.[9] Crucially, no *Eigenname* can be a *Begriffswort* and *vice versa*, because the *Begriffswort* is essentially unsaturated and is only completed by a *Eigenname*.

This analysis presupposes the Tree of Life, for concept-expressions will always be VPs acting as predicates, either containing a full verb or a grammatical copula. The logical copula is thus eliminated from logical analysis. Predication is explained in terms of the unsaturatedness of concepts. The hopeless ambiguity of the Aristotelian copula could in Frege's system be neatly captured by the notations for identity, predication, existence, and class-membership (= , Fx, ∃x, Fx⊃Gx).[10]

One great advantage of Frege's account was that the heterogeneity view supposedly guaranteed the unity of the proposition. For on the homogeneity view, a copula is needed to glue together two terms. But what is gluing together the copula and the term? Once the copula is understood as signifying a real relation, an infinite regress will turn any such theory into a metaphysical Hydra.[11] However, Frege's account runs into difficulties, too. Since for Frege every expression that linguistically functions as a singular term refers to an object (in a true sentence), no concept can be referred to by a singular term. So, for example, "the concept horse" cannot refer to what it appears to refer to.[12] The fundamental logical distinction on which Frege's theory rests is one that cannot be stated from within Frege's theory without incurring a paradox.[13]

Frege thinks that you may give up on the concept-object distinction, but as soon as you give up heterogeneity, the unity of the proposition problem arises.[14] But why should the predicate be unsaturated, and not the subject, or indeed the copula?[15] Oscillating between heterogeneity and homogeneity, thinkers in the Arabic tradition developed innovative accounts of the semantic role of the copula to address the problem of the unity of the proposition.

For the Graeco-Arabic Tree Three is a hybrid of the Forbidden Tree and the Fregean Tree of Life.[16] On the Arabic theory, derived names that include the signification of the nexus to a subject are essentially like unsaturated concept-expressions. If in Arabic there is no copula to pin the ambiguity upon, were Arabic logicians saved from the successive corruptions of logic Geach described? Yes and no. They had a clear sense that attributes and their expressions are distinct from substances and their expressions. But it is of course true that traditional logic East or West, at least until in the wake of George Boole (1815–1864) the project of mathematizing logic began in earnest, never abandoned the Aristotelian syllogistic that presupposed homogeneity.[17]

It is however also true that the Aristotelian *Organon* on which traditional logic is based is "the ricketiest of constructions."[18] While the *APr* certainly occupied a central position in it, the *DI* has likewise been an integral part. Yet we know next to nothing about the relative genesis and intended use of the short texts (lecture notes?) that came to make up the *Organon*.[19] What is clear, however, is that they were never intended to be what they became.[20] The later traditional ordering of those texts under the unifying title of *Organon* (Tool) began with the *Categoriae* (*Cat*), *DI*, and *APr*, as dealing with terms, propositions, and syllogisms in an ascending order of complexity. These were followed by the *Analytica Posteriora* (*APo*), *Topica, Sophistici Elenchi*, as treating the different kinds of syllogisms. This ordering entirely obscured several important independencies between these texts. At no point do the syllogistic texts presuppose the *Cat* or the *DI* in such a way that they could be systematically integrated. Nor does any other text presuppose the *Cat* in any way whatsoever.[21]

Traditional logic was the product of treating the chance survivals of Aristotle's logical writings as a coherent and systematically structured whole that was to serve as a pedagogically organized textbook for the budding philosopher to acquire the "tool" for correct reasoning.[22] But there was no such whole intended for those texts. And, in fact, we may even question whether the parts of the respective texts were supposed to be composed in the way they have come down to us. For chapters 1–4 of the *DI*, the chapters we are primarily concerned with, Montanari has coined the sub-title *"sezione linguistica"* and suggested that they belong to a different textual stratum than the rest of the *DI*.[23]

From what we know about the texts of the *Organon*, we may make here two observations. As far as Geach's accusation regarding Aristotle's fatal change of mind is concerned: it is at least conceivable that Aristotle wrote the *DI* after the *APr*, and there is no hard and fast evidence to tell one way or the other. Concerning the history of Aristotelian logic: if the homogeneity of the *APr* was part of Aristotelian logic, so was the heterogeneity of the *DI*. The medieval Latin logicians developed ways of accommodating the ambiguity of the copula. This story has been studied in detail by Nuchelmans.[24] I here propose to revisit Geach's Paradise Lost to reconstruct the emergence of the notion of the copula with the Greek commentators before embarking on the untold medieval Arabic story of the problem of predication.

"NAME" (ὀνόμα), "VERB" (ῥῆμα), AND "TO BE" (εἶναι)
IN ARISTOTLE'S *DE INTERPRETATIONE*

Aristotle himself had no theory of the copula. It was the ancient commentators who began to theorize about the semantic role of the word "is." The seminal passages for Aristotle's ideas about APs and their constituting elements are the first four chapters of the *DI*. In this introductory section to the *DI*, Aristotle first presents a rudimentary theory of meaning (*DI* 1), and then defines the two constituting elements, the naming-word (*DI* 2) and the statement-word (*DI* 3), that uniquely make up an AP (*DI* 4). That there is no copula in Aristotle's account of APs should not come as a surprise. Even in languages that do employ a copula in some predicative sentences, the simplest truth-apt sentences are noun-verb combinations.

The *DI* itself is a peculiar work with a peculiar title. Its focus is not "interpretation" as the title would suggest, but the theory of contradiction.[25] However, to develop a theory of contradiction, Aristotle had to lay some preliminary groundwork. That groundwork consisted in clarifying what the items that contradict each other are, and what they are made up of. In other words, this groundwork is the analysis of APs.

Much of the story I am going to tell depends on the rich and difficult text of Aristotle's *DI*. Hence, I begin by offering new translations of pertinent passages, which I use to unpack what I think Aristotle's theoretical commitments are. More importantly, I want to show where important interpretative spaces open up that the later tradition could then fill in specific ways.

The Naming-Word

Following the introductory chapter on the relation between language, thought, and the world, the second chapter is dedicated to the name (*onoma*), or naming-word.[26] Aristotle seems to first give a definition, then presents examples to clarify the definition, and closes by pointing out two exceptions to the definition:[27]

TEXT 1 (ARIST. *DI* 2): ARISTOTLE, *DE INT.* 2 (WEIDEMANN), 16A19–16B5

A naming-word then is a sound of the voice significant by convention, and without [reference to] time, no part of which is significant in isolation. For in [the naming-word] "Fairsteed," "steed" does not signify—like [it would] when saying "fair steed"—anything by itself. To be sure, with compound [naming-words] it is not [the same] as it is with simple ones; for in the case of the latter, the part is never significant, whereas in the case of the former, it wants to signify something, just not in isolation, as for example "ketch" in the [naming-word] "cutter-ketch."

"By convention" [I added], because none of the naming-words is [such] by nature, but only once it has become a token. For even the unwritable noises—of wild beasts, for example—indicate something, [yet] none of them is a naming-word. "Non-human" is not a naming-word. There is in fact no name that we can call it by; so, let it be an "indefinite naming-word." "Philo's" or "to-Philo" and the like are not naming-words, but inflections of a naming-word. The rationale (*logos*) of this is in other respects the same, except that [even together] with "is" or "was" or "will be" [an inflected naming-word] is not true or false (whereas a naming-word always is) like in the cases of "Philo's is or is not"; for nothing is so far either true or false.

Aristotle presents five criteria to determine what a name is: (a) a sound in the voice that is (b) significant, not by nature but (c) by convention, whose meaning (d) does not include time, and (e) no part of which is significant in isolation. Criteria (a)–(c) are properties that the name shares with both the statement-word and the sentence; (d) will be discussed in the following chapter on the statement-word, for which it is the pertinent criterion; (e) is presumably specifically clarified at this point since it is primarily names that can occur as compounds.

The point of the examples has mystified most readers.[28] The only thing that seems certain is that Aristotle uses them to clarify criterion (e). A plausible and minimally committal reading is this. The naming-word is defined as the smallest unit of spoken sound that has a meaning unconnected to time. Some strings of sound, however, may appear to have such a meaning when in fact they do not. A decision procedure for identifying naming-words is to check whether the meaning of a given string of sounds (no part of which has any further meaning) is not superseded by the meaning of the next-larger meaning unit in the string of sounds. "Fairsteed" (*Kalippos*) is a proper name—one of Aristotle's colleagues at the Lyceum was so called.[29] As such, none of the parts of which the name is made up ("fair" and "steed") contributes anything to the meaning of "Fairsteed."

"Cutter-ketch" is a compound in which "ketch" *wants* (*bouletai*) to mean something. What "ketch" (*kelēs*) means by itself contributes to the meaning of "cutter-ketch," which refers to a ketch with headsails typical of the cutter.[30] "Ketch" appears in the exact same form as it would if encountered by itself. This is different from the case of proper names, for here the parts of the compound make up the compound meaning, but they still do not mean anything when they are separated: whereas "ketch" means something, "-ketch" does not.[31]

With his explication of (c), i.e., that a naming-word is significant only by convention, Aristotle makes explicit what was already implicitly stated in 16a4–9, alluding to the related debate in the *Cratylus*.[32] To clarify what the conventional character of the naming-word's semantic properties is, he contrasts such meaningful sounds with the sounds of beasts that also indicate something. Yet in this case the relation between an animal sound and what it indicates is not established by convention. It is, presumably, natural.

It is illuminating to point out what distinction Aristotle does not make: as the examples show, there is no attempt to distinguish between proper names and common nouns, or between proper names and proper nouns. But clearly the naming-words "Kalippos" (or "Alexander the Great" [*Alexandros ho megas*] as a proper name consisting of two proper nouns) and "cutter-ketch" are not only different in terms of whether or not their parts appear to be significant. Proper names denote specific objects whereas common nouns do not. Aristotle does not make this central logical distinction here.[33]

The Statement-Word

The third chapter is dedicated to the statement-word. Aristotle begins by distinguishing the statement-word from the naming-word. Then, in parallel fashion to the preceding chapter, he excludes indefinite statement-words and their inflections from being statement-words *sensu strictu*, before he discusses the semantic function of isolated statement-words.

TEXT 2 (ARIST. *DI* 3): ARISTOTLE, *DE INT.* 3 (WEIDEMANN), 16B6–25

A statement-word is that [word] which co-signifies time, and no part of which signifies [anything] in isolation. And it is a sign of that which is said of something else. [When] I say that it co-signifies time, [I mean that] "recovery," for example, is a name, whereas "recovers" is a statement-word; for it co-signifies that it applies now. And it always is a sign of that which applies [to something else], i.e., of that which is [said] of a subject. "Non-recovers" or "non-suffers" I do not call statement-word; for while it co-signifies time and always applies to something [else], [there is a difference between this and the statement-word] for which we have no ready name. But let it be an "indefinite statement-word," since it applies equally to things that exist and that do not. Similarly, "recovered" or "will recover" are not statement-words, but inflections of statement-words. They differ from statement-words in that while the latter co-signify the present time, the former [co-signify] a time outside [it]. These statement-words, then, when said by themselves, are names and signify something—for the speaker halts the thought, and the listener pauses—but it does not yet signify whether [that which it signifies] is or not; for it is not a sign for the being or not being of the thing [meant], nor is "being" if you say it in isolation. For in itself it is nothing, but it [only] co-signifies some combination, which is impossible to think without its components.

While both naming-words and statement-words share the property of having no parts that are significant in isolation, the statement-word is distinguished by two criteria. It co-signifies time, and it is such that it ascribes something to something else, instead of simply naming something.

As Aristotle intimates in 16b20, statement-words have this ascriptive force only in the context of a proposition, for when "said by themselves, [they] are names." This has been seen as problematic, for Aristotle indiscriminately uses "white" (*leukon*) as a statement-word.[34] But you need a copula (*esti*) to turn it into a predicable.[35] To capture both options, I translate *rhēma* by "statement-word." This particular issue will be important for the commentators.

There is a textual problem in 16b11 that was already discussed in antiquity and had far-reaching consequences. Weidemann is right to assume that some scholiast later added "or *in* a subject" (*ē en hypokeimenō*) thinking of *Cat* 5 2b3–5 and 2a34.[36] It is however unlikely that this is what Aristotle had in mind. In *Cat* 5 Aristotle distinguishes between two types of predication: universals are *said of* particulars, but accidents are said to be *in* their substances. Mentioning *being-in* predication at *DI* 3 16b11 would defeat the purpose of the passage, because Aristotle has just distinguished the statement-word "recovers" (*hygiainei*) from the naming-word "recovery" (*hygieia*) to bring out the difference between the *ascriptive* force of the former as opposed to the mere naming function of the latter. To say that statement-words may also predicate in the sense of *being-in* would introduce an entirely different distinction not apposite to the context.[37] This variant proved, however, momentous for the Arabic reception.

The last paragraph of the chapter Kahn called "full of difficulties"; that seems an understatement, given the amount of literature it has produced, and it will be important for the commentators' understanding of the passage.[38] Aristotle states that "being" in itself is nothing, but only co-signifies a combination that is impossible to think without its components. We will return to this claim time and again to see what that could mean for the conception of a copula.

The Copula

Of the copula we have said nothing so far because Aristotle has said nothing explicit about it. In fact, Aristotle nowhere says anything explicit about the copula. Geach is right that Aristotle had no theory of it, nor did he need one—the technical term "copula" is a much later coinage.[39] (Though Aristotle likely did understand *desmos* as denoting a syntactically relevant expression.) The seminal passage in the *DI* on the copula for the Latinate tradition is this:[40]

TEXT 3 (ARIST. *DI* 10): ARISTOTLE, *DE INT.* 10 (WEIDEMANN), 19B19–22

> But when "is" is additionally predicated as a third item, there are already two [pairs]
> of contradictory statements. I mean, for example, [statements of the form] "[A] man
> is just." I take "is" as a third item to be compounded with a naming-word, or [rather?]
> a statement-word, in an affirmation.

In this passage Aristotle distinguishes statements of the form "[A] man is just"
from statements of the form "[A] man is [i.e., exists]." The latter treats "is" as a
statement-word and there are exactly two possible contradictory statements. The
former presumably treats "is" as a copula, and here both the predicate and
the copula can be negated, so that there are exactly four possible contradictory
statements. This distinction between *secundum adiacens* and *tertium adiacens*
propositions is going to play an important part in the Arabic reception history.

The main interpretative problems in this passage revolve around the questions
of what "as a third item" should be taken to be relative to (words, elements of the
proposition, or something else altogether?), and of how to grammatically construe the last sentence. Does Aristotle here say that the copulative "is" is either a
naming-word or a statement-word, or a statement-word rather than a naming-
word, or just that it is compounded with either of them, or that it is compounded
rather with the statement-word?[41] A little later in *DI* 12 he states that "there is no
difference between saying that a man walks and that a man is walking" (21b9–10),
suggesting that all statement-words may be analyzed as consisting of a copulative
expression and a participle. This is further illuminated by the following passage:

TEXT 4 (ARIST. *DI* 10): ARISTOTLE, *DE INT.* 10 (WEIDEMANN), 20A3–5

> But for those [statement-words] with which "is" does not fit together, like with "re-
> cover" or "walk," since they take the same place that "is" would take [in the sentence],
> they play the same role [as it].

It appears that verbs themselves have a copulative function. How then does the
copula fit into the logical grammar of the *DI*? Is it a statement-word, a naming-
word, both, or neither? Or perhaps some logical element common to the logical
form of statement-words?

A little earlier in *DI* 10 it would appear that Aristotle counted not only *einai* but
also other "copulative" expressions as statement-words on the grounds that they
co-signify time.

TEXT 5 (ARIST. *DI* 10): ARISTOTLE, *DE INT.* 10 (WEIDEMANN), 19B12–14

> Without a statement-word there is no affirmation or negation; for "is" or "will be"
> or "was," or "becomes" or other such more, are, according to what was laid down,
> statement-words; for they co-signify time.

But here he refers to non-copulative uses of those verbs, as in sentences of the form
"[A] man exists." Given that *einai* is clearly different from other statement-words
in some crucial respects, it does not follow that the same will apply to copulative uses. All will depend on the grammatically impenetrable *to esti triton phēmi*

synkeisthai onoma ē rhema en tē kataphasei (19b22).[42] One respect in which the copulative *einai* seems to be crucially different from statement-words was especially influential for an interpretation of the copula as a logical element distinct from the parts of speech outlined in the *DI*. In the passage in *DI* 3, Aristotle said that "being" when uttered by itself not only had no truth-value, but also did not even function as a name in the way that other statement-words do when uttered in isolation. While, presumably, "walking" signifies walking, "being" "in itself […] is nothing, but it [only] co-signifies some combination, which is impossible to think without its components" (17a4–6).[43]

Another notorious passage shows that Aristotle distinguishes the semantic role of *einai* in copulative and existential uses.

TEXT 6 (ARIST. *DI* 11): ARISTOTLE, *DE INT.* 11 (WEIDEMANN), 21A25–28

Homer, for example, *is something*, let us say a poet. Does it then follow that he *is* (i.e., exists), or not? [Of course not.] For "is" is predicated accidentally of Homer—since he *is a poet*; but "is" is [here] not *per se* predicated of Homer.

Aristotle had previously dealt with multiple predication and here warns against the confusion arising from the assumption that you can infer from a statement in which two predicates are said of one subject that each of the predicates must hold individually. What makes the passage difficult to interpret is that it seems unfortunate that Aristotle uses "is" as an accidental predicate, and "poet" as another predicate. For example, when you say "Callias is a good cobbler," you cannot infer that "Callias is good," because he is only good inasmuch as he is a cobbler. Exactly what the example is supposed to bring out, however, remains a matter of debate, for it seems that "is" in many ways functions differently from "good" so that it is doubtful whether they can be treated alike as instances of multiple predication.[44]

These passages raise several questions: Is the copula a part of the proposition? Does *einai* change its meaning or its role in the sentence, depending on where it appears? What are its syntactic properties? What are its semantic properties? What part of speech is it? A statement-word, a naming-word, or something else altogether? It is those questions and those passages that the commentators felt the need to clarify.

PROBLEMATIZING THE COPULA: THE GREEK COMMENTATORS

The *DI* was perceived as obscure already in antiquity, and even though it is in no way presupposed by the syllogistic of the *APr*, it kept being read and commented upon.[45] Aspasius's is the first of the three early attested commentaries on the *DI*, compiled in the first half of the second century. Neither this commentary nor those attested for Herminus (*fl.* mid-2nd century), a teacher of Alexander of

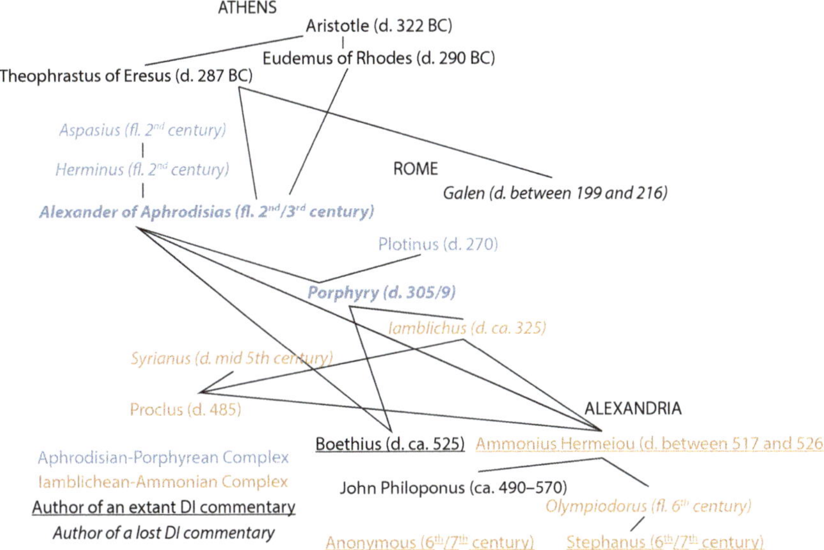

FIGURE 4. Hellenic Commentators on the *De interpretatione.*

Aphrodisias, and for Alexander himself, who held a chair of Peripatetic philosophy (at Athens?) at the bequest of Septimius Severus and Caracalla between 198 and 209, have survived.[46]

After Alexander, of the attested *DI* commentators most are Neo-Platonists, beginning with Porphyry (234–305/9) and his student Iamblichus (*ca.* 240/5–325), and later followed by Syrianus (d. mid-5th century) and Olympiodorus (*fl.* 6th century). None of their commentaries is extant.[47] All we have are the four commentaries by (1) Ammonius Hermeiou (d. between 517 and 526), (2) Stephanus (6th/7th century), (3) an anonymous author, who was probably a contemporary of Stephanus, and (4) the two versions of Boethius's (*ca.* 480–525) commentary written in Latin.[48]

From those four commentaries and some fragments and scholia we can reconstruct a fair amount of the reception history of the linguistic passage of the *DI* up to the end of late antiquity. The texts of the early Peripatetics were known and used by Alexander and later Porphyry. Porphyry, who studied with Longinus in Athens and then with Plotinus in Rome, largely incorporated Alexander's commentary into his own detailed (*polystichon*: "long-winded") commentary on the *DI.*[49]

Even though Alexander's contribution to the interpretation of the *DI* was immense, Porphyry's extensive use of it may have led to the commentary's eventual disappearance. Porphyry's lost commentary, in turn, served as the model for Boethius's *Second Commentary*, which preserves a good part of it. Ammonius's commentary came to be highly influential with the Alexandrian school, but it is unlikely that Boethius knew it. Figure 4 shows the relations between commentators of the *DI*. The Stoics and Boethius would merit a study of their own, but they had a negligible direct influence on the Arabic tradition—or none at all.[50]

The Early Peripatos and the Aphrodisian-Porphyrean Commentary Complex

The first to critically engage with Aristotle's text were his immediate students. Of Theophrastus of Eresus (d. 287 BCE), who succeeded Aristotle at the helm of the Lyceum, and Eudemus of Rhodes (d. 290 BCE), a fellow student and co-author of Theophrastus in most logical works, only fragments survive.[51] However, their writings certainly were an important source for Alexander, and we have evidence that he was acquainted with Eudemus's work.

We have a scholium that reads: "Eudemus in the first book of his *On Expression* [*Peri lexeōs*] shows *at some length* that the 'is' in simple propositions such as 'Socrates is,' 'Socrates is not' is predicated and is a term"; this appears to be mentioned by Alexander in his commentary on the *APr* (see Text 10).[52] There it would however seem that Alexander read Eudemus arguing not for the position that in existential propositions "is" is a term, but for the position that "is" in propositions like "Socrates is pale" is in some sense predicated. Scanty though the evidence may be for the early Peripatos, it seems warranted to say that the role of *einai* in predication was problematized "at some length" by Aristotle's students.

Between Eudemus and Alexander of Aphrodisias, there lies of course almost half a millennium, in which not only Christendom appeared on the scene. Stoic logic rose to prominence, both Greek and Latin grammatical theory developed into full-fledged sciences,[53] and by the time of Alexander, Galen had codified a medical corpus—which included logic—which was to remain a point of reference well into early modern times.[54]

We will have to skip most of this. But in many ways Alexander can be seen as continuing the tradition of the early Peripatos. His engagement with intermediate commentators was limited (although we have to assume a fair amount of influence from his teacher Herminus, whom he sometimes criticizes), and his attitude toward Stoic logic was on the whole dismissive.

For the ancient commentators, APs were linguistic items. But they are defined in quite different terms in the *DI* and the *APr*. Alexander was acutely aware of this:

TEXT 7 (ALEX. *APR* 1): ALEXANDER, *IN AN. PR.* (WALLIES), 10.13–11.27

One account of propositions will be the account Aristotle gave of statements in *On Interpretation*, namely: an utterance "in which there is truth and falsity." But here now, he gives a definition specific to propositions; for even if propositions and statements are the same in what underlies them, they differ in account: inasmuch as they are true or false, they are statements; inasmuch as they are expressed affirmatively or negatively, they are propositions. Or: the declarative statement is what it is simply in virtue of being true or false, whereas the proposition [is what it is] in virtue of *how* it is so [i.e., true or false]. Hence statements which are true or false, but not in the same way, may be saying the same, but not be the same propositions. For when uttered, the proposition "justice is good" is the same as "injustice is bad" in terms of what is said [as a statement], i.e., they are both true and both are affirmations, but they are not the same propositions, for in them their subjects and predicates differ. But also: both a true affirmation and a true negation may in this respect be the same statement, yet not the same proposition, since the quality [affirmative/negative] of the statement is different in them.[55] While they are not the same proposition, they are the same declarative statement.

What is underlying both definitions, that of the statement in the *DI* and that of the proposition in the *APr*, must surely be the utterance token. Alexander's synthesis was an original and lasting contribution to Aristotelian logic. For him, the *DI* and the *APr* do not differ in any fundamental logical assumptions about the analysis of language, but only in their respective perspectives on utterance tokens. A sentence has certain features if considered inasmuch as it has a truth-value, and others if considered inasmuch as it is part of a syllogism.

On this two-terminologies reading, Alexander must bring clarity to Aristotle's remarks on the role of *einai*. In another passage from the commentary on *APr*, Alexander argues that *prima facie* it might seem that at least in existential propositions like "Socrates is," "is" is the predicate term. However, this is misguided, he says:

TEXT 8 (ALEX. *APR* 1): ALEXANDER, IN *AN. PR.* (WALLIES), 15.15–22

For here "is" seems to be the predicate term. But in fact, if you consider the case precisely, "is" is not even here a term in its own right. For the proposition that says "Socrates is" is equivalent to "Socrates is a being," in which not "is" but "being," together with "is," becomes the predicate term. Since "is" seems to be equivalent to "being" (for it is an inflected form of it), for the sake of brevity and in order not to say the same thing twice, it alone is connected to the subject. And when it is connected in this way it becomes a term and a part of the proposition.

Alexander distinguishes between copulative and predicative uses of *einai*—as Aristotle had done, though less clearly, perhaps. However, Alexander claims that "is" never is a term, not even in "Socrates is," which Aristotle had treated as a statement of the form "S Φs." But if "is" is not a term, what is it? Commenting on *DI* 3, Alexander says that since statement-words and naming-words are distinct, but statement-words can be called naming-words inasmuch as in their uninflected form they signify an object (e.g., "walking" designates the tenseless action of walking), then *einai* is a statement-word just as any other, so that it is correct to call "being" (*ōn*) a name:

TEXT 9 (ALEX. *DI* 3): AMMONIUS, *IN DE INT.* (BUSSE), 57.18–34

But if someone does not agree with this interpretation of "additionally signify," let him be persuaded by Alexander when he says that in the words "for by itself it is nothing" etc., Aristotle is again speaking about the word "is" after having spoken parenthetically about "being," and saying that not even this, when it is said by itself, is capable of signifying anything true or false, and also that the word "is" or also "is not" (for the same story goes for each of them), when said just by itself, is not such that it signifies anything true or false. But being a name, just as are the other verbs too, it primarily has a power to signify (*dynamis semantikē*) participation in or deprivation of being, but also secondarily to signify the predicate's joining with the subject, and when added to them it makes the sentence complete and significant of truth or falsity.

In fact, even if it is immediately predicated of the subject, even then the word "is" potentially signifies its joining with "being," e.g., "Socrates is a being," and "is not" potentially signifies its division, or actually both of them signify, for it was said in *On the Soul*: "even he who says that something is not pale has put together not being pale with the subject."

So *einai* is, for Alexander, apparently a statement-word. As for its logical role, Alexander holds, as we have seen, that "is" is not really a term and he is said to have repeated a similar example ("Socrates is a being") in his *DI* commentary. He also thinks that quantifiers are annexed to the subject, whereas "is" is annexed to the predicate. Taking the syntactical role of "is" to be on a par with that of quantifiers, Alexander can coherently claim that "is" is not a part of the proposition. And in fact, in the commentary on the *APr* he says as much explicitly:

TEXT 10 (ALEX. *APR* 1): ALEXANDER, *IN AN. PR.* (WALLIES), 16.7–17

Or else he adds "when you add or divide 'is' or 'is not'" in order to indicate that these items, i.e., "is" and "is not," are neither parts of the proposition nor terms, but that both "is" and "is not" are external to the terms, either being added externally to the predicate terms when propositions are divided into terms or else being separated from them. For the addition or subtraction of these items contributes nothing to the division of propositions into terms: the terms in "Socrates is white" seem to be "Socrates" and "white." His expression would be more congruous if it were put this way: "when you add 'is' or 'is not' or divide them." Or is it absurd to claim that the "is" in these propositions is not predicated in any sense? Eudemus, in the first book of his *On Expression*, shows this at some length.

His explanation for this is to be sought in his conception of the semantics of *einai*. According to his interpretation of the lemma "for by itself it ['being'] is nothing" (16b24) as reported by Ammonius (Text 9), "*einai*" is a name and as such primarily signifies participation in or deprivation of being. It has semantic force (*dynamis semantikē*, Text 9) and in a secondary way it signifies the predicate's joining with the subject. Additionally, and this seems to be his interpretation of the notorious word "*prossēmainei*" (16b10), it also makes the sentence complete and significant of truth and falsehood. Boethius, however, reports that Alexander's view was that "is" by itself signifies nothing, but has its semantic function only activated when it occurs in its correct place in a proposition.

TEXT 11 (ALEX. *DI* 3): BOETHIUS, IN *DE INT.* (MEISER), II 77.1–12

As to the addition "nor if you say simply 'this is'" or the alternative reading "nor if you simply say 'being'" Alexander says "is" or "being" are equivocal. For all predicates which do not come under a common genus are equivocal and "being" is predicated of everything; for substance is, quality is, and quantity etc. Therefore, he now seems to be saying: "being" or "is," from which is derived "to be," signifies nothing in itself; for every equivocal [word] signifies nothing when on its own. Unless it is applied to specific things at the instigation of the one who signifies in itself it signifies none just because it signifies many.

The reason why it is not signifying on its own as other verbs are is that "being" is equivocal, and no equivocal word signifies anything in isolation; since being can be said of everything, by itself it means nothing. Whether Alexander had offered two different interpretations, or whether Ammonius and Boethius misreported his positions, is difficult to say. But having semantic force need not mean that it signifies *something*. He denies that "is" is a term and thus that it constitutes a part of a proposition. His response is that "is" is annexed to the predicate, effectively offering a parsing of the form NW+[cop+NW].

This semantic analysis of *einai* suggests that in a proposition it can function in two distinct ways: First, it can be a purely syntactical marker annexed to the predicate as an indicator of the predicate's joining with the subject, thus making the sentence complete and significant of truth or falsity. Second, in its participial forms it can occur in the predicate place ("Socrates is a being"), which is also the correct analysis of existential propositions ("Socrates is"), in which case it signifies in the same way other equivocal verbs signify, i.e., its initially indeterminate meaning is defined by the subject of which it is predicated. "Socrates is a being" thus signifies something like "Socrates participates in the things-that-are as Socrates (as a rational animal)."[56]

The Iamblichean-Ammonian Commentary Complex

Of Iamblichus's writings we have very little connected to the *DI*, but Ammonius in his commentary on the *APr* reports how Iamblichus explained the difficult passage about the copula in *APr* 1. After giving Alexander's interpretation of *APr* 24b12, Ammonius mentions an alternative reading by Iamblichus, "the great philosopher [who] having done a more profound and more careful exegesis says that 'adding or dividing to be or not to be' signifies the different forms of the propositions."[57] What that means is the following:

TEXT 12 (IAMB. *APR* 1): AMMONIUS *IN AN. PR.* (WALLIES), 23.11–14

For of the propositions we are concerned with here, some have the predicate term taken together with the subject, some have "is" additionally predicated, and some are qualified by a modality; then again, some are simple, and others metathetic.

Iamblichus's point is that every proposition is analyzed as consisting of two terms: subject and predicate. "Adding or dividing to be or not to be" means to add "is" or "is not" to the subject and predicate terms in the sense that it is adjoined (*prosthesis*) to the predicate, analogous to the way in which modal or metathetic qualifications are adjoined to terms. Iamblichus appears to have conceived of APs like "Socrates is just" as having the form NW+[cop+NW].

Ammonius's father, Hermeias, studied with Syrianus and became the first professor of Platonic philosophy at Alexandria. Ammonius himself was educated in Athens under Proclus and upon his return succeeded his father, holding the chair of Platonic philosophy from about 470 until his death sometime between 517 and 526.[58] However, according to the last Athenian scholarch, Damascius, Ammonius lectured predominantly on Aristotle.[59] The only commentary we have from Ammonius's own hand (as opposed to *ex voce* notes that students took from his lectures) is the commentary on the *DI*. From it we may extract a view of the role of *einai* in predication that emphasizes heterogeneity in the logical analysis of simple sentences.

Ammonius, like Alexander, distinguishes statements from propositions. For him, "the proposition in itself is to be understood not inasmuch as it is a *logos apophantikos*, but inasmuch as it is a part of a syllogism."[60] Not surprising for a Platonist, in his comments on *DI* 3 he cites a passage from the *Sophist*.[61] Ammonius understands the heterogeneity of naming-words and statement-words as some words fitting together whereas others do not. This is explained by the peculiar force of the verb:

TEXT 13 (AMM. *DI* 3): AMMONIUS, *IN DE INT.* (BUSSE), 49.7–14

The word "always" is also not added in vain in "and it is always a sign of things said of another." For this especially makes the particular property of verbs clear, since nothing prevents names too from being predicated, as "animal" is predicated of "man," but they neither belong to those which are only and always predicated nor, when they are predicated by themselves without some verb, e.g., "is" or "is not," are they such as to effect a complete sentence, while verbs, as long as they preserve their proper force, come to be predicated always and only by themselves.

This goes back to his initial clarification about the definition of the name in *DI* 2, where he marks the difference between NWs and SWs by saying that any vocal sound, including names like "pale," are called "verbs" (i.e., statement-words), when they occur in the predicate position.

TEXT 14 (AMM. *DI* 1): AMMONIUS *IN DE INT.* (BUSSE), 28.5–10

Thereby he decided to count "pale" among the verbs not according to the usual definition, but according to the definition which directs that any vocal sound which forms a predicate in a proposition be called a verb.

Ammonius thinks that any regular verb can be analyzed into (is+participle), so that (is+pale) is to be treated analogously to the analyzed structure of regular verbs. However, this does not force him to regard "is" as not being a verb itself. For "is" has a primary signification, namely "being so or not being so" (*hyparchein*), or, in other words, truth or falsity. But it also has a secondary signification of time, since it is tensed as any other verb. It just does not signify "being so" when said in isolation—but no other verb does! It is just a special case, because its primary signification is the same as that which nothing signifies in isolation, unless "is" is added.

This is perhaps not a good interpretation of Aristotle, but an original reading to which he gets by way of his explanation of the notorious *passus* in *DI* 3.[62] He analyzes "For not even 'to be' or 'not to be' is a sign of the thing" as an *a fortiori* argument aimed at showing that since the verb that would be the most likely candidate to signify being so or not being so, i.e., "to be" and "not to be," cannot be said to actually signify this when said in isolation, then—*a fortiori*—all those verbs that can be analyzed into "is" and a participle will not signify that either.

In a second step, even the most primitive form of "to be," its participle, which is a name, does not signify anything being so or not. All grammatical forms of "to be" still signify something (here he mitigates the Aphrodisian-Porphyrean position), but not truth or falsity.

TEXT 15 (AMM. *DI* 3): AMMONIUS, *IN DE INT.* (BUSSE), 55.10–56.13

"But whether it is," Aristotle says, "or is not" is not yet clear.[63] For him "it is" signifies affirmation, and "or is not" signifies negation, or rather "it is" signifies truth, "or is not" signifies falsity. For he who in accordance with nature says that what is "is" speaks the truth, and he who says that "it is not" speaks falsehood. So, verbs signify something, Aristotle says, a suffering or activity, but they do not yet signify truth or falsehood. And he adds this by way of a syllogism: "For not even 'to be' is a sign of the thing, nor is 'not to be.'" This is an *a fortiori* argument that verbs do not admit the true and false. For, if the most primitive and general of verbs, those into which all the rest are analyzed, since they immediately signify being so or not being so itself, are not true or false when said by themselves, then clearly other verbs would accept these properties much less. And, in fact, the first is so; thus, so is the second.

He assumes that of all verbs "is" and "is not," which he calls "to be" and "not to be," are most primitive, since each verb could be analyzed into a participle and one of these, definite verbs into "is" and indefinite verbs into "is not"; for example: "he runs" = "he is running," "he thrives" = "he is thriving"; "he runs not" = "he is not running," "he thrives not" = "he is not thriving." If, therefore, as these verbs are such and by themselves signify nothing true or false, how could it be reasonable for the verbs posterior to these, which would signify being so or not being so entirely by their participation in these, to indicate anything true or false?

And that "is" or "is not" by themselves signify nothing true or false is perhaps self-evident: for one who has said ten thousand times "is, is . . ." or "is not, is not

. . . " has signified neither of these. But he establishes this too by a similar *a fortiori* argument, taking something more primitive than "is," namely, "being," from which "is" and "is not" are derived. For he says that not even this "being," which is a name, is a sign of the thing, just like the verb derived from it, "is." That is to say, it is not revelatory of the thing's truly existing, when it is said by itself. For "is" signifies something when said by itself, and "being" likewise; but neither of these posits itself and says that it exists, even when said ten thousand times, will it signify something true or false. For, as has been said many times, only sentences, consisting of names and verbs, are such to accept either of these, and each of these, i.e., "being" and "is," is simple and far from any such composition.

Syntactically, Ammonius understands the role of "is" to be best represented in a verbal phrase (is+noun/participle). Commenting on *DI* 10, which is the same passage that Bäck uses as evidence for Ammonius's subscribing to the copulative theory,[64] he applies Iamblichus's interpretation of *APr* 24b12 to the notorious passage in the *DI* (16b21f.):

TEXT 16 (AMM. *DI* 10): AMMONIUS, *IN DE INT.* (BUSSE), 162.17–35

[Aristotle] says "when 'is' is additionally predicated as a third" not to imply that among the predicates in the proposition "is" occupies the third place, but that "is" is third in the proposition relative to the two terms. In relation to the subject and the predicate it occupies second place as itself being predicated and, as it were, being additionally predicated. For when we say "man is just," we predicated antecedently "just" of the subject "man," since we proposed that this be asserted of that, but, because the former is not sufficient to interweave with the latter for making an assertion, "is" has been attached to them as binding them, as has been said before, and is supplementally predicated of the subject. In fact, we say the whole about it ["man"], i.e., that he "is just."

It is clear from this quote that "is" is not an independent part, not even a part of the proposition at all, but that it rather always goes with the predicate and turns it into a verbal phrase. Ammonius thinks that the surface structure of language may not always exhibit this. Yet the distinctive force of "is" to make a predicate such that it goes together with a subject is shown by the possibility to analyze regular verbs into (is+participle).

This being so, for Ammonius the "is" of the predicative expression, which in analogy to the parts of names does not signify anything in isolation, has—as part of the statement-expression—two distinct semantic functions. Ammonius accepts, against Porphyry, the amplifying textual variant at 16b11, and thus the reference to *Cat* 5 distinguishing essential/homonymous and accidental/paronymous predication.[65]

After Ammonius the *DI* continued to be taught and written on.[66] However, Ammonius's commentary wielded such influence that the extant commentaries of

Stephanus and Anonymous—which in contrast to Ammonius's written exposition are *ex voce* renderings from lectures—as well as the fragments of Olympiodorus's commentary hardly contain anything on the copula that is not already in Ammonius.

Both Stephanus and Anonymous agree with Ammonius that "is" by itself signifies something—just not truth or falsity—and that there are only two parts of speech that are necessary to form a statement: NWs and SWs.[67] And just like Ammonius, both Stephanus and Anonymous agree that all verbs are in principle analyzable into (is+participle). But Stephanus introduced new terminology that will be important for understanding the Arabic reception: he calls the verb "*einai*," which he takes to be an archetypal statement-word, a *hyparktikon rhēma* (*hyparctic verb*).[68] This technical term is formed from the verb (*hyparchein*) that Aristotle typically uses in the *APr* to express that a predicate holds of a subject.[69]

Moreover, Stephanus has no reservations against verbs in the subject-position:

TEXT 17 (STEPH. *DI* 3): STEPHANUS, *IN DE INT.* (HAYDUCK), 13.15–18

[And Aristotle said] that [statement-words] are always said of something else: either *of a subject*, when it is synonymously predicated, like "To walk is to move" or "To philosophize is to eudaimonize," or else as *in a subject*, like "Socrates thrives."

Epitomizing Ammonius, Stephanus employs the distinction from *Cat* 5 to explain Ammonius's infinitival predications with a verb in the subject-place. For Anonymous, this seems to have been a commonplace reading:

TEXT 18 (ANON. *DI* 3): ANONYMOUS, *IN DE INT.* (TARÁN), 7.11–8.4

And [Aristotle] said the statement-word is a sign of predicates, and as the form of the predicate is either such that it is predicated substantially and essentially of the substance of the subjects, or else accidentally, he says that it is a sign of both. "Animal" is predicated substantially of "man," and "moving" of "walking" [. . .]. "Walking," however, is accidentally predicated of "Socrates," and so is "pale" and the like. Substantial predicates are said *of the subject*, and accidental ones *in the subject*.

Arabic commentators were puzzled by this and Fārābī took this idea as a point of departure for his own theory of propositions.

CONCLUSIONS

Even though the *DI* is a treatise on the theory of contradiction, in the linguistic section Aristotle presents his most thorough account of what a proposition—in the sense of an utterance token with a truth-value—is, what its elements are, and how it is that we can use such sentences to describe the world truly or falsely. He distinguishes two elements of speech, the naming-word and the statement-word, that uniquely make up a proposition. These two elements are heterogenous, not merely because they have different definitions, but crucially because they play distinct roles in statements. The SW, and only it, is used to signify that whatever it means applies to what the NW names.

We cannot tell what the relation of the text of the *DI* was to any of the other texts we have of Aristotle. It was the jerry-building of the early editors and commentators that produced the *Organon* as a supposedly coherent logical corpus with a defined pedagogical structure and purpose. In such an environment, the linguistic section of the *DI* was perceived to be in tension with the core of the syllogistic, i.e., the requirement in the *APr* that the two terms of a proposition be homogenous and thus interchangeable.

The tension between the *DI* and the *APr* did not go unnoticed by the Greek commentators. They tried to make the two texts coherent. Any attempt to do so had to come to grips with the scattered remarks Aristotle makes about *einai*. It is the *DI* that forces the Aristotelian tradition to puzzle over the copula. In the *APr* itself the copula is hardly problematic. Instead of simply giving up the *DI* as an obscure text that adds nothing to the understanding of the syllogistic, the commentators tried not only to understand the text, but also to read it in a way that would further reinforce the cohesion of the *Organon*.

Alexander of Aphrodisias's commentary significantly shaped the reception history of the *DI*. He explained the apparent tension by a difference of perspective on the same object under scrutiny. Whereas the *DI* looks at utterances insofar as they have a truth-value, the *APr* looks at them with a view to how they have a truth-value. For Alexander, *einai* is a SW that functions pretty much like any other. In statements, however, its syntactical role is alike to that of a quantifier: just as a quantifier is attached to the subject, "is" is attached to the predicate, and hence not a part of the proposition. Only terms make up a proposition and "is" is not a term. In one sense there are clearly two heterogeneous elements. We may write: NW+[cop+NW]. Frege, too, considered the copula at times a part of the *Begriffswort* that could be substituted by the verbal ending.[70]

Ammonius synthesized several strands of interpretation, arguing against the Aphrodisian-Porphyrean position that "is" or "being" when said in isolation does in fact signify something, just not truth or falsity. Taking the cue from Aristotle, Ammonius developed the idea that all verbs potentially contain "is," since every verb can be rephrased as "is" plus a participial form. His analysis, then, was also clearly of the form NW+[cop+NW].

The linguistic section of the *DI* had thus a peculiar fate in antiquity. Even though it never had the same importance as the *Cat* or the *APr*, it proved recalcitrant in the face of the seemingly contradicting logical analysis of propositions in the *APr*. You may want to condemn the *APr* (which we need not, at least not for Geach's reasons: the shortcomings of the syllogistic are not in principle due to a two-term theory and they can be and have been amended), but you may not, on historical grounds, charge Aristotle with a fatal change of mind.

The commentators were right to say that the *DI* had a different perspective on the sentence. This peculiar situation at the end of late antiquity explains some of the peculiar turns in the fate of the *DI* over the course of its Arabic reception. For Semitic languages do not naturally use a copula—yet the philosophers of the classical period insisted on an artificial copula to make conspicuous the logical form of a statement.

2

———

Historical Prelude

Fārābī's Philosophical Project

The idiosyncratic development of the problem of predication in the Arabic tradition can only be appreciated in the peculiar historical context of its appropriation. It is first necessary to understand the ways in which the conception of linguistic meaning became a contested issue. Then, how certain new but fundamental grammatical and logical notions emerged as part of the development of Arabic grammar. And how this development unfolded in tension between a descriptive and normative approach to language that itself was in competition with the emerging "foreign" Aristotelian logic. Only then can we fully appreciate Fārābī's original approach to the semantic role of the copula as being central to his overall philosophical project. Taking a step aside from the discussions on the copula, this chapter is a prelude to the Arabic story, providing the background to situate Fārābī's interpretation of the *DI* and his reconceptualization of the copula in his overall philosophical project. The impatient reader may skip this chapter and return to it later.

HISTORICAL CONTEXT: A CONFLUENCE OF TRADITIONS

The formative period of medieval Islamic civilization is marked by a historically peculiar situation that Gutas has called the "war of signification."[1] In the time leading up to the 4th/10th century, as some of the major autochthonous Arabic sciences—like grammar (*naḥw*), dialectical theology (*kalām*), and jurisprudence (*uṣūl al-fiqh*)—were coming of age, and a host of "foreign" scientific texts was being made available in Arabic, new technical terminologies were being forged. With them arose the need to explain them. The translations of Greek texts posed problems, as the "vocabulary whose specialized meanings and implicit sense and

36

reflection of the way things are [. . .] not only did not arise congenially out of native Arabic usage but were in many instances dissonant with it and awkwardly superimposed upon it."[2] The question not only of what but also of how words mean became central to virtually all scientific disciplines. This preoccupation with linguistic and semantic questions across the Islamic scientific curriculum was tied to the translation movement and peculiar to the Arabic tradition. There is arguably no equivalent in medieval Europe.[3]

How much of a continuous story we can tell of the transmission of Greek learning from Alexandria to Baghdād remains an open question in scholarship.[4] Concerning the *Organon*, Gutas argued that there were two traditions of teaching the *Organon* in late antiquity and early Islam.[5] One was primarily Greek and the other primarily Syriac. The former comprised the first four books of the *Organon* with the exception of modal logic at *APr* A8–22. The latter excluded everything after *APr* A7.[6]

In light of recent research this needs to be revised. Instead of two distinct traditions, we rather must assume a widespread diglossia among scholars in the 6th and 7th centuries, so that we should speak of a continuous existence, from Alexandria to Baghdād, of Graeco-Syriac and predominantly Syriac environments.[7]

The abridgement of the *Organon* exhibited in the sources may just indicate certain teaching practices already present in the Alexandrian context.[8] We have to assume that all of the *Organon* was available and studied in several places, only not as part of introductory logic curricula. More generally, recent research indicates that there was a much livelier Aristotelian tradition in Syriac than our sparse sources suggest, and that the broader development from the Alexandrian veneration of Plato to the focus on Aristotle among the Baghdād Peripatetics took shape already in the Graeco-Syriac tradition.[9]

The first known Syriac commentator on Aristotle was Sergius of Rēsh ʿaynā, a priest and physician (d. 536) who had himself studied, likely under Ammonius, in Alexandria (in Greek).[10] The first Syriac translation of the *DI* was made by Probus, archiater of Antioch, in the 6th century; the second by George, bishop of the Arabs (d. 105/724), in the 1st/7th.[11] Probus also wrote a commentary on the *DI*, the only one extant in Syriac.[12] Paul the Persian (*fl.* 6th century) composed an epitome, written in Middle Persian (Pahlavi) and translated into Syriac by Severus Sabokht, bishop of Qenneshre.[13] The earliest Arabic writings on Aristotle's *Organon* we know of are by Ibn al-Muqaffaʿ (d. shortly after 139/756).[14] The earliest known commentarial work on the *DI* in Arabic is by the East Syriac Metropolitan of Moṣul, ʿAbdīshū Ibn al-Bahrīz (d. *ca.* 212/827).[15]

These scholars were multilingual and of diverse backgrounds with distinct perspectives. In their pioneering work they preconfigured in many ways the Arabic reception of Aristotelian logic already before the organized translation efforts began. The first such effort was led by Abū Yaʿqūb b. Isḥāq al-Kindī (d. *ca.* 257/870) and sponsored by the caliph al-Maʾmūn (*reg.* 198–218/813–833).[16] Next was the workshop of Ḥunayn b. Isḥāq (d. 259/873), who with his son Isḥāq b. Ḥunayn (d. *ca.* 297/911), Abū ʿUthmān al-Dimashqī (d. ca. 308/920), and Ibrāhīm b. ʿAbd Allāh al-Kātib (d. *ca.* 328/940), in a mammoth effort spanning two generations (*ca.* 230–290/840–900), produced the standard Arabic translations for the entire *Organon* (except the *APo* and the *Poetica* (*Poet*)).[17]

The Baghdād Peripatetics, a third group of translator-philosophers consisting of Abū Bishr Mattā b. Yūnus and his pupils, the Muslim Fārābī and the Jacobite Christian Yaḥyā Ibn ʿAdī (d. 363/974), were no longer as multilingual (Abū Bishr did not know Greek, and Fārābī probably neither Greek nor Syriac), but building on the terminological and exegetical work of their predecessors, they completed the translations of the *Organon*, and first fully appropriated it in an Arabic context.

Grammar and the Traditional Sciences on (the Arabic) Language

At the same time, in this period the traditional Islamic disciplines developed into their mature form, both in tension and in conversation with the translated sciences. Arabic grammar, a discipline first formalized in Sībawayhi's (d. 180/796) *al-Kitāb* (The Book), developed between antagonistic camps of grammarians in Kūfa and Baṣra and found a mature expression in the work of Ibn al-Sarrāj (d. 316/928). Ibn al-Sarrāj was Fārābī's contemporary and the first representative of the Baghdād school to synthesize the Kūfan and Baṣran approaches to grammar. His *al-Uṣūl fī l-naḥw* (Principles of Grammar) clearly shows the influence of Greek logical and grammatical thought.[18]

The early Baṣrian grammarians had approached the Arabic language of pre-Islamic poetry and the Qurʾān on the supposition that language in some substantial sense mirrored a rational reality.[19] Their efforts were thus aimed at a rational systematization of language in order to provide a normative grammar. Any linguistic phenomenon defying subsumption under the system had to be rationalized as an exception to the rule. While the Baṣrians sought to explain all linguistic phenomena by appealing to a paradigm (*aṣl*) and rules of derivation that could be employed by analogy (*qiyās*), the Kūfans, generally speaking, paid more attention to linguistic usage and thus sought to explain well-attested irregularities not in terms of regular deviations, but on a case-by-case basis.[20]

As a result, the two approaches often produced quite different theories. But for both, at the beginning of any grammatical theory, there stood a comprehensive theory of morphology as governed by inflection and derivation (*taṣrīf* and *ishtiqāq*) and an exhaustive classification of linguistic items into noun (*ism*), verb (*fiʿl*), and particle (*ḥarf*).[21]

A major point of controversy was how to apply the notion of derivation (*ishtiqāq*) to the infinitival forms (*maṣādir*) and active participles (*asmāʾ al-fāʿil*) on the one hand, and to nouns and verbs on the other.[22] Derivation (*ishtiqāq*) may be translated with "etymology" and the only extant early work dedicated exclusively to *ishtiqāq* is in fact a work on etymology.[23] However, given the particularities of Arabic word formation, *ishtiqāq* is closely tied not only to historical word formation, but also to word formation by grammatical inflection (*taṣrīf*). Perhaps the first to systematize the notions of *taṣrīf* and *ishtiqāq* was Ibn Jinnī (d. 392/1002).[24]

The close relation between the two notions could arise naturally only because Semitic word formation is systematic in a way in which in Indo-European languages it is not. In Arabic, virtually all vocables consist of three root consonants. These may be modified by changing the intervening short vowels (which need not be written), or by adding augments, to nuance their semantic force. The semantic spectrum of the trilateral root is considered basic. Modifications, like any of the fourteen different verbal forms (expressing, for example, causative, reciprocal, or passive modifications of the basic meaning), participial or infinitival forms, as well as tensed conjugations or declinations, are considered derivative. They are derivative both on the level of morphology and on the level of meaning. One assumption was, as we will see later for Fārābī, that, historically, words signifying basic meanings came first. Derivations of words by means of *ishtiqāq* signify meanings that were later derived from basic meanings. It is here that for Arabic grammarians etymology and grammatical inflection converge: grammatical forms are seen as having etymologies.[25]

Depending on the rules for grammatical inflection (*taṣrīf*) and the conception of historical word formation (*ishtiqāq*), infinitival and participial forms of verbs will be classified differently. The Baṣrians derived the inflected verbal forms from the supposedly more basic tenseless infinitive. The Kūfans considered the tensed verbal forms primary and the infinitival forms secondary derivations.[26] Ibn al-Muqaffaʿ, for example, in line with the grammarians of Kūfa, had grouped the participial forms under *ḥarf* (particle) and taken them to signify an extended time (*fī ʾl al-ḥāl/fī ʾl dāʾim* in the grammarians' terminology).[27]

Discussions on semantic matters were central to other traditional disciplines as well, often cross-pollinating one another. In theology and especially in jurisprudence, at stake was not only the success of a theory, but serious implications for dogmatics or even criminal law.[28] A prime example is the debate about the createdness of the Qurʾān resulting in the inquisition of the *miḥna* (218–232/833–847). The question was here about the nature of the Arabic language understood as one of God's attributes (*ṣifāt*)—the Qurʾān being an expression of His pre-existing "speech"—and had far-reaching political consequences.[29]

Another example is the debate on the extensions of general terms in Islamic theology and jurisprudence. Beginning with the Baṣrian Muʿtazilite Wāṣil b. ʿAṭāʾ (d. 131/748–9) and the Kūfan Abū Ḥanīfa (d. 150/767), eponym of the Ḥanafī school of law, Schöck has shown how Qurʾānic exegesis, Arabic grammar, and Aristotelian logic mutually influenced one another in a quest for hermeneutical theories all the way down to Avicenna. The theory of derived nouns (*asmāʾ mushtaqqa*) as presented in Ibn al-Muqaffaʿ's theory of judgment or in Fārābī's position on propositional quantification was informed by both their readings of the *DI* and the current debates of the grammarians. As controversial contributions to the ongoing confrontation between *kalām* and *falsafa* they ultimately had palpable consequences for criminal law.[30]

Or, as a third example, Marwan Rashed has explored the algebraic-combinatorial theory of language propounded by the influential Muʿtazilite theologian Abū Hāshim al-Jubbāʾī (d. 321/933), which may have influenced Fārābī's theory of inference.[31]

Questions about the meaning and reference of words were thus debated across many disciplines. A particularly interesting case are works on *adab*, a genre of writing that had, by Fārābī's time, developed into a *sui generis* form of learned and witty belle-lettrism. Ibn al-Muqaffaʿ may be seen as pivotal in broadening the conception of *adab* with his works. Abū ʿUthmān ʿAmr al-Jāḥiẓ (d. 255/868–869) already presented a full-fledged theoretical discussion of meaning in his *Kitāb al-Bayān wa l-tabyīn* (Book of Eloquence and Exposition) that may be seen as a rival account to the Peripatetic one.[32]

One text is especially relevant here: Fārābī's younger contemporary Abū Hayyān al-Tawḥīdī (*fl.* mid- to late 4th/10th century), himself an *adīb* and admirer of al-Jāḥiẓ, recorded a public debate—said to have taken place in 326/937 at the court of the vizier Ibn al-Furāt—between the chief grammarian of Fārābī's time, Abū Saʿīd al-Sīrāfī (d. 368/979), and Fārābī's fellow Peripatetic Abū Bishr Mattā on the relative merits of Arabic grammar and Aristotelian logic.[33]

The Debate between Abū Bishr Mattā and Abū Saʿīd al-Sīrāfī

At the heart of the dispute as presented by al-Tawḥīdī is the question of which science can claim privileged access to understanding meanings (*maʿānī*). Abū Bishr holds that only logic deals with meanings to begin with, because it is in the business of clarifying the rules of thought irrespective of the language they are expressed in, as it investigates the intelligible meanings by scrutinizing their affections in the soul (111.1ff.). Logic thus deals primarily with meanings (*maʿānī*), and only accidentally with the forms of utterances, whereas grammar is said to deal with the forms of utterances of a specific language only (i.e., with *iʿrāb, taṣrīf, ishtiqāq* in Arabic). But as we have seen, especially the Baṣrians had made it their business to systematize the forms of utterances based on their *maʿānī*. Abū Saʿīd then retorts that the grammarians do in fact deal with *maʿānī*, and that their access to them is not only privileged but exclusive.

As Endreß has argued, Abū Bishr's claim was based on a semantic theory extracted from *DI* 1, and extracted in such a way that the Arabic *maʿnā*, which Isḥāq b. Ḥunayn had used to translate the Greek *pragma*, referred to things, as opposed to the meanings of linguistic signs.[34] Abū Saʿīd, on the contrary, takes the meaning (*maʿnā*) of a linguistic sign to be a reality in the mind that is first formed by linguistic mediation (111.1). It is thus only through language that meanings arise. Hence, according to Abū Saʿīd, it is absurd to claim *a priori* validity for logic as a tool to discern the true from the false by directly dealing with meanings, for the logician must use language to form those meanings (*maʿānī*), and the rules of Aristotelian logic are rules devised for and from within the Ancient

Greek language (110.11f.). Even if perfect translation were possible, the rules of logic would be the rules of a language long dead (111.13f.). However, since no two languages are exactly the same as to how they allow for meanings to be formed and conveyed, exact translation is virtually impossible to begin with (112.1–9).

Neither Abū Saʿīd nor Abū Bishr seems to be aware of their different conceptions of "*ma ʿnā*," but I think that they differ not only on some minute terminological detail. In the translations of Aristotelian logic familiar Arabic words became technical terms, and often the simultaneous use of such words in traditional and translated sciences led to confusion.[35] This particular confusion is paradigmatic of the different conceptions of "*ma ʿnā*" in Arabic grammar and Aristotelian logic. Abū Saʿīd's hostile remarks on Abū Bishr's poor Arabic are not mere *ad hominem* arguments. As a Syriac speaker with no knowledge of Greek and poor knowledge of Arabic (from a grammarian's point of view), Abū Bishr lacked the linguistic expertise to even notice such confusions.

One way to avoid terminological confusion was to create neologisms. Abū Saʿīd ridicules the Baghdād Peripatetics for that practice (123.6–124.6). His invective partly serves to show that he himself is well versed also in Aristotelian logic (in contrast to Abū Bishr, who repeatedly admits that he has not studied Arabic grammar), but it is noteworthy that his list of ridiculous and empty neologisms includes many of the key concepts of Aristotelian philosophy, and all are construed by adding the suffix "*-iyya*" to form abstract meanings from particles.[36] That procedure was, for Fārābī, a crucial tool for forging new concepts formerly non-existent in Arabic usage. It was also evidence for his theory of concept-formation.[37]

The historical background of the Graeco-Syriaco-Arabic transmission of the *Organon*, the "war of signification," the grammatical discussions about the notion of *ishtiqāq*, and the specific arguments about privileged access to meaning help better understand how Fārābī conceived of his philosophical project. He saw himself as the direct heir of a continuous Aristotelian tradition for the expression of which he felt he needed to construct a new technical language in Arabic that allowed talking *about* language in a logically perspicuous way.

FĀRĀBĪ AND HIS PHILOSOPHICAL PROJECT

Abū Naṣr Muḥammad b. Muḥammad al-Fārābī was born in the second half of the 3rd/9th century, likely in Fārāb, a district by the middle Syr Darya (Jaxartes) in modern-day Kazakhstan.[38] At some point he moved to Baghdād, where he sought out Abū Yaḥyā Ibrāhīm al-Marwazī and Yuḥannā ibn Ḥaylān from Moṣul to study Aristotelian logic. On his own testimony, he read with them all books of the *Organon*. Fārābī had several students in his later years in the capital, among whom the most important was the Jacobite Christian Yaḥyā Ibn ʿAdī (d. 363/974). Sometime between 330/942 and 331/943 Fārābī moved to Damascus and subsequently spent several years in Syria. He stayed at the court of the Ḥamdānid prince Sayf al-Dawla in Aleppo, where he dictated his commentary on the *APo* to his student Ibrahīm Ibn ʿAdī (Yaḥyā's brother?). Around 337/949 Fārābī was in Egypt. He died in Damascus in Rajab 339, between December 950 and January 951.

We still lack a critical inventory of Fārābī's works.[39] But it is clear that most of his writings on philosophical matters (his other great interest was music) deal with language and logic broadly, and many of them with the *Organon* specifically.[40] In fact, probably a good half of his output deals with logic. It can be classified into (1) epitomes of the *Organon* following the model of late antique prolegomena, (2) Alexandrian-style commentaries on most books of the *Organon*, (3) minor writings.[41] How are we to make sense of this unprecedented gravitational pull toward Aristotle, and to language and logic, in Fārābī's œuvre? An answer will have to involve an assessment of how Fārābi interacted with his immediate historical context, especially vis-à-vis the translation movement, the war of signification generally, and the grammatical tradition specifically.

Fārābī's "Alexandria to Baghdād" Narrative and His Knowledge of the Tradition

Reading Fārābī's account of the emergence of Aristotelian philosophy in the Islamic world may provide the basis for an explanation. As historically unreliable as his account in *Fī Ẓuhūr al-falsafa* (On the Emergence of [Aristotelian] Philosophy) may be, it is an important source for how Fārābī presented his own role in the historical context of his time.[42]

In the context of the translation movement and the Graeco-Syriaco-Arabic transmission process of Aristotle, Fārābī perceived his scholarly task to be—at a crucial moment in history—to facilitate the introduction of Aristotelian thought, and especially logic, into the Islamic scientific canon. It has been noted that the subtext of his account is clearly anti-Christian, anti-Byzantine, and phil-Hellenic.[43] Fārābī presents himself—in a direct lineage from Aristotle through Alexandria, Antioch, Marw, and Ḥarrān—as the savior of philosophy at the crucial moment in history when philosophy had come to an end everywhere else under Christian censorship.[44]

This is peculiar. First, why should Fārābī, who closely worked with several Christians in Muslim Baghdad, stylize himself as the savior of Aristotle from Christian censorship? And why should he insist on a continuous and single line of transmission from Aristotle to his own school—which he likely knew was historically inaccurate? The following is a possible explanation. As Gutas suggested, the anti-Christian element, which Fārābī's account shares with all others we have, may stem from intermediary sources written in the spirit of the Maʾmūnid ideology of "anti-Byzantinism is philhellenism."[45] Fārābī used it to the same effect for which the imperial propaganda had been designed: to contrast himself with the benighted and fanatic Byzantine Christians of the past who prohibited the study of the ancient sciences—and especially logic—for religious reasons.

In the intellectual climate intimated by the account of the Sīrāfī-Mattā debate, and at a time when the Byzantine threat was far greater than under al-Ma'mūn, Fārābī's self-representation then served to pit him against the enemies of Greek logic, like al-Sīrāfī, whom he implicitly assimilates to the Byzantine fanatics.[46] The same may hold for his insistence on the continuity of the transmission and his singular role in it. At any rate, it clearly was an appeal to authority, framed in terms of the Islamic notion of an uninterrupted chain of *ḥadīth* transmitters (*isnād/musnad*), which would have been more readily acknowledged in a majority Muslim context.

Thus, Fārābī's account may be read as a self-representation of his role as the savior of philosophy in the historical process. For the veneration of Aristotle instead of Plato, Fārābī might have found precedence in the Graeco-Syriac tradition. But, in any case, his concern with pleading the case for the utility of logic would have found little help in Plato.[47] It was the *Organon* that held the promise. That Fārābī not only presented himself as the savior of Aristotle, and specifically of his logic, but also perceived himself as such is borne out by the fact that he wrote more on Aristotle's logic in Arabic than anyone before him.[48]

The tendentious nature of Fārābī's account of the history of philosophy raises the question of how much he actually knew about the tradition. He likely read neither Syriac nor Greek and himself made no translations.[49] Concerning the *Organon*, we know from quotations in his extant works that he read the *Isag, Cat, DI, APr, APo, Top, Soph. El.*, and some version of the *Rhet*, all in Arabic translations.[50] Even though the Arabic translations of the *Organon* that Fārābī had at his disposal were far from perfect and in some cases outright spurious, there can be no doubt that he knew most of the *Organon*, and that he knew it very well.

The matter stands differently with Fārābī's knowledge of the commentaries. Almost all of Fārābī's references to the "commentators"—he hardly ever names individuals—were clearly not based on any knowledge of primary texts.[51] The most plausible scenario is that he was acquainted with their contributions through fragments and paraphrases he may have found in the margins of his Aristotelian text, like in the Parisinus Ar. 2346, and in didactic abridgements.[52]

Overall, however, his knowledge of the commentary tradition was rather thorough, and his sources must have come from both the Aphrodisian-Porphyrean and the Iamblichean-Ammonian commentary complex.[53] But Fārābī's access to the tradition was through Arabic alone, and his philosophical project was conceived on the basis of a theory of (the Arabic) language.

The Kitāb al-Ḥurūf: *The Origin of Language, Linguistic Constructivism, and Translation*

In the war of signification, the central issue at stake was how to claim privileged access to meanings (*ma'ānī*). One way to do this was to provide a theory of language to support such claims. I think this is what Fārābī does in what is perhaps his most independent philosophical work, the *Kitāb al-Ḥurūf* (Book of Letters/Particles, henceforth *KḤ*).[54] The theory of language developed there I call "Linguistic

Constructivism," and I think Fārābī employs it to justify the Aristotelian method. According to Linguistic Constructivism, language is essentially the product of a linguistic community's combining of signs to express meanings as need arises. In the process new concepts are formed for which then new signs are created, until gradually different sciences are constructed. Linguistic Constructivism is continuous with Fārābī's own philosophical project of forging a new terminology and language for Aristotelian philosophy in Arabic.[55]

On my reading of the *KḤ* Linguistic Constructivism casts the development of all sciences in a progressive historical account of the development of human language, based on a constructivist view of the formation of both words and concepts. On this theory the socio-historical development of language leads, on one hand, via new words and new concepts to new knowledge and new sciences. On the other hand, it leads to a usage of language that, even though sanctioned as "correct" by grammarians in accordance with the habits of its speakers, is however misleading as to the meanings and their arrangements it used to, and should for the purposes of demonstrative science, express.

Fārābī's mistrust of the surface structure of language is rooted in the idea that humans are inclined to use utterances metaphorically. Utterances are becoming increasingly estranged from the meanings they were initially forged for in connection to immediate experience. Only philosophy (*falsafa*) has the tools to unravel language and make it fit for demonstrative science. Without giving here, for lack of space, a sustained argument for this reading, the following summary may at least make the overall idea plausible.[56]

The *KḤ* consists of three parts (*abwāb*), the order of which is disputed.[57] What I take to be the first part (Mahdi's part 2) lays out the historical basis for Linguistic Constructivism, explaining how words came to be ambiguous. In the remainder of the work Fārābī applies the theory by working back to disambiguate the notions central to logic (part 1) and metaphysics (part 3). What I take to be part 1 is a detailed account of the origin and development of (the Arabic) language and the syllogistic sciences, from gesture and ostension in primitive communities to the rise of demonstrative science in Fārābī's day.

This story is remarkable for the fact that language is depicted as entirely conventional—in opposition to most contemporary theological arguments about the origin of language.[58] The two principles driving linguistic change are what I call the principle of inertia (§§115,118), according to which humans tend to choose the easiest path to arrive at their goals, and the principle of alignment (§122), according to which humans by their nature are inclined to systematize, and thus seek to align utterances and meanings in such a way that similar meanings are expressed by similar utterances. (§§123–124)

Different linguistic communities develop different languages because they have distinct physical features and some will find certain sounds easier to produce than others, so that, by the principle of inertia, they will then use the sounds they find easy to produce in the early stage of language development where phonemes are joined to ostension (§§117–118). Similarities between different languages are presumably simply due to similarities of human experience. As there are fewer distinct phonemes (*ḥurūf*) than meanings, humans began to combine phonemes that are gradually accepted in a linguistic community (§119).

In this early stage of language development, speakers begin to form concepts as follows (§§120–123). By pointing at something and accompanying it with the speech-sound communally accepted for it, and then pointing at a similar thing using the same speech-sound, a crucial step from referring to particulars toward a conception of universals is made. The community, or an individual, will continue to institute names for all meanings relevant for the necessities of life (§120).

Moving gradually from phenomena immediately accessible to perception to more abstract mental phenomena, at a certain point speech-sounds come to be instituted to signify actions (§121). With verbs at their disposition, it is supposedly at this point that the linguistic community acquires the ability to communicate APs (that is, beyond propositions only involving 1-place being and ostension, like pointing at a stone asking "Stone?"—and someone nodding, saying "Stone."). In the intermediary stage of language development, the existing vocabulary becomes increasingly systematized. The community begins to hierarchically organize universal terms into genera and species. As some speech-sounds signify meanings that are fixed and stable, but have changing accidents, they seek to reflect this in the forms of the utterances (§§123–127).

This is crucial, because I take this to refer to what the grammarians were to call *taṣrīf* and *ishtiqāq*. For example, the trilateral root BYḌ becomes instituted as *bayaḍ* to deictically refer to "this-white," then turning into the universal term "white." Gradually, new morphologies are derived to express changing accidents of the basic meaning. The root BYḌ and the meaning of "white" remain fixed. But with, e.g., *abyaḍḍa* (to whiten) or *bayāḍ* (whiteness), the changing accidents of the basic meaning are reflected by the changing intermittent sounds around the basic root consonants. Abstract terms ending in "-*iyya*" are formed by derivation, too, but may then be considered basic. Fārābī calls them *maṣadir*, not because they are grammatically infinitival forms, but because they come to be used to signify the source (*maṣdar*) meaning, abstracted from all changing accidents (*cf.* §83).

This process will at some point inevitably lead to ambiguity. Some utterances will be used for quite dissimilar meanings or different utterances for the same meaning, and homonymy and synonymy arise, followed by metonymy and metaphor. The mode of expression of the linguistic community is now rhetorical, increasingly developing the resources for poetic expression (§127). This is the beginning of the emergence of the practical syllogistic arts (Rhetoric, Poetry).

Language will increasingly be used to tell and orally transmit stories that matter to the linguistic community, until the tradition becomes too extensive to be memorized and writing is invented (§131). Subsequently the art of the knowledge of language begins to emerge (§132).[59] Then—and this I take to be a description of the emergence of Arabic grammar—people who inquire into utterances in the record will systematize them in terms of the similarities or differences they exhibit among one another (§136). Here, another crucial step is taken. To talk about the characteristics of utterances, new utterances to express these new meanings are required. These can be forged by either neologisms or metaphors (§136). Both are admissible and common practice, but Fārābī urges that it is best to use an existing utterance whose meaning is most similar to the new one (§136).

It will become clear that the utterances used to talk about utterances are utterances of second imposition, signifying secondary intelligibles. And this, as we shall see in the next chapter (see Texts 27–31), is precisely what Fārābī does by investing "*mawjūd*" with a new technical signification to express what he thinks the Greek *esti* expressed: the secondary intelligible of a predicative function. Fārābī has thus shown grammar its place in the development of the sciences.

Later, the community will gradually develop dialectical argumentation to validate their opinions (§140). They will come to distinguish sophistical from truly dialectical arguments and perfect the dialectical method. Fārābī thinks that this stage was reached in Greek civilization at the time of Plato (§142). The process continues until it reaches its goal, as it had with Aristotle: the method of demonstrative science in theoretical and practical philosophy (§143). The truths of philosophy are then taught by demonstrative proofs to the scholarly elite, and disseminated to the people in the more easily accessible guise of rhetorical or poetical discourse (§143).

Here, Fārābī puts the theologians into place. Only when the truths of philosophy are used to run a society can an excellently valid religion arise. If, however, religion arises before philosophy is perfected, it likely includes many false doctrines and will be corrupt (§§147–149). Both a religion and philosophy may be taken over from another society (§§149–152). It seems clear that Fārābī saw himself at the forefront of promulgating the already perfected philosophy of the Greeks to a society that had a religion before reaching philosophical perfection.

Fārābī's closing remarks connect his programmatic self-representation discussed above with his project of Linguistic Constructivism: "It is obvious that in every religion (*milla*) that is opposed to philosophy (*falsafa*), it is the discipline of theology (*kalām*) that opposes philosophy, the adherents of the former being pitted against the adherents of the latter, to the degree that the religion is opposed to philosophy" (157.1–3). To this statement, perhaps alluding to the *topos* of the "Byzantine fanatics," is appended a last chapter on coining and transferring names.

Fārābī offers a set of guidelines for the constructivist project—interestingly first framed by a scenario in which not philosophy is imported to a linguistic community, but religion—for how to proceed in cases when a certain philosophical meaning has no equivalent in that linguistic culture (§154; §§155–158). If the technical meaning of a philosophical term in the source language is derived from an ordinary meaning, then the translator should use an equivalent term in the target language that has the same ordinary meaning and institute it as a technical term. If there is no such equivalent, either a similar term with an ordinary meaning may be instituted as a technical term, or a neologism may be forged. A neologism may be forged either by transliterating the foreign word, or by creating a new word in the target language. These guidelines read like a considered response to al-Sīrāfī's ridiculing of Peripatetic neologisms.

This technique is continuous with the historical process described by Linguistic Constructivism. You just need to agree on, or stipulate, a sign to be used for a certain meaning. Hence the same problem arises: new technical terms are then used homonymously, synonymously, or else by virtue of other similarities may be used ambiguously. This ambiguity arises between technical and ordinary meanings of words, but also within the technical terminology, and it is the task of the philosopher to disambiguate language to make it fit for demonstrative science.

All this I take to be a *prolegomenon* providing the theory of language needed to ground the claim that Aristotelian logic is not only the best but the only way to access meanings in such a way as to allow for the certainty resulting from demonstration. Parts 2/3 (Mahdi's 1/3) then put theory into practice and in an exemplary fashion disambiguate the meanings of the particles that are most important for Aristotelian philosophy. Part 2 itself deals with particles relevant to logic, mainly the particles used to ask about the categories, while Part 3 deals with particles used to ask the questions relevant to demonstrative science described in *APo* B 1–2.

The notion of derivation (*ishtiqāq*) is central to Part 2, and it is here spelled out in connection with terms of first and second imposition. Based on his historical account of word formation, Fārābī thinks that the morphologically simplest forms of the Arabic language, the simple substantive noun or the Form I *maṣdar* (verbal noun), historically were coined first and used to name substances. He calls them, likely a calque from the Greek, prototypes (*al-muthul al-ūlā*).[60] From those prototypes names and verbs that always name attributes and thus co-signify an indeterminate subject were derived.

The grammarian will classify those derived words, but the logician will have to determine where among all the expressions of a language (that the linguistic community has tried to make resemble their meanings, resulting in ambiguity) morphology goes against logical syntax. The logician has developed a vocabulary to talk about the things that signify substances and attributes in the way that concept-formation is described, a meta-language to describe the object-language, so to speak.

The vocabulary of the meta-language refers to secondary intelligibles that unlike primary intelligibles have no reference to anything outside the soul. Examples are "genus," "prototype," "noun," "verb," "copula." This, I think, is how Fārābī conceives of his philosophical project. How, on that account, does Fārābī demarcate logic from Arabic grammar?

Grammar versus Logic

We have a treatise dedicated specifically to the difference between Aristotelian logic and Arabic grammar by Fārābī's younger contemporary and fellow student of Abū Bishr's, Yaḥyā ibn ʿAdī. It may have been redacted as a response to the debate between Abū Bishr and al-Sīrāfī.[61] In it, Ibn ʿAdī distinguishes the two disciplines along the same lines as his teacher Abū Bishr had done: grammar deals with the forms of linguistic signs of a particular language, while logic deals with meanings.

Fārābī did not write such a treatise, but the demarcation of logic from grammar features prominently in several of his works, notably in his *Iḥṣā' al-ʿulūm* (Enumeration of the Sciences).[62] Fārābī thinks that grammar deals with the rules for linguistic utterances insofar as they are manipulated in accordance with the arrangements and inflections peculiar to the practice of a particular linguistic community. Logic, in turn, deals with the rules for meanings insofar as they are expressed by linguistic utterances, or, which comes down to the same, with the rules for linguistic utterances insofar as they refer to meanings (17.5–7).[63]

This is slightly different from Abū Bishr's and Yaḥyā's claim: just like grammar, logic also deals with linguistic items, only from a different angle. And Fārābī was acutely aware that the grammatical rules of a particular language might be misleading with regard to the rules of logic. Whereas the rules of grammar are contingent on a given linguistic community, the rules of logic are universal (18.4–7).

In the case of simple predication, for example, a phenomenon common to all languages, this would mean that the grammarian investigates the issue only insofar as it arises in a particular language, whereas the logician investigates it insofar as it is common to all languages and as such a universal feature of thought (18.11ff.). Particular languages might differ in terms of the accuracy with which they reflect these universal features. It is therefore legitimate for the logician to turn to the grammarians, of different languages, if possible, for help in understanding these underlying features.

Much of Fārābī's philosophical project can be seen as an attempt to make conspicuous these traps of natural language, and he does turn to grammarians, Greek, Syriac, and Arabic, for help. Fārābī believes, for example, that the division of utterances into names, verbs, and particles is a feature common to all languages, reflecting a universal feature of thought; and it would seem that he thought the same of morphological derivation (*ishtiqāq*).[64] The use to which he puts this threefold division, and especially the role he assigns to the particles, as well as to the notion of morphological derivation (*ishtiqāq*), is however foreign to Aristotle. The theory should be seen as a result of the mutual influence between grammarians and logicians in the formative period of their respective disciplines, when fundamental classifications and the specific technical vocabularies were being developed.[65]

As Karimullah has convincingly argued, Fārābī held that the subject-matter of logic was primary intelligibles, and the most general of those, which Karimullah identifies with the ten categories.[66] On that picture, the logician is concerned with those utterances which signify intelligibles that have arisen from likenesses in the soul of things in the extramental world. These intelligibles are universals, abstracted from the experience of several similar *concreta*, as described by Linguistic Constructivism.

Of those, the most general are of the greatest importance to the logician: these most general intelligibles are the categories. This explains why Fārābī in the *KḤ* belabors the particles with which you ask about the categories. Secondary intelligibles, i.e., those that are true of first intelligibles, but not of anything in the extramental world, are those that the logician needs to use in order to describe the properties of and rules for combining first intelligibles. The utterances with which these secondary intelligibles are signified, e.g., "name," "statement-word," "universal," "copula," are the logician's vocabulary. And many of those are discussed in the *DI*.

SUMMARY

In the historical context of the translation movement, Fārābī saw himself as constructing a framework in Arabic with which Aristotelian logic could be imported to his own Arabo-Islamic civilization. A firm grasp of the demonstrative method would ensure a just and good society based on certain knowledge of philosophical truths. Casting his own philosophical project within his historical account of scientific progress, Fārābī ties his theory of the development of language and science to his own work as a logician engaged in Linguistic Constructivism. Under the pressure of theologians and grammarians he clearly demarcates logic from grammar in a way that ensures the universal applicability of the former—on the grounds that it deals with certain utterances insofar as they signify the most general first intelligibles, namely, the categories—whereas the latter has the parochial character of a specialized science only applicable within a given linguistic community.

At the same time, Fārābī engaged in what we may call a project of linguistic archaeology. By analyzing language from the standpoint of its historical formation, Fārābī sought to unravel the ambiguities of linguistic signs. That required making two fundamental distinctions. One with regard to the morphology of Arabic words (prototypal/derivative) and the other with regard to intelligibles (primary/secondary intelligibles). The prime example of a meaning for which Arabic had no ready equivalent, much less a linguistic sign, was the meaning expressed by the copula as discussed by the Greek commentators. Fārābī institutes *"mawjūd"* as a technical term, signifying the secondary intelligible of a predicative relation. But more than any other, this word was misleading on account of its morphology.

3

Greek Logic Arabicized
and the Copula Transformed

The *DI* is the only text of the *Organon* for which we have Fārābī's commentary in its entirety—and additionally his *Mukhtaṣar* (Epitome).[1] Fārābī's overall approach to the text has rightly been described as novel: he thinks that the *DI* is first and foremost concerned with the *formal composition* of utterances insofar as they signify meanings, that is, especially with the predicative relation signified by the copula.[2] The interpretation of the linguistic section evinces the influence of a number of ideas that Fārābī had formed, at least partly, elsewhere. Some of them have been introduced in the preceding chapter: the tripartite classification of linguistic items, his idea of paronymy as rooted in the development of language, his mistrust in linguistic surface structure, his notion of second-order concepts, the idea of logic as a universal grammar of thought, and his stance on which words co-signify tense.

Fārābī thinks there are three types of linguistic signs: nouns, verbs, and particles. Equating Aristotle's notion of paronymy from *Cat* 1 with the theory of morphological derivation (*ishtiqāq*) of the Arabic grammarians, Fārābī roots his fundamental distinction between utterances that signify attributes and utterances that signify substances in his theory of the development of language. No verb can signify a substance, nor can it function as an essential predicate, and it always co-signifies time.

Hence, Fārābī thinks, he needs to institute a new technical term with which to express that a predicate is said to hold of a subject absolutely and regardless of time. For these are the kinds of statements needed to express the timeless truths of philosophy. The word he uses as a timeless copula is the derived name "*mawjūd*," signifying in one of its senses the secondary intelligible of a predicative relation. That "*mawjūd*" is a derived name is a prime example of linguistic usage that is misleading with regard to logical form. In a logically perfect language, the predicative relation should be expressed by a particle—which is why Fārābī spends much of the *KH* disambiguating the different senses of "*mawjūd*."

FĀRĀBĪ AND ISḤĀQ B. ḤUNAYN'S TRANSLATION OF THE *DE INTERPRETATIONE*

As much as Fārābī's immediate historical context sketched in the preceding chapter may have led him to make a theory of translation integral to his philosophical project, he lacked the expertise in both Greek and Syriac to prepare his own translations. In any case, with enough professional translators around, there was no need. While Fārābī in some cases undoubtedly played a role in establishing the Arabic text and especially its technical terminology, his own initial access to the *DI* was dependent on what he understood from the Arabic translation in which he first read it.[3] Hence we must afford a brief look at some of the particularities of the Arabic translation that may have influenced Fārābī's novel way to conceptualize the copula.

The Arabic Translation: Sources and Methods

The translation, apparently the first to be made into Arabic, was prepared by Isḥāq b. Ḥunayn (d. 289/911), probably from an intermediary Syriac version made by his father, Ḥunayn b. Isḥāq (d. 260/873).[4] The text was edited (with an extensive glossary) from the MS Paris: Bibliothèque nationale, Arabe 2346 (*P*) by Pollak in 1913.[5] The manuscript represents a type of Baghdād school-canon of the Arabic *Organon*. Sometimes it contains several translations of the same text and running annotations in the margins, many of which were already accessible to Fārābī. Thus, *P* bears witness that the creation of a unified Arabic text for Aristotle's logical writings, with a coherent technical terminology that was both accurate and understandable, was an ongoing and collaborative effort of both translators and philosophers.[6]

The fact that the Arabic text itself appears to be full of "barbarisms" need not indicate an inferior quality of the translation. Rather, at least in the case of the *DI*, this fact reflects a theory of translation underpinning a highly professionalized praxis that carefully negotiated between intelligibility and faithfulness to the original text.[7] We know of Ḥunayn b. Isḥāq—who reportedly had learned Greek in Alexandria and was able to recite Homer[8]—that he applied rigorous philological methods, including the collation of several manuscripts in different languages, in order to establish a given text before translating it. He employed the *sententia pro sententia* method of translation (instead of *verbum pro verbo*), which he is said to have perfected.[9] It stands to reason that Fārābī's theory of translation was influenced by the hands-on experience of translators.

Ḥunayn's son Isḥāq, who (in contrast to Abū Bishr, for example) had a reputation for being even more accomplished in the Arabic language (*faṣīḥ*) than his father, would apply the same critical methods. It is not unlikely that he—as did Ibn Suwār, for example—compared Greek manuscripts with the Syriac text in the process of translating the *DI*.[10] As opposed to his father, who had specialized in the Galenic corpus, Isḥāq's focus was on Greek philosophical works. Hence, he must have been even more versed in the different terminological choices other scholars had made in translating Aristotelian logical works into Arabic.

By Isḥāq's time, several key terms seem to have had one, or sometimes several, counterparts in Arabic that were already established as technical terms. The problematic title of the *DI*, for example, was either transliterated or unanimously translated as *al-ʿIbāra* (perhaps literally from the Greek [diction, interpretation]; but it regularly also means expression).[11]

The Translation of DI *2–4: Terminology and the Term* "Kalima"

Concerning the translation of *DI* 2–4, the terms for name, statement-word, and declarative phrase are rendered as "*ism*," "*kalima*," and "*qawl jāzim*," respectively. "*Ism*" and "*qawl jāzim*" are straightforward translations by means of the technical vocabulary of Arabic grammar. However, "*kalima*" is precisely not the technical term of Arabic grammar for "verb" (*fiʿl*), but a more general term, perhaps modeled on the Greek *rhēma*, signifying "word." Translators may have followed the same inclination as I have in instituting a new technical term ("statement-word") to designate the type of word Aristotle defines (whether or not that may include words that are not grammatical verbs).

The school notes in the margins of *P* show that translators and philosophers were indeed troubled by this: "Among the Greeks, 'verb' (*kalima*) corresponds to what is called 'verb' (*fiʿl*) by Arabic grammarians. A *kalima* signifies acting, like 'beat,' or being acted upon, like 'was beaten,' or mere existence, like 'was' (*kāna*) or 'will be' (*yakūn*)."[12] This does not, however, square with Aristotle's use of examples.[13] Another school note reads: "Aristotle can call *yūjad*, which is a verb (*fiʿl*), a name (*ism*) because the Greek grammarians call, in a general way, every word a name."[14]

There was confusion about the relation between Arabic grammatical terminology and the terminology of the *DI*. The particular choice of translating "*rhēma*" by "*kalima*" provided a steppingstone for Fārābī's new understanding of the copula. For it allowed him to construe Aristotle's "*kalima*" as an ambiguous term that, in its strict sense, only designated any sign signifying the copulative force.

The Translation of "Einai" *in the* DI

Apart from the particularities of Isḥāq's translation of *DI* 2–4, it is in the ways that the Greek word "*einai*" itself is translated in the passages discussed in chapter 1 that we find some hints to better understand Fārābī's new conception of the copula and his interpretation of what he thought Aristotle must have understood by "*kalima*." Throughout the *DI* the word "*einai*" is—when it is not omitted—usually translated by locutions involving either the root KWN (to be) or a passive form of the root WJD (to find).[15] Both strategies were of course applied in other translations of Aristotle (especially of the *Cat*) and were already established by Isḥāq's time.

The problem in translating *"einai"* into Arabic (or Syriac) does not lie in the task of translating Greek sentences in which a conjugated form of the word is used. For inflected forms of the roots KWN and WJD, like *"kāna"* (was) and *"yakūnu"* (is/will be) or *"yūjadu"* (is-found-as) and *"mawjūd"* (passive participle: [is-]found-as), even though they are semantically superfluous and grammatically improper in present-tense statements, are perfectly understandable in Arabic and convey pretty much the same sense as the Greek when used in a *verbum pro verbo* translation. And, of course, on the *sententia pro sententia* method, the sense of a Greek present-tense sentence containing *"einai"* can be rendered perfectly accurately in impeccable Arabic without mentioning a copula. (Another way to translate such sentences into Arabic is to use the partitive pronoun *"huwa"* [he] between subject and predicate term. This was done and is mentioned by Fārābī, but it does not appear in Isḥāq's translation of the *DI*.[16] It was more frequently used after Fārābī and became the standard example for the Arabic copula in the later tradition.)

Rather, the problem arises in one of two cases: (a) when it appears that the use of *"einai"* in a present-tense declarative statement matters for the logical analysis of a sentence, or (b) when in the Greek text the word *"einai"* is mentioned rather than used. Both (a) and (b) arise in the notorious *tertium adiacens* passage:

TEXT 19 (ḤUNAYN *DI* 10): *DI* 19B19–22 = ARISṬŪṬĀLĪS, *KITĀB AL-ʿIBĀRĀ* (POLLAK), 18.11–15

But when "is" is additionally predicated as a third item, there are already two [pairs] of contradictory statements. I mean, for example, [statements of the form] "[A] man is just." I take "is" as a third item to be compounded with a naming-word, or [rather?] a statement-word, in an affirmation.

As for when the statement-word signifying hyparxis is a third [component], predicated [in addition] to what is predicated, then contradiction is said in this case of two contradictories.[17] An example of this is "A man is-found-as just." "Is-found-as" is a third thing connected to [the statement-word "just"] in this affirmation, being either a name, or a statement-word [or, reading *bimā* instead of *bihā*, as in Fārābī's lemma: "is-found-as" is a third thing connected to what is affirmed].

To deal with (b), Isḥāq here uses the circumlocution "the statement-word signifying hyparxis" (*al-kalimatu l-dāllatu ʿalā l-wujūdi*) to render the Greek mention of *"esti"* (marked by the definite article *to*). The locution *"al-kalimatu l-dāllatu ʿalā l-wujūdi"* as a description of *"esti"* is a reflection of how far the interpretive history of the *DI* had come: *"al-kalima"* is a technical term, distinct from the term for "verb" used by Arabic grammarians; the notion of copulae as hyparctic statement-words—nowhere explicit in Aristotle—had found its way, likely via Stephanus's *hyparktikon rhēma*, to the Arabic translators.

With "*to esti*" so understood, the point of this passage is precisely (a), i.e., that the role played by "*esti*" in a categorical statement does matter for its logical analysis. Given the main point made in the passage, namely that in statements of the form "[A] man is just" there are two possible contradictory statement pairs (and not one, as with, e.g., "[A] man runs") precisely because "is" can be negated, it was impossible to omit the copula in the Arabic translation of the examples. The Arabic word to translate "*esti*" as used in the example is "*yūjad*," strangely placed at the beginning of the sentence. For the mention of "*esti*" immediately following its use, the translator choses "*yūjad*" again. But he marks it out by "*qawlunā*" (our saying), a way to express in Arabic what we commonly express by quotation marks.

As for the question that the Greek text had raised, i.e., relative to what "*esti*" was to be considered a third item, Isḥāq's Arabic was perhaps aiming at preserving the ambiguity (*bihā*), but Fārābī "corrected" the text so that its sense could now be taken to be that the hyparctic statement-word was a third item in an affirmative proposition and could be either a name or a statement-word. Nonsensical as this may at first sound, I think this is what Fārābī understood from the Arabic here, and he bent the definition of "*kalima*" to accommodate his understanding of this passage.

Another passage shows the same strategy for rendering a mention of "*esti*," and helps to see how one could think that what "*kalima*" really means for Aristotle is the copulative force:

TEXT 20 (ḤUNAYN *DI* 10): *DI* 20A3–5 = ARISṬŪṬĀLĪS, *KITĀB AL-'IBĀRĀ* (POLLAK), 19.10–13

<table>
<tr><td>

But concerning those [statement-words] with which "is" does not fit together, like with "recover" or "walk," since they take the same place that "is" would take [in the sentence], they play the same role [as it].

</td><td>

And that for which it is not correct that there be a hyparctic statement-word in it, as is the case with "recovers" or "walks," this type of statement-word plays the role—since the position of that verb is the same—which the particle "*yūjad*" or its likes play, if it is connected to them.

</td></tr>
</table>

Further, in the translation of the second occurrence of the mention of "*esti*" in this passage, "*yūjad*" is called a particle—even though clearly, in grammatical terminology, it is a verb (*fiʿl*). Fārābī, I am going to suggest, ultimately conceived of the copula as a particle, and he might have been pushed to this position by such translations.

But that position was difficult to reconcile with other passages in the *DI*:

TEXT 21 (ḤUNAYN *DI* 10): *DI* 19B12–14 = ARISṬŪṬĀLĪS, *KITĀB AL-ʿIBĀRĀ* (POLLAK), 18.4–6

Without a statement-word there is no affirmation or negation; for "is" or "will be" or "was," or "becomes" or other such more, are, according to what was laid down, statement-words; for they co-signify time.

There is no affirmation and no negation in the absence of a statement-word. For "was" or "is" or "will be," or "becomes" and others like this, they are—from what has been laid down—statement-words. That is because they signify, along with what they signify [to begin with], a time.

In both Greek and Arabic, it would appear that copulative words are statement-words, or in fact real *verbs*, because they co-signify time. A way to circumnavigate this problem was to interpret "*kalima*" as only signifying the copulative force.

It is noteworthy that in the passage in which Aristotle stated that "*esti*" need not have existential import in *tertium adiacens* propositions, Isḥāq uses not "*yūjad*," but "*mawjūd*" for "*esti*":[18]

TEXT 22 (ḤUNAYN *DI* 11): *DI* 21A25–28 = ARISṬŪṬĀLĪS, *KITĀB AL-ʿIBĀRĀ* (POLLAK), 23.21–25

Homer, for example, *is something*, let us say a poet. Does it then follow that he *is* (i.e., exists), or not? [Of course not.] For "is" is predicated accidentally of Homer—since he *is a poet*; but "is" is [here] not *per se* predicated of Homer.

An example of this is "Homer is-found-as something" (*mawjūd*), like when you say "a poet." Is he then existent or not? [In this case,] we predicated "is-found-as" of Homer only accidentally, meaning that we only said that he is-found-as-a-poet, and "is-found" is not predicated of Homer himself [essentially].

We shall see that it was Fārābī's contention that "*mawjūd*" was to be used in logic to signify the copulative force, without existential import and regardless of time.

FĀRĀBĪ'S COMMENTARY: THE AMPLIFYING VARIANT,
PARONYMY (*ishtiqāq*), AND TENSE

Another textual particularity, not so much due to translation, but more due to the textual transmission, was crucial in shaping Fārābī's reading of the *DI*. In his commentary, Fārābī explains the ascriptive force of the statement-word in terms of the semantic properties of derived nouns. The latter notion was more familiar from Arabic grammar and more fundamental, given Fārābī's theory of language, than that of the copula. It ultimately is the notion of derivation (*ishtiqāq*) that provided the basis for Fārābī's logical syntax:

TEXT 23 (FARAB. *DI* 3): AL-FĀRĀBĪ, *SHARḤ AL-ʿIBĀRĀ* (KUTSCH & MARROW), 33.13–26 (Z 22)

It [i.e., the statement-word] is always a sign of being said of something else:[19] We must take it to mean that statement-words are like derived expressions. For like a derived noun, a statement-word signifies an indeterminate subject. It also signifies its connection with the subject of which it is predicated, without requiring a hyparctic verb as a copula. Furthermore, it signifies something whose proper function is never to be a subject by itself but always a predicate.

Always a statement-word is a sign of being said of something else, such as what is said of a subject or what is in a subject: we must understand that a statement-word *qua* predicate is always a sign of being predicated of something else, that is, a sign of the predicate's connection with the subject. For a predicate is inevitably either a statement-word or a name. If it is a statement-word, it combines two things: the notion predicated and the predicate's connection with the subject. If it is a name—and a name does not become a predicate of a name unless it is connected by a hyparctic verb—then it is either the predicate which defines a subject's essence, or the kind that is in a subject. In either case, it is the statement-word that signifies that the predicate *qua* predicate is connected with the subject. It signifies a predicate as such, no matter whether it is predicated of a subject or in a subject.

The Amplifying Variant

The translation Fārābī is reading includes the amplifying variant that was already present in Ammonius, as we saw, and transmitted by Ibn al-Muqaffaʿ. It glosses the definition of the statement-word as always being a sign of what is said of something else with "*such as what is said of a subject or what is said in a subject.*"[20] Like Ibn al-Muqaffaʿ and earlier Ammonius and Stephanus, Fārābī understood this amplifying variant with reference to *Cat* 1–2 and 5.[21]

According to Fārābī's claims in this passage, a statement-word is always a predicate by dint of its semantic structure (and, conversely, no subject can be a statement-word). This claim applies to finite verbs only, and as such would be trivial, were it not for some peculiarities of the Greek and Arabic languages. Following Ammonius and the amplifying variant, Stephanus had explained the lemma in question: "And that [verbs] are always said of something else, either of a subject, when they are predicated synonymously, as in 'walking is moving,' or 'philoso-phizing is eudaimonizing,' or as being in a subject, as in 'Socrates recovers.'"[22] For Stephanus it was possible for verbs to predicate synonymously, and thus essentially. And it was not a problem for verbs to take the subject position in a sentence, as his examples show. In Greek, infinitives are tensed just like finite verbs, and thus do not violate the definition of a verb.

Arabic, however, does not have tensed infinitives. The only grammatical form comparable to a Greek infinitive is the *maṣdar* (verbal noun). We have seen the discussions between the Kūfan and Baṣrian grammarians concerning the temporality of the *maṣdar* and participial forms. Ibn al-Muqaffaʿ, in line with the grammarians of Kūfa, had grouped the participial forms under *ḥarf* and taken them to signify an extended time (*fiʾl al-ḥāl*/*fiʾl dāʾim* in the grammarians' terminology).[23] For Fārābī, they do not co-signify time and hence are not verbs. Reading the amplifying variant in Isḥāq's text, Fārābī had no doubt that this was a reference to *Cat* 1–5, where Aristotle explains the notion of paronymous predication. But what does paronymous predication have to do with verbs?

Paronymy and Morphological Derivation (ishtiqāq):
Signifying Substance vs. Attributes

In the beginning of the *Cat* Aristotle had distinguished between homonymous, synonymous and paronymous names: a homonym is a name applied to multiple referents under different definitions in each case ("animal" to a real man and a man in a painting); a synonym is a name applied to multiple referents with the same definition in each case ("animal" to a man and an ox); and a paronym is a name derived from the name of a quality by inflection ("courageous," as derived from "courage"). Next, he had distinguished between something being said *of* a subject and something being *in* a subject.

As it was commonly understood in the Greek tradition, Aristotle in *Cat* 2 had proposed a fourfold division of beings into (1) universal substances (being said of a subject, but not inhering in a subject = "secondary substance"), (2) particular substances (neither said of nor inhering in a subject = "primary substance"), (3) universal accidents (both said of a subject and inhering in a subject), and (4) particular accidents (inhering in a subject, but not said of a subject). (1) and (3) are essentially predicated, whereas (4) is accidentally predicated.[24] Concerning this distinction, as we have seen, the commentary tradition Fārābī had at his disposal had distinguished two main senses of "is" in predication. Universals are said *of* their particulars "homonymously," whereas accidents are said to be *in* their substances "paronymously."

The first fundamental distinction is thus that between word-classes that signify substances and those that signify attributes. Equating Aristotle's notion of paronymy with the notion of morphological derivation of the Arabic grammarians, Fārābī came to think that verbs are always predicates. Following Ammonius, he takes them to be always analyzable into [cop+NW] (e.g., "is Φing"), except that for Fārābī, a NW is then a derived name (*ism mushtaqq*: IM for short). But any IM, being a word derived from a basic trilateral root in Arabic in order to signify not a substance as the original word, but a property of a substance, implies that there is some substance in which that property inheres. It is this fact that explains why any statement-word co-signifies an indeterminate subject in which the notion it primarily signifies inheres (just as any IM does). Thus, the first fundamental distinction Fārābī makes is that between prototypal expressions signifying a substance, and derivative expressions signifying accidents, where verbs are derivative.

On this basis, Fārābī thinks that the semantic structure of a verb itself is four-fold. By virtue of its form (analyzable as [cop+IM]) it signifies

1. an indeterminate subject (as any IM does),
2. the notion it signifies,
3. a circumscribed time,
4. that the notion it signifies is in a subject at the circumscribed time.

This last signification is the copulative function. Hence, verbs can only paronymously be predicated of a subject, and only in relation to a circumscribed time. Thus, verbs only predicate accidentally, not essentially, an attribute of a subject. However, for Fārābī, it is still always a verb that signifies that the predicate is connected to the subject. If the predicate is a regular verb, it co-signifies that *qua* predicate it is connected to the subject. If it is a name, then a hyparctic verb (*kalima wujūdiyya*) is needed to signify that the predicate is connected to the subject.[25]

Fārābī here claims against Ammonius and Stephanus that a verb—defined as co-signifying time, an indeterminate subject, and the copulative function—can only occur in the predicate-place, and hence no subject-place can be filled by a verb. Against Ibn al-Muqaffaʿ, he claims that participial forms do *not* co-signify time, as every verb can be analyzed into [cop+IM], where IM stands for a derived name, and tense is co-signified by the copula. He follows Ammonius's argument about the analysis of verbs into [cop+NW].[26]

In general, if the predicate is a name, it either is a prototypal noun and synonymously predicates an essential attribute of the subject; or it is a derived noun and paronymously predicates an accidental attribute in a subject. Fārābī merges the notion of *ishtiqāq* from Arabic grammar with Aristotle's notion of paronymy. As a result, verbs can only be paronymously predicated.

Traps of Linguistic Form: An Exemplary Semantic Analysis of a Misleading Derived Name

On that account, although Arabic is far more systematic than other languages in this regard, there may be traps of linguistic form. Derived names may be used for non-derived meanings, and it is not always clear how to take a given noun. An exemplary case of tracking down the misleading structure of natural language is the semantic analysis of the derived name "*ḥayy*" (alive) that Fārābī carries out next:[27]

TEXT 24 (FARAB. *DI* 3): AL-FĀRĀBĪ, *SHARḤ AL-ʿIBĀRĀ* (KUTSCH & MARROW), 34.23–35.5 (Z 22)

Names of secondary substances are clearly not to be verbalized at all since they are not used derivatively or signify any subject whatever.

Someone might ask about *ḥayy* [alive], a name used to signify the same as *ḥayawān* [animal], namely, a secondary substance, despite being a derived noun. Moreover, *yaḥyā* [lives] is a verb. How has "animal" come to be the substance of something named by a derived noun? And how has it come to be signified by a verb?

If this is so, then here is a substance that has a subject since a derived noun signifies a subject. Similarly, if *yaḥyā* is a verb, it too signifies a subject: it always signifies being predicated of something else.

The answer is that *ḥayy* is [indeed] of derivative shape, and that this derivative shape can be shared by notions with a derived name and such with an underived name. For one of the stipulations as to what a notion with a derived name is is that it should signify a subject.

In such cases, there is ambiguity, and we have to ask what we mean when we use a word like "*ḥayy*." Sometimes, Fārābī continues, we mean by "*ḥayy*" that something has breath (*dhū nafas*), in which case the derivative noun "*ḥayy*" is used in its derivative meaning to predicate a differentia, signifying a subject that has breath.[28] There seems to be no problem here, but:

TEXT 25 (FARAB. *DI* 3): AL-FĀRĀBĪ, *SHARḤ AL-ʿIBĀRA* (KUTSCH & MARROW), 35.17–21 (Z 24)

Sometimes, when we say something is *ḥayy*, we mean to say that it is a union of a body and a sensitive soul, that is, of matter and form. In this case, it signifies, not a differentia or an accident in an animal, but the same as "animal." When so used, "*ḥayy*" is the name of a secondary substance, does not signify a subject, is not derived albeit of derivative shape, and is not to be verbalized.[29]

The logician can thus make conspicuous the logical structure of a statement by analyzing the semantics of a derived name.

The Problem with Signifying Untensed Statements in Arabic

The second fundamental distinction is that between word formations that by their very grammatical form co-signify time or not. What can go into the predicate-place always contains a verb, either a proper verb or a hyparctic one, and if time is co-signified, predication will be accidental. Fārābī's account so far makes it impossible to make well-formed untensed statements in Arabic.

But he needs such statements to account for synonymous and essential predication. He alludes to the discussions of Arabic grammarians concerning the question whether the present time can be signified at all.[30] Discussing whether uninflected verbs (present tense verbs for Aristotle, *maṣādir* for Fārābī) signify time, he writes:

TEXT 26 (FARAB. *DI* 3): AL-FĀRĀBĪ, *SHARḤ AL-ʿIBĀRA* (KUTSCH & MARROW), 41.19–28 (Z 32)

Others believe that derived nouns are uninflected verbs, and that it is derived nouns that signify that something is taking place in the present time. But this is not the case, because formation and shape of a derived noun do not signify any time whatever, except perhaps in an accidental way in which some nouns that are prototypes signify time.

This is the proof: if derived nouns were verbs by essence and formation, they would also have the signification of hyparctic verbs. There would be no need for them to be connected, when predicated, by a hyparctic verb being expressly articulated or tacitly understood. But we find that they are not connected with a subject unless a hyparctic verb is manifestly expressed or tacitly supplied in the soul. Examples are "Zayd is just" and "Zayd is walking." If we articulated the hyparctic verb in addition to the predicate, it would be nonsensical and redundant, as in "Zayd is walks," "Zayd will be walks," "Zayd was walks," or " . . . is will walk."

On Fārābī's account, the analysis of APs can always be formalized as

[name [(hyparctic verb) (prototype/derived name)]]

and there is always a tense co-signified. Whenever a tense is co-signified, the predication might express that something is said of something else synonymously, but not essentially, for it is only said to be holding for the time signified. Fārābī's idiosyncratic interpretation of Aristotle's claim that every well-formed statement needs a verb provides the conceptual framework to account for essential predication. The timeless truths sought in the sciences can be expressed by redefining the copula as a syntactical marker.

THE COPULA AND SCIENTIFIC PROPOSITIONS

Fārābī thinks that in Arabic an expression for the timeless copula is crucially missing. He uses the technical term *"mawjūd"* to make up for this deficiency, because the copula "is necessary in the theoretical sciences and in the art of logic."[31]

The Copula and Its Signification

Fārābī presumably gets the cue for his theory of the copula from the notorious passage in *DI* 3 (16b22–25).[32] He begins by relating how "the commentators" interpreted the passage. We can identify "the commentators" here with the Iamblichean-Ammonian tradition, and almost certainly with Ammonius himself, for Fārābī rehearses Ammonius's argument.[33] Fārābī voices his discontent with this reading but admits that in his opinion the question whether or not any verb in isolation, hyparctic or not, signifies affirmation or negation is a very obscure matter (*fa-amruhā aghmaḍ*; 44.12f., Z 35). Especially so when it is used as a copula.

He suggests to read this passage not as an *a fortiori* argument in the way Ammonius had done, but as an explanation of the force of the hyparctic verb as such (44.14–15, Z 35). Fārābī admits that hyparctic verbs can be used existentially—but then signify in the way all other verbs do. In the copulative use of hyparctic verbs, however, there is no referent or meaning that is signified by the hyparctic verb. All that is signified is the composition, i.e., that subject and predicate are so combined. This is why Fārābī can take the following clause that had so troubled commentators in an idiosyncratic way. He comments on the lemma "for in itself it [i.e., "being": *un/to on*] is nothing," reverting to the Aphrodisian-Porphyrean position that the copula is a mere *Formwort*:

TEXT 27 (FARAB. *DI* 3): AL-FĀRĀBĪ, *SHARḤ AL-ʿIBĀRA* (KUTSCH & MARROW), 44.24–27 (Z 36)

> The words *un* [i.e., *to on*], *mawjūd* [found], *yūjad* [is-found], and *wujida* [was-found] by themselves do not signify a thing, but they signify a composition. Composition is a relation; and this composition, being a relation, cannot be understood without the components, namely, the predicate noun and the subject noun, in accordance with the fact that a relation cannot be understood unless the things related are taken into account.

After having given an answer to the question of what the components of a statement are, i.e., noun and verb, Fārābī here spells out how the components of a statement are put together, and what it is that connects them: it is a relation (*iḍāfa*) that is expressed by the copula. Relations are, as we shall see in the next section, primarily expressed by particles. The discussion of relations occupies an important part in the *KḤ*.[34] There Fārābī says that "*mawjūd*"

TEXT 28 (FARAB. *KḤ*): AL-FĀRĀBĪ, *KITĀB AL-ḤURŪF* (MAHDI), 125.13–126.12

> serves to connect the predicate with the subject in affirmative statements […] as an expression in which is implied a subject of a predicate or a predicate of a subject—in a word: two things so combined. […]
>
> In the force of this expression are two quiddities thus related. […] It comprises not the two things themselves, but a subject of a predicate or a predicate of a subject. Thus, it makes no difference whether we state from the subject to the predicate or from the predicate to the subject by saying "A is B" or "B holds of A."[35]

The copula "*mawjūd*" expresses a relation between subject and predicate. It does not signify anything besides this relation. For Fārābī it is a syntactical marker of a predicative function with two argument places (*__mawjūdun__*). But what can go into each argument place is not arbitrary, for if we switch the arguments, we have to account for that switch by also converting "is" (*alifun mawjūdun bāʾan*) into "holds of" (*bāʾun mawjūdun li-alifin*), so that we should rather write (… *mawjūdun__*). That Fārābī conceived of the relation between subject and predicate term as inherently asymmetrical is shown by the definition of relation (*iḍāfa*) in a passage from the *KḤ*.[36] Presenting the copula as a syntactical marker in these terms is novel in the tradition.

The Copula as Signifying a Secondary Intelligible

Following the comment on the lemma quoted earlier, Fārābī anticipates a number of objections someone could raise against the idea that the copula "*mawjūd*" signifies a relation. The first objection is this. If the copula (*yūjad, wujida, mawjūd*) signifies the relation of the predicate to the subject, then in the sentence "Zayd is existent" (*Zaydun yūjadu mawjūdan*) we would have to say that the predicate is related to the subject twice. Fārābī responds that here only "*yūjad*" is the copula that behaves like a hyparctic verb, whereas "*mawjūd*" in this case is the predicate, i.e., a derived noun that does not signify the relation. It here only signifies "existent."[37]

The second objection is a version of the unity of the proposition problem. If there is a relation connecting subject and predicate that is expressed by the copula, how then is that relation connected to the subject? There would have to be a relation between the relation expressed by the copula and the subject, and between that relation and the subject, and so *ad infinitum*. Fārābī responds that that is true, but does no harm, because the notion of the copula expressing a relation is a secondary intelligible (*ma ʿqul thānī*) and the regress is not vicious.[38]

Having established that the copula signifies a relation and as such is a secondary intelligible, Fārābī tries to reconcile the Aristotelian text with his own grammatico-logical framework. Anticipating two further objections, he establishes how "*mawjūd*," even though grammatically a derived name, can function as a copula for tenseless scientific statements.[39]

"Mawjūd" as a Tenseless Copula for Scientific Statements

Aristotle says that "no statement is proper without a verb" (19b12). But according to what Fārābī has laid out so far, the sentence "*Zaydun mawjūdun ʿādilan*" is well formed, even though it contains no verb. His exegetical argument is based on observations in comparative grammar:

TEXT 29 (FARAB. *DI* 3): AL-FĀRĀBĪ, *SHARḤ AL-ʿIBĀRĀ* (KUTSCH & MARROW), 46.13–20 (Z 38)

We find the same situation in all languages. We find that there are hyparctic verbs that signify the present, future, and past times. We find that a noun which derives from the verbal noun (*maṣdar*) of the hyparctic verb and which, like other derived nouns, does not signify a time is employed, like the hyparctic verbs, as a copula in statements whose predicates are nouns. This noun is represented by the word *mawjūd* in Arabic, in Greek by *astin* and *ūn*, in Persian by *ast* and *hast*, and by corresponding expressions in other languages. These expressions are employed as copulae when a circumscribed time is not to be signified. They serve to signify that the predicate-noun is to be connected with the subject-noun without qualification, either without [considering] time, or in time absolutely [i.e. eternally].

Even though Fārābī is mistaken about the details of Greek grammar, his observations are illuminating as to his own logico-linguistic thinking. It seems likely that Fārābī's conviction that both *ast/hast* (is/there is) and *astin* (a transliteration of *estin*, which is also third-person singular, meaning "is," or sometimes existentially "there is") are nouns stems from an oral source who knew Syriac, but not Greek or Persian (perhaps Abū Bishr). In Syriac *īth* means "existence" and is grammatically a noun and hence does not have any reference to time.[40]

Since, according to Fārābī's conception, "in Arabic, from the very outset of its formation, there was no expression to take the place of *hast* in Persian or of *astin* in Greek," the (Peripatetic) philosophers, once they started to do logic and philosophy in Arabic, saw the need to forge a new term and began using "*huwa*" (he) instead.[41] But "*huwa*" was presumably a less elegant solution, as it could not be inflected to serve as tensed and untensed copulae or as a 1-place predicate, so that later it was replaced by "*mawjūd*."[42] We have seen that the question whether participial forms co-signified time or not was a heated discussion among Arabic grammarians. That Fārābī had to maintain that participial forms precisely do not co-signify time may well have been determined by the need he saw for "*mawjūd*" to play the role of a timeless copula in the otherwise deficient Arabic language.

Having argued that essential predication is possible by way of the timeless copula "*mawjūd*"—if taken to play the same role as Fārābī thought the copulae did in Persian, Greek, or Syriac—Fārābī still has to explain why a statement of the form

Zaydun mawjūdun ʿādilan (Zayd [is]-found-as just)

can be well formed, even though it does not contain a verb. He suggests, referring to *DI* 10 (19b19–26), that what Aristotle means by "statement-word" (*kalima*) is not always the same:

TEXT 30 (FARAB. *DI* 3): AL-FĀRĀBĪ, SHARḤ AL-ʿIBĀRĀ (KUTSCH & MARROW), 47.16–18 (Z 39)

In this case *kalima* would be a term usable in a wider or narrower sense. First of all, *kalima* [in the non-technical sense of "word"] means any significant expression. This meaning is familiar in the language of every nation. Secondly, *kalima* means an expression "which signifies hyparxis" and which is employed as a "third component" connecting the predicate to the subject. And the third meaning is the one he [Aristotle] defined after [defining] the noun.[43]

This reading would have appeared much less plausible from the Greek text, but since the ordinary use of *kalima* in Arabic is much broader than the way in which Aristotle used *rhēma*, it is easy to see how Fārābī was led to it.[44] As a result, Fārābī awards the copula a special place in his logical theory.

To reconcile this with the Aristotelian text, he attributes to Aristotle a view according to which what Aristotle most generally meant by the word *kalima* was no more than a sign signifying the relation between subject and predicate. In other words, what Aristotle really understood by *kalima* is whatever it is that carries the signification of the copulative force, without which no statement is complete. Fārābī says:

TEXT 31 (FARAB. *DI* 3): AL-FĀRĀBĪ, SHARḤ AL-ʿIBĀRĀ (KUTSCH & MARROW), 47.19–48.8 (Z 39–40)

Aristotle uses the term *kalima* in each context in the appropriate sense. In saying that a statement "is not without a *kalima*," he means: [it is not] without an expression to signify the notion of hyparxis connecting the predicate when it is either [a verb] like "walks" or [a derived noun] like "walking" (*māshin*) [*scil.*: where "walks" signifies this notion by itself]. "Walking" is connected to the subject either by "is" (*yūjadu*) or by "exists-as" (*mawjūd*): by "is" (*yūjadu*) if we wish to signify that the predicate holds in a present or a future time; and by "exists-as" (*mawjūd*) if we wish to signify that it is connected with the subject timelessly. Hence if we say "Zayd is just" (*Zaydun yūjadu ʿādilan*) and "Zayd exists as just" (*Zaydun mawjūdun ʿādilan*), the copula (*al-rābiṭ*) is a *kalima* in both cases, albeit not in the sense defined above. Without our explanation, [the stipulation that every statement needs a verb] would be in conflict with Aristotle's own usage in the sciences, when he discusses necessary matters. For he employs the notion of hyparxis in statements without reference to time, as is appropriate in scientific discourse. Hyparctic verbs signifying circumscribed times are properly employed only in rhetorical and poetical statements. The same applies to statements about particulars (*shakhṣiyyāt*).

In defining the parts of speech, Aristotle confines himself to just these two, the noun and the verb. For at this stage, he needs only them, not the particles (*al-adawāt*). With the particles (*al-adawāt*) he deals in the *Poetics* and the *Rhetoric*.[45]

For philosophers, then, the only relevant copula is "*mawjūd*" and, according to Fārābī, it is a *kalima* in the general sense that it signifies the copulative force. It is curious that Fārābī refers to the *Poet* and *Rhet* for a more in-depth treatment of particles, for in those works Aristotle is not at all concerned with logic, but mainly with style. It is however clear from Fārābī's extant works that particles played an important role in his own logical thinking, and it is tempting to understand "*mawjūd*" as a particle. Given the above argument, it seems clear that for Fārābī the copula "*mawjūd*" is not a verb (*fiʿl*) in the grammatical sense, nor can it be a name, because it does not signify anything but a relation. How to understand that relation we learn in the *Book on Particles* (*KH*).

THE PHILOSOPHICAL SIGNIFICANCE OF PARTICLES

Fārābī found precedents for the comprehensive tripartite classification of the parts of speech into noun, verb, and particle both in the Aristotelian logical and Greek grammatical traditions on the one hand, and in the Arabic grammatical tradition on the other. As with other grammatical phenomena, like the notion of derivation, Fārābī must have thought that particles were a feature common to all languages and somehow gave us a clue about the underlying universal logical structure it was an expression of.[46] In his writings on the *DI*, Fārābī does not offer any detailed discussion of the particle.[47] But Fārābī thought that it was an important task to describe and classify them, not only to better understand their use in logic, but also for the metaphysical implications of their use.[48] He does that in *al-Alfāẓ al-mustaʿmala fī l-manṭiq* (Utterances Employed in Logic, henceforth *AM*) and the *KH*.

In the *AM*, as Eskenasy has pointed out, Fārābī takes his departure from the Greek grammatical tradition. He probably knew its Syriac intermediaries like Sergius of Reshʿaynā, who adhered to the Dionysian octopartite division of speech.[49] Fārābī considered this division superior to the Arabic one, for he used it to classify and elucidate the use of particles in logic in the *AM*. In contrast to contemporary grammarians like al-Rummānī, who had organized his *Kitāb ma ʿānī al-ḥurūf* (Book on The Meanings of Particles) according to the number of letters of a particle and laid out their grammatical use in terms of governance etc., Fārābī in the *AM* divides, again comprehensively, all meaningful utterances into noun, verb, and particle, and their simple categorical combinations.[50]

Then, he (roughly) groups what in the Dionysian tradition had been the remaining five parts of speech under the different types of particles.[51] He distinguishes *khawālif* (pronouns: *antonomata*), *wāṣilāt* (joints/relatives: *arthra*), *wāsiṭāt* (media/prepositions: *~protheseis*), *ḥawāshī* (glosses/adverbs: *epirrhēmata*), *rawābiṭ* (connectors/conjunctions: *sundesmoi*). Each of these types of particle qualifies the expressions—i.e., nouns, verbs, or combinations thereof—to which they are syntactically attached, in a logically significant way.[52] We may say that *khawālif* function like indexicals in that they are context-dependent, *wāṣilāt* like quantifiers, and *rawābiṭ* like logical connectors. The *wāsiṭāt* (*min, ʿan, ilā, ʿalā*/of, from, to, on, etc.) may be seen as logically important in that they signify relations (*nisab*).

By far the most differentiated group of particles is however that of the *ḥawāshī*, which can be characterized as including the logical constants very broadly construed. We find anything from the notion of assertion (*inna, naʿam*) or negation (*laysa, lā*) to the particles expressing the categories, or the interrogative particles with which we ask about things in the categories, plus the particle with which we ask about the existence of a thing (*hal*).

The purpose of the *AM* is descriptive. It aims at comprehensively laying out its subject-matter, the eponymous *Utterances Employed in Logic*, as a pedagogical introduction for the student of logic. For Fārābī this is an important task, since the way utterances are employed in logic often deviates from the way common people employ them. Explicating the latter is the task of grammar, explicating the former the task of logic.[53] Particles play an important role especially in logic and metaphysics, because we use them to signify meanings that neither nouns nor verbs can indicate, that is, syncategorematic or transcendental notions like the logical constants, or being, unity, cause, and God. Nothing of that is explained in the *AM*; the theory underpinning the descriptive effort in the *AM* is to be found in the *KH*.

The *KH* is, in contrast to *AM*, not primarily a logical work. Part of it deals with the *Cat* and parts of it are structured somewhat like *Metaphysics* Δ. Yet its general thrust is clearly metaphysical. Along the lines of Menn's reading,[54] I think the *KH* is a project similar to Aristotle's in *Metaphysics* Δ, where the latter explains the supposedly equivocal notions central to this science. But Fārābī faces a more formidable task since confusion is bound to arise to a much greater extent along the way of translating Aristotle from Greek to Syriac and to Arabic. Moreover, for Fārābī, the notions central to metaphysics are—or at least were initially—expressed not by nouns or verbs, but by particles. That he must have thought this is supported by the overall theory of the simple categoric statement so far laid out.

Verbs and derived names always co-signify an indeterminate subject, and non-derived nouns (*maṣādir*) are prototypes signifying a substance. None of them, by dint of their semantic structure, can signify what Fārābī takes to be the central notions of metaphysics, e.g., existence, unity, or God, which do not fall under the categories. Notably, Fārābī thought that the Greek neuter and masculine participles *un/on* and *ūn/ōn* were particles in Greek.

But in any case, if a heading in *Metaphysics* Δ was clearly a noun, or one of the headings in the *KH* is not grammatically a particle, Fārābī would have thought that each of these notions that are syncategorematic should, in a proto-language, or an ideal language for that matter, be expressed by particles, precisely because they do not refer to anything extramentally. Such syncategorematic notions include, in addition to the notions of the categories, existence and other transcendent notions, especially those that we would call logical constants.[55]

Now from the *KH* it would appear that Fārābī conceived of the term "*mawjūd*" as being a particle, regardless of its grammatical form as a derived noun—or at least as a term that should have been a particle in an ideal language for the sense that we are concerned with. He thinks that it was a particle in Greek, and he clearly thinks in the *Sharḥ* that it is not a verb. And from what he says about "*mawjūd*," i.e., that it signifies nothing but a syntactic relation, it seems that it cannot be a noun either. The only remaining possibility is for it to be a particle, and that would explain why he treats it at length in the *KH*. As such, it plays an important role not only in logic, but in metaphysics as well, because more than any other particle, it has invited gross misconceptions based on its misleading grammatical form.

Menn has presented a salient point of Fārābī's treatment of "*mawjūd*" in the *KH* that is worth repeating in this context.[56] On the model of *Met* Δ7 and *APo* B 1–2, Fārābī distinguishes two fundamental senses of "*mawjūd*": *being-as-circumscribed-by-the-categories* and *being-as-truth*. Fārābī's main worry here is that one might be led to think that since "*mawjūd*" is (grammatically) a derived noun, there must be an indeterminate subject through whose *wujūd* something is said to be "*mawjūd*." But this is not generally the case, and even when it is, then that *wujūd* is nothing other than the essence of the subject. But often it is not the case, because when "*mawjūd*" is used to signify a secondary intelligible, there is nothing extramental that could be the indeterminate subject co-signified by derived names.

The position that Fārābī thinks is a result of the confusion caused by the grammatical form of "*mawjūd*" and that he wants to guard against is the misconception that there is a univocal notion of "existence" (*wujūd*) that is a first-order concept and a real attribute extrinsic to the essences of things, and that is thus truly predicated of all things. That is why he distinguishes these two senses of "*mawjūd*" and insists that in one of them "*mawjūd*" signifies a secondary intelligible.

In the sense of "*mawjūd*" as *being-as-circumscribed-by-the-categories* a concept is represented in the mind as it is circumscribed by the categories. The *wujūd* through which that concept is *"mawjūd"* is that it has a quiddity outside the soul. In that sense, *"mawjūd,"* as a derived name, does co-signify an indeterminate subject, namely, the extramental instance of the concept. Existence is here a primary intelligible, because it is predicated directly of that extramental instance, not of a concept in the mind. Yet it is nothing other than the thing's quiddity.

By contrast, in the much broader sense of *being-as-truth*, "the *wujūd* of what is true is a relation of the intelligibles to what is outside the soul."[57] What that means is that when I say that something is *"mawjūd"* in the sense of its being true, I predicate existence not of any extramental thing, but of something in the mind, be it a concept or a predication (Fārābī does not systematically distinguish between 1-place and 2-place being here), saying that there is something of which that concept holds. In that sense 1-place *"mawjūd"* signifies, basically, what is expressed by the existential quantifier. As Menn suggests, for 2-place being we may write a Fregean function with two arguments, an object and a concept, whose value is the True, iff the object falls under the concept: $f(\mathrm{F}(\mathrm{x}))$.[58]

CONCLUSIONS: LANGUAGE AND LOGIC

Fārābī's conception of his philosophical project as Linguistic Constructivism granted him the poetic license, so to speak, to invent or postulate a new vocabulary in Arabic with which to do Aristotelian logic as he understood it. The way he understood Aristotle, however, was equally influenced by his engagement with Arabic grammar, and the texts cited in this chapter betray Fārābī's willingness to bend Aristotle's text to fit what he presupposed were universal features of thought reflected in the structure of all languages.

The most remarkable innovations in his account of predication in the commentary on the *DI* are (i) the distinction of word-classes signifying substances and those signifying attributes based on the grammatical notion of *ishtiqāq*, (ii) the institution of the technical term *"mawjūd"* as a copula to express untensed statements, (iii) the idea that the copula is a syntactical marker or mere *Formwort*, (iv) the importance of particles as expressing central metaphysical notions and logical constants, and, finally, (v) the notion of *"mawjūd"* as a particle expressing a secondary intelligible.

All these innovations were highly influential and, in some way or other, conditioned the standard position in the subsequent tradition. But only (i) proved to be intuitive enough to become fully integrated within Arabic logical theory. Both (ii) and (iii) were controversially discussed, (iv) does not seem to have been a position that, except by Avempace, garnered much interest, and (v) was rejected by Avicenna. Fārābī's account of predication is remarkable for the formalist approach to language, arguably showing awareness of what today is called the principle of compositionality. The relation the copula signifies is presented in terms of a predicative function that is however not simply that of taking two terms to make a statement, thus presupposing homogeneity, but clearly conceived of as an asymmetric relation that presupposes heterogeneity, that is, the type of heterogeneity reflected in derived names, giving the following general form of the sentence: [name [(cop) (prototype/IM)]].

4

———

Avicenna

Radical Reshaping in the East

Avicenna's œuvre represents the cusp between the most thorough engagement with the Aristotelian system yet (in his early works) and the beginning of a truly Arabic tradition of philosophy and logic (in his late work) that in many respects provided a radically different point of departure for the later tradition. As we are gradually getting a better picture of the post-Avicennan tradition, it might emerge that Avicenna is better understood as a transformer of the tradition rather than its culmination.

Concerning the problem of predication, Avicenna's role is doubly interesting, both for his contributions and for the role he played in its transmission. While he responded to and developed the Fārābīan theory in his early works, he is largely silent on the issue in his later and more influential works. I deal elsewhere in more detail with Avicenna's views on the analysis of APs across his *summae*.[1] Here I want to bring out the differences between his early and late work regarding the problem of the copula. The point of reference for the later tradition was his late work, and later philosophers tended to turn to his early work, where he engages with Fārābī, only for clarification. It is in the tensions between Avicenna's remarks about the copula and derived nouns that a critical question arises: What is the relation between linguistic expressions and the logical structure of what they signify?

I argue that we must acknowledge that a host of fundamental philosophical problems—even though they were perceived as peripheral to the central metaphysical or cosmological questions that were hotly debated between *falāsifa* and *mutakallimūn*—nevertheless made their way past Avicenna and, due to the specific dynamics of transmission in the 5th/11th and 6th/12th centuries, were able to develop a life of their own. The problem of predication is a case in point and should stand as a *pars pro toto* for a general feature of the post-Avicennan tradition up to the end of the 9th/15th century. Once this fact is acknowledged, it becomes hard to square with Gutas's assessment that a general development in this period was a tendency toward "paraphilosophy."[2]

AGAINST THE WESTERNERS

Avicenna begins, in the *Shifā'*, by redefining the subject-matter of logic, notably in opposition to Fārābī and the Baghdād Peripatetics. In that work he further developed the notion of *ishtiqāq* as a syntactic constraint on propositions dictated by Arabic grammar, further explored the relationship between logical syntax and the structure of the Arabic language, and rejected—for metaphysical reasons— Fārābī's claim that "*mawjūd*" signified a second-order concept. Yet nothing of that seems of importance in his own synthesis of philosophy presented in *al-Ḥikma al-mashriqiyya* (Eastern Philosophy, henceforth *Easterners*) and the far more influential *Ishārāt*. The restructured logic of the *Ishārāt* had finally broken the spell of the supposed textual unity of the *Organon*.

There can be no doubt that Avicenna knew Fārābī's commentary on the *DI* and that he was influenced by it. However, Avicenna rejected a crucial aspect of Fārābī's work on logic, with wide-ranging repercussions. In the introductory part (*Madkhal*) of the *Shifā'* that corresponds to Porphyry's *Isag* Avicenna might well have had Fārābī in mind when he launched an invective against "the one who says that the subject-matter of logic is the inquiry into utterances insofar as they signify meanings."[3] To Avicenna this position was stupid and confused. While Fārābī had held that the subject-matter of logic was primary intelligibles and the utterances signifying secondary intelligibles its vocabulary, Avicenna turns this conception of logic on its head, arguing that the subject-matter of logic is in fact secondary intelligibles.[4] Secondary intelligibles are concepts that are true only of primary intelligibles, not of things in the extramental world, whereas primary intelligibles are concepts that are true of things in the extramental world.

Logic as a science is concerned exclusively with the accidents or properties that accrue to secondary intelligibles. But not generally—for then the subject-matter of logic would be no different from the subject-matter of grammar. Rather, logic considers the properties of secondary intelligibles insofar as they allow proceeding from the known to the unknown. There are two kinds of compounding operations that lead from the known to the unknown. The first is conception (*taṣawwur*) through restriction (*taqyīd*) by compounding genus and species terms. The second is assent (*taṣdīq*) through predication (*ḥaml*) and syllogisms (i.e., compounding subject and predicate to form a proposition, compounding propositions to reach a conclusion).

Examples of secondary intelligibles the logician is concerned with are "universal," "predicate," "genus," "proposition," and the like.[5] Those secondary intelligibles form a distinct subset of all things. This is the subject matter of logic and the proper domain of the logician.[6]

Thus, there is a sharp contrast between Avicenna's and Fārābī's conception of the relation between logic and language. While for Fārābī the logician studies utterances insofar as they signify meanings, Avicenna would have preferred to dispense with utterances altogether:

TEXT 32 (AVIC. PORPH. EISAGOGE): IBN SĪNĀ, *KITĀB AL-SHIFĀʾ, AL-MANṬIQ, AL-MADKHAL* (MADKŪR ET AL.), I.4, 22.13–23.4

As for the inquiry into utterances, this is something prompted by necessity; utterances are not the logician's primary occupation—inasmuch as he is a logician—if it were not for talk and conversation.

If it were possible to learn logic by pure thought, expressing in it the meanings alone, then this would be enough; and if it were possible for an interlocutor to read by other means what is in another's mind, utterances could be entirely dispensed with. But since necessity requires the use of utterances, and especially since it is inconceivable for reason to arrange meanings without imagining their utterances alongside them, reasoning being almost a dialogue between a man's mind and imagined utterances, it follows that utterances have various features on account of which the features of the meanings corresponding to them in the mind vary, to the effect that the latter acquire qualifications which, were it not for utterances, they would not have. It is for this reason that the art of logic must—at least part of it—inquire into the features of utterances; if it were not for that we would not have said that it needs to also have this part. This necessity notwithstanding, talking about utterances corresponding to their meanings is like talking about their meanings, except that imposing utterances is just more practical.

The logician deals with utterances only because a medium is necessary to communicate meanings. Utterances just happen to be used for this purpose. What the logician is really concerned with are meanings and how the mind can perform operations on them to proceed from the known to the unknown. From this passage it also appears, however, that Avicenna acknowledged some substantial influence of linguistic practices on thought itself, for he clearly states that meanings have qualifications (*aḥkām*) that they would not have if it were not for utterances.

Sabra took the qualifications that the features of utterances bring about in the meanings corresponding to them as referring to the "secondary properties which concepts acquire when they constitute definitions and arguments."[7] They may also be understood as referring to the secondary intelligibles accruing to the meanings of utterances when they are expressed by specific grammatical forms, like derived names, different types of verbal nouns (*maṣādir*), or verbs. Avicenna nowhere states this explicitly, but I think we can read *al-ʿIbāra* as giving substance to this claim, because there Avicenna discusses formal patterns that Arabic grammar foists upon utterances in a way that appears to be logically significant.

It is worth pointing out that Avicenna's conception of the subject-matter of logic is entirely non-psychologistic, even though it consists of secondary intelligibles without extramental referents. Neither do the rules for compounding operations depend on psychological facts, nor do particular linguistic structures or conventions impinge on these rules. Avicenna's remark on the influence of linguistic practice on thought itself must be understood not as an expression of linguistic relativism, but as a claim to the effect that, broadly, language may exhibit a certain structure, however minimally construed, that reflects some deeper structure of thought. This structure is reflected by what the notions discussed in the *DI* signify. Besides the notions of naming-word and statement-word, in the *Shifā'* Avicenna discusses particles, hyparctic statement-words, and the verbal noun (*maṣdar*).

THE ANALYSIS OF PROPOSITIONS IN THE *SHIFĀ'*

Even though Avicenna comments on most points raised by Aristotle in the linguistic section of the *DI*, he includes his own reflections and changes the relative emphasis between the issues he treats. It is revealing that Avicenna here adds an entire chapter on the Arabic verbal noun (*maṣdar*), even though he otherwise strictly follows the structure of Aristotle's text. This addition serves to elaborate more fully Fārābī's theory of derived names, relating the notion of predicability to the semantics of statement-words, verbal nouns, and derived names.

Avicenna on the Statement-Word

Avicenna begins the chapter on the statement-word by reproducing Aristotle's definition: A statement-word "signifies time along with what it otherwise signifies, and no part of it signifies in isolation; and it is always a sign of something being said of something else."[8] He notes that for the statement-word—which he says the Arabic grammarians call "verb" (*fi ʿl*)—in contrast to the Greek language, Arabic does not customarily use a distinct inflection to express the present tense (17.10–18.2). However, in Arabic you may express "(he's) walking" (*māshin*) by a derived name, but then it is no longer a statement-word (18.5). According to Avicenna, there are in fact three utterance types that can occur in simple categorical statements, for

> here we have the subject naming-word, the derived naming-word, and the statement-word. The subject naming-word signifies that which is talked about, but it does not signify a subject at all. The derived naming-word signifies an indeterminate subject which has the derived quality that the name signifies, so that it signifies a meaning and a quality and an indeterminate subject for it, and a nexus between the two [i.e., the quality meant and the indeterminate subject]. (18.6–8)

While the derived naming-word is not tensed, the statement-word signifies the same as the derived naming-word, plus the time when its meaning is said to be connected to the subject (18.10–12). Avicenna points out that not everything that is a verb for the Arabic grammarians is also a statement-word for the logicians. For a statement-word is by definition semantically simple, as no part of it signifies in isolation, but Arabic grammarians consider for example "(I) walk" (*'amshī*) and "(you) walk" (*tamshī*) to be verbs (18.12–14).

However, these cannot, *per definitionem*, be statement-words for the logician, because they both contain a determinate subject and a predicate said of it, and thus must have a truth-value. In fact, these one-word expressions signify exactly the same as the two-word expressions "I walk" (*ana 'amshī*) and "you walk" (*anta tamshī*) (18.14–16).

This is no different from Greek or Persian, but Avicenna takes this as a point of departure for some critical remarks on the semantic simplicity criterion for statement-words. For Avicenna, "this is in fact an issue to investigate. For these utterances are not exclusively either simple or compound" (18.16), Whether a given meaning is simple or compound was an issue of paramount importance for the logician to clarify. Hence, Avicenna dedicates almost the entire remainder of the chapter to this investigation.

Avicenna reasons as follows. If we take these utterances to be simple, then they cannot have a truth-value. If we take them to be compound, then we are committed to the following. If the augments *hamza* (*'a-*) or *tā'* (*ta-*) signify a determinate subject (i.e., "I" or "you"), then the remaining letters *-mshī* would signify some meaning (and begin with a silent letter [*sukūn*], which in Arabic is generally not possible) (19.1–7). This raises four issues:

1. In what sense are we then to consider utterances of the type "(I) walk" (*'amshī*) to be compound?
2. If those utterances are compound, do we have to say that all verbs are compound?
3. If yes, would then not "(he) walks" (*yamshī*) also have to be considered a compound utterance with a truth-value?
4. Are then derived names not also compound in a certain sense?

Avicenna's answer to (1) is that we should consider first- and second-person inflected verbs to be compound utterances for two reasons.

First, these types of utterances violate the definition of the statement-word. Not, in fact, simply because they consist of two significant parts, but because one of the parts (*'a-*) signifies a determinate subject on which judgment is passed. This would violate the definition even if "*-mshī*" had no separate signification (23.10–15). These types of utterances simply are not statement-words for the logician.

Second, these types of utterances may not be different from other compound utterances. Just like compound names, their parts do not signify anything in isolation. They only jointly signify what they signify as a compound (23.15–24.1). I take this to mean that, just as, once "-ketch" is removed from "cutter-ketch," it does not signify anything, no more does "-*mshī*." However, in the compound, both elements contribute to the overall meaning of the utterance, only with "(I) walk (*'a-mshī*)" one part signifies a determinate subject and the other a predicate said of it. It thus may be an utterance without proper significant parts, yet it may still be a compound in the same way as "cutter-ketch" *and thus* violate the definition of the statement-word by the fact that "*'a-*" and "-*mshī*," even though not significant in isolation, contribute two meanings that however in this case are a subject and a predicate.

As for (2), Avicenna responds by saying that this question is not really the logician's business to answer. Languages generally differ as to whether or not they employ compound utterances for certain meanings (19.16–20.3). For example, Arabic has a simple utterance signifying the meaning of "ignorant" (*jāhil*), whereas Persian has a compound one (*nādān*; literally, not-knowing, like i-gnorant) (20.4–8). As for statement-words, Arabic verbs in the past tense (like *saḥḥa*) have no part that signifies an indeterminate subject (as opposed to the imperfect tense, where the *yā'* in *ya-mshī* signifies an indeterminate subject). In that respect they are just like Persian verbs in the future tense (*bo-konad*; literally, "will-be") (20.8–11).

However, in Persian simple statement-words are much rarer. For example, a translation of *saḥḥa* would be *dorost shod* (literally, became healthy) (20.11–16). Since the matter of whether a given meaning is expressed by a simple or by a compound utterance is arbitrary between specific languages, it is not the logician's task to make general claims about that. Rather she "must know that [a given] meaning is signified by a simple utterance" (20.7–8). For generally, Avicenna says,

TEXT 33 (AVIC. *DI* 3): IBN SĪNĀ, *KITĀB AL-SHIFĀ'*, *AL-MANṬIQ*, *AL-'IBĀRA* (EL-KHODEIRI ET AL.), I.3, 20.17–21.6

Since logical inquiry is not concerned with a language *qua* language, so that if in a given language there is no statement-word signifying the present tense, logicians [just] stipulate the signification of the three [temporal] divisions of statement-words, therefore likewise logicians do not require that [Arabic] philologists acknowledge that there is no statement-word, but instead of the statement-word a naming-word connected to another expression that signifies what [otherwise] the statement-word would signify.

Rather, the logician must consider what the definition [of the statement-word] demands, and this can occur in [any] language. For it is without doubt possible that there be an expression univocally signifying a meaning and the time of its occurrence and that [this expression] be simple—that will then be the statement-word. But if there is no such [expression] in the Arabic language, that is not an objection.

In keeping with his conception of the subject-matter of logic, Avicenna emphasizes that the logician must examine the meaning of an utterance and then figure out whether that meaning is compound, no matter how it may be expressed on the level of language. If one language or other does not conspicuously express the structure of a given meaning, that of the statement-word for example, *tant pis*. The logician is content with the possibility of paraphrase.

That still leaves us with (3). While as logicians we might not be interested in the fact that the Arabic for "(he) walks" (*yamshī*) is a single word, we still must ascertain whether or not its meaning is simple or compound. That is, we must be able to say whether it has, by dint of its structure analogous to utterances like "(I) walk" (*'amshī*), a truth-value (19.7–12). If we take these two utterances to be in fact similarly structured, then we would have to say that, just like the *hamza* in "(I) walk" (*'a-mshī*), the *yā'* in "(he) walks" (*ya-mshī*) signifies a determinate subject. If this were so, we would have to construe this statement, in the same way as we may refer to a determinate subject by saying "man" (*insān*) without designating a specific object, as actually meaning "there is something in the world that walks." Then it would be an existential statement, like ∃(x)M(x) where M stands for *mashī* (walking), and as such have a truth-value.

However, Avicenna contends, this is wrong (21.10–11). It is wrong because what the "*yā-*" in "(he) walks" (*ya-mshī*) really signifies is an indeterminate subject. Only by actually mentioning that object does it become fully determinate (21.12–23.5). Third-person inflected verbs are hence not compound, have no truth-value (yet), and thus count as statement-words.

If this is so, what about derived names (4)? For they too signify an indeterminate subject—should we then consider them to have compound meanings? Avicenna had earlier raised this specific possible line of argument. Derived names consist of two parts: their matter, i.e., the root letters, and a form (presumably their morphology). The matter *m-sh-y* signifies the basic meaning *walk*. Once molded into the form of *māshī* or *māshin*, the form signifies an indeterminate subject in which the basic meaning inheres (19.12–15). Avicenna dismisses this line of argument on the grounds that it presupposes a notion of "part" that is not at all relevant to the issue under consideration.

The hylomorphic notion of part required by this line of argument has nothing to do with the notion of ordered parts in utterances, i.e., the sequence of their syllables and letters, sounded or unsounded (21.7–10). This does not strike me as a satisfying response, because it seems that the morphology does contribute precisely that meaning. However, Avicenna could have said, as he did in the earlier quotation, that derived names have the same semantic structure as third-person statement-words, minus the co-signification of time, as he has shown that the meanings of third-person statement-words are not compound (18.10–12). So neither are the meanings of derived names.

What the logician must discern, then, is which accidents accrue to the meanings used in logical reasoning. One type of meaning the logician must be able to recognize is that of the statement-word, and she must know that a statement-word signifies a certain meaning, an indeterminate subject, and that the meaning is connected to the indeterminate subject at a particular time. Avicenna had mentioned that derived names have similar features. Both include the signification of an indeterminate subject in their morphology.

Regarding the question whether the definitional phrase that a statement-word is "always a sign of something being said of something else" is a necessary part of the definition, Avicenna insists that, while not required to uniquely mark out statement-words, it is an important part of the definition (24.6–12). Urging that definition be conceived in the broader sense as aiming at staking out the real nature of the *definiendum*, instead of simply demarcating its extension, then,

> when seen that way, it is adequate that this addition [is understood as] signifying one of the conditions by which the statement-word is constituted, namely the nexus to an indeterminate subject needed for it and for the mode of the signification of time to be completed. The need of the statement-word for [such] a nexus is no smaller than its need for a tense. How could [the nexus] not be primary, given that if there were no nexus, there could be no time for that nexus! (24.13–16)

Avicenna on the Verbal Noun (al-maṣdar), *Auxiliaries* (al-adawāt), *and Hyparctic Verbs* (al-kalimāt al-wujūdiyya)

The signification of a nexus to an indeterminate subject is for Avicenna a feature common to statement-words, verbal nouns (*maṣādir*), and derived names—all utterance types that can go into the predicate position. In an additional and separate chapter, Avicenna sets out to explain how these three are related to the notion of "being said of something else." In fact, "the meaning which the verb indicates as existing for the subject (*ʿalā wujūdihi li-l-mawḍūʿi*) is something that is signified by a name: either an absolute name, or a name which is a *maṣdar*" (25.5–6). The name is thus semantically basic so that, syntactically, the above three types of word formation turn the meaning that the name merely brings up into a meaning that is connected to another meaning. In this chapter, Avicenna picks up where Fārābī had left off, giving a systematic account of the semantic role of Arabic verbal nouns of which the derived names that Fārābī had discussed are a subclass. For Avicenna distinguishes between two types of verbal nouns (*maṣādir*).

The first type of *maṣdar* is formed from the first and basic verbal pattern (*wazn*). In this case it functions as an absolute name, like "hitting" (*al-ḍarb*) (25.6–7). It is called an "absolute" name, because it merely brings up whatever its meaning is, without signifying that that meaning is in any way connected to another meaning. While "hitter" (*ḍārib*) signifies hitting *and* someone who does the hitting, "hitting" by itself just brings up the idea of hitting. In other words, absolute names do not—in contrast to derived names, verbs, and *maṣādir* of the second type—signify a nexus to an indeterminate subject (26.3–5).

The second type of *maṣdar* is formed from any of the remaining verb patterns (*awzān*). For example, *al-taḥarruk*, from Form V (*tafaʿʿala*), signifying intransitive "moving"; *al-ibyiḍāḍ* from Form IX (*ifʿalla*), signifying intransitive "whitening," that is, "paling"; or, *al-taḥrīk* and *al-tabyīḍ*, from Form II (*faʿʿala*), signifying transitive "moving" and "whitening," respectively. In contrast to the first type of *maṣdar*, expressions of this type signify that the meaning of the basic *maṣdar* ("motion" [*al-ḥaraka*] and "whiteness" [*al-bayāḍ*]) is connected by a nexus (*mansūb*) to a subject to or in which that meaning occurs (25.8–10).

Even if the terminology may in practice not always be accurate, because sometimes a *maṣdar* of the second type may also act like an absolute name, for example, when the basic verb pattern is not generally used, like with "splitting (*al-iftirāq*)," Avicenna thinks the distinction is generally apt (25.10–26.2). It helps us to distinguish, on the level of utterances, those that are a sign of something being said of something else and those that are not. The notion of the second-type *maṣdar* as the semantic structure of utterances that are predicable is thus basic for Avicenna.

In fact, he continues,

> mostly, in Arabic, it is the case that when there is a specific expression for the *maṣdar*, then the statement-word signifies the presence of the meaning of that *maṣdar* expression for some subject, and at a known time. That may include the meaning of the absolute name as well, as when one says [intransitively] "he whitened" (*ibyaḍḍa*), "he whitens" (*yabyaḍḍu*), from "whitening" (*al-ibyiḍāḍ*), for what signifies whitening (*al-ibyiḍāḍ*) also signifies whiteness (*al-bayāḍ*). (26.5–8)

In Arabic, the distinction between utterance types that include the signification of a nexus to an indeterminate subject is neat. The meanings that both statement-words and derived names signify are based on the meanings signified by *maṣdar* expressions. Meanings of second-type *maṣdar* expressions are hence always accidents accruing to a substance, and, conversely, no second-type *maṣdar* can, in principle, signify a substance (26.8–12).

That is also why statement-words in Arabic cannot be used to signify a substance. Avicenna here takes up a discussion we have seen in Fārābī and agrees that statement-words, in Arabic and by their primary signification, never signify substances.[9] In Arabic, if we want to use a statement-word to express that Zayd is a substance, e.g., the intransitive verb "substance-ing" (*tajawhara*; this is a neologism also in Arabic), we have the trouble that by the very force of the *maṣdar* laid out above, we would always be saying, paradoxically, that Zayd's being a substance somehow is an accident occurring to or in him. But Avicenna is open to the idea that other languages might not be so constrained (*muḍā'iq*) and actually have a way of making tensed substance predications by means of statement-words (26.13–27.9).

After cursorily treating indefinite and temporally inflected statement-words, Avicenna gets to another point that is not in Aristotle, but that he thought was crucially missing. In his words, "it is shameful of the First Teacher [Aristotle] that he mentions among the simple utterances the name and the statement-word but leaves aside the auxiliaries (*adawāt*) and what resembles them" (29.15–16).

The reason for Avicenna's complaint may well be that he was aware of the tradition of Arabic grammatical theory and of Fārābī's incorporation thereof in his logical vocabulary. In Arabic grammar, there are three fundamental word-classes, nouns, verbs, and particles. In Fārābī's logical vocabulary there were names, statement-words, and particles (which he sometimes calls auxiliaries).[10] And, the copula "*mawjūd*" was likely a particle for Fārābī.

Avicenna here distinguishes between auxiliaries proper, like "from" (*min*) and "on" (ʿalā), and hyparctic verbs (*al-kalimāt al-wujūdiyya*), like "become" (*ṣāra, yaṣīru*) and "be" (*kāna, yakūnu*) (28.14–15). Both types of expression are semantically incomplete. But their semantic incompleteness is different from that of statement-words, derived nouns, or *maṣdar* nouns of the second type. For those, when uttered in isolation, do signify a meaning and a nexus. They are semantically incomplete, because they do not signify the subject to which their meaning is connected. Auxiliaries and hyparctic verbs, when uttered in isolation, do not signify anything except a nexus (29.5–8). For example, if you ask "Where is Zayd?" and someone answers "in," your mind does not settle on anything. The same goes for the question "What is Zayd doing?" being answered by "becomes" (29.3–12).

According to Avicenna, "the relation of auxiliaries to nouns is the same as the relation of hyparctic verbs to [grammatical] verbs" (29.5–6). Auxiliaries and hyparctic verbs can grammatically become predicates (*khabar*) of a subject (*mubtadaʾ*), only if that deficiency is met by supplying a value for x in "is x"/"became x" and "from x"/"on x" expressions. This, Avicenna urges, is how "you ought to understand this issue [. . .], and not pay attention to what they say" (29.14–15).

Avicenna on the Copula

Based on the foregoing theory of verbal nouns, Avicenna has no need for a copula. The copulative element is included in the signification of all predicative forms (except absolute names—but any absolute name can easily be turned into any *maṣdar* of the second type). Nevertheless, in *al-ʿIbāra* I.6 Avicenna says a good deal about the copula and under what circumstances it is needed. He begins the chapter on the simple declarative statement (corresponding to *DI* 5) by discussing the differences between Greek and Arabic when it comes to the use of the copula.

TEXT 34 (AVIC. *DI* 5): IBN SĪNĀ, *KITĀB AL-SHIFĀʾ, AL-MANṬIQ, AL-ʿIBĀRA* (EL-KHODEIRI ET AL.), I.6, 37.6–38.11

Every declarative phrase, be it categorical or hypothetical, requires, in the language of the Greeks, the use of hyparctic statement-words; these are the statement-words which signify a nexus and a time, without however the meaning connected to the indeterminate subject actually obtaining in them, if the root in itself is not a statement-word. [. . .]

As for predicative statements, in the language of the Greeks, the judgment about them is thus, so they are forced to say "Zayd was such, or is such"; however, this is not necessary in the language of the Arabs.

What is however necessary with regard to the matter itself, is that the predicative proposition be completed by three things. These are: the meaning of the subject, the meaning of the predicate, and a nexus between the two. It is not the case that the joint presence of meanings in the mind makes [these meanings] subjects or predicates in the mind, but rather there is a need for the mind to believe that there is, along with that, a nexus—affirmative or negative—between the two meanings.

The utterance too, if I want it to capture what is in the mind, needs to consist of three significations: the signification of the meaning which the subject has, another of the meaning which the predicate has, and a third of the relation and the bond that is between them. It is not necessary from assembling "man" and "animal" in the mind and from considering these two, in how far this is a man and that an animal, that from that it results that one of them is a predicate or a subject, or in general connected to anything. If the utterance signifying this relation is left out, you only leave out a reminder for the mind or a dependency on one of the features of utterances which attaches to one or both of them [i.e., "man" and "animal"] for the encompassing of this meaning. In that case it may signify this meaning by a spoken signification, even if it is not by a simple utterance specified for this.

While Greek grammar, as Avicenna (wrongly) thinks, always requires that in simple categorical statements a copula is used to signify the nexus between subject and predicate, Arabic grammar does not. This does not, however, mean that on the level of meanings that the logician is concerned with we can neglect the meaning of the copula in the logical analysis of such statements. For it is possible to entertain two meanings together in one's mind without them being so connected as to be correctly expressed by a simple categorical statement.

Avicenna does not, as Fārābī did, insist that technical terminology be invented to express this meaning on the level of the Arabic language. Rather, he says that, even though leaving the copula implicit may not cause any harm, if one aims at conspicuity on the level of language, there are different ways of achieving this. As he will explain, one way is to use auxiliaries or hyparctic verbs in Arabic to signify that meaning, or as seems to be suggested here, it might just be enough to pay attention to the overall morphology of a statement, by which that nexus may also be signified, without the use of a specific word.

But first, this reflection of the force of the copula for Avicenna raises the problem of the unity of the proposition. Formulated in terms entirely different from Fārābī's worries about Bradley's regress, the following passage seems to suggest a deflationary solution that is however very different from that of Fārābī, who as we saw maintained that the copula signified the secondary intelligible of a predicative function. Avicenna says:

TEXT 35 (AVIC. *DI* 5): IBN SĪNĀ, *KITĀB AL-SHIFĀ'*, *AL-MANṬIQ, AL-ʿIBĀRA* (EL-KHODEIRI ET AL.), I.6, 38.11–39.3

As for the succession itself of one utterance to another in a short time, it is not by means of signifying the feature of one of them for the other that it is a signification obtaining by [their] assemblage. Likewise with the composition present in definitions. If it were not for an additional thing connected to it, it would not be necessary for the succession itself of one of its parts to another to be a sign of the assemblage and its unity. Rather, our saying "living walking having two legs" would come to signify a single meaning by its mere assemblage, because you mean by it "the living [thing], which is walking and has two legs." This would be signified by the form of the composition, so that the phrase becomes one [unity], because you consider the descriptions to be of one [thing], and mark out some of them from others. And if it were not for this reason additional to the succession itself, the succession would not be a unity. Likewise, if someone said "the sky the earth the griffon the circle." But there is a need to connect to the succession something else signifying the bond of the elements to one another by connecting predication and subjection, or connecting the restrictions [in definitions] to one another. The matter ought to be understood in this way. Do not waste time with the improbable exertions [at explanation] that they are attempting.

It is unclear whether Avicenna has Fārābī in mind in this last sentence. For Fārābī, the unity of the proposition was guaranteed by one of the two senses of the artificial copulative term "*mawjūd*," i.e., the sense of *being-as-truth*. In this sense, the meaning of "*mawjūd*" is that of a second-order concept, a function taking the concept of the predicative relation between the meaning of the predicate and the meaning of the subject to its instantiation.[11] For Avicenna, the distinct nature of meanings loosely assembled in the mind and of meanings assembled in the mind forming a larger unity of definition or of predication must then somehow be expressed in language, too. Avicenna extends the problem to definitions and descriptions, fitting the problem into the framework of compounds the logician is concerned with. That is, that of descriptive restriction which aims at conception, and that of predicative statement, which aims at assent.

Avicenna's solution is that in predication there is a meaning additional to the meaning of the subject and the meaning of the predicate, which is called the nexus (*nisba*), and it is the nexus that provides the bond that unifies these two meanings to become a proposition. The nexus may be implicit in Arabic, or else may be signified by verbal or nominal copulae:

TEXT 36 (AVIC. *DI* 5): IBN SĪNĀ, *KITĀB AL-SHIFĀ'*, *AL-MANṬIQ*, *AL-ʿIBĀRA* (EL-KHODEIRI ET AL.), I.6, 39.4–40.4

It has become clear from this that there is a meaning which is not the meaning of the subjected thing, and not the meaning of the predicated thing, and of which it is only right that it should be signified—and this [meaning] is the nexus. The utterance signifying the nexus is called copula, and the account of it is the same as the account of auxiliaries. As for the language of the Arabs, the copula may be omitted relying on the mind's discernment of its meaning, or it may be mentioned.

When it is mentioned, it may be in the form of a name, as in "Zayd, he (is) alive." The utterance "*huwa*" comes in not to signify by itself, but to signify that Zayd is something that is not mentioned afterwards. Its signification is not understood as long as only "*huwa*" is said—until [what it refers to] is made explicit. Thus, it fails to signify by itself a complete meaning and belongs to the auxiliaries, even though they are similar to names. Or in the form of a verb as in "Zayd was such or is such (*Zayd kāna kadhā aw yakūnu kadhā*)," when they are hyparctic verbs. In Arabic it is common to use [the temporal copula] for something that is not temporal, like the words of Him Exalted: "And Allah is (*kāna*) forgiving and compassionate." And [also] for what is not temporally specified, like when they say: "Every three is (*yakūnu*) is odd."

As for the Persian language, they do not use propositions in which [the copula] is only imagined. Either [it is indicated] with a simple expression, when they say "Someone is (*hast*) such and such," or by the vocalization, when they say "[Someone] is such and such ([*fulān*] *chinīn-e*)," with a *fatḥa* on the *nūn*. And the *fatḥa* signifies that *chinīn* is the predicate of *fulān*. Hence, the copula, be it expressed or implicit, is what makes unity out of a plurality, and since the declarative statement is one, in predication, the copula, whether explicit or implicit, signifies a single bond, and the bond in a predicative statement is that you say that the subject is the predicate.

This assessment allows Avicenna to reconceptualize Aristotle's distinction in *DI* 10 between what the Latin tradition has called *secundum adiacens* and *tertium adiacens* propositions:

TEXT 37 (AVIC. *DI* 10): IBN SĪNĀ, *KITĀB AL-SHIFĀʾ*, *AL-MANṬIQ*, *AL-ʿIBĀRA* (EL-KHODEIRI ET AL.), II.1, 76.8–78.1

Either in the proposition there is stated explicitly a copula as mentioned, be it temporal or non-temporal, or there is not. If it is stated explicitly, it is called ternary; if not, it is called binary. The binary ones may be abbreviations [of ternary ones] unless their predicates are verbs. For it is not unlikely that verbs are copulated through themselves since they signify the subject in virtue of their morphology. Moreover, there is a need for a copula to signify the nexus of the predicate to the subject when there is a name that is by itself separate. When a signification of the subject is found to occur in the verbs, their need for the copula is different from that of underived names. Derived names are analogous to the verbs here. Accordingly, this is also not a general judgment about verbs. For even though verbs signify a subject, they do not signify a determinate one. There must be something that copulates it to a determinate [subject].

Arabic does have a nominal particle to express this copulation [to a determinate subject]. But it lacks a verbal particle for this purpose. So when they say: "Zayd (he) is alive [*Zayd huwa ḥayyun*]," "he" refers to Zayd and contains an indication of him alone. Moreover, when it is said "Zayd was alive [*Zayd kāna ḥayyan*]" there is no indication of the determination of Zayd in "was" [*kāna*]. On account of that, what learned men say about their language is that here there is an ellipsis, and its sense is "He is alive." Other languages differ in that respect.

Therefore, there are three classes of propositions: (i) the class in which the determination of the nexus is signified [*Zayd huwa ḥayyun*], (ii) the class in which an indeterminate nexus is signified [*Zayd kāna ḥayyan*], (iii) and the class in which no nexus is signified at all [*Zayd ḥayyun*].

This last division is perfectly binary, while the other two are ternary. However, the first of them is perfectly ternary, while the second is ternary but does not have a perfectly ternary structure.

In general, the ternary structure is that in which the copulation is made clear, as when we say, "man exists-as-just" [*al-insānu yujadu ʿadilan*] or "man (he) is just" [*inna al-insanu huwa ʿadilun*]. So the expression "exists" [*yūjadu*] and "he" [*huwa*] are not included in virtue of being predicates in themselves, but rather so as to signify that the predicate is present to the subject.

The utterance "he'll-be" [*yūjad*] signifies the existence of the predicate in the future. The utterance "he" [*huwa*] signifies the existence of the predicate for the subject absolutely. The copula signifies the nexus of the predicate, and the quantifier signifies the quantity of the subject. That is why the copula is counted as belonging to the predicate, and the quantifier as belonging to the subject.

Ranging the copula with the predicate and the quantifier with the subject is reminiscent of Alexander. Otherwise, all this—except the division of categorical statements in complete and incomplete ternary and binary propositions—is close enough to Fārābī's account. Verbs and derived names co-signify an indeterminate subject, while non-derived names do not.

It is important to note, however, that Avicenna makes a distinction Fārābī did not make. Besides the signification of an indeterminate subject that is included in the meaning of verbs and derived names, a copula may signify the linking to a *determinate* subject. In Arabic, this can be explicitly expressed only by "*huwa*," even though it may be understood implicitly by other formulations.

Hence, Avicenna's version of the *secundum/tertium adiacens* distinction is nothing like Aristotle's, or that of any of the Greek commentators. Aristotle arguably had distinguished, as we have seen, existential from predicative statements ("Socrates is [i.e., exists]" = *secundum adiacens* vs. "Socrates is pale" = *tertium adiacens*), or at least that is how the Latin commentators came to understand him.[12] Avicenna's distinction is solely based on whether a copula is mentioned and what kind of copula is mentioned—the structure of the propositions expressed seems to be the same. This doctrine was later criticized by several logicians, including Fakhr al-Dīn al-Rāzī and Quṭb al-Dīn al-Taḥtānī.

AVICENNA'S LATER WORK AND THE BREAKING OF THE *ORGANON*

Like that of the *Ishārāt*, the logic part of the *Easterners* is structured very differently from Avicenna's earlier logical works, which were modeled on the structure of the *Organon*. One organizing principle seems to be the different kinds of subject-predicate relations.[13] The work was partly lost already in 425/1034 and thus had a lesser influence on the ensuing Avicennan logical tradition.[14] The structure of the logic part may however be taken to reflect the centrality of the subject-predicate relation for Avicenna's "true" conception of the discipline.

In the short chapter on the naming-word, statement-word, and auxiliary of a proposition, Avicenna again describes certain utterances, when used as a copula, as semantically incomplete.

TEXT 38 (AVIC. *DI* 10?): IBN SĪNĀ, *AL-ḤIKMA AL-MASHRIQIYYA* (AL-KHAṬĪB & AL-QATLĀN), 58.18–59.4 (= MS CAIRO: DĀR AL-KUTUB ḤIKMA 6 M [UṢṬAFĀ FĀḌIL], FOLS. 116V–138R)

There are also utterances that are sometimes used with a simple and complete signification, and sometimes with a simple and incomplete signification. For example, when you say "he (*huwa*)" or "is-found (*mawjūd*)," they may only signify the name [previously mentioned]. Then you say "Zayd, he [is] a writer" and "Zayd is-found-as-a writer" and you use them as attachments and copulae, so that if you were to stop [upon pronouncing them] the statement would not be complete in terms of the statement's signification, when you do not intend "he (*huwa*)" or "found[-thing] (*mawjūd*)" as that which you intend by a name.

Rather, you intended by it something following another utterance that needs to be expressed, like when you say "Zayd on or in." Likewise you sometimes say "Zayd was" and you mean "his existence in itself," and then the statement is complete. And sometimes you say "Zayd was a writer," and then "was" functions as an attachment and a copula.

It is thus obvious that some nouns and verbs signify incomplete significations. If you say "was a writer," by that alone you do not signify "being" of a meaning, but rather just "writing." For you signified a time for a thing that is not mentioned afterwards. Those are called temporal statement-words.

But a little later, he states: "There are two parts in a predicative statement. One of them is the bearer of predication commonly known as 'subject,' like 'Zayd' in our example, and the second is the predicate, like 'writer' [*kātib*] in our example."[15] Here the nexus that is supposed to be signified by the copula is left out of the picture. Fakhr al-Dīn al-Rāzī later accused Avicenna of contradicting himself, for in the *Ishārāt* he insisted that the copula "*huwa*" must be mentioned to properly express a determinate nexus, even in cases where the predicate is a derived name:

TEXT 39 (AVIC. *DI* 3?/*APR* 1?): IBN SĪNĀ, *AL-ISHĀRĀT WA L-TANBĪHĀT* (AL-ZĀRʿĪ), 78.14–79.3

You must know that the true account of the predicative proposition is that together with the meaning of the subject and the meaning of the predicate, there is the meaning of the composition between the two. This is a third meaning in addition to these two. As one should seek to have utterances and meanings correspond in number, this third meaning deserves a third utterance signifying it. It may be omitted in some languages, as it occasionally is entirely omitted in Arabic, like when we say "Zayd [is] a writer," where it really should be said "Zayd, he [is] a writer." But in some languages its omission is not possible, as is the case in proper Persian, for example with "is [*ast*]" in "Zayd is a writer [*Zayd dabīr ast*]."

Here, Avicenna insists that the copula "*huwa*" must—or should—be used even when the predicate is a derived name. This appears to contradict what he said in the *Easterners*. Taking the cue from these two passages, Rāzī argued that the nexus is already co-signified by derived names, and thus need not be mentioned again: "*Zayd kātib*" is perfectly fine.

It seems that Avicenna in his late period had no need for Fārābī's theory of derived names to accommodate the different types of predication set out in *Cat* 1–5. His overall reconceptualization of Aristotelian logic rejects the *Cat* in its entirety and avoids several problems arising from it, like that of singular predication, multiple predication, or quantified predicates.[16] It also incorporated the reconceptualization of the notorious distinction between *said of* and *said in* predication that Fārābī, following Ammonius, had made a central notion for the Arabic *DI* and the pivot of his theory of derived names.

As Kalbarczyk has pointed out, the fourfold predicative scheme not only was an invention of the commentators, but actually was at odds with Aristotle's doctrine of hylomorphism laid out in *Met* Z–H.[17] Avicenna was troubled by this tension already in *al-Mukhtaṣar al-awsaṭ*: in order not to confuse essence and existence claims he suggests beginning by distinguishing the two different kinds of nexus (*nisba*) with which a given subject (*mawḍū ʿ*) may be described (*yuṣāfu*) by a predicate (*maḥmūl*), namely, either (1) as being it (*bi-annahu huwa*), or (2) as having it (*bi-annahu dhū huwa*).[18] In *al-Maqūlāt* of the *Shifāʾ* Avicenna criticizes an anonymous "logician" as well as Fārābī for having equated "being said of a subject" with "being a universal." More blatantly, Avicenna accuses Fārābī of having equated it with "being predicated essentially" (as Fārābī did in the context of his theory of prototypes/derived nouns, as we have seen).[19] An anonymous predecessor, likely Porphyry, or the Neo–Platonic tradition in general,[20] had equated the notion of "being said of a subject" with both.

One problem Avicenna points out is that by equating "being in a subject" with non-essential predication *tout court* they both confuse the ontological account of what it means to be an accident (*ʿaraḍ*) subsisting in a substrate (*mawḍū ʿ*) and the predicative relation between logical subject (*mawḍū ʿ*) and predicate (*maḥmūl*) applying to the former accidentally (*ʿaraḍī*).[21] In *al-Maqūlāt* I.3 Avicenna then proposes an entirely new system based on the basic distinction between "being it" and "having it" types of attributes put forward in *al-Mukhtaṣar al-awsaṭ*.

According to Kalbarczyk, Avicenna was concerned that "under the fourfold classification scheme we might be forced to swallow the attributive identity between two ontologically very distinct types of beings, namely a substantial form inhering in matter and an accident inhering in a subject which is ontologically prior."[22] The new fivefold scheme repairs what Avicenna saw as a broader failure of the *Cat*, which has likewise troubled modern readers of Aristotle, namely, a confounding of linguistic, logical, and ontological notions. While the fourfold scheme of the commentators was "a division of *things* by means of *predicative* relations," the new fivefold scheme gives an exhaustive account of the types of relation (*nisba*) in which a predicate may stand to a subject.[23]

The new scheme is much clearer in keeping apart not only the logical and the ontological level, but also the notions of substance, essence, and accident. It gives clear criteria for checking whether a given predication is essential or accidental—

which the fourfold scheme had not. Avicenna might just not have needed Fārābī's theory any longer.

If we take the linguistic section of the *DI* as conceived by Avicenna in the *Shifāʾ* as providing substance to the claim that linguistic practice influences thought, we may be led to think that Avicenna in his mature thought abandoned that idea together with the old fourfold scheme of predicative relations. One might say that when Avicenna writes in the *Ishārāt*, "Because there is a certain relation between the utterance and the meaning, and [because] some features of utterances often affect some features of meanings, the logician must also pay attention to the aspects of the utterance taken by itself insofar as that is not specific to one language or another,"[24] he does not mean the same thing as in the passage from the *Shifāʾ*.

Or, alternatively, if we take it to mean the same thing, we might say that Avicenna simply thought that the Fārābīan-inspired theory of utterance types in *al-ʿIbāra* was still right, but not pertinent to his restructured presentation of logic as it naturally is. Be that as it may: in the ensuing tradition, which accorded the *Ishārāt* the bulk of the attention, there is no clear answer to this, and often commentators turned back to the text of the *Shifāʾ*.

A WORD ON THE ANDALUSIAN TRADITION
AND A PRELIMINARY CONCLUSION

Of those Ibn Khaldūn (d. 808/1406) considered the four greatest Muslim philosophers,[25] we have seen that the first, Fārābī, played a crucial role in the Graeco-Arabic transformation process of Aristotelian logic in the face of the "war of signification" fought out between the different scientific disciplines that were coming of age around the 4th/10th century.[26] The second, Avicenna, radically changed the philosophical tradition inherited from the Baghdād Peripatetics.

It must at least be mentioned that the project of the Baghdād Peripatetics had a more or less direct continuation in the textual Aristotelianism of Ibn Bājja (Avempace) and Averroes, the third and fourth of Ibn Khaldūn's greatest philosophers, in Muslim Spain. However, while Averroes was to become an important source for Latin Aristotelianism in 13th-century Paris and Padua, his influence in the Islamic East was eclipsed by Avicenna.[27]

The work of the Andalusian philosophers on the analysis of APs and the role of the copula in predication is characterized by an increasing readiness to closely engage with the text of Fārābī and Aristotle himself. Some of the central doctrines shaped by Fārābī were accepted by Ibn Bājja, Averroes, and Ibn Ṭumlūs.[28] For example, they all subscribe to Fārābī's general outlook on the subject-matter of logic, the role of the *Cat*, the distinction between primary and secondary intelligibles, and likely the theory of the copula (*mawjūd*) as a second-order concept. Especially Ibn Bājja and Averroes further developed Fārābī's logical theories: Ibn Bājja in his development of a theory of relations,[29] and Averroes with his criticism of Fārābī's conception of the semantics of statement-words and derived names.[30] Despite Averroes's self-proclaimed Aristotelian purism, his presentations are indebted to a significant extent to Fārābī's reading of Aristotle, and to a considerable extent to the *Notes* by Ibn Bājja.

In stark contrast to the continuity of the Fārābian tradition in the West, we see a radical re-conception of the Aristotelian *Organon* already in Avicenna's *Shifā'*. By breaking with the Fārābian tradition and proclaiming the subject-matter of logic to be secondary intelligibles, the inquiry into the analysis of atomic propositions, the question of the relationship between language and logic, and the role of the copula took on a new shape.

With Avicenna, propositions became firmly rooted in the realm of meanings of sentences. In the part corresponding to the *DI* Avicenna examines at length issues like the criteria for semantic simplicity, and the relation between Arabic word formation and logical properties accruing to secondary intelligibles. Overall, his theory of the Arabic verbal noun is a development of Fārābī's theory of derived names that provides clear criteria based on features of Arabic grammar for distinguishing names from predicables. Avicenna followed Fārābī in distinguishing three classes of utterances, not two as Aristotle had, and in characterizing the copula as belonging to one of two types of auxiliaries, the third class of utterances whose meanings are incomplete. However, Avicenna does not think, as did Fārābī, that "*mawjūd*" in the sense of *being-as-truth* signifies a secondary intelligible and thus nothing in extramental reality.

I suggested that Avicenna's elaborations in *al-ʿIbāra* give substance to his claim that some features of utterances determine some properties of the meanings they signify. For there, Avicenna deals with cases in which the grammatical form of an utterance determines some logical properties of the meanings they signify, for example, when an utterance in a second-type *maṣdar* form determines that the meaning it signifies is an attribute, not a substance, and implies a nexus to an indeterminate subject. Yet it seems that in his late period all of the Fārābian-inspired theory was lost. Avicenna did—*malgré lui*—change his mind about some central issues.

In the logic part of the *Easterners* Avicenna presents philosophy, as he says in the introduction, not according to any partisan account, but in the way it naturally is. We may see the first part of the Logic of the *Easterners* as fleshing out the subject-predicate relation by introducing and clarifying the properties that the notions of secondary intelligibles used to describe them have.

Avicenna's work left the Eastern philosophers who were working in his wake with the curious situation of two quite dissimilar approaches to the analysis of atomic propositions and the role of the copula. Adding to the curiosity of the situation is the fact that much of the *Easterners* was lost already before Avicenna's death, and never widely received. Rather, later generations focused their attention almost entirely on the *Ishārāt*, turning to the *Shifā'* mainly for clarification of this terse and often cryptic text.

PART TWO

An Overture Rather Than a Coda

The Copula and the Development of Arabic Philosophy of Language in the East (1200–1500)

5

The "New Logicians" Stirring Things Up

Recent research has begun to explore the highly dynamic intellectual history between the 6th/12th and 9th/15th centuries in the Islamic world.[1] The remainder of this study follows discussions on the problem of predication through this period—long seen as marked by scholastic ossification in the rational sciences—making a larger historical argument that we should perhaps conceive of the history of philosophy, and of logic in particular, in this period as a new overture, rather than a coda to the great Arabic philosophers discussed in the preceding chapters.

The overall historical argument of part 2 is however more specific. Dimitri Gutas, who has arguably done more than anyone to promote the study of post-Avicennan Arabic philosophy, has recently argued that even though philosophy was alive and well long after Avicenna, the kind of philosophy practiced was, after all, no longer the kind of open-ended scientific inquiry into reality that Avicenna had pursued. Instead, it became "para-philosophy," a pursuit that—albeit formally beholden to the method and aims of the Aristotelian/Avicennan tradition—was employed merely to prove the doctrines of faith by philosophical means.[2] While Gutas's partial reversal to the view of 19th/20th-century orientalists is suggested from a much-better-informed vantage point, we still know too little about the contents of too many philosophical works to make such a claim.

The discussions on the problem of predication in the period up to the early 10th/16th century provide a powerful example of how logic, the rational (and Aristotelian) science *par excellence*, not only emancipated itself from its Greek roots but became an independent research discipline. The discussions on the copula show that philosophical investigations into abstract logical problems—utterly useless for any doctrinal purposes—were pursued with vigor and sophistication. Gutas grants that one or the other science may have been able to "burst the scholastic cocoon" of para-philosophy.[3] The specific point of the material presented here is to suggest that the very idea of a scholastic cocoon may be questionable. Instead, Arabic logic developed, in conversation with other disciplines like *balāgha* or *'ilm al-waḍ'*, a strand of research that we can properly call philosophy of language.

EARLY AVICENNISMS

Between Avicenna's death in 428/1037 and the beginning of Fakhr al-Dīn al-Rāzī's scholarly activity in the last third of the 6th/12th century there was in the Islamic East, even more so than was the case in al-Andalus, a lively engagement with Avicenna's works.[4] Until recently, scholarship focused on the fierce opposition to Avicenna, and to Aristotelian philosophy as a whole, by the famous Ash'arī theologian Abū Ḥamīd al-Ghāzālī (d. 505/1111).[5] For a long time al-Ghāzālī was seen to have dealt the deathblow to philosophy in Islam.[6] However, it has by now become clear that he was instrumental not only for the institutionalization of logic within the scientific canon of the emerging *madrasa* system, but also for the naturalization of the Avicennan version of the Aristotelian philosophical method within what was to become mainstream Sunnī rational theology (Ash'arī *kalām*).[7]

In that period there were distinct Aristotelian philosophical programs in the Islamic East being carried out in critical conversation with Avicenna.[8] There was, for example, the Aristotelian philosopher and Jewish convert to Islam Abū al-Barakāt al-Baghdādī (d. 556/1164–5), who worked in a more Aristotelian vein largely critical of Avicenna's reshaping of the discipline.[9] Perhaps on the other end of the spectrum there was the influential Philosophy of Illumination (*Ḥikmat al-ishrāq*) by Shihāb al-Dīn al-Suhrawardī (d. 587/1191), presented as a Neo-Platonic alternative to Aristotelian/Avicennan philosophy, while incorporating many of its elements.[10] Yet another example would be the slightly later philosophical works of 'Abd al-Laṭīf al-Baghdādī (d. 629/1231).[11] The genealogical line of students spanning from Avicenna to the 7th/13th-century thinkers we are concerned with next represents a more orthodox strand of early Avicennism.[12] It is this latter strand that, spreading from the lands of Khurāsān and Transoxania, was to develop into an intellectual tradition proper, ushering in different forms of antagonistic Avicennisms.[13]

This early "school Avicennism,"[14] characterized by attempts to refine the Avicennan system without leveling fundamental criticisms against it, was mainly represented by Avicenna's direct student Bahmanyār b. al-Marzubān (d. 458/1066) and his student Abū al-'Abbas al-Lawkarī (d. *ca.* 517/1123). The latter wrote the philosophical compendium *Bayān al-ḥaqq* (The Clear Exposition of Truth), which closely resembles the works of Avicenna and Bahmanyār.[15] Al-Lawkarī is credited with having brought Avicennan philosophy from his hometown Marw to Khurāsān.[16] 'Umar al-Khayyām (d. 517/1126), who frequented Marw but was mainly based in Nīshāpūr, and Sharaf al-Zamān al-Īlāqī (536/1141)—reportedly a student of both al-Lawkarī and al-Khayyām—as well as his student ʿUmar ibn Sahlān al-Sāwī (d. mid 6th/12th century) continued to spread the tradition to Transoxania and likely westward, too, until the mid-6th/12th century, when Rāzī was born.

As Shihadeh has convincingly argued, there was, much in the polemical spirit in which al-Ghazālī's *Tahāfut al-falāsifa* (The Incoherence of the Philosophers) was written, an Ashʿarī trend incorporating methods and parts (like logic) of the Aristotelian tradition into theological discourse (as happened, e.g., with al-Baghdādī's *al-Kitāb al-Muʿtabar*), and at the same time criticizing, often harshly, that very same tradition.[17] One representative of this trend is the jurist and theologian Afḍal al-Dīn ʿUmar b. ʿAlī ibn Ghaylān al-Balkhī (d. *ca.* 590/1194).[18] Rāzī met and debated with Ibn Ghaylān in Bukhārā around 582/1186 and in his *Munāẓarāt* (Debates) describes him as "a Shaykh who is famous in *falsafa* and skillfulness."[19]

Another representative, who was personally acquainted with both Ibn Ghaylān and Rāzī, was Sharaf al-Dīn Muḥammad ibn Masʿūd al-Masʿūdī (d. *ca.* 585/1189–590/1194). Not only did he write a polemic commentary (*shukūk wa-shubah*) on Avicenna's *Ishārāt* that had a formative impact on Rāzī's early understanding of Avicennan philosophy, but he was at the same time highly respected by Ibn Ghaylān for his "thorough knowledge of logic, firm grounding in *kalām*, and a disposition to deal with rational matters, paralleled only by *Hujjat al-Islām* Muḥammad al-Ghazālī," so that he would not be fooled by the Aristotelian philosophers, but could effectively criticize them.[20]

It is in this milieu of a gradual and contested appropriation of Aristotelian philosophy by Ashʿarī theologians, mainly through the works of Avicenna and al-Ghazālī, and to some extent through al-Baghdādī's *al-Kitāb al-Muʿtabar*, that we have to understand Rāzī's work. His education and scholarly activity may be seen as a confluence of traditions, from al-Juwaynī (d. 478/1085) through al-Ghazālī, Muḥammad b. Yaḥyā al-Nayshabūrī (d. 548/1153), his teacher Majd al-Dīn ʿAbd al-Razzāq al-Jīlī (d. after 555/1160), and his own father, on the one hand, and from Avicenna through his students and al-Masʿūdī on the other. His own influence on the tradition was mainly due to his commentary on the *Ishārāt*, which sought to steer a middle path between the early school Avicennism and the entirely polemic approach of al-Masʿūdī. A similar approach is exhibited by his commentary on *ʿUyūn al-ḥikma* and his *al-Mulakhkhaṣ*.[21]

Modern scholarship, as well as historical Islamic sources, have tended to depict Islamic intellectual history in the 7th/13th century in terms of an antagonism between the anti-Avicennan Sunnī theologian Rāzī and the influential Shīʿī theologian Naṣīr al-Dīn al-Ṭūsī (d. 627/1274), who figures as the savior of Avicenna's philosophy from Rāzī's attacks.[22] This view came to be embodied in a statement by Ṭūsī that later became proverbial, namely that Rāzī's commentary (*sharḥ*) was nothing but a calumny (*jarḥ*). However, this statement was in fact not pronounced by Ṭūsī himself but attributed (though approvingly) to an anonymous wit (*ẓarīf*).[23] More generally, it has become clear that this statement can only be properly understood from the perspective of a reverential attitude toward Avicenna that both Rāzī and Ṭūsī shared.[24]

The scholarly narrative concerning the history of post-Avicennan Arabic logic, mainly established by Nicolas Rescher's pioneering work in the 1960s and 1970s, assumed that Rāzī was a largely unoriginal logician and that his originality only lay in the re-organization of existent material and the anti-Avicennan thrust of his work.[25] Rescher further thought that there were antagonistic "Western" and "Eastern" developments in the 7th/13th century until the tradition ossified in later centuries.[26] Recent research has begun to revise and refine Rescher's assessments. Rāzī must be seen, in fact, as a very imaginative logician who propelled forward the development of Arabic logic as a research discipline independent from the exegesis of Aristotle's *Organon*.[27] He was, for example, the first to include the fourth-figure syllogism alongside the traditional three in a major philosophical work.[28] That said, Rāzī's younger contemporary Khūnajī now appears to have been an even more innovative logician.[29]

Beginning with Rāzī, the antagonistic nature of appropriating Avicenna's works was played out not so much between an anti-Avicennan Western tradition initiated by Rāzī and a pro-Avicennan Eastern tradition spearheaded by Ṭūsī, but rather between two camps that both read, taught, commented on, and criticized Avicenna from an equally reverential attitude, but disagreed on the method and appropriate extent of critiquing Avicenna. Nor were these camps neatly divided by geography. The tradition most influential in later centuries that we are following was geographically centered around the astronomical observatory of Marāgha in the Western part of modern-day Iran.[30] However, logicians in conversation with this tradition were active as far west as Sicily and as far east as the easternmost part of what is today Uzbekistan.

Tony Street has introduced the term "revisionist" Avicennism for the camp that was ready to substantially revise Avicenna's logic, in opposition to the "orthodox" Avicennans, who tended to defend Avicenna against such revisions.[31] Of course, not all logicians discussed here will neatly fit into one or the other camp—and, of course, not everything they wrote was directly responding to Avicenna: they also wrote independent treatises and commented on one another's works, a process in the course of which new problems and issues could be raised. But many of them align—with or against Avicenna—on some crucial controversial issues, as for example the subject-matter of logic, the immediate implications of conditional and disjunctive propositions, the conversion of possibility propositions, or the productivity of first-figure syllogisms with possibility minors. Thus, we may say that Rāzī and Khūnajī (this chapter), as well as Abharī, Urmawī, and Kātibī (discussed in the next chapter), belong to the "revisionist" camp. On the other hand, Ṭūsī (also discussed in the next chapter) and his student Ḥillī, who in turn taught

Quṭb al-Dīn al-Rāzī (both discussed in chapter 7), all were "orthodox" Avicennans. With the authors treated in chapter 8 the matter is less clear.

The term "revisionist" Avicennism is useful as a tool for historical analysis not only because it allows us to group together certain logicians, but also because it reflects a watershed moment in the 7th/13th century that Ibn Khaldūn captured with the terminology that later logicians would use to group themselves and others. Street's "revisionists" tally well with what Ibn Khaldūn meant to capture by "new/later logicians" (*al-mutaʾakhkhirūn*), who in polemical contexts are often simply designated as "the author of *al-Kashf* [i.e., Khūnajī] and those who follow him."[32] These are pitted against the "old/earlier logicians" (*mutaqaddimūn*), whom Street's "orthodox" Avicennans aspire to rehabilitate. Ibn Khaldūn writes, in the late 8th/14th century, about this watershed moment in the history of the science of logic in his *Muqaddima*:

> The *later scholars* came and changed the technical terms of logic; and they appended to the investigation of the five universals its fruit, which is to say the discussion of definitions and descriptions which they moved from the *Posterior Analytics*; and they dropped the *Categories* because a logician is only accidentally and not essentially interested in that book; and *they appended to On Interpretation the treatment of conversion* (even if it had been in the *Topics* in the texts of the ancients, it is nonetheless in some respects among the things which follow from the treatment of propositions). Moreover, they treated the syllogistic with respect to its productivity generally, not with respect to its matter. They dropped the investigation of [the syllogistic] with respect to matter, which is to say, these five books: *Posterior Analytics, Topics, Rhetoric, Poetics,* and *Sophistical Fallacies* (though sometimes some of them give a brief outline of them). *They have ignored [these five books] as though they had never been*, even though they are important and relied upon in the discipline. Moreover, that part of [the discipline] they have set down they have treated in a penetrating way; they look into it in so far as it is a discipline in its own right, not in so far as it is an instrument for the sciences. Treatment of [the subject as newly conceived] has become lengthy and wide-ranging—the first to do that was *Fakhr al-Dīn al-Rāzī* and after him *Afḍal al-Dīn al-Khūnajī*, on whose books the Eastern logicians rely until this day. He has in this discipline the *Disclosing of Secrets*, which is long, but there is also an abridged version entitled *The Concise*, which is good for teaching, and another, *The Sentences*, which consists of only four pages giving a synopsis of the discipline and its principles. Contemporary students use it and profit from it. The books and ways of the ancients have been abandoned as though they had never been, even though they are full of fruits and useful points of logic as we said. God is the Guide to that which is correct.[33]

Ibn Khaldūn's appraisal of the more recent history of Arabic logic is not without some remorse, perhaps indicating an inclination to the more orthodox Avicennans, like Ṭūsī, who did include all of the Aristotelian *Organon* in his Persian summa. He might not be entirely right about the extent to which the "new logicians" eradicated the contents of the other books of the *Organon* from the discipline. Some found their treatment within the new structure of the science.

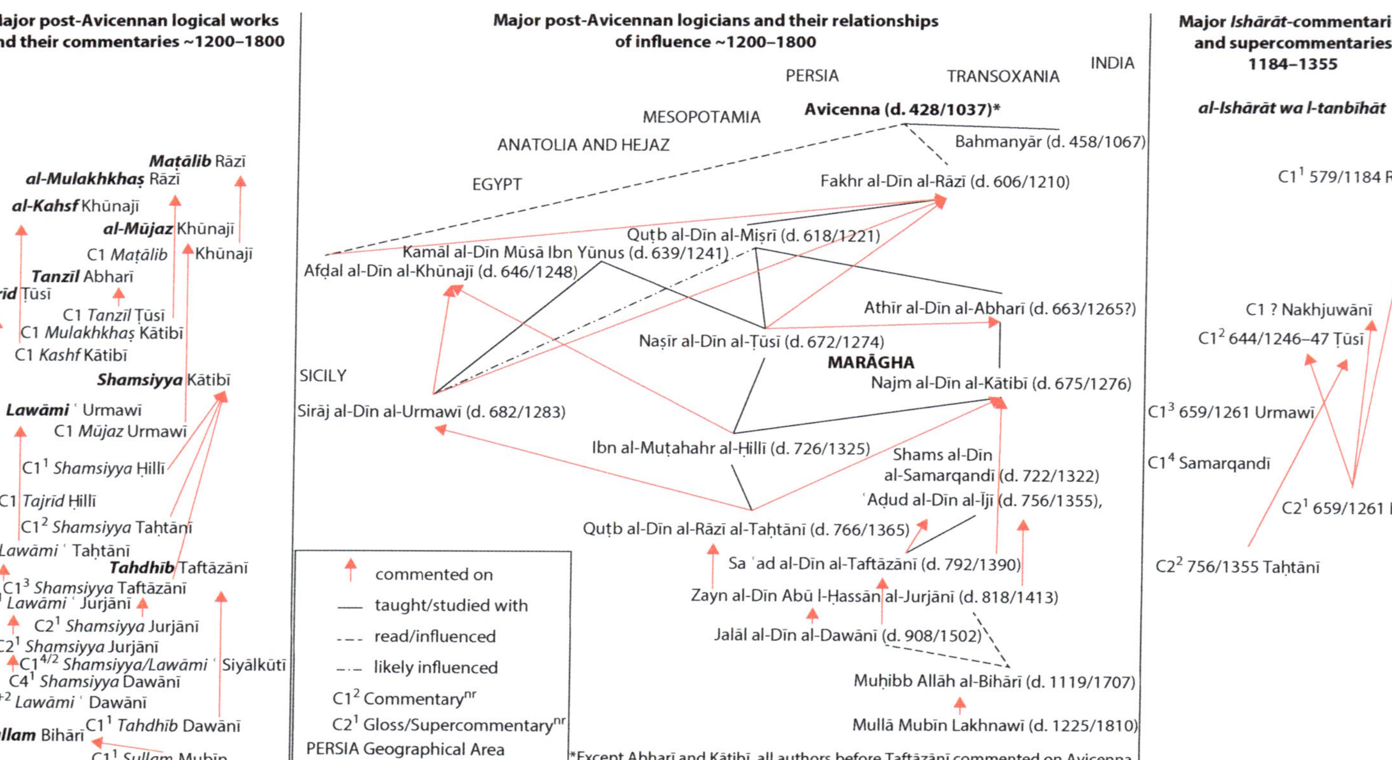

FIGURE 5. Major Post-Avicennan Logicians and Their Relations of Influence.

And there were movements urging a return to the old structure, both within the period discussed and later.[34] But overall, the historicity of the watershed moment Ibn Khaldūn tries to capture and tie to the logicians Rāzī and Khūnajī is borne out by recent studies and indeed the discussions on the problem of predication.[35] The problematizing approach of Rāzī and Khūnajī affected the works of all other authors studied here. Their move away from a largely exegetical to a more problematizing approach ushered in a reconfiguration of logic as a research science, dramatically increasing the scholarly output. The diagram visualizes the relationships of influence between these authors.

THE CHALLENGE OF FAKHR AL-DĪN AL-RĀZĪ

Fakhr al-Dīn Muḥammad al-Rāzī was born in 544/1149 in Rayy.[36] His father, Ḍiyāʾ al-Dīn ʿUmar al-Makkī (d. 559/1163–64), a prominent Ashʿarī theologian and Shāfiʿī, taught him in theology and law. Al-Makkī had studied with Abū al-Qāsim al-Anṣarī (d. 504/1110), who in turn was a student of al-Juwaynī's (d. 478/1085) and thus represented the later Juwaynian phase of Ashʿarī theology.[37] This theological tradition in which Rāzī was raised is reflected in his early works, for example, in his lengthy summa, probably titled *Uṣūl al-dīn* (Principles of Religion).[38]

His father passed away when he was still young, so Fakhr al-Dīn traveled to Nīshāpūr and Marāgha to study with other teachers, like Majd al-Dīn al-Jīlī, a teacher of philosophy and author of a logic book. Majd al-Dīn had studied with one of Ghazālī's most eminent students, Muḥammad b. Yaḥyā al-Nayshābūrī (d. 548/1153), and he taught the Illuminationist philosopher al-Suhrawardī (d. 587/1191). When Majd al-Dīn was invited to teach at the Mujāhidiyya madrasa in Marāgha, Rāzī accompanied him.[39] Rāzī appears to have traveled elsewhere in Persia, Central Asia, and India, receiving the patronage of the Khwārazmshāhs and the Ghūrids. He died in Herāt in 606/1210.

Rāzī was a prolific scholar. In contrast to Khūnajī, who was primarily known as a logician and of whom we have no more than a handful of works, Rāzī was first and foremost a theologian and wrote numerous works on a wide range of subjects, mainly on theology (*kalām*), scriptural exegesis (*tafsīr*), jurisprudence (*fiqh*), and Avicennan philosophy (*falsafa*), but including works on literary criticism, physiognomy, and chemistry. However, his output on logic was still substantial. Among his more influential writings on logic are, first and foremost, the commentary on Avicenna's *Ishārāt* (completed after 579/1183–1184 and before 582/1186), together with a critical epitome of it (*Lubāb al-Ishārāt* = *The Kernels of Pointers*) that he completed in 597/1201, and a commentary on Avicenna's *ʿUyūn al-ḥikma* (Elements of Philosophy) that he composed later in his life (604–605/1208–1209).[40] Further, he wrote a short handbook on logic titled *al-Āyāt al-bayyināt* (The Evident Signs), on which Sirāj al-Dīn al-Urmawī (d. 682/1283) wrote a commentary.[41]

The most systematic presentation of Rāzī's logic we find in the Logic part of his summa titled *al-Mulakhkhaṣ* (The Summary), completed shortly before his commentary on the *Ishārāt* in 579/1183–1184. In this work, Rāzī refers the reader to another summa of logic he wrote, by the title of *al-Manṭiq al-kabīr* (The Long Logic), but the unicum manuscript—listed in the catalogue of the Topkapı Palace Library as MS Ahmet III 3401, copied in 667/1268—that is supposed to contain that work appears to be a misattribution.[42] It is however one of the longest works of Arabic logic ever written and must be dated to the mid-7th/13th century.[43]

Reading Avicenna: Annotations on the Shifāʾ, and Rāzī's Challenge in the Commentaries on the Ishārāt and ʿUyūn al-ḥikma

Rāzī studied and taught logic largely by reading Avicenna. Even though evidence for close textual engagement with the *Shifāʾ* has been conspicuous by its absence between the 5th/11th and 10th/16th centuries, Di Vincenzo has recently drawn attention to several newly discovered identical marginal glosses (*ḥāshiyāt*) in nine MSS preserving the *Shifāʾ*. These can be identified as coming from Rāzī's hand, pointing to a lively exegetical practice of the text, likely in a madrasa context.[44] While the glosses on the *Shifāʾ* seem to have been intended for study purposes, they at least indicate that Rāzī considered Avicenna's discussion of third-person inflected verbs to stand in need of explanation.[45] The commentaries on the *Ishārāt* and the *ʿUyūn al-ḥikma* provided space for a more critical engagement. In the chapter on metathetic and positive predicates (*al-ʿudūl wa-l-taḥṣīl*) of the commentary on the *Ishārāt*, Rāzī explains an apparent discrepancy between what Avicenna says about the need to express the copula in the *Ishārāt* on the one hand, and in the *Easterners* on the other. Rāzī insinuates that Avicenna might have been indulgent with his wording in the former, urging that his considered opinion be taken as the one expressed in the latter:

TEXT 40: FAKHR AL-DĪN AL-RĀZĪ, *SHARḤ KITĀB AL-ISHĀRĀT WA L-TANBĪHĀT* (NAJAFZĀDE), I.3.7, 154.12–155.6

Know that the words of the Shaykh [Avicenna] "it is said 'Zayd [is] a writer' where it should be said 'Zayd, he [is] a writer'" invite further reflection. For "writer" is one of the derived names, and we just explained that their likes are predicated [by themselves] and that they do not need another utterance signifying that [they are being predicated]. [Avicenna] was explicit about that in the *Eastern Philosophy*, where he said: "As for the case when the proposition is not ternary, i.e., when it is only binary, the copula is not mentioned in it and [one] is able to dispense with it, because its predicate is a statement-word or a derived name. It then includes the mentioned nexus on account of the language, or else it is not mentioned for reasons of economy of expression. And the negational particle attaches only to the predicate."

Here we have an explanation of derived names as including the signification of the nexus; perhaps [Avicenna] was being indulgent in this book [i.e., the *Ishārāt*], because his goal here is to teach the metathetic and positive expressions, not to verify the distinction between binary and ternary propositions. What he says in detail is what he means, what he says in summary is not. In any case, the truth is as we presented it.

Rāzī takes issue with Avicenna's use of the copula "*huwa*" (he), which Rāzī thinks must not be used when the predicate is a verb or a derived name. Strangely, in the later *Lubāb* he himself uses the copula "*huwa*" with a derived name (*baṣīr*, i.e., sighted/seeing) in his examples. But that might be charitably read in the same way that Rāzī read Avicenna: his considered opinion was what he said when discussing the point in detail.[46] In the *Mulakhkhaṣ*, which was completed in 579/1183–1184 before the commentary on the *Ishārāt*, the criticism is also voiced. In the commentary on the *Ishārāt* itself, just before the passage quoted earlier, Rāzī had put the matter thus:

TEXT 41: FAKHR AL-DĪN AL-RĀZĪ, *SHARḤ KITĀB AL-ISHĀRĀT WA L-TANBĪHĀT* (NAJAFZĀDE), I.3.7, 152.10–153.4

[Avicenna] said: And you must know [. . .] the second case, [if] the copula precedes the [negative particle], it makes [the negative particle] a part of the predicate.

I say: Every statement inevitably consists of something that it makes a statement about and something else with which it makes a statement, and of a nexus of one of the two to the other, either affirmatively or negatively. The utterance signifying that which the statement is about is called the subject, the one signifying that with which the statement is made [is called] the predicate. You should know that predicates fall under one of two types. Some contain the signification of the copula, and some are not like that. The first are the statement-words and the derived names, for we explained that derived names and statement-words have in common that they signify meanings accruing to indeterminate subjects. "Writer," for example, signifies not only "writing," but also that writing accrues to some [one] thing, and that [signification] is the nexus obtaining between "writing" and its subject.

Since the nexus is one of the things internal to the concepts of derived names and statement-words, surely there is no need to mention a simple utterance signifying this nexus. Rather, they are predicated by themselves without the need to mention a simple utterance signifying that nexus. If it is made explicit by mentioning the utterance signifying that nexus, then this would be a useless repetition.

This is, in essence, Rāzī's challenge. It is not the case that a proposition—in the sense of an utterance with a truth-value—consists, when fully analyzed, of three items. We may note that for Rāzī, subject, predicate, and the copula are expressions. That about which judgment is passed, that with which judgment is passed, and the nexus, be it affirmative or negative, are the concepts signified by those expressions. While for Rāzī it is correct to say that the nexus is a concept distinct from the meanings of both subject and predicate, this does not mean that a third utterance is needed to signify it. Rather, the majority of predicates is such that what they signify includes as part of their essence (*dhāt*) the signification of the nexus. To someone insisting that the number of concepts signified by a proposition should be mirrored by the number of expressions, he counters:

TEXT 42: FAKHR AL-DĪN AL-RĀZĪ, *SHARḤ KITĀB AL-ISHĀRĀT WA L-TANBĪHĀT* (NAJAFZĀDE), I.3.7, 153.5–154.2

If it is objected that when we say "Man is-a-writer" (*al-insānu kātibun*), then *man* is a concept distinct from the concept *writer*. When two concepts are distinct, inevitably there must be a connecting relation (*intisāb*) of one to the other that is additional to the two concepts, and that requires a third utterance—then we respond as follows.

First, this is absurd as far as the statement-word is concerned, for it is predicated all by itself, even though what you mentioned does apply [i.e., that the nexus is a concept additional to the concepts signified by subject and predicate]. And also, because the nexus, even if the concept of it is distinct from the concept of the subject, is connected to it by its essence. And likewise, whatever [meaning] comprises the nexus as internal to its concept is connected to the subject by its essence.

When, however, predicates are non-derived names, there must be an utterance signifying that nexus. For that nexus, since it is a third meaning distinct from both subject and predicate, surely must be singled out by an utterance signifying it, be it explicitly or implicitly.

Hence it is clear that there are propositions which are binary by nature and do not permit of being turned into ternary ones, and others that are ternary and do not permit of being turned into binary ones. The matter is not as superficial thinkers thought, namely, that binary propositions are those that do not mention the copula with an [additional] utterance, so that once [the copula] is made explicit they become ternary.

Some propositions are binary because their predicate includes the signification of the nexus. However, this does not apply to all predicates *qua* predicates, but depends on the type of concept that occurs in the predicate-place. If the predicate is signified by a statement-word or a derived name, it will be a concept such that it is never a substance. If the predicate is signified by a non-derived name, it does not by its own essence connect to the subject but needs the nexus to be signified by a copula. For Rāzī, such propositions consist—when fully analyzed—of three items.

But only those do, and hence there is no liberty in mentioning or leaving implicit the copula, as Avicenna had supposed. In his later commentary on *ʿUyūn al-ḥikma* Rāzī criticizes Avicenna from yet another angle:

TEXT 43: FAKHR AL-DĪN AL-RĀZĪ, *SHARḤ ʿUYŪN AL-ḤIKMA* (AL-SAQQĀ), I.125.1–18

There are questions here. The first question is this. Every affirmative proposition has three parts: the essence of the subject, the essence of the predicate, and the specific nexus obtaining between them. One of them is a subject for the other, and that other [thing] is a predicate for the former. The proof for this is that when we say "The sky [is a] sphere," then what is understood from "sky" is one thing, and what is understood from "sphere" is another. What is understood from the sky being described as a sphere is a third thing. The proof: It is perfectly possible to conceive of the sky and the quiddity of a sphere without knowing that the sky is described as a sphere. And what is known is distinct from what is not known.

Further: What is affirmed when one affirms that the sky is a sphere is the affirmation of the nexus. And what is denied when it is denied that the sky is a sphere is likewise the nexus. [For the sake of argument, assume] it is affirmed: then [it is affirmed that] this nexus is a third concept distinct from the essence of the subject and the essence of the predicate. Now, when we say "the body has blackness," the body is the subject, and blackness is in reality its predicate. And "has" is the description signifying this specific nexus. However, the Shaykh [Avicenna] said that blackness was not a predicate, but that the predicate was [in fact] "black."

What Rāzī adds in this passage is that contrary to what Avicenna said, blackness (*sawād*), which is treated as a non-derived name, may well be a predicate, and then just needs a copula to signify the nexus ("*lahu*," i.e., "to it/it has" in Rāzī's example). Rāzī's argument here is roughly the same as in the commentary on the *Ishārāt*. In both commentaries Rāzī advances what I shall call the "Repetition Argument":

TEXT 44: FAKHR AL-DĪN AL-RĀZĪ, *SHARḤ ʿUYŪN AL-ḤIKMA* (AL-SAQQĀ), 1.125.18–25

In my opinion this is weak. For here we have an essence present in the soul and an attribute present in that essence, and that essence is described by this attribute—the subject is just this: the aptitude for being described. As for the attribute: it is nothing other than "blackness," or "whiteness."

Now that you know this, we may say that if what is meant by "predicate" is what we just said, then the nexus is external to the thing named, and in this case a third expression is needed to signify the nexus. If, however, what is meant by "predicate" is what the Shaykh said, then the specific nexus is one of two parts of the meaning that is understood from "predicate." If the matter is thus, then it would be impossible to single out the nexus by [employing] an additional third expression. For it is not correct to say "Zayd he [is] a writer," because the expression "writer" by containment signifies that nexus. Hence, singling it out by [employing] another expression is mere repetition.

For Rāzī, there are two types of predicates. First, it may be a concept to which the nexus is external (which is signified by non-derived names), and in that case a copula is needed to signify that nexus. Second, the predicate may be what Avicenna referred to in his *Eastern Philosophy*, namely, a concept that contains the nexus. In that case it is impossible to signify the nexus by an additional expression (as Avicenna thought you could). If you tried to signify the nexus by a copula in the second case, that would amount to a repetition, because the nexus would be signified twice.

The Logic of al-Mulakhkhaṣ

In the *Mulakhkhaṣ*, even though broadly following the Avicennan format, much of Rāzī's presentation of logic, both on a general level and on a level of detail, is still idiosyncratic. It is noteworthy that the Repetition Argument already features in this relatively early work, completed over twenty years before the commentary on *ʿUyūn al-ḥikma*. The chapter on simple categorical propositions in the *Mulakhkhaṣ* provides a more comprehensive picture of the problem of predication, suggesting why Rāzī might have insisted on the Repetition Argument. He divides the issue of the copula in two. First, one can ask about the elements of propositions either regarding their form or regarding their matter. Rāzī equates the form of a proposition with the nexus. And with regard to the nexus, we may inquire either about the utterance signifying it, or about the meaning itself.

TEXT 45: FAKHR AL-DĪN AL-RĀZĪ, *MANṬIQ AL-MULAKHKHAṢ* (QARĀMALIKĪ), I.129.1–130.5

As for the elements [of the proposition], they are either its form, and this is the nexus which is between its two terms, or its matter, and this is the subject and the predicate. As for the form, the investigation is concerned either with its [i.e., the nexus's] meaning, or with the utterance signifying it.

[A] Concerning the meaning, there are two investigations.

First: In every proposition there are no doubt the essence of the subject, the essence of the predicate and the nexus between the two, which is distinct from them because of the possibility to conceive each of the two without conceiving [the nexus] or conceiving [the nexus] without conceiving the specificity of each of the two [i.e., of predicate and subject]. And [also,] because the nexus between the two things is posterior to them, and what is posterior is distinct from what is prior.

Second: The nexus of one of the two to the other is not [the same as] the nexus of the other to it, because the nexus of one of the two to the other is the nexus of being-a-subject and of being-a-locus, while the nexus of the other to the first is the nexus of being-a-description and of being-a-state. One of the two [nexus] may be necessary while the other is contingent. That's why propositions do not preserve their modalities when they are converted. But the nexus which is part of the quiddity of the proposition is the aptitude of the essence of the subject for being described by the predicate, while the other [nexus, i.e., that of predicate-hood] is an extrinsic implicate [of the quiddity of the proposition].

As in the earlier passages, Rāzī makes clear that the nexus is distinct from the meaning of subject and predicate. Here he states that there are in fact two nexus, because the modal qualities may differ depending on which term is in the predicate-position. Only the subject-nexus is part of the quiddity of the proposition. Concerning the investigation of the utterance, he continues:

TEXT 46: FAKHR AL-DĪN AL-RĀZĪ, *MANṬIQ AL-MULAKHKHAṢ* (QARĀMALIKĪ), I.130.6–132.10

[B] Concerning the utterance, there are five investigations.

First: If the nexus is signified by containment through the predicate-name, as is the case with derived names and statement-words, on pain of repetition it is not permissible to single it out by correspondence [between simple utterances and simple concepts signified]. This proposition is by nature binary on the level of utterances.

Second: The natural place for the copula is in the middle between subject and predicate because the nexus is between the two. Hence, the utterance signifying it inevitably should be between them, [too].

Third: Every proposition is in itself quaternary, because the copula by itself inevitably has a specific quality—either necessity or non-necessity. This may or may not be the case for the utterance.

Fourth: When we say "Man is necessary-that-it-is-an-animal" it is possible that necessity is a predicate, and what comes after ["necessary"] is mentioned so that [the predicate] is further specified, because necessity is a relational matter (*amr nisbī*) and it is not possible to mention it in its specificity, except by mentioning that to which it is related (*mansūb*); or because it is a part of it; or, finally, because it is external to it. On the first and second account the proposition is not modalized on the level of language, but rather it is absolute. It is only modalized on the third account. [. . .]

Fifth: Even though the quantifier is, as will soon be explained, God willing, a part of the proposition when it is heard, it is however not a part of the proposition when it is intellected. [The quantifier] is nothing but an utterance signifying the quantity for which the predicate subsists, and that quantity is the same as the subject. But in [extramental] reality the quantifier has no expression distinct from the subject— in contradistinction to the copula and the modality. That's why they classified propositions—because of [the quantifier]—as quinary, just as they classified them— because of the copula and the modality—into binary, ternary and quaternary.

Rāzī here both provides a new conceptual framework to think about propositions as hylomorphic compounds in which the meanings of subject and predicate are the material parts, and the nexus the formal part. He closely ties modality to the discussion of the nexus signified by the copula. A proposition for Rāzī is something to the utterer of which it is said that she speaks truly or falsely. But a proposition may be intellected or heard, and Rāzī presupposes a certain isomorphism between the two. When intellected, a proposition consists of the meaning of the subject, the meaning of the predicate, and a nexus that is a concept distinct from these two.

The nexus has an intrinsic modal quality, no matter whether it is mentioned in a spoken proposition or not. Given that the modal quality of the nexus may change when a proposition is converted, Rāzī insists that there are two distinct nexus between any two terms depending on which of them is assumed to be the predicate. Both the nexus and its modal quality find an expression in extramental reality. The reason why Rāzī insists on the Repetition Argument is that on his account some meanings of predicates (those signified by verbs and derived names) are such that they include the meaning of a copula (i.e., the nexus). The nexus is however still distinct from the notion primarily signified by the predicate. Khūnajī responded to most of these points.

AFḌAL AL-DĪN AL-KHŪNAJĪ:
A CHAPTER ON THE COPULA

Afḍal al-Dīn Muḥammad b. Nāmāwar b. ʿAbd al-Malik al-Khūnajī was born in 590/1194 in Khūnaj, a town between the cities of Zanjān and Marāgha in the province of Azerbaijan.[47] We know little about his upbringing and studies. The chronicler and polymath Bar Hebraeus (d. 685/1286) mentioned him as one of Fakhr al-Dīn al-Rāzī's students. This is however with justification doubted by

El-Rouayheb.[48] We know that Afḍal al-Dīn was in Mecca in 624/1226–1227, where he wrote *al-Jumal* (The Sentences). A couple of years later, in 632/1234–1235, he was in Cairo, where Ibn Abī Uṣaybiʿa, the famous author of the biographies of philosophers and physicians, was among his students.[49] When the Ayyūbid ruler of Egypt al-Malik al-Kāmil (*reg.* 615/1218–635/1238) died, Afḍal al-Dīn was forced to move to Seljuk Anatolia, where he served as a judge. After the Mongol invasions of 641/1243 he returned to Cairo where he was appointed chief judge by al-Malik al-Ṣāliḥ (*reg.* 637/1240–647/1249) a year later and died there in 646/1248.

Khūnajī wrote three works on logic. As Ibn Khaldūn stated, *al-Jumal* is a very short (four leaves) handbook useful for students.[50] It was popular especially in North Africa, and Ibn Khaldūn likely studied logic with it himself. Naturally, given its brevity, Khūnajī does not engage in criticism in this work. He simply states that a proposition needs a nexus by which the predicate is true of the subject, either affirmatively or negatively, and that if the copula (*huwa/laysa huwa*) is mentioned, the proposition is called ternary, and if not, binary.[51] Further, he states that the nexus inevitably has a modal quality, i.e., necessity (*ḍarūra*) or lack thereof, or perpetuity (*dawām*) or lack thereof, which, when expressed by a simple utterance, makes the proposition quaternary.[52] It is noteworthy that he includes a section on the quantification of the predicate.[53] The second work, an intermediate length handbook titled *al-Mūjaz* (The Concise), has not yet been edited.[54] It elicited a commentary by Sirāj al-Dīn al-Urmawī (d. 682/1283), as well as by Fakhr al-Dīn b. Badīʿ al-Bandahī (d. 657/1258), and Sayf al-Dīn Dāʾūd b. ʿĪsā al-Baghdādī (d. 705/1305).[55] The third logical work, a summa titled *Kashf al-asrār ʿan ghawāmiḍ al-afkār* (Disclosing the Secrets of the Obscurities of Thoughts), is, as Ibn Khaldūn noted, very long and contains Khūnajī's most in-depth confrontation with the positions of his predecessors.

The Kashf al-asrār *and the Subject-Matter of Logic*

One of the most influential works of Arabic logic ever written, Khūnajī's *Kashf al-asrār* was first edited in 2010 and remains to be thoroughly studied.[56] While the momentous importance of the work was appreciated by contemporary scholars and near-contemporaries like the historian Ibn Khaldūn, the later tradition grew increasingly oblivious of the origin of many of Khūnajī's logical innovations, which came to be absorbed into the standard logical textbooks written in the 7th/13th and 8th/14th centuries.[57]

However, this substantial and self-standing work on logic (adding up to some four hundred pages in the printed edition, even though it remained unfinished) certainly stands out from the usual tripartite presentations of philosophy where the logic part serves as the *propaedeuticum* for the parts on metaphysics and physics. It is roughly structured after the logic of the *Ishārāt* and was likely written between 624/1227 and 634/1237, after *al-Jumal* (composed 624/1226–1227 in Mecca) and probably before *al-Mūjaz*.[58] In the words of Kātibī, who wrote a monumental commentary on it, Khūnajī presents in the *Kashf al-asrār* noble investigations, subtle rules and general principles that are absent from the works of people of the discipline, especially in modality propositions, their contradictories, converses and contrapositions, and the modal and hypothetical syllogisms. He uniquely presented outstanding innovations and truthful discoveries that were not indicated by people before him.[59]

What Kātibī refers to here are some of the major innovations that were to shape Arabic logic for centuries to come.[60] Another point on which Khūnajī in the preliminaries of the *Kashf al-asrār* presents a radically new idea is his conception of the subject-matter of logic. For him, logic investigates not secondary intelligibles but the objects of conception and assent. Even though not paraded as a novelty by Khūnajī himself, this conception of the subject-matter of logic was perceived by later logicians, like Kātibī and Khūnajī's student Ibn Wāṣil al-Ḥamawī (d. 697/1298) for example, as fundamentally distinct from and decidedly superior to the Avicennan position.[61]

On this conception, logic as a science in the typical Aristotelian fashion investigates the *per se* accidents (*a ʿrāḍ dhātiyya*; here: *awāriḍ lāḥiqa limā huwa huwa*) of its subject-matter (8.13–9.2).[62] Yet whereas for Avicenna logic investigates the *per se* accidents of its subject-matter, that is, of secondary intelligibles such as "being-a-genus" or "being-a-predicate," insofar as they lead from the known to the unknown, Khūnajī considers the subject-matter of logic to be more general than secondary intelligibles. This is precisely because for him it is not only the *per se* accidents of secondary intelligibles that are relevant to logic, but also, in some cases, the *per se* accidents of primary intelligibles and, if Samarqandī's reading is correct, tertiary intelligibles.[63]

Khūnajī's Criticism of Avicenna on the Statement-Word

As far as the notion of the statement-word is concerned, Khūnajī closely engages with Avicenna's ruminations in the *Shifāʾ* and criticizes some of the points Avicenna had made there. After discussing the types of signification and the distinction between simple and compound utterances (10.12–14.14), Khūnajī introduces the types of simple utterances: name (*ism*), statement-word (*kalima*), and auxiliary (*adā*). He reproduces and explains the definitions of name and statement-word given in Avicenna's *al-ʿIbāra* (14.15–15.5).[64] Fully alive to the importance of Avicenna's addition to the definition of the statement-word, Khūnajī remarks:

> As a last addition to the [definition of] the statement-word the Shaykh [Avicenna] claims that, even if not needed for precise specification, but nonetheless to fully circumscribe its real nature, [the statement-word] signifies a nexus to a subject. The statement-word needs this nexus no less than it needs a tense, for as long as there is no nexus, there will be no tense for the nexus. (15.5–8)[65]

Khūnajī then discusses Avicenna's considerations concerning the statement-word in Arabic as being different from Greek, and as being different from what Arabic grammarians understand by "verb" (*fiˤl*). He reports three of the four issues raised by Avicenna, and summarizes:[66]

> This is a synopsis of what Avicenna said. He further refines [the definition of] the proposition by declaring the past and present third-person conjugated verb forms to be statement-words (not propositions) and all remaining verb conjugations to be propositions (*kalām*). And he also judges the declined noun to be composite on account of the hidden inflectional pronouns signifying an additional meaning. (20.3–5)

With all of this Khūnajī emphatically disagrees:

TEXT 47: AFḌAL AL-DĪN AL-KHŪNAJĪ, *KASHF AL-ASRĀR ˤAN GHAWĀMIḌ AL-AFKĀR* (EL-ROUAYHEB), 20.6–17

> And we say that the matter is not like that for Arabic speakers, for "I walk" (*amshī*) or any of the other [inflected verb forms], are by themselves not propositions (*kalām*) susceptible to truth and falsehood. Rather, [these become propositions only] together with the noun concealed in them. [The grammarians call] this the agent pronoun. It is the expression "I" (*ana*) in "I walk" (*amshī*), and "you" (*anta*) and "we" (*naḥnu*) in the other [examples]. What is heard is by itself not a proposition but a part of a proposition consisting of what is heard and the concealed noun, just as is the case with "he walks" (*yamshī*) which is a proposition (*kalām*) together with an explicit noun or else with an implicit pronoun for the third person, and that is the expression "he" (*huwa*).
>
> And if it is said that even if the *hamza* is not a noun or a pronoun for the first-person agent, it is still a sign for this pronoun and has a signification in the context of the sentence necessitating a composition, then we say: so likewise for the *yāʾ*! It has a certain signification because it is a sign for the third-person pronoun. Some of them stick to this position to the extent that they think that there is no statement-word in the Arabic language, and that present-tense statement-words are composed of two names or of a name and a letter/particle (*ḥarf*) as their position requires—clinging to the idea that what comes after the letters [signaling] the present-tense is neither a past nor future-tense verb, but a name, and that every single one of the letters [signaling] the present-tense is either a name or a particle. Space does not allow for an extensive treatment of the issue, but whoever wants a thorough examination of it has the books on Arabic [grammar] at his disposal.

Khūnajī simply does not buy Avicenna's arguments that first- and second-person inflected verbs are not statement-words, but complete propositions with a truth-value. His criticism cuts at the first juncture (1) so that neither (2), whether or not third-person inflected words would then also have to count as compound utterances and hence as propositions with a truth-value, nor (3), the same question in relation to derived names, can even arise. For Khūnajī, all these cases are structurally indistinguishable: none—by itself—counts as a proposition. Rather, such utterances only implicitly contain personal pronouns whose reference needs to be fixed by context—that's no different for an implied "you" or "he." To ostensibly fix that reference, the implied pronouns need to be made explicit. But then they are no longer part of the simple utterance.

Khūnajī's Criticism of Rāzī concerning the Copula

Khūnajī is the first to dedicate a chapter specifically to the copula in a substantial work on logic in Arabic (75.1–77.11). In it he presents largely traditional material, but also explicitly criticizes Rāzī. He begins by stating the common ground that both Avicenna and Rāzī shared. A proposition consists of three things: the meaning of the subject, the meaning of the predicate, and a nexus (*nisba*) between them (75.2–3). As the nexus is a conception that is irreducible to subject or predicate (we can conceive of them without being so combined), it is only right to express this fact also on the level of language; and that which signifies said nexus on the level of language is called the copula (*rābiṭa*) (74.3–6). But some languages, like Arabic, do not customarily use a copula. Hence, if the copula is expressed, the proposition is called ternary, and if it is implicit, binary (75.6–9). He continues: The copula is an auxiliary and may be in the form of a statement-word (hyparctic), in which case it is temporal, or in the form of a naming-word (i.e., pronoun: *faṣl/ 'imād*), in which case it is atemporal (75.10–13). Whereas Greek always explicitly expresses a temporal copula, Arabic does so only in conditionals, not in categoricals; Persian only uses ternary propositions, with either additional temporal or non-temporal copulae, or else with an inflection at the end of the predicate (75.14–76.2). So far, nothing of this was controversial in the tradition. However, the remainder of the chapter has a more critical tone.

Khūnajī cites Avicenna from the *Shifā'* where he distinguishes between binary, incomplete ternary, and complete ternary propositions, depending on whether and what kind of copula is expressed (76.3–13).[67] Only non-temporal copulae signify a nexus to a determinate subject (*mushār ilayhi*: indexically; 76.9). Statement-words and derived names signify a nexus, but only to an indeterminate subject (76.6–7). Hence, Avicenna classified propositions into complete ternary (expressing a copula that signifies a nexus to a determinate subject), incomplete ternary (with a copula implying an indeterminate subject), and binary (where no copula is expressed) (76.7–12). This, according to Khūnajī, is why in the *Ishārāt* the non-temporal copula is needed in propositions like "Zayd[, he] is a writer" to determine the subject (76.13–16).[68]

However, as we have seen, Avicenna in the *Easterners* had also said that the statement-word may contain the signification of the nexus, including that to a determinate subject (76.16–77.2).[69] Khūnajī credits Rāzī for resolving doubts about the consistency between Avicenna's *Ishārāt* and the *Easterners*. In his commentary on the *Ishārāt* Rāzī said that Avicenna here might have said that *"huwa"* is needed, but in fact this might just be due to carelessness or negligence, or else the exigencies of the context at hand, and that what he really meant is what he says in *al-Ḥikma al-mashriqiyya*.[70] Yet Khūnajī criticizes Rāzī's position:

TEXT 48: AFḌAL AL-DĪN AL-KHŪNAJĪ, *KASHF AL-ASRĀR ʿAN GHAWĀMIḌ AL-AFKĀR* (EL-ROUAYHEB), 77.3–7

> The Imām [al-Rāzī] in his books maintains that if the predicate of the proposition is a statement-word or a derived name, then it is true of [the proposition] that it is binary, because of the nexus being signified by containment. Consequently, it is not permissible—on pain of repetition—to single out [the nexus] by mentioning [the copula]. If [the predicate] is a non-derived name, then it is true of [the proposition] that it is ternary. This goes against what we transmitted from the Shaykh [Avicenna], so how can he [Rāzī] acknowledge in the commentary on the *Ishārāt* that the statement-word only signifies a nexus to an indeterminate subject?

For Khūnajī, Rāzī is himself being incoherent here. Rāzī held that if the predicate is morphologically derived (an IM, or a verb), then the proposition is binary (*fī l-lafẓ bi-l-ṭabʿ*), because the signification of the nexus to the subject is contained in the predicate. As we have seen, in support of this, Rāzī had provided the Repetition Argument.[71] Khūnajī's critique is this:

TEXT 49: AFḌAL AL-DĪN AL-KHŪNAJĪ, *KASHF AL-ASRĀR ʿAN GHAWĀMIḌ AL-AFKĀR* (EL-ROUAYHEB), 77.7–78.2

> But from what is said—if we say "Zayd writes," the expression "he" is implied at the end of the statement-word, being concealed in it according to the Arab grammarians, but if we also put it in the middle, we would say "Zayd, he writes, he" (*Zayd huwa yaktub huwa*), and that is a repetition—none of this follows. For the expression "he" which is at the end of the statement-word is not a copula for [the grammarians], but an agent noun (*ism fāʿil*), whereas the middle one is a copula, and each of the two is unlike the other. Therefore, [the grammarians] do not doubt that the last one is a name (*ism*), and some of them maintain that the other is an auxiliary.
>
> We find in the Qurʾān the explicit statement of a copula even though the predicate contains the nexus, like the words of Him Exalted "You are the All-Observer" (*kunta anta al-raqība*) [Q5:117], recited with the accusative ending. But it is possible that the statement-word alone is not a predicate for them, but rather the sentence (*jumla*) obtaining through it *and* the agent noun (*ism fāʿil*) coming after it. The statement-word, even if alone it does not signify a determinate subject, together with the silent pronoun that refers back to the preceding [grammatical] subject (*al-mubtadaʾ*), signifies a determinate subject (*mawḍūʿ*). But generally speaking, the controversy about this is ultimately a linguistic inquiry that is outside the scope of the logician. It is only incumbent upon the logician that he makes it obligatory to mention whatever signifies a determinate subject. If the Arabic statement-word is assumed to do this, then it is not necessary to mention the copula along with it. If it signifies [only] an indeterminate [subject], then it is necessary.

The Repetition Argument does not hold, for what statement-words or derived names signify by containment is different from what is signified by a non-temporal copula. The Qur'ānic verse *"Kunta anta al-raqība"* is cited to invalidate the Repetition Argument. Here we have both a temporal copula in the form of a second-person singular hyparctic verb *and* an accusative case-ending inflecting the predicate to signify, Khūnajī speculates, the nexus to an indeterminate subject in this way. If the copula *"anta"* is here mentioned, then it must be that leaving it out would not sufficiently specify the subject of the nexus implied by the inflection. The subject becomes specified only by the inflection understood as a hidden pronoun referring back to the grammatical subject. But that is ultimately a matter for grammarians to resolve. Khūnajī's verdict is that the logician has to make sure the determinate subject is signified, whatever that may require.

Two brief rejoinders are annexed to the chapter that are both also found in Rāzī. First, temporal copulae may be used to signify non-temporal nexus and *vice versa* (78.3–4). Second, the nexus of a subject to its predicate is not the same as that of the predicate to the subject, for similar reasons that Rāzī had adduced. The nexus of the predicate to the subject may have different qualities in terms of affirmation/negation and a different modality—otherwise a proposition would be indistinguishable from its converse (78.5–11).

The latter point came to be extensively discussed by later logicians, especially by Kātibī and Urmawī, as we shall see in the next chapter. The problem may be seen as arising from the "interchangeability thesis." Post-Avicennan logicians noticed that there was a fundamental problem with assuming that it is possible to take two terms and switch them around between subject- and predicate-place. One of the reasons they became aware of the problem was that when places are switched, the modal quality of the nexus may no longer be the same. Some logicians in the later tradition thus distinguished four different nexus by which two terms may be connected.

CONCLUSIONS

With Rāzī and Khūnajī, the first two of Ibn Khaldūn's new logicians, Arabic logic had begun to emancipate itself from its Aristotelian roots. This happened not only in the sense that the Aristotelian text was no longer the point of reference (this development had begun with Avicenna himself), but also in the sense that Avicennan logic as the new point of reference was being approached with a critical spirit aimed not at mere polemics, but rather at ameliorating the logical system as a whole, scrutinizing argument for argument.

The revisionist Avicennans approached Avicenna in a similar spirit to the one Avicenna used to approach Aristotle. While Avicenna, especially in his later works, had not given much attention to the copula, Rāzī, by criticizing Avicenna's seemingly contradicting remarks in the *Ishārāt* and *Easterners*, made the copula central again to discussions of predication, of the parts of the proposition, and of issues with modality and conversion.

Rāzī conceptualized the nexus between the meanings of subject and predicate as the form of a proposition and not a material part. His Repetition Argument claims that there are linguistic items that only occur as predicates, signifying at once two distinct concepts, i.e., the meaning they have *and* the distinct concept of a nexus to a subject, and hence must not be used with a copula in categorical statements.

Khūnajī, who had reconceptualized the Avicennan subject-matter of logic, just as Avicenna had done with Fārābī's, making it an independent science with a larger scope, criticized Avicenna's idea that, in Arabic, some inflected verbs are not statement-words but propositions. However, concerning Rāzī's Repetition Argument, Khūnajī insisted that there was a distinction to be made between the meaning of the copula signifying a nexus to a determinate subject and the meaning included in statement-words and derived names that implies a hidden pronoun and thus only signifies a nexus to an indeterminate subject.

6

The Marāgha Generation of Logicians

The forty years or so between the completion of Khūnajī's *Kashf al-asrār* (most probably by 634/1237) and Urmawī's *Bayān al-ḥaqq* (written in 675/1276) were extraordinarily prolific in terms of new logical works produced in the East. Most of these works were compiled after the Mongols sacked Baghdād in 656/1258. A closer look at their contents will disperse any prejudice that may remain against philosophical works written after the fall of the ʿAbbāsid capital. With the terms of the debate set by Razī and Khūnajī, four scholars were instrumental in shaping a truly Arabic logical tradition. Three of them were connected to the astronomical observatory at Marāgha near present-day Tabrīz: Athīr al-Dīn al-Abharī, Naṣīr al-Dīn al-Ṭūsī, and Najm al-Dīn al-Kātibī. Another scholar of the same generation, Sirāj al-Dīn al-Urmawī, was not connected to the observatory but played an important role in synthesizing the logical tradition in an advanced handbook.

Against widespread skepticism among scholars of Islamic studies, the work of these logicians shows that Arabic logic did not degenerate into scholastic school science. On the contrary, by the end of the 7th/13th century, they had reinvented the canon of Arabic logic to include controversial issues in textbooks and established a dialectical praxis that encouraged original research in logic. An important aspect of this development was the emerging discipline of formal disputation that shaped the critical engagement with Rāzī.

PROBING RĀZĪ: ATHĪR AL-DĪN AL-ABHARĪ AND NAṢĪR AL-DĪN AL-TŪSĪ

Athīr al-Dīn al-Abharī was a contemporary of Khūnajī's, probably about the same age, and it is not unlikely that they met. Going by his toponym, he was likely born in the town of Abhar near Qazwīn northwest of Tehran.[1] Contrary to what Bar Hebraeus claims, he was probably not himself Rāzī's student, but studied with the latter's student Quṭb al-Dīn al-Miṣrī (d. 618/1221) in Nīshāpūr.[2] He further pursued studies in astronomy and dialectics (with the luminary Rukn al-Dīn al-ʿAmīdī [d. 615/1218]) in Samarqand, and later in Mosul.[3] Mosul was a vibrant center of learning at the time, and there he also studied Ptolemy's *Almagest* at the Badriyya madrasa with Kamāl al-Dīn Mūsā Ibn Yūnus (d. 639/1242), whose teaching fellow (*muʿīd*) he became.[4] Ibn Yūnus also taught Ṭūsī and Urmawī, and he reportedly read Fārābī and Avicenna with the Christian philosopher Theodore of Antioch.[5]

In 625/1227–1228, Abharī came to Irbil, where he settled a year later to teach at the Dār al-Ḥadīth. There, the biographer Ibn Khallikān (d. 681/1282) was among his students.[6] Information on his later life is scarce. A colophon written by one of his students suggests that he traveled or lived in Seljuk Anatolia at the same time as Khūnajī, returning to Mosul in 643/1245, and later went to Persia (*al-ʿajam*), where he died, probably in Shabistar near Marāgha.[7] The traditional date of his death, 19 Rabīʿ II, 663/February 8, 1265, is likely inaccurate, for it appears from manuscript evidence that he was no longer alive in 656/1258 when Ṭūsī wrote his *Taʿdīl al-miʿyār* (Recalibrating the Measure), a refutation of Abharī's *Tanzīl al-afkār* (The Revelation of Thoughts).[8]

In his overall philosophical outlook, Abharī largely followed Rāzī's revisionist course.[9] In logic, he was substantially influenced by the revisionist ideas of Khūnajī: the recent edition of Abharī's *Muntahā l-afkār fī ibānat al-asrār* (The Ultimate Thoughts in Explicating Secrets), a work that survives in two recensions, shows that the earlier recension lacks many of the idiosyncratic revisionist innovations from Khūnajī's *Kashf* that are however included in the later recension.[10] He was also somehow connected to Ṭūsī and may have had a hand in preparing the foundation of the astronomical observatory at Marāgha, even though it is doubtful that he ever worked there.[11]

Abharī's writings on astronomy and mathematics, as well as his connections to Frederick II of Hohenstaufen, have attracted the interest of scholars for a while now.[12] Yet his considerable output on logic remains largely unstudied and even unedited.[13] Next to his enormously influential tripartite presentation of philosophy titled *Hidāyat al-ḥikma* (The Guidance of Wisdom/Philosophy)—the logic part of which seems however to have been neglected by the later tradition—he is best known for his short introductory epistle on logic (*Īsāghūjī, eisagōgē*). It covers, in a highly succinct manner, all of the traditional logical corpus—not just the five *praedicabilia*, as had the texts by Porphyry and his epigones.[14]

Far from the esoteric appeal of the logic in the *Ishārāt*, it clearly was intended as an accessible "introduction" to all of logic that was to be read by budding logic students together with their teachers in a madrasa context. While the traditional

Eisagoge served as a propaedeutic to the Aristotelian *Organon*, Abharī's *Īsāghūjī* may be considered the first of several Arabic handbooks on logic whose purpose it was to introduce students to the principles of logic as was the state-of-the-art in the subject developed by the "later logicians (*al-muta'akhkhirūn*)."[15]

Abharī's lasting influence as a logician is largely due to the contribution he made to "school science" with his handbook, but it is his less-studied and more-advanced logical texts that help us better understand the emergence of logic as a research science in the second half of the 7th/13th century. Among the more influential of those texts are, first and foremost, the self-consciously revisionist tripartite presentations of philosophy, the *Kashf al-ḥaqā'iq fī taḥrīr al-daqā'iq* (Disclosing Truths in Revising Subtle Points) and the *Tanzīl al-afkār fī ta'dīl al-asrār* (The Revelation of Thoughts in Recalibrating Secrets).[16] On the latter Ṭūsī wrote a detailed refutation in the spirit of a more orthodox Avicennism.[17]

Of his other substantial logical works, the two recensions of his *Muntahā al-afkār* mentioned earlier appear to represent an intellectual turning point toward a more revisionist, specifically Khūnajīan position in logic.[18] It is noteworthy that Abharī wrote extensively on and reportedly taught dialectics (*jadal wa ādāb al-baḥth*) and juridical eristics (*'ilm al-khilāf*), both of which he had studied with the expert al-'Amīdī. For in the course of the century, we see an important increase in the influence of formalized rules of debate on logical commentaries.[19]

Ibn Khallikān reports that he himself studied *'ilm al-khilāf* with Abharī at the Dār al-Ḥadīth in Irbil, where he would probably have read Abharī's *Ta'līqa fī l-khilāf* (Notes on Juridical Eristics) and *al-Mughnī fī 'ilm al-jadal wa-ādāb al-baḥth* (Summa of Dialectic and Disputation Theory).[20] Abharī also taught Kātibī, whose formulations in the commentaries on Rāzī and Khūnajī are marked by strategies of formal disputation. But before we turn to Abharī's student, let us introduce his fellow scholar Ṭūsī.

Naṣīr al-Dīn al-Ṭūsī was born in 597/1201—about five years after Khūnajī and ten years before Rāzī's death—in the town of Ṭūs in Khurāsān.[21] Schooled by his father, a Twelver-Shi'ī jurist, he later—like Abharī—went on to study philosophy at the Niẓāmiyya madrasa in nearby Nīshāpūr with Rāzī's students Quṭb al-Dīn al-Miṣrī and Farīd al-Dīn Dāmād.[22] Around the time of the Mongol sacking of Nīshāpūr in 618/1221 he left for Baghdād and Mosul, where—again like Abharī—he studied with Ibn Yūnus.

He then spent about thirty years at Alamut, the Isma'īlī fortress of the "Assassins." After the Mongols captured Alamut in 654/1256, he was able to secure the patronage of Genghis Khān's grandson and future Īlkhān Hülegü, who in 657/1259—just a year after the fall of Baghdād—entrusted Ṭūsī with directing the astronomical observatory at Marāgha. Ṭūsī then spent over a decade at Marāgha, attracting numerous astronomers, philosophers, and mathematicians. He died in Īlkhānid Baghdād in 672/1274.

Even though Ṭūsī studied with the same teachers as Abharī, and perhaps read the *Ishārāt* under Abharī,[23] his resistance to Rāzī's revisionism developed into an intellectual program that went far beyond Abharī's critical attitude toward his predecessors. This phenomenon may at least be partly explained by sectarian affiliations, and, by implication, Ṭūsī's political agenda in his quest for patronage. However, even though he is much less of an obscure figure than Khūnajī or Abharī, Ṭūsī's role at the interstices of scholarship, academic administration, and politics remains difficult to reconstruct considering the tendentious nature of the sources.[24]

At any rate, it is beyond doubt that Ṭūsī's influence on Twelver-Shiʿism—and Islamic intellectual history more broadly—as the great synthesizer of Avicennan philosophy and Twelver-Shiʿī theology has been such that it is still felt today. Two works, the *Tajrīd al-manṭiq* (Extracted Points of Logic), an abridgement of the eight books of the *Organon* completed upon arrival at Hülegü's court in 656/1258, and the *Tajrīd al-iʿtiqād* (Extracted Points of the [Twelver-Shiʿī] Creed), were still being widely read along with the commentaries by his student al-ʿAllāma al-Ḥillī in Twelver-Shiʿī colleges until around 1950.[25]

Among Ṭūsī's other substantial works on logic is the *Asās al-iqtibās* (The Foundation of [Knowledge-]Acquisition), a Persian summa completed 642/1244–1245 dealing exclusively with logic and reverting to the organizing structure of the Aristotelian *Organon*, the departure from which Ibn Khaldūn had bemoaned.[26] Further, there is the slightly later *Ḥall mushkilāt al-Ishārāt* (Solving the Problems of the Pointers), an *Ishārāt* commentary completed in 644/1246–1247 while still in the Ismaʿīlī context of Alamut, refuting numerous interpretations and modifications Rāzī had presented in his own commentary. Finally, the *Taʿdīl al-miʿyār fī naqd Tanzīl al-afkār* (Recalibrating the Measure in Criticizing the Revelation of Thoughts) is a systematic criticism of Abharī's revisionist presentation of the three parts of philosophy, completed in 656/1258 (the same year as the *Tajrīd al-manṭiq*) probably already under the patronage of Hülegü.[27]

It is especially the *Taʿdīl* that, together with Abharī's *Kitāb al-shukūk* and Ṭūsī's *Ishārāt* commentary, provides an insight into the logical controversies in the lead-up to the foundation of the Marāgha observatory.[28]

The Beginning of Adjudication: Ṭūsī's Ishārāt *Commentary*

When Ṭūsī in 644/1246–1247 completed the *Ḥall mushkilāt al-Ishārāt*, the reception history of the *Ishārāt* changed significantly.[29] Even though he was not the first to write an *Ishārāt* commentary after Rāzī, Ṭūsī's commentary inaugurated a new era of adjudicative commentaries, *al-Muḥākamāt* (Adjudications), in which the relative merits and shortcomings of different *Ishārāt* commentators were being weighed.[30] This contributed to an increased scrutiny also of more peripheral issues like Rāzī's Repetition Argument. Here is Ṭūsī's criticism of Rāzī:

TEXT 50: NAṢĪR AL-DĪN AL-ṬŪSĪ, *ḤALL MUSHKILĀT AL-ISHĀRĀT* (FAYḌĪ),
241.3–15

The distinguished commentator [Rāzī] raised an objection against the Shaykh [Avicenna] by saying: "writer" demands a connection to something else all by itself, because it is one of the derived names, so that his [Avicenna's] saying "but it really should be said 'Zayd, he [is a] writer'" is not correct. Rather, it is only correct for non-derived names. He may have been careless in this objection because the verb only connects to its agent-noun when [the agent-noun] precedes it, but the agent-noun does not [normally] precede the verb in Arabic. Thus, [the agent-noun] does not connect by itself to a name that precedes it in any possible case, like with the grammatical subject and others. Hence, [the agent-noun], in order to connect to its like when it attaches to it needs another copula, i.e., not the one [the agent-noun] contains in itself. How could this not be, when this is the case with the non-derived name? If his words "Zayd [is a] writer" were exchanged for "Zayd writes" for example, so that the predicate is the verb itself, then similarly it should really be said "Zayd, he writes," because the connection of "writes" to "Zayd" preceding it is not the [same as the] connection of the verb to its agent-noun that connects to it all by itself, but rather it is the connection of the grammatical predicate to the grammatical subject. The verb is here together with its agent-noun in the position of a simple grammatical predicate connected to the grammatical subject by a copula that is not the connection of the verb to its agent-noun.

Ṭūsī's criticism is reminiscent of Khūnajī's treatment in the *Kashf*—but not quite the same. To recapitulate: Rāzī had argued that statement-words and derived names have a semantic structure such that they include in their overall signification the signification of the nexus. Hence, propositions with statement-words or derived names as predicates are binary by their own nature on the level of language, so that mentioning a copula would result in superfluous repetition. Khūnajī had attacked Rāzī for misrepresenting and unduly accusing Avicenna of incoherence while he, Razī, was being incoherent himself.

The crucial point for Khūnajī was that what needs to be signified in any expression of a proposition is the nexus to a determinate subject, and not only that to an indeterminate subject (which is the one implicitly signified by verbs and derived names). Khūnajī made a distinction between the signification of "*huwa*" as the agent-noun (*ism fā ʿil*) implicit in the verb and its signification as the copula, the former being a noun and the latter an auxiliary.

Ṭūsī nowhere mentions Khūnajī, but at its core his criticism of Rāzī's Repetition Argument is the same. However, Ṭūsī's distinction between two kinds of connection, one a connection (*isnād*) between the verb (*fi ʿl*) and its agent-noun (*fā ʿil*) that is implicitly signified by verbs, the other the connection (*isnād*) between the grammatical subject (*mubtadaʾ*) and predicate (*khabar*), is slightly different, and so is his argument for it.

Contrary to Indo-European grammar where word order tends to require that the subject be put first with the verb subsequently qualifying it, in Arabic verbal sentences always begin with a verb. The verb's inflection signifies an indeterminate agent that is only subsequently specified. Just as non-derived names do not connect by themselves, verbs also do not if the word order is reversed. For once a sentence starts with a noun, there is no expectation for the specification of an implied indeterminate agent. Ṭūsī claims that in such cases it will also be necessary to mention a copula in order to signify the connection of the grammatical predicate to its subject.

A fortiori, and against Rāzī, propositions with derived names in the predicate place will also require the copula to be mentioned in order to signify a nexus to a determinate subject, for even though "writer" (*kātib*), just like "writes" (*yaktub*), implies "he" (*huwa*), the "he" so implied is distinct from the "he" that is needed to signify the nexus of the predicate meaning to a determinate subject.

The Tanzīl *and the* Ta῾dīl

Ṭūsī's refutation of Abharī's *Tanzīl al-afkār*, the *Ta῾dīl al-mi῾yār*, written more than a decade after the *Ishārāt* commentary, restates the same position. We do not know when exactly Abharī wrote the *Tanzīl*, but he was probably dead by the time Ṭūsī finished the *Ta῾dīl*. It is noteworthy, especially given that the issue did not feature in the likely earlier *Kitāb al-shukūk*, that Abharī succinctly but explicitly presents the position of Khūnajī/Ṭūsī:

TEXT 51: NAṢĪR AL-DĪN AL-ṬŪSĪ, *TA῾DĪL AL-MI῾YĀR FĪ NAQD TANZĪL AL-AFKĀR* (MUḤAQQIQ & IZUTSU), 159.1–160.11

[Abharī's] words: If the predicate in a proposition is either a verb or a derived name, it signifies a nexus to some subject. If the copula is mentioned, it signifies a nexus to a determinate subject. If you say "Zayd writes," the utterance "he" is implied in the parts of the statement-word, but it is an agent-noun, and the copula signifies the nexus. What is signified by one is not what is signified by the other.

I [Ṭūsī] say: The verb, when it is the predicate, signifies the nexus to some subject when it is taken in isolation, which is what happens when we say for example "Zayd writes" [the grammatically proper word order in Arabic is reverse, i.e., "*yaktubu Zayd*"]. Here, the utterance "writes" signifies in its essence the nexus to some subject, which is then specified by the utterance "Zayd." As for what happens when we say for example "writes Zayd" [here the Arabic word order is the grammatically improper "*Zayd yaktub*"], there is no difference in the meaning mentioned between this and our saying "Zayd [is a] man," since both are connected by the [hidden] pronoun "he" on the level of meaning, so that what is implied is "Zayd, he writes." They only differ in that "writes" needs "he" yet another time, whereas "man" does not, and this is the "he" implied in the statement-word which is the agent pronoun—which is different from the copula, for it is a noun while the other is a particle. The grammarians call one the partitive and adjuvative copula, and the other a nominative pronoun. Hence, the derived name is analogous to the verb. When we say for example "[Is] Zayd a writer?" [the word order in Arabic is "A Writer Zayd?" with an interrogative particle prefixed to "writer"] it connects by itself, and when we say "Zayd [he is a] writer" it connects by means of the implied utterance "he."

His words: When the copula in a proposition is a verb, the proposition is called incomplete ternary, because it does not signify a nexus to a determinate subject; it is only the atemporal copula that signifies that.

I say: In terms of meaning, the verb does not signify the nexus to a determinate subject essentially; it nonetheless signifies it accidentally, because its agent specifies that subject which the verb does not signify by specification, like when we say, for example, "Zayd is (*yakūnu*) a writer." Here, the utterance "is" signifies the necessity of its being connected to some subject, whereas the utterance "he"—which is implied in the verb and refers back to Zayd—specifies the subject connected to it. This proposition, on the level of meaning, signifies the same as that which is signified by "Zayd, he [is a] writer" (*Zayd huwa kātib*), with the additional signification of time because of the utterance "is" that is added to it.

In terms of the utterance, the proposition whose [copula] has the morphology of a verb is called defective ternary, and that whose [copula] is in the form of a noun is called complete ternary. One in which no copula is mentioned is called binary. The utterance alone, without considering hidden pronouns and implied [meanings], requires in one of the two [cases] the nexus to an indeterminate subject, and in the other the nexus to a determinate subject, and in the third, it does not signify a subject.

Ṭūsī does not disagree with Abharī here but seems to be fleshing out Abharī's position by way of his own argument. Again, he makes a clear distinction between the copulative and the pronominal "*huwa*." The signification of the latter is contained in verbs, that of the former is not—or at least not essentially. Interestingly, Ṭūsī here further elaborates the distinction between these two significations in terms of essential and accidental features of word-classes. Verbs essentially signify a nexus to an indeterminate subject—and so do derived names—by dint of the implied pronoun.

But, once in the context of a sentence, verbs and derived names may accidentally signify a determinate subject. As with the anaphoric use of indexicals, the signification of the implied pronoun, i.e., the indeterminate subject, may become specified by mentioning the subject if the implied pronoun refers back to that subject. In that sense, "*Zayd yakūnu kātib*" signifies the same proposition as that expressed by "*Zayd huwa kātib*," except that in the former case a tense is specified. That is because in "*yakūnu*" the pronominal "*huwa*" is implied, and once it refers back to the subject in the context of a sentence, it determines the subject and thus acts like the copulative "*huwa*."

Other Works by Abharī and Ṭūsī

Abharī's position on the issue seems to have been consistent across his other works. In his *Kashf al-ḥaqāʾiq* (completed before Ṭūsī wrote his *Ishārāt* commentary, but after his own revisionist turn of the *Muntahā*) Abharī had stated:

TEXT 52: ATHĪR AL-DĪN AL-ABHARĪ, *KASHF AL-ḤAQĀ'IQ FĪ TAḤRĪR AL-DAQĀ'IQ* (SARIOĞLU), 58.4–11

The predicate, if it is a statement-word or a derived name, may connect to the subject by itself, because [in that case] it signifies a nexus to some subject, yet it does not signify a nexus to a determinate subject. So when the copula is mentioned, the nexus to the subject is specified and hence there is no repetition.

But if you say that in "Zayd writes" (*Zayd yaktub*) the expression "he" is implied at the end of the statement-word in Arabic, so that if we mention the copula, there will be repetition—then we say we do not concede that. This is because what is implied at the end of the statement-word is an agent-noun and the other is a copula and there is no repetition.

As for Ṭūsī, it is worth noting that in his most substantial logical work (even though not nearly as influential as the *Tajrīd*), the Persian *Asās al-iqtibās*, he summarizes his discussion on the declarative statement and how the combination of simple expression works as follows:

TEXT 53: NAṢĪR AL-DĪN AL-ṬŪSĪ, *ASĀS AL-IQTIBĀS* (MUDARRIS RAḌAWĪ), 67.4–10

What is to be retained from this discussion is that the primary parts of any proposition are not more than two. These two together with the composition make three things, but not three parts. For the composition is not a part, but the nexus of one part of the proposition to the other. If the composition were a part, there would be a need for a new nexus. As we cannot possibly count the composition as a proper part, we will have to consider it a formal part and not a material part, whereas the other parts are material parts. Attention to this fine point is important, for the slightest negligence about these points leads to grave error.

This is clearly a reworking of the conceptual structure in Rāzī's chapter on the proposition in the *Mulakhkhaṣ* (additionally noting a version of Bradley's Regress), but it need not contradict his criticism of Rāzī's challenge.[31] In the *Tajrīd*, he simply states that every proposition consists of two parts, and that the copula may be omitted (even though in Persian it must be mentioned, he adds), depending on whether the proposition is binary or ternary.[32]

It appears that Abharī, and then Ṭūsī, who provided new arguments, both reacted in the same vein as Khūnajī to Rāzī's Repetition Argument. They both insisted that what is implied by statement-words and derived names is an agent-pronoun and hence distinct from the copula. The former signifies the nexus to an indeterminate subject, while only the latter signifies the nexus to a determinate subject. For both, mentioning the copula did not cause repetition.

According to Ṭūsī, however, statement-words and derived names that imply an agent-pronoun may be understood as containing a pronoun that refers back to a subject already mentioned, thereby specifying the nexus to a determinate subject. Abharī's student Kātibī not only applied his critical attitude to his teacher but went back to the works of Rāzī and Khūnajī themselves to form his opinion on logical matters. He discussed his views in exchanges with Ṭūsī, who employed him as a professor at the Marāgha observatory.

NAJM AL-DĪN AL-KĀTIBĪ AT THE MARĀGHA OBSERVATORY

Najm al-Dīn ʿAlī b. ʿUmar al-Kātibī (Dabīrān) al-Qazwīnī was born in 600/1204 in the town of Qazwīn in modern-day Iran.[33] According to the Ottoman historiographer Kātib Çelebi (d. 1067/1657), Kātibī studied not only with Abharī, but also with Ṭūsī.[34] This is however not corroborated by earlier sources. At any rate, Kātibī and Ṭūsī knew each other and must have influenced each other, for Ṭūsī hired Kātibī along with three other philosophers when he set up the Marāgha observatory in 657/1259.[35]

It seems that Kātibī was teaching at Marāgha from 658/1260 until at least 670/1271–1272. Among his students were the polymath Quṭb al-Dīn al-Shīrāzī (d. 710/1311) and the famous Shīʿī scholar Ibn al-Muṭahhar al-Ḥillī (d. 726/1325), who were both also students of Ṭūsī's. According to El-Rouayheb, "al-Ḥillī described al-Kātibī as a Sunnī Shāfiʿī, and there is no reason to doubt this description, even though other early sources are silent concerning al-Kātibī's sectarian affiliation."[36] He died in 675/1276 and was buried in his hometown.

Kātibī was one of the most prolific and influential logicians in the Arabic tradition, and a pivotal figure in the burgeoning revisionist Avicennism in 7th/13th-century Arabic logic. He penned what was to become the arguably most influential logical text in the Arabic tradition: the short handbook dedicated to the Īlkhānid vizier Shams al-Dīn al-Juwaynī (*reg.* 661–83/1262–1284), whose patronage he enjoyed. Titled *al-Risāla al-Shamsiyya* (Epistle for Shams [al-Dīn]), it was simply known as the *Shamsiyya* and it elicited more commentaries than any other non-introductory logical work. It was used, together with some of the major commentaries, for teaching well into the 20th century.

In addition, Kātibī authored several holistic presentations of philosophy that begin with a part on logic, a number of independent works on logic, and many commentaries on logical works by others as well as on his own shorter works. He also engaged in written discussions with Ṭūsī (and others) on several issues. One exchange concerns the nature of the proposition.[37] Kātibī remains one of the most severely understudied logicians relative to his output and merit.

In the years that Kātibī was active at Marāgha (from 658/1260 until at least 670/1271–1272), he not only wrote some of his most important works, but also taught a significant number of students. Next to Shīrāzī and Ḥillī, several influential scholars are reported to have come to Marāgha to study with him. Fakhr al-Dīn Abū al-Fatḥ al-Qazwīnī al-Ḥakīm (the Philosopher) studied logic with Kātibī from 665/1266–1267 until dying prematurely two years later (his father was nicknamed al-Athīrī and was probably Abharī's *famulus*).[38] Qawām al-Dīn Abū ʿAlī al-Yazīrī al-Ḥakīm also studied logic with Kātibī in 667/1267–1268.[39] Muḥyī al-Dīn Abū Faḍl al-Kūfī al-Baghdādī (d. 703/1303–1304) studied with Ṭūsī and Kātibī at Marāgha from the age of twenty-three (beginning in 670/1271–1272).[40] As for Shīrāzī, he arrived at Marāgha shortly after its foundation in 658/1259–1260 to study with Kātibī.[41] And Ḥillī came to study the works of Rāzī, Khūnajī, and Abharī together with Kātibī and Ṭūsī.[42]

The *Shamsiyya* is clearly a Marāgha text, because its dedicatee, Shams al-Dīn, became vizier in 661/1262, and it is likely that Kātibī used it for teaching there.[43] Another Marāgha text is Kātibī's commentary on Rāzī's *Mulakhkhaṣ*. Even though only completed in 671/1272–1273, he must have worked on it while at Marāgha. In the proem Kātibī says that he first commented on the logic, and some years later on the philosophical and theological parts, and then revised the logic before dedicating it to Shams al-Dīn.[44] For Kātibī's commentary on Khūnajī's *Kashf* we have no absolute dating, but given its length, he may have still worked on it at Marāgha.

These commentaries are not intended for beginners or intermediate students, if they were used for teaching at all. They betray a concern with what we would have to classify as "research science." In these texts, Kātibī quibbles with advanced and sometimes minute details of logic in a way that cannot in the main have been intended as mere exegetical work or as a running commentary for students. The fact that during his tenure at Marāgha Kātibī wrote both an accessible handbook clearly intended for intermediate teaching and substantial and critical advanced commentaries suggests that at Marāgha logic was conceived not merely as a school science, but also as a research science for its own sake. So let us look at these commentaries.

The Analysis of Simple Categorical Statements in Sharḥ Kashf al-asrār *(Commentary on the Disclosing of Secrets)*

Kātibī's commentary on Khūnajī's seminal summa *Kashf al-asrār* is a mammoth work, one of the longest works on formal logic ever written in Arabic.[45] It is not a typical lemmatic commentary. Instead of quoting and then treating the main text (*matn*) lemma by lemma, in this work the *matn* is incorporated in Kātibī's continuous prose. Besides explicating and frequently criticizing Khūnajī's text, Kātibī also completed what Khūnajī had expressly planned to include but left unfinished, adding sections on induction, analogy, and the matters of the syllogism (demonstration, dialectics, rhetoric, sophistry, and poetics).[46] The commentary of the chapter "On the Copula" is largely intended to be explicatory, not polemical. But two points are noteworthy.

First, even though Kātibī agrees with Khūnajī that the question whether in Arabic the copula needs to be mentioned is an issue for grammarians to resolve, he does present an argument in support of Rāzī's Repetition Argument. Kātibī thinks that Khūnajī's criticism of Rāzī's Repetition Argument is fair granted that the copula *"huwa"* has a signification distinct from that of the agent-noun. The argument only works if the elided pronoun *"huwa"* implied by statement-words and derived names does in fact not signify a nexus to a determinate subject.

But, Kātibī points out in a way very similar to Ṭūsī's position, the implied agent-noun may well signify a nexus to a determinate subject once in the context of a sentence, because then it refers back to the subject and thereby makes the subject to which it signifies a nexus determinate. In that case, mentioning the copula should be considered a repetition (which Ṭūsī had denied):

TEXT 54: NAJM AL-DĪN AL-KĀTIBĪ AL-QAZWĪNĪ, *SHARḤ KASHF AL-ASRĀR* (MS ISTANBUL: SÜLEYMANIYE CARULLAH 1417), FOL. 58R13–18

[As for the copula] "he (*huwa*)": If we say for example "Zayd writes" or "Zayd [is a] writer," for them [the grammarians/logicians?] the predicate is in reality not the statement-word alone in the first case, nor the derived name alone in the second case. Rather, the predicate in the first case is the entirety of what is expressed by the statement-word. That means it includes the agent-noun implied after it. In the second case, it likewise is the entirety of what is expressed. That means it includes the name and the hidden pronoun contained in it.

Hence, for the statement-word and the derived name, even if nothing in them by itself signifies the nexus to a determinate subject, the entirety of what is expressed by them and what is implicit after them in terms of hidden pronouns that refer back to the preceding grammatical subject may still signify the nexus to a determinate subject. If this is so, then mentioning the copula another time will be a superfluous repetition.

Second, Kātibī is most vocal in his criticism on the passage where Khūnajī states that the nexus of the subject to the predicate must be conceptually distinct from the nexus of the predicate to the subject. While Abharī seems to have been the first to offer a substantial criticism of conversion rules, it appears that Kātibī was important for tying the issue of conversion to the debates on the nexus and the copula.[47] In Kātibī's words, Khūnajī had claimed that we know that the nexus of one term of a proposition to the other by subject-hood is not the same as its nexus by predicate-hood, because "if the two nexus were in fact one and the same, then there would be no distinction between what is understood from a proposition and what is understood from its converse," and this is obviously not the case (fol. 58r24–25).

In other words, if there were no such conceptual distinction, then "Humans are writers" would be the same as "Writers are humans." But this is not so, because—as Khūnajī argued—from a modal point of view, the propositions have different truth-conditions: writers are necessarily humans, but humans are not necessarily writers. Finding fault with the conditional, Kātibī criticizes the *modus tollens* argument:

TEXT 55: NAJM AL-DĪN AL-KĀTIBĪ AL-QAZWĪNĪ, *SHARḤ KASHF AL-ASRĀR*
(MS ISTANBUL: SÜLEYMANIYE CARULLAH 1417), FOL. 58R25–32

Thus did the author [Khūnajī] present it, but there is room for discussion here. For the mentioned conditional [i.e., if the two nexus are . . .] is faulty.

[This is so] for the subject-term, because [the conditional] is only true [if both of the following are true]. [First,] what is understood from the original proposition is an expression of the nexus of the proposition's subject to its predicate by way of subject-hood, and[, second,] what is understood from [the original proposition's] converse is an expression of the nexus to it by predicate-hood—but this is not so! Rather, the first nexus is external to what the original proposition expresses, and the second is internal to what makes up the quiddity of the converse. It does not follow from the identity of two things, one of which is external to a quiddity and the other internal to what makes up another quiddity, the conceptual identity of both quiddities.

And for the predicate-term, [the conditional is faulty,] because it is only true [if both of the following are true]. [First,] what is understood from the original proposition is an expression of the nexus of its predicate to its subject by predicate-hood, and[, second,] what is understood from its converse is an expression of the nexus to it by subject-hood—but this is not so, either! From the identity of the two there follows no conceptual identity of quiddities. This is evident.

Kātibī does not disagree with the general idea that there should be a conceptual distinction between the relation the subject bears to its predicate and the one the predicate bears to its subject. But he faults Khūnajī with having failed to see that only one relation is internal to the quiddity of a proposition, and for consequently having committed a formal fallacy. There is no logical implication between the parts of the conditional on which the *modus tollens* argument depends:

> If the two nexus were in fact one and the same, (P)
> then there would be no distinction between what is understood from a
>   proposition and what is understood from its converse, (Q)
> but there is such a distinction. (¬Q)
> Therefore, the two nexus are not one and the same. (¬P)

For Kātibī, P does not imply Q to begin with—or it only does if we have a mistaken idea of what the properties of the two nexus are. The relation between "humans" and "writers" may well be one relation, no matter whether one is predicated of the other or *vice versa*, if we consider that only one aspect of this relation, i.e., "_being a predicate for_," is ever relevant for the proposition, or in Kātibī's words, "internal to the quiddity of the proposition."

If the two nexus are one and the same in this sense, this identity would not imply that we cannot distinguish between a proposition and its converse, because we can still make that distinction based on the different roles this nexus has. When "writers" bears the predicate-relation to "humans," the relation that "humans" bears to "writers" is irrelevant to the proposition. It only becomes relevant when the proposition is converted, so that now "humans" bears the predicate-relation to "writers." None of this implies that a proposition and its converse are identical, for the same nexus is in one case internal to the quiddity of the proposition, and external in the case of conversion. Kātibī has more to say on this issue in his commentary on Rāzī's *Mulakhkhaṣ*.

The Analysis of Simple Categorical Statements in al-Munaṣṣaṣ fī Sharḥ al-Mulakhkhaṣ *(The Precise Commentary on the Summary)*

According to Kātibī, after having treated preliminary matters like the definition of "proposition" and its classification into different types, Rāzī now takes on the intrinsic properties (*arkān*) and immediate implications (*aḥkām*) of propositions themselves (fols. 31v31–32r16).[48] An intrinsic property of a proposition is what makes up its essence, i.e., its form and matter. Immediate implications are properties that are extrinsic to a proposition, but that are nonetheless determined by intrinsic properties, i.e., a proposition's contradictory, its *salva veritate* conversion, and so forth. The form of a proposition is its nexus, and its matter are subject and predicate.

The ensuing discussions deal, according to Kātibī, with issues to do with the form of propositions, first with questions about the nexus itself, then with questions about the utterance signifying it, i.e., the copula. Concerning the nexus, there are two issues. First, the claim that the nexus is a concept distinct from the concepts of subject and predicate, for which Rāzī offers two different arguments. Second, the claim that there are two conceptually distinct nexus in a proposition, for which Rāzī offers again two arguments. Kātibī first explains each of the arguments, and then advances his own criticism of each. I shall treat them in turn, and dwell a little on the last argument, about which Kātibī has the most serious misgivings.

The first argument for the claim that the nexus is a concept distinct from the concepts of subject and predicate is expressed, Kātibī thinks, by a conditional with two disjunctions:

> If the concept of the nexus were the same as the concept of the predicate, or
> if the concept of the nexus were the same as the concept of the subject,
> then it would be impossible for us to conceive of the predicate separately, or
> it would be impossible for us to conceive of the subject separately.

Both disjuncts of the consequent are false, for we are in fact able to conceive of both predicate and subject separately without at the same time conceiving of a nexus. If the conditional is evidently (*ẓāhiratayn*) true, as Rāzī must have thought, the falsity of the consequent implies the falsity of the antecedent. However, Kātibī adds, rather tersely: "there is room for discussion here, for we reject the possibility of conceiving the nexus that is between the two" (fol. 32r11). He does not elaborate this comment further, and we may only speculate what this criticism was supposed to amount to. He might have meant to directly question the conclusion that the nexus is a concept distinct from the concepts of predicate and subject, by saying something like this:

> If the nexus is a distinct concept, it must be possible for us to conceive of it separately.
> But it is impossible to conceive of the nexus separately.
> Therefore, the nexus is not a distinct concept.

The second argument is given by Kātibī as follows: "The nexus which is between [subject and predicate] is posterior to both, for a nexus between two things is posterior to them, and what is posterior to something is necessarily distinct from it" (fol. 32r11–13). Here Kātibī takes issue with the first premise, i.e., that the nexus is posterior to subject and predicate. The way I read his counterargument is this. Take the totality of all nexus as a subject term of a proposition: "all nexus are posterior to their subject and predicate." Now think of the nexus to this subject, i.e., to "all nexus"—this nexus cannot be posterior to the subject, because it is also part of the subject. If this nexus is not posterior to the subject, it cannot be true that all nexus are posterior to subject and predicate (fol. 32r12).

He closes by saying:

TEXT 56: NAJM AL-DĪN AL-KĀTIBĪ AL-QAZWĪNĪ, *AL-MUNAṢṢAṢ FĪ SHARḤ AL-MULAKHKHAṢ* (MS MASHHAD: KITĀBKHĀNA-YI MARKAZĪ-YI ĀSTĀN-I QUDS-I RAḌAWĪ 1201), FOL. 32R13–16

Now that you have learned this, we say: as for the fact that every proposition inevitably needs to have a subject and a predicate, this is obvious; as for the nexus, it is internal to the quiddity of the [proposition], for if it were not, then anyone who conceived of the meaning of the subject and the meaning of the predicate without this nexus, would then conceive of the meaning of a categorical proposition—but it is obvious that this is not so.

The third argument Kātibī analyzes is the first Rāzī gives in support of the claim that in a proposition there are two conceptually distinct nexus. Kātibī presents the argument thus: "The nexus of the subject to the predicate is the nexus of the thing described to the description, and the nexus of the locus to that which occurs in it" (fol. 32r18). From this, says Kātibī, Rāzī intimates four syllogisms in the second figure that all produce the conclusion that the nexus of the subject to the predicate is not the same as the nexus of the predicate to the subject.

Kātibī objects:

TEXT 57: NAJM AL-DĪN AL-KĀTIBĪ AL-QAZWĪNĪ, *AL-MUNAṢṢAṢ FĪ SHARḤ AL-MULAKHKHAṢ* (MS MASHHAD: KITĀBKHĀNA-YI MARKAZĪ-YI ĀSTĀN-I QUDS-I RAḌAWĪ 1201), FOL. 32R23–26

There is room for discussion here, because we do not concede something in the premises mentioned in these syllogisms. For when we say "Every such-and-such is so-and-so," we do not mean that the first is the thing described and the second is a description, and not that the first is a substrate and the second what inheres in it, even if in some kinds of propositions the first may be either something described or a substrate and the second either a description or what inheres in a substate. Rather, what we mean by it is that everything of which the first is true in actual fact, of that the second is also true. If this is so, then what he mentioned in terms of a proof for showing that the two nexus mentioned are distinct crumbles.

Rāzī's argument for a proposition's having two distinct nexus was based on the idea that there is a substantial logical distinction to be made between a description and the thing described by it. Kātibī counters that the logical form of a true proposition does not require any such distinction. Instead, what we mean when we say, for example, "All writers are humans" is that for all objects x of which it is true to say that they are a writer, it is also true to say that they are human. Whether or not *writing* is a description and *human* the thing described is simply irrelevant. Hence, Rāzī cannot build a proof on this distinction. It appears that Kātibī would here urge to treat both "human" and "writer" effectively as predicates, as we would do in modern logic. He does not, however, develop this idea further in the remainder of his discussion.

Whereas with regard to the first claim, i.e., that the nexus is a distinct concept, Kātibī's criticism was directed against the argument and not the claim itself, it seems that Kātibī was more seriously unhappy with the idea that in a proposition there are two conceptually distinct nexus. After refuting the first argument, Kātibī goes to some lengths to also refute the second. Kātibī understands the argument from distinct modalities as twofold, just like in his commentary on Khūnajī's *Kashf*. The first aspect is to say that if the nexus of the subject to the predicate were the same as the nexus of the predicate to the subject, then we could make no difference in the modal qualities of these relations. But the consequent is false, because, for example, in the proposition "Every writer is a human" the nexus of the subject to the predicate is necessary, whereas the nexus of the predicate to the subject is contingent.

The second aspect of the argument makes direct reference to conversion. Kātibī formulates it as follows: "To give an idea of what he means is to say that if the two nexus mentioned were identical, then propositions would retain their modalities in the converse. The consequent is false, as you will learn in the chapter on conversion, and hence the antecedent is rejected" (fols. 32r33–32v1). Kātibī has nothing more to say on this, but he strongly disagrees with Rāzī in the next lemma he quotes, where Rāzī states: "But the nexus which is a part of the quiddity of the proposition is that of the subject's essence being described by a predicate, whereas the other is necessarily external to it."[49] Kātibī appositely objects that the matter is more fittingly described as being the opposite: what matters, and what is part of the quiddity of a proposition, is not the nexus of the subject to the predicate, but the nexus of the predicate to the subject—though he does give Rāzī credit for having said as much in his *Ishārāt* commentary (10.11–11.4). He closes this section by saying:

TEXT 58: NAJM AL-DĪN AL-KĀTIBĪ AL-QAZWĪNĪ, *AL-MUNAṢṢAṢ FĪ SHARḤ AL-MULAKHKHAṢ* (MS MASHHAD: KITĀBKHĀNA-YI MARKAZĪ-YI ĀSTĀN-I QUDS-I RAḌAWĪ 1201), FOL. 32V12–20

In general, this is an issue that needs reflection. Inquire for yourself and seek the truth about it. My opinion is that the nexus of one of the two terms of the proposition to the other as being a subject for it is not the same as the nexus to it as being a predicate for it. If the two nexus were identical, then they would also have to be identical in their implications. But the consequent is false, because the nexus of the subject to the predicate as being a subject for it is external to the quiddity of both the original proposition and its converse. And its nexus to it as being a predicate is internal to the quiddity of the converse. The nexus of the predicate to the subject as being a predicate for it is internal to the quiddity of the original proposition and its converse. And the nexus to it as being a subject for it is external to the quiddity of both the original proposition and its converse together. The nexus of one of the terms of a proposition to the other as being a subject for it is thus not the nexus of the other to it as being a predicate for it. Hence, if these two nexus were identical, then there would be no difference between the subject of a proposition and its predicate inasmuch as they are subject and predicate. The consequent is obviously false. But one of these two nexus is the other *potentialiter*, and those cannot differ in quality or modality, because when "writer," for example, insofar as "human" is affirmed of it is necessary, then "human" is, insofar as it is affirmed of "writer," also necessary.

For Kātibī, there are four ways in which we can conceptualize the nexus as a relation between two terms. This is because you can convert any given proposition that consists of two terms. By exchanging subject and predicate you have two propositions, (2) and (4), in which the nexus may carry different modalities. While the nexus ($\leftarrow$) in (2) carries the modality of possibility ($\diamond$), because humans are only possibly writers, the nexus in (4) carries the modality of necessity ($\square$), because a writer is necessarily human. But you may also consider these two propositions in a different way, namely, by asking what modal relation the subject bears to the predicate. I distinguish these two types of nexus by writing ($\rightarrow_{\text{subjecthood}}$) and ($\leftarrow_{\text{predicatehood}}$). "Human" is necessarily a subject for "writer," but "writer" is only possibly a subject for "human."

(1) $S(\text{human})\square(\rightarrow_{\text{subjecthood}})P(\text{writer})$ (2) $S(\text{human})\diamond(\leftarrow_{\text{predicatehood}})P(\text{writer})$

(3) $S(\text{writer})\diamond(\rightarrow_{\text{subjecthood}})P(\text{human})$ (4) $S(\text{writer})\square(\leftarrow_{\text{predicatehood}})P(\text{human})$

Kātibī's position is that none of these nexus are in fact identical. First, he argues against Rāzī that the type of nexus in (1) and (3) is not part of the quiddity of these propositions, whereas the type of nexus in (2) and (4) is part of their quiddity. What we mean when we say "All writers are human" is not that *writing* is only possibly true of *human*, but rather that *human* is necessarily true of *writing*. Hence, the nexus in (1) is not identical to that in (2), and that in (3) not identical to that in (4). Second, Kātibī adds that while the nexus in (1) and (3) viz. (2) and (4), respectively, do not necessarily have the same quality and modality, the nexus in (1) is potentially the nexus in (4), and that in (2) potentially that in (3), for in those pairs quality and modality are the same.

There follows a discussion on the copula that contains Kātibī's criticism of the Repetition Argument. He quotes Avicenna to the effect that, even though derived names and statement-words implicitly signify a nexus, they only signify a nexus to an indeterminate subject; but since a proposition requires a nexus to a determinate subject, Kātibī continues, this would mean that—if we follow Avicenna—in propositions in which the predicate is a derived name or a statement-word, a copula is still required to signify that nexus (fol. 32v23–25). But, in fact, in such propositions, it is not the derived name or statement-word alone that makes up the predicate, but also the agent-pronouns implied by them. Once in the context of a sentence, they do signify a nexus to a determinate subject, because they refer back to the subject already mentioned, in which case no copula is required (fol. 32v25–23).

As for Rāzī's argument itself, i.e., that, since the agent-pronoun is implied by derived names and statement-words, mentioning the copula would amount to repetition (e.g., "*Zayd huwa ʿālim huwa*" [Zayd, he is knowing he]), Kātibī does not concede that this is in fact a repetition, because that would only be the case if the second mention of "*huwa*" were not an agent-noun (fol. 32v31). But Rāzī did say it was an agent-noun, even though some grammarians call it an auxiliary (fol. 32v31–33). In any case, Kātibī says—just as he does in the commentary on Khūnajī's *Kashf*—that this is a question for grammarians to resolve; all that matters for the logician is that in some way or other the nexus to a determinate subject is signified (fols. 32v33–33r6).

SIRĀJ AL-DĪN AL-URMAWĪ AND THE NEW LOGIC HANDBOOKS

Sirāj al-Dīn Maḥmūd b. Abī Bakr al-Urmawī likely hailed from Urmia in the modern-day Iranian province of Azerbaijan.[50] He was born in 594/1198 and only twelve when Rāzī died. Hence, Bar Hebraeus's report of a teacher-student relationship is, again, likely false.[51] But he did study, like Abharī and Ṭūsī, with Ibn Yūnus, their fellow Shāfiʿī jurist, who was highly respected for his ability to explain Rāzī's texts.[52]

Little is known about Urmawī's early years. Later he migrated, like Khūnajī, first to Ayyūbid Egypt, where he enjoyed the patronage of al-Malik al-Kāmil and al-Malik al-Ṣāliḥ.[53] The latter sent him on a mission to the Hohenstaufen king of Sicily and Holy Roman emperor Frederick II.[54] According to his own testimony[55] in 655/1257 he moved, like Khūnajī, from Cairo to Seljuk Anatolia, where he spent the last decades of his life and was later appointed chief judge (*qāḍī*) of Konya. He died in Konya in 682/1283.

Urmawī came from the same historical region of Azerbaijan as Khūnajī. About the same age, later in their lives they were active at the same courts in Cairo. It is not unlikely that they met, but neither seems to mention the other in his writings. In terms of logical doctrine both authors are closely aligned in their revisionist ideas, and on grounds of the circumstantial evidence about the direction of influence, El-Rouayheb suggests that Urmawī was more likely a follower of Khūnajī's than the other way around, and that we might want to see "the logic part of the *Maṭāliʿ al-anwār* as [. . .] an abridgement of Khūnajī's *Kashf al-asrār*."[56]

At any rate, Urmawī's approach to the logical tradition was still critical overall. His most influential logical work was no doubt the *Maṭāliʿ al-anwār* (The Dawning of Lights), a more advanced handbook on logic and metaphysics (the metaphysics part fell out of use soon after Urmawī's death) significantly more detailed than Kātibī's *Shamsiyya*. Together with the lengthy commentary by Quṭb al-Dīn al-Rāzī al-Taḥtānī (d. 766/1365), it remained the standard handbook for advanced logical studies in the Eastern Islamic world well into the 19th century.[57]

Of the three handbooks written in the second half of the 7th/13th century—that is, Abharī's *Īsāghūjī*, Kātibī's *Shamsiyya*, and Urmawī's *Maṭāliʿ al-anwār*—the latter brought "school science" in logic closer to "research science." With it, many of the logical issues that had been raised in the course of the 7th/13th century became part of the advanced logic curriculum. These three logic handbooks institutionalized Arabic logic as a scientific discipline with a standard curriculum to be studied in the madrasa or outside of it. Logic had now not only completed the process of emancipation from the Aristotelian *Organon*, but also dissociated itself from the direct exegetical engagement with Avicenna.

With the *Īsāghūjī*, students had an easily accessible introductory textbook to the Arabic logic of the "later logicians." Kātibī's *Shamsiyya* was to become the standard intermediate textbook, and Urmawī's *Maṭāliʿ* the advanced work of reference for students who were interested in going beyond the expository textbooks. It was largely due to the commentaries together with which these texts were studied that they became so successful as teaching texts. By the early 10th/16th century it was virtually impossible that an accomplished scholar would have studied logic and not read any of these texts. The Ottoman scholar and judge Aḥmed Ṭāşköprüzāde (1495–1561), for example, reports that he studied the *Īsāghūjī* together with Kātī's commentary, the *Shamsiyya* with Quṭb al-Dīn al-Rāzī's commentary, and the the *Maṭāliʿ* together with Quṭb al-Dīn's commentary and al-Sayyid al-Sharīf al-Jurjānī's glosses.[58]

But not only was there now a readily available logic curriculum. The development of the genres of writing through which logic was presented was increasingly marked by the influence of the emerging science of formal disputation (*ādāb al-baḥth*), so that students who studied these handbooks together with advanced commentaries were at the same time trained to criticize logical arguments themselves. In the centuries to come, the study of logic would, for many scholars, culminate in the redaction of their own commentaries or glosses, which were—arguably more often than not—not necessarily exegetical and intended for teaching, but intended to advance the science of logic. They may often be seen as contributions to original research.

Urmawī wrote widely on logic, and most of his works remain unedited.[59] A good example to show how scholars in the latter half of the 7th/13th century engaged with the history of a given logical problem and at the same time contributed their own original thoughts by challenging their predecessors is Urmawī's treatment of the copula in his summa *Bayān al-ḥaqq*. As the text gives a succinct history of the problem of the copula and remains unpublished, it is worth citing it in full:

TEXT 59: SIRĀJ AL-DĪN AL-URMAWĪ, *BAYĀN AL-ḤAQQ WA LISĀN AL-ṢIDQ* (MS ISTANBUL: SÜLEYMANIYE ATIF EFENDI 1567), FOLS. 13R9–13V11

Second Section: On the Copula
The categorical [proposition] is made up of three things: the subject, the predicate, and the nexus by which one of them is connected to the other, in [the sense] that it is it, or it is not it. If we conceive of both terms but do not conceive of the nexus as we mentioned, then there is no conception of a proposition. Concerning this nexus between them, from each of [the terms], it is only right that it be signified by an expression, and this expression is called the copula.

[First inquiry:] If it is omitted in some languages or in certain contexts, then it is just shorthand for what in principle must be expressed. It is only omitted on the level of expression when it can be expected to be understood in the soul, either from a [particular] language or in certain contexts. In that case the proposition is binary on the level of expression. But it is ternary on the level of thought; if the [copula] is expressed, then it is called ternary also on the level of expression.

Second inquiry: The copula is no doubt one of the auxiliaries, but it may be in the form of the hyparctic verbs mentioned earlier, in which case the copula is called a "temporal copula" because of its signification of tense; or, it may be in the form of a name, like any of the pronouns. Then the copula is—in the Arabic language—a partitive or adjuvative copula, which [in logic] is called a "non-temporal copula." Languages are different with regard to the use of the copula. In Greek it is necessary to mention a temporal copula in all propositions, be they categorical or hypothetical. In Arabic this is only necessary in conditionals like "If the sun is up, it is day." It is not necessary in categoricals like "Zayd [is] in the house," when the proposition is binary. When we say "Zayd was free," then [the proposition] is ternary, and the copula temporal; when we say "Zayd, he [is] free," then the copula is atemporal. In Persian, it is necessary that any proposition be ternary. The copula is either temporal as in "Zayd was a writer" and "Zayd will be a writer," or atemporal, in which case it may be an expression as in "Zayd is [*hast*] a writer," or a vocalization at the end of the predicate as in "Zayd a writer [is]" [*Zayd dabīr-e*].[60]

Third [inquiry]: the Shaykh [Avicenna] said in the *Shifāʾ* that when the predicate is a verb or a derived name, it is not unlikely that it connects by itself to the subject, as it contains a nexus to the subject. Hence, the need of verbs and derived names for a copula [Avicenna continues] is not [the same as] the need of non-derived names [for it]. Then he said that indeed the verb and the derived name signify a nexus to a subject, but they do not signify a nexus to a determinate subject. Here, what is needed is something that connects the predicate to the subject, but the temporal copulae in Arabic do not signify a nexus to a determinate subject. Only atemporal copulae signify the nexus to a determinate subject. As they do in fact signify that, [Avicenna] distinguished three classes of propositions:

First: the complete ternary, which is the one in which a nexus to a determinate subject is signified, like the propositions in which there is a non-temporal copula.

Second: the incomplete ternary, which is the one in which an indeterminate subject is signified, like when the predicate contains a verb or derived name that includes, as mentioned, a temporal nexus.

Third: the binary—from this we know what he meant in the *Ishārāt* where he said that when we say "Zayd [is] a writer" it is necessary to [actually] say "Zayd, he [is] a writer," for by this the nexus is specified. He had explained that the nexus needs to be specified; but the need of verbs and derived names is not the [same as] the need of non-derived names, for there is nothing in the [latter] that signifies a nexus.

The Imām [al-Rāzī] falsely assumed that this was different from what [Avicenna] said in *al-Ḥikma al-mashriqiyya*, [namely] that the verb implicitly signifies the nexus to the subject. But I have ascertained that the two [passages] agree and there is no difference between them. The Imām said in his books that if the predicate is a verb or a derived name, then the proposition is in reality binary, because the nexus is signified by containment, and it is not permitted—on pain of repetition—to mention it separately. And if [the predicate] is a non-derived name [says Rāzī], then it is in reality ternary. On the basis of what you learned this is a weak argument.

In the commentary on the *Ishārāt* he ascertains that the verb only signifies the nexus to an indeterminate subject. Indeed, he said that if we say "Zayd writes," then the expression "he" (*huwa*) is hidden at the end of the verb—"concealed in it" as the Arabic grammarians say—and if we were to also place it in the middle, then we would have to say "Zayd, he writes, he." And because of this particle, the Imām believed that a repetition would follow.

I said: There only follows a repetition if each of the two expressions, the "he" in the middle and the "he" at the end, are copulae; but this is not so for the Arabic grammarians. Rather, the one at the end is an agent-noun and the one in the middle is a copula. Hence, they do not differ in that the one at the end is a name, but they differ with regard to the one in the middle—of which some [grammarians] say it is a name and others that it is an auxiliary. There appears in the Glorious Qurʾān a mention of the copula together with a predicate containing the nexus. This is in the word of the Exalted "And when You took me up, you were the Observer over them" [Q5:117]. Since ["Observer"] is being put in the accusative, the analysis of this on the part of the grammarians is that they say that the verb alone is not a predicate, but, together with putting it into the accusative of the agent-noun and the verb, even if it does not signify a determinate subject on its own, they do so together.

But this is a linguistic inquiry—for the logician it is only necessary that he mentions whatever signifies a determinate subject, and if the verb and the derived name signify a determinate subject, then it is not necessary to mention the copula, and if not, then it is necessary to indicate it.

The temporal copula may be used for what is not temporal, like the words of Him Exalted: "He is [literally, was] compassionate and merciful," as well as for what has no specified time, like when we say "Every three is odd" and "Every four is even."

Fourth [inquiry]: The nexus of each of the terms to the other as being a subject for it is not [the same as] the nexus to it as being a predicate for it. Otherwise, a proposition would be the same as its converse, and the two would not imply each other. For they may differ in quality, like "Every human is an animal," but not "Every animal is a human," and in modality, like "Every human is possibly a writer," but "Every writer is necessarily a human." [. . .] The difference is [clear] in every proposition that does not convert. But every proposition has a converse that is not of their kind.

Further: The nexus of each of the two [terms] to the other by subject-hood is not [the same as] the nexus of the other to it by predicate-hood. Do they imply each other so that one of them is the other *potentialiter* and there is no difference in quality and modality?[61]

As for the quality, this is evident, because if A is a subject for B, it is impossible that B is not a predicate for A, no matter whether the subject-hood [of A] is affirmative or negative.

As for the modality, it has been said [by Kātibī] that if A insofar as B is affirmed of it is necessary, and B insofar as it is affirmed of A is necessary, then it is impossible that the two differ in modality.

There is room for discussion here: If the subject is more specific than the predicate, like "human" and "animal" for example, then "human" insofar as "animal" is affirmed of it is necessary, but "animal" insofar as "human" is affirmed of it is not necessary. This is with a view to their essences. As for the view to particular subjection and predication, like "This human is this animal," here it is necessary that each of the two nexus be necessary or non-necessary. It is impossible that there be a difference between them.

The Imām said: The nexus of one of them to the other by subject-hood is not [the same as] the nexus of the other to it by predicate-hood. It is because of this that the proposition does not preserve its modality in conversion. But this is weak. For in the converse subject-hood and predicate-hood differ.

Urmawī gives a detailed description of the history of the problem of predication up to his time. At several junctures of the story, Urmawī intervenes to criticize a position and propose an improvement. He also organizes the discussions on the copula into four inquiries: (i) the copula and whether it needs to be expressed, (ii) the copula and its grammatical description, (iii) the nexus and whether it is signified as part of the signification of verbs and derived names, (iv) the nexus and whether there are distinct nexus in a proposition.

It is noteworthy that Urmawī in his handbook reduces the inquiries to (ii) and (iv). However, even in the handbook, Urmawī criticizes Rāzī and includes a critical discussion of (iv). Rather than the *Bayān al-ḥaqq*, scholars in the later tradition often took the abridged version of the handbook (which is substantially the same) as their point of departure.[62]

CONCLUSION

The development of the discussions on the analysis of categorical propositions in the four decades between Khūnajī's *Kashf* (probably 634/1237) and Urmawī's *Bayān al-ḥaqq* (675/1276) may stand as a *pars pro toto* for the evolution of Arabic logic. The critical attitude fostered among Rāzī's disciples engendered discussions on logical issues big and small (in logic, there are no small distinctions, one might want to say) among leading scholars. All scholars in these chapters owe a great deal to Rāzī, and it was by no means Ṭūsī alone who became highly critical of the Rāzīan intellectual milieu in which he was nourished. Reading closely more of the unedited texts of this period will likely yield a picture more nuanced about not only the traditional Ṭūsī/Rāzī divide, but also the more recent distinction between orthodox and revisionist Avicennans.

Rāzī's challenge of Avicenna's position that a copula must be expressed in order to fully signify a complete proposition elicited critical reactions from all scholars discussed. Ṭūsī rejects it by giving arguments both from grammar and from semantic intuitions of natural language use. Ṭūsī is probably the first to substantially attack Rāzī on this point. Ṭusī sided with Abharī on the issue, as far as we can tell. But Abharī in his later work was highly critical of Rāzī's (and others') treatment of conversion rules for categorical propositions.

Kātibī seems to have been the first to offer substantial discussions of the subject-predicate nexus in relation to conversion and modality. All these discussions became, especially in the last two decades of the period under consideration, when Ṭūsī and Kātibī were active at Marāgha, both more sophisticated in advanced logical texts and synthesized (first and foremost by Urmawī, who was not connected to the observatory) into logic handbooks intended for students. The next generation of scholars was going to perpetuate this dual concern of teaching and research by producing some of the most influential commentaries to go with the new handbooks.

7

———

The Great Dialectic Commentaries

Until recently, the 8th/14th century had been described by scholars of Islamic intellectual history as the beginning of a period of decline and scholastic ossification in the rational sciences, especially in logic. This assessment was mainly supported by the largely armchair assumption that after the 7th/13th century hardly any independent works were written in philosophy, especially in logic, and that the works listed in bibliographies are, merely by the fact that they are commentaries, necessarily pedantic and unoriginal. By looking at these works, many of which first have to be edited, and by analyzing their contents, recent scholarship has begun to show that original research was being carried out within the format of the commentary.

The post-Marāgha generation of scholars contributed to both a multiplication and an intensification of original research in logic. As we saw in the last chapter, the lively and critical engagement with the Avicennan-Rāzīan heritage by scholars connected to the Marāgha observatory led to a number of logical innovations that became enshrined in the new logic handbooks. The next generation of scholars, both Sunnī and Shīʿī, shaped a new commentatorial praxis that was intimately linked to the formalization of dialectics (*ādāb al-baḥth*) advanced by Shams al-Dīn al-Samarqandī.

In addition to the new genre of the *Muḥākamāt*—adjudicative commentaries on earlier *Ishārāt* commentaries—scholars like al-ʿAllāma al-Ḥillī and Quṭb al-Dīn al-Rāzī wrote monumental commentaries on the new logic handbooks. Conceived in a critical spirit influenced by disputation theory, they set the standard for later generations—up to the eve of modernity—against which scholars were to probe their arguments and further their original research in logic. With regard to discussions on the problem of predication, this development helped scholars to formulate

131

a fresh set of problems and insights and, with Quṭb al-Dīn, led to the first and most forceful rejection yet of the Aristotelian-Avicennan doctrine of the copula.

DIALECTICS AND LOGICAL RESEARCH IN COMMENTARIES: SHAMS AL-DĪN AL-SAMARQANDĪ

A significant development in 7th/13th- and 8th/14th-century Islamic intellectual history was the formalization of dialectics. Emerging from the traditions of juridical eristics (*'ilm al-khilāf*) and the dialectics of Aristotle's *Topics* (*jadal*), the new formalized theory of disputation (*ādāb al-baḥth/munāẓara*) was based on the principles of propositional logic set out by the new logicians.[1] The process of an increasing cross-pollination between the developing *ādāb al-baḥth* and the form of argumentation within logical commentaries was already underway at the turn of the 7th/13th century when Abharī studied with al-'Amīdī. It was more clearly in evidence in the commentaries of Abharī's student Kātibī, who criticized arguments by using the dialectical method, presenting in a formulaic way possible objections and responses with expressions like "there is room for discussion here (*fīhi naẓr*)," "we do not concede x (*lā nusallim*)," "to the one saying x, we say y (*li-qā'il . . .*)."[2]

While it is beyond the scope of this chapter to thoroughly study this development, by briefly introducing a figure—arguably the single most important author for the formalization of *ādāb al-baḥth*—as a paradigmatic example of an esteemed logician who formalized and first integrated the new science into logic, the significant interconnections between the development of *ādāb al-baḥth* and logic proper may at least be brought to attention.

This scholar, named Shams al-Dīn Muḥammad b. Ashraf al-Ḥusaynī al-Samarqandī, was born sometime in the mid-7th/13th century and likely hailed from Samarqand.[3] Even though he wrote several highly influential works, he hardly features in the near-contemporary biographical sources.[4] It seems that he studied with the expert on *khilāf* and *jadal* at the time, Burhān al-Dīn al-Nasafī (d. 687/1288), a Central Asian-born scholar who taught in Baghdād (al-'Allāma al-Ḥillī and Ibn al-Fuwaṭī were among his students), and on whose *al-Fuṣūl al-burhāniyya* (The Burhānian Chapters) he wrote a commentary, completed in 690/1291 in Mardīn.[5] He dedicated his extensive auto-commentary on his logical summa *Qisṭās al-afkār* (The Balance of Thoughts) to 'Imād al-Dīn Khiḍr b. Ibrāhīm al-Mu'minī an Īlkhānid grandee in Tabrīz. Later he appears to have moved to Khujand in Central Asia. The preferable date of his death is now 722/1322, based on a correction in an early manuscript.[6]

We do not know much more about his life, but both his *al-Ṣaḥā'if al-ilāhiyya* (Theological Papers; completed in 680/1282–1283) and his auto-commentary thereon, *al-Ma'ārif fī al-ṣaḥā'if* (The Knowledge [Contained] in the Papers), were important works of Maturīdī theology.[7] He was also a skilled mathematician and astronomer.[8] In logic, his most important works include the substantial logical summa *Qisṭās al-afkār* (completed 683/1283–1284) and a lengthy auto-commentary on it, showing some independent thinking on the analysis of the proposition (completed 692/1293–1294).[9] He also wrote an *Ishārāt* commentary titled *Bishārāt al-Ishārāt* (The Good Tidings of the Pointers; completed 688/1289), which appears to have influenced Quṭb al-Dīn al-Rāzī.[10]

However, Samarqandī was primarily known to posterity for his foundational treatise on disputation theory, the eponymous *al-Risāla al-Samarqandiyya fī ādāb al-baḥth* (The Samarqandian Treatise on Disputation Theory).[11] In it, he lays out the formal rules for an orderly debate and the kinds of objections one may raise against one's opponent.[12] While Samarqandī wrote other works on dialectics, it is important to note that he considered this newly codified science a proper part of logic. He dedicated the entire twelfth section of his *Qisṭās* to it, making it the first work on logic to include the new science.[13]

The influence of *ādāb al-baḥth* on the style of commentary writing became more pronounced in the course of the century, especially in the commentaries of Quṭb al-Dīn al-Rāzī. In what follows we shall first survey Samarqandī's treatment of the Repetition Argument in his *Qisṭās* from 683/1283–1284, his *Ishārāt* commentary from 688/1289, and the *Sharḥ al-Qisṭās* from 692/1293–1294, and then provide brief reflections on his method and his contribution, which will serve as the basis for a tentative argument about his influence on Quṭb al-Dīn al-Rāzī, discussed at the end of this chapter.

Samarqandī on Copula and Nexus: Responses to Rāzī

Samarqandī was neither an orthodox nor a revisionist Avicennan. But on the major issues regarding the analysis of propositions discussed in the tradition, he critically engaged with Rāzī and proposed solutions that he either eclectically pieced together from both revisionist and orthodox logicians, or else that he seems to have come up with himself. In the *Qisṭās*, Samarqandī begins the part on the Acquisition of Assent by compiling the accounts of the parts of propositions by Avicenna, Rāzī, and Khūnajī. Often quoting his predecessors verbatim, he first offers a comprehensive account of the uncontroversial parts of the tradition on the analysis of propositions, and then tackles controversial issues. First, he discusses the Repetition Argument:

TEXT 60: SHAMS AL-DĪN AL-SAMARQANDĪ, *QISṬĀS AL-AFKĀR* (PEHLIVAN 2010), 63.5–12 (= PEHLIVAN 2014, 175.18–177.8)

The Imām [al-Rāzī] claimed that the proposition whose predicate is a statement-word or derived name is binary on the level of expression, but ternary by nature, because the nexus is signified by containment. And that mentioning it causes repetition.

The response to this is the following: We have explained that these [i.e., statement-words or derived names in the predicate-place] do not signify the determination of the subject and that, therefore, a copula is needed. For the pronoun contained in the predicate is the agent-pronoun and its position is at the end of the predicate. This [pronoun] is a name—as agreed by grammarians—and its signification of the nexus to some subject is different from [that of] the copula. They disagree about whether [the copula] is a name and about its place in the middle, but in the Qur'ān there is an explicit mention of the copula together with the predicate implicitly containing the [signification of] the nexus: "You are the All-Observer" [Q5:117].

This inquiry is in reality outside the scope of the logician, since it is not on him [to figure this out], except insofar as it is necessary that that which signifies a determinate subject be mentioned. And if derived names in Arabic are such, then it is not necessary to mention the copula—and if they are not, it is necessary.

Samarqandī here clearly takes Khūnajī's line of response. While it is correct to say that a part of the verb or derived name signifies an indeterminate subject, this does not make mentioning the copula obsolete. For what the copula contributes to the meaning of the sentence is precisely to determine the subject that verbs and derived names signify only implicitly and indeterminately. Like Khūnajī, Samarqandī cites grammarians in support, and like Khūnajī, he dismisses the issue—beyond the point that in propositions a determinate subject must be indicated—as being irrelevant to logic.

He quotes the same Qur'ānic example as Khūnajī, giving however some valuable explanation as to the point that he takes it to illustrate. The example is "You are the All-Observer [Q5,117: *Kunta anta al-raqība*]," where, according to Samarqandī, the predicate *al-raqība* is a derived name (and declined [*manṣūb*], as Khūnajī had pointed out) and thus implicitly signifies an indeterminate subject, while the copula—"*anta*" (you) in this case—is still explicitly mentioned. If Rāzī were to insist that this was a meaningless repetition, he would have to explain this verse with regard to the doctrine of the perfection and inimitability of the Qur'ān.

The next controversial issue Samarqandī picks up also contains a criticism of Rāzī. As Khūnajī had already pointed out, a nexus between subject and predicate is not symmetrical, for, depending on a given subject and predicate, the modal quality of the nexus in the direction from predicate to subject may be different from that in the direction from subject to predicate. Samarqandī considers different positions before he gives his own opinion.

TEXT 61: SHAMS AL-DĪN AL-SAMARQANDĪ, *QISṬĀS AL-AFKĀR* (PEHLIVAN 2010), 64.4–65.4 (= PEHLIVAN 2014, 177.15–179.15)

The Imām [al-Rāzī] seeks to prove the distinction [between the two distinct nexus] by the difference of modality between the default [proposition] and its converse.

There is an issue here. For that only follows if the nexus of the predicate is also by predicate-hood in the converse, but this is not the case; for it is then by subject-hood.

Their views waver on the question of whether it is subject-hood or predicate-hood that is a part of the proposition. The Imām [al-Rāzī] in the *Mulakhkhaṣ* holds that it is subject-hood, and that predicate-hood is necessarily external [to the proposition]. In the *Sharḥ al-Ishārāt* he said: The copula expresses the nexus of the predicate to the subject; therefore, its quality is the modality of the proposition. These two [claims] are contradictory. Some scholars of our time agree with the first [claim], and perhaps this is based on the fact that when the subject-hood is necessary, then the proposition is necessary, even if the predicate-hood is not necessary, like with the general necessity [proposition]; and when [the subject-hood] is not necessary, the proposition is [also] not necessary, even if the predicate-hood is necessary, like with the separable property. This is the account of what they are saying on this issue.

Rāzī's argument had been that since you cannot convert "Humans [are] writers" to "Writers [are] humans" without thereby changing the modal quality of the nexus, there must be two distinct nexus, one in the direction from predicate to subject, and one in the direction from subject to predicate. Samarqandī now points out that Rāzī's argument does not show that there are two nexus, because once converted the relation between "writer" and "human" does not change: it is still necessary that a writer is a human and contingent that a human be a writer.[14] It is still the case that human is the subject, in the sense of underlying thing, in which writing, in the sense of an attribute, inheres. Hence, Samarqandī's reply to the controversy is that "being-a-subject" and "being-a-predicate" are conceptions dependent on something prior: what is relevant to, and in fact part of, the proposition is the occurring or not of the nexus affirmed by the judgment.

What changes, then, in conversion is the nexus affirmed by the judgment. The modality of the resulting proposition is dependent on that, not on its subject- or predicate-nexus. The distinction between a nexus that is affirmed by a judgment and the nexus between the meaning of subject and predicate appears—even though presented as an Avicennan position—novel in the tradition. It should be a central point for Quṭb al-Dīn al-Rāzī's revised account of the analysis of the proposition—even though Samarqandī makes no mention of this idea in his comment on the lemma in question in the *Bishārāt*:[15]

TEXT 62: SHAMS AL-DĪN AL-SAMARQANDĪ, *BISHĀRĀT AL-ISHĀRĀT* (MS ISTANBUL: CARULLAH 1308), FOLS. 28V1–28V9

I say: When he clarified that when the negational particle is a part of the predicate, the proposition is metathetic, and otherwise positive, he needed to explain by what [criterion] one knows the difference between the negational particle that is part of the predicate and that which is not.

So we say: The quiddity of a categorical [proposition] is composed of three parts, the subject, the predicate, and the nexus between the two, by means of which subject and predicate are connected. And just as it is only right for the subject and the predicate to be signified by an utterance, it is only right that the nexus also be signified by an utterance, so that the utterance corresponds to the meaning. This utterance [signifying the nexus] is called "copula." The copula may be left out in some languages, like in Arabic, as it is correct to say "Zayd [is] a writer." In this case the proposition is called binary; and if the copula is mentioned, as when it is said "Zayd, he is a writer," it is called ternary. In some languages leaving it out is not permitted, as for example in Persian, for one cannot leave out "is" (*hast*) from the sentence "Zayd is a writer."

The copula belongs to the auxiliaries, because it signifies a nexus and a nexus is not independent in itself. It may be found in the form of a name as one of the pronouns like "he" or "she" etc., in which case we call it a non-temporal copula, or else it may be found in the form of one of the hyparctic statement-words, i.e., the [semantically] defective verbs like "to be" or "exist," in which case we call it a temporal copula, because of its signification of time.

Like Urmawī's, Samarqandī's *Ishārāt* commentary appears here purely expository. The main interest of the passage lies in the intertextual connections between Samarqandī's works and that of Quṭb al-Dīn al-Rāzī. The wording here is very close to the expository paragraphs in Samarqandī's *Qisṭās* and its commentary, as well as to the *Ishārāt* commentary by Quṭb al-Dīn.[16]

In the commentary on the *Qisṭās*, Samarqandī does not add much to the discussion of Rāzī's Repetition Argument, except that he explains in greater detail why the Qur'ānic verse "You are the All-Observer (*kunta anta al-raqība*)" serves as a proof for the falsity of the Repetition Argument. According to Samarqandī, the Qur'ānic example shows that "*anta*" is the copula that does however not cause repetition, for if it were not, it would have to be the grammatical subject (*mubtadā'*) and "*al-raqīb*" its grammatical predicate (*khabar*), or if "*al-raqība*" is lifted from the sentence, it would be the predicate of "*kunta*" (*khabar kāna*). Neither option is plausible for Samarqandī, nor is the idea that the pronouns ("*huwa*," "*anta*") have no signification but only function to separate subject and predicate (*faṣl wa ʿimād*). But in any case, this is for grammarians to sort out. As he said in the *Qisṭās*, adopting Khūnajī's phrasing, all that matters for the logician is to know that a nexus to a determinate subject must be signified.

Just before, however, he sets out his thoughts about the difference in the use of the copula between Persian and Arabic:

TEXT 63: SHAMS AL-DĪN AL-SAMARQANDĪ, *SHARḤ AL-QISṬĀS* (MS BERLIN: STAATSBIBLIOTHEK LANDBERG 1035), FOLS. 42V31–43R4 (= MS YALE: BEINECKE ARABIC 11, FOLS. 30V13–19)

If you were to say: Why is it not possible that the copulae in Arabic are just the signs of declension, be it short vowels or letters, and that this [just] is the truth of it, for they signify the compound by dint of the conventions (*waḍʿ*) of the Arabic language. The proof for this is that when simple expressions are mentioned and then there is a pause before another [is mentioned], no connection and no compound obtain; and when they signify the compound by convention, then they are copulae. In this case there is no difference between Arabic and Persian with regard to the necessity of mentioning the copula.

Then I say: We know by necessity that the statement-words we mentioned are copulae connecting the predicate to the subject on account of the language and [its] convention. In this case it is not correct to say that the signs of declension are a copula by convention. For if it were like that, then it would not be possible to mention along with them the copulae that we have mentioned—yet it is well agreed that it is possible. As for the antecedent: because if they are mentioned, they are mentioned either in order to connect, or in order to affirm the connection that the signs of declension signify, or else in order to distinguish the attribute from the predicate by agreement. But there is no way to any of those. As for the first: it is impossible to make obtain what is already obtaining; as for the second: the affirmation cannot precede the thing affirmed; as for the third: there are cases in which there is no need to mark the distinction, like in *"Zayd huwa kātib."* Hence, it is not allowed to treat as a copula the [short vowel] *kasra* at the end of the predicate in Persian. The signs of declension have only been set down by convention for the meanings of simple expressions that do not signify the compound of their own account in terms of being a subject, being an object, and being a genitive-construct, as the grammarians explain. Hence it is not prohibited to mention them, as they are set down by convention for the judgment-nexus, its occurrence or lack thereof.

We may note that Samarqandī here raises an objection that—whether hypothetical or not—has not been discussed in the authors surveyed so far. The idea is that, given the intuition from Arabic grammar that found its expression in Rāzī's Repetition Argument, namely that the artificial copula introduced by the earlier logicians is not at all needed to properly express a proposition, one might argue like this: granted that the nexus is a concept distinct from those of subject and predicate and thus needs to be expressed somehow on the level of language, why should that task not be taken care of by the grammatical inflections that simple expressions take in the context of a sentence? Quṭb al-Dīn will make use of it, as we will see at the end of the chapter.

Note on Samarqandī's Method: Logic and Dialectics (ādāb al-baḥth),
Auto-Commentaries, and Eclecticism in the Qisṭās al-afkār

From this short survey of passages dealing with the analysis of propositions and the copula, we may tentatively note three important points. First, as we have seen in Kātibī's commentaries, Samarqandī's commentaries make extensive use of locutions and argumentative strategies from the new *ādāb al-baḥth*. While the *Ishārāt* commentary may be described as primarily expository or exegetical in approach, in both the *Qisṭās* and the auto-commentary on it the style of writing is essentially dialectical, using devices like "A said *x*, B said *y*, but the truth is *z*," "if you were to say *x* . . . I say *y*," etc. Objections raised may be objections made by scholars in writing or orally, or hypothetical objections that the author himself anticipates. Both are treated in the same way following the formalized protocol of *ādāb al-baḥth*.

This leads to the second point: It is important to note that with Samarqandī's dialectical method, the genre of the auto-commentary appears to be particularly conducive to what we should describe as original work or research. The claim that commentaries were pedantic and unoriginal rested on the idea that their authors merely reproduce, perhaps in a more accessible fashion, the material presented by other authors. While one might find a reason to write such a commentary on one's own work, the commentary on the *Qisṭās* seems to be more concerned with deepening questions than with making them more accessible.

The third point, then, is that since both independent works and commentaries routinely engage with the positions of predecessors, even including an author's own earlier work (there is little difference between the independent *Qisṭās* and its commentary in that the commentary would contain fewer original ideas— rather the contrary), we should see the eclectic presentations of logical issues together with this deepening of questions as the main thrust of at least some of the writings of most logicians, including commentaries, from that period.

IBN AL-MUṬAHHAR AL-ḤILLĪ: COMMENTING ON RĀZĪ, ṬŪSĪ, AND KĀTIBĪ

Ḥasan b. Yūsuf Ibn al-Muṭahhar al-Ḥillī, known by the honorific al-ʿAllāma al-Ḥillī, was a contemporary of Samarqandī, born in 648/1250 to an Imāmī Shīʿī family in Ḥilla, Iraq.[17] His father belonged to the scholarly and political elite of Ḥilla and appears to have been, together with his maternal uncle Najm al-Dīn al-Ḥillī, who was the *"muḥaqqiq al-awwal"* (foremost scholar) of the town, the most important teacher in his youth.[18] After studying the works of the Shīʿī Muʿtazilites with various renowned teachers, he read with Ṭūsī and Kātibī—likely at Marāgha[19]—the philosophical works of Avicenna and Rāzī, and, especially, with Kātibī the logical works of Khūnajī, of Abharī, and of Ṭūsī and Kātibī themselves. Ḥillī spent a later period of his life at the court of the Īlkhānid ruler of Persia Öljaitu (*reg.* 704/1304–716/1316) and played some role in the ruler's conversion to the Shīʿī Islam.[20] He died in his hometown in 726–727/1325.

Ḥillī was one of the most influential Shīʿī scholar-theologians of the medieval period. His works, especially on theology and jurisprudence, continued to be revered by Shīʿī readers until modern times.[21] His orientation seems to have tended more toward the orthodox Avicennism of his teacher Ṭūsī than toward the revisionist Avicennism of his teacher Kātibī.[22] He wrote commentaries on the key logical works of both his teachers. On Kātibī's *Shamsiyya*, he wrote *al-Qawāʿid al-jaliyya fī sharḥ al-Risāla al-Shamsiyya* (The Clear Principles in Commenting upon the Epistle for Shams al-Dīn), completed likely before 676/1277.[23] His most widely read logical work is *al-Jawhar al-naḍīd fī sharḥ manṭiq al-Tajrīd* (The Tiered Jewel in Commenting upon the Logic of the Extracted Points) on Ṭūsī's *Tajrīd al-manṭiq*, completed after 680/1281.

Further, he wrote an *Ishārāt* commentary, titled *Muḥākamāt* (Adjudications), completed shortly before 720/1320 and still unedited, in which he critically compared the commentaries of Rāzī, Ṭūsī, and Najm al-Dīn al-Nakhjuwānī (7th/13th century). Other than in his unfinished commentary on Avicenna's *Shifāʾ*, he extensively treats logic in his tripartite summae of philosophy, notably in the Logic of *al-Asrār al-khafiyya fī l-ʿulūm al-ʿaqliyya* (The Hidden Secrets in the Rational Sciences), completed around 679/1280, and in *Marāṣid al-tadqīq wa-maqāṣid al-taḥqīq* (Observation Points of Precision and Destinations of Verification), of which only the Logic part survives.[24]

Between Revisionist and Orthodox Logicians: Commenting on His Teachers Kātibī and Ṭūsī

Ḥillī has been considered a foremost theologian and a formative legal theoretician, but a largely unoriginal philosopher.[25] While it is fair to say that the virtues of his commentaries on logical works lie in the clear exposition of the positions of their authors rather than in original contributions by Ḥillī himself, this does however not mean that Ḥillī had no contributions to make to logical theory. Even though his two early logical commentaries are in the main expository teaching texts, we see Ḥillī, who must have been in his twenties or early thirties when he wrote them, embracing the teachings and general approach to the Avicennan tradition of his orthodox teacher Ṭūsī, while criticizing the positions of his revisionist teacher Kātibī.[26]

In the *Qawāʿid*, which Ḥillī says he wrote at the request of logicians who found the *Shamsiyya* difficult to understand—a typical *topos* to introduce expository commentaries—he at the end refers his readers to the *Asrār* for his own positions.[27] The chapter "Parts and Classifications of Propositions" does not raise problematic issues, but Ḥillī there does mention Rāzī's Repetition Argument, simply dismissing it by saying "Fakhr al-Dīn claimed that [predicates that are statement-words or derived names] are connected by themselves to the subject of a proposition. But this is false."[28]

In the *Jawhar*, Ḥillī is already, as Street has remarked, "less full-throated in his support for Ṭūsī's positions" than in his earlier works, and on occasion reverts to a Rāzian or Khūnajīan position on specific issues.[29] In the chapter on the Parts of the Proposition, Ḥillī does not mention the Repetition Argument, but explains that propositions consist of two primary parts, that about which judgement is passed and that by which judgment is passed. A proposition is true, iff that of which the former is true, of that the latter is also true, i.e., if "man" is true of x, and "writer" is true of x, then "man is a writer" is a true proposition. The copula is a formal part (*juzʾ ṣūrī*) that may or may not be mentioned in Arabic (but must be mentioned in Persian).[30]

While in these early commentaries Ḥillī's inclination toward the orthodox strand of Avicennism is discernible, and there may already have been a development toward a more balanced approach to the legacy of both his logic teachers, they were certainly not the place to discuss controversial logical issues in detail. The much later *Muḥākamāt* (completed around 720/1320) did provide space for that.

The Adjudications between Rāzī's and Ṭūsī's Ishārāt Commentaries

In the *Muḥākamāt*, commenting on the lemma that Rāzī had used to advance his challenge, Ḥillī first presents an account of the proposition and its parts in terms of a hylomorphic compound, just as Rāzī had.[31] According to Ḥillī, a proposition—just like any other compound—in reality (*fī l-ḥaqīqa*) needs both formal and material parts. In a simple categorical proposition, there are thus exactly two material parts, namely, what is signified by subject and predicate, respectively, and exactly one formal part, namely, the combination of the two material parts (*ijtimā'*) signified by the copula (fol. 96v8–11).

That the meaning of the copula, i.e., the combination of the two material parts, is a concept additional to the concepts signified by subject and predicate is shown by the fact, and here Ḥillī again follows Rāzī, that the latter two can very well be conceived of without conceiving of the former. This formal part is strictly necessary for there to be a proposition. While the copula is a mental concept (*amr 'aqlī*, fol. 96v15), for there to be correspondence in number between utterances and concepts, it should be mentioned in sentences expressing propositions (fol. 96v11–16).

However, in his exegetical presentation of the Avicennan lemma, Ḥillī says that languages differ as to the necessity or not of expressing the copula, so that while in Persian it indiscriminately has to be mentioned, in Arabic it is not needed as long as the predicate is a verb or a derived name. Hence, one should say "Zayd, he [is a] writer" instead of merely "Zayd [is a] writer." This was the point Rāzī had used to mount his criticism. Consequently, the way Ḥillī classifies propositions into binary and ternary differs slightly from his predecessors. On his account, a proposition is called binary either if a proposition is such that its predicate is a verb or a derived name, so that it naturally does not have a copula, or else if the copula is simply omitted. Here, he does not distinguish between complete and incomplete ternary propositions (fols. 96v16–97r11).

After this lengthy exposition, Ḥillī presents the challenge that Rāzī had posed in his own commentary together with Ṭūsī's rejection of it. He quotes Rāzī verbatim, then charitably presents his objection: What is understood from verbs and derived names contains, in addition to the action or property they primarily signify, a concept distinct from that. This is the nexus between this primary signification and a subject in which it inheres. Hence, if in such cases a copula is mentioned, there would be useless repetition. Ḥillī also faithfully reproduces Rāzī's anticipated objection (*i'taraḍa*, fol. 97v1): One might say that since the concept of "man" and the concept of "writer" are distinct and the concept of the linkage (*intisāb*, fol. 97v3) of one to the other is a concept additional (*zā'id*, fol. 97v3) to these two, then necessarily there must be an additional expression signifying this concept (fols. 97r11–97v3).

But then, as Ḥillī reproduces Rāzī's response (*ajāba*, fol. 97v4), even if the concepts of the nexus and of the predicate are concepts distinct from the concept of the subject, this does not entail that the nexus needs a separate expression to signify it. For the concept of the predicate is such that it connects to the subject by its own essence. The nexus is part of the predicate and, thus, that which signifies the predicate includes the signification of the nexus. Ḥillī quotes (again verbatim) the Most Eminent of the Verifiers (i.e., Ṭūsī), objecting that the verb only connects by itself to its agent-noun when nothing comes before it, and the agent-noun never precedes the verb in Arabic, so that it never by itself connects to a name preceding it. On Rāzī's argument, if we change "Zayd [is a] writer" (*Zayd kātib*) to "Writes Zayd"[32] (*Zayd yaktub*), the predicate is a verb and even in this case we would have to change to "Zayd, he writes" (*Zayd huwa yaktub*), because when the verb follows the agent-noun it does precisely not by itself connect to it. So there is a difference between what connects the verb to the agent-noun and what connects the grammatical predicate to the grammatical subject (fol. 97v4–14).

Ḥillī's judgment (*wa l-ḥaqq*, fol. 97v15) falls squarely on the side of Ṭūsī. He justifies his adjudication by saying that the copula implicit in verbs and statement words does not signify the connection to a specific subject, but just to any subject, and that what is needed in a proposition is something that signifies the connection to a determinate subject. For him, the implicit pronouns are names, and the copula an auxiliary. Ḥillī thus advocates the position that the copula is needed, and goes on to explain that the correct place for it in the sentence is in the middle between subject and predicate expressions—even though in Persian it usually comes at the end. Then, Ḥillī adds some more general remarks of his own on the analysis of the proposition. Every proposition, says Ḥillī, is in fact quaternary, because any nexus has in itself a determined modal quality, even if a modality is explicitly expressed in the proposition. Further, as has been pointed out since Khūnajī, the nexus of the subject to the predicate is not the same as the nexus of the predicate to the subject, for their modal qualities may differ (fols. 97v5–98r13).

In contrast to Samarqandī, Ḥillī here formulates a new doctrine according to which there are not two distinct nexus in a proposition, but in fact four. Samarqandī had rejected the idea that any of the two nexus are part of the proposition in favor of the idea that what is in fact part of the proposition is the judgment-nexus (Text 63). Ḥillī claims that since every proposition contains a subject and a predicate, and each of them has a nexus to the other either as being-a-subject or as being-a-predicate, there is a total of four distinct nexus in a proposition (and its converse). He might have gotten this idea from Kātibī, who did not explicitly state this position, but did distinguish four ways in which one can think of a nexus between two terms (fols. 98r13–98v3).

The Logic of the Summae

At the end of the *Qawā ʿid*, Ḥillī had referred the reader to his *Asrār* for fuller treatment of his criticisms of Kātibī.[33] In this early work, Ḥillī introduces the distinction between hypothetical and categorical propositions and then lays out his view on the parts of the proposition.[34] A categorical proposition consists of three parts: that about which judgment is passed (subject), that with which judgment is passed (predicate), and the nexus between them which is required to turn the former two parts into a proposition and which is signified by the copula (56.9–10).

The copula, too, is in principle required for a sentence to express a proposition, but because it is often obvious that its signification is intended, it has ceased to be mentioned in many languages (56.12–13). Ḥillī does not mention Rāzī's Repetition Argument here, but clearly reacts to it in line with Ṭūsī's response. He states that, generally, no matter whether the predicate is a name, derived name, or statement-word, the copula—be it nominal (*huwa*) or verbal (*yakūn/yūjad*)—needs to be expressed, and that "*Zayd huwa kātib*," "*Zayd yakūnu kātiban*," and "*Zayd yūjadu kātiban*" all signify the same proposition (56.14–16).

Oddly, Ḥillī makes no distinction between temporal and atemporal propositions here. However, that general rule notwithstanding, predicates that are verbs may connect by themselves to the subject. This is because even though the pronoun implied by verbs and derived names is not the same as the copula, so that the correct analysis of "*Zayd yaktub*" is "*Zayd huwa yaktubu huwa*," the second "*huwa*" specifies the nexus to a determinate subject by referring back to it: "*Zayd kātib*" thus ultimately expresses the same proposition as "*Zayd yakūnu kātiban*" and hence in such cases the copula is already expressed and there is no need to express it again (56.17—57.3).

Following Ṭūsī, Ḥillī proposes what is basically Rāzī's position, namely that predicates that are statement-words and derived names connect by themselves to the subject, only for different reasons: it is not part of the essence of the concepts signified by these word-types that they connect to a subject in themselves, but as Abharī and Ṭūsī had suggested, it is the context of the sentence that allows for such word-types to signify the nexus to a determinate subject by referring back to a subject already mentioned. So far, this is nothing entirely new.

There follows a paragraph on the question of whether there are distinct nexus in a proposition. It is titled "Secret," a formal device of the *al-Asrār al-khafiyya* (Hidden Secrets) appended to the exposition of a chapter in which Ḥillī advances what he holds to be the truth on certain controversial issues. Ḥillī begins by rehearsing Kātibī's position: the nexus of subject to predicate by subject-hood is not the same as that of the predicate to the subject by predicate-hood; they are distinct in that the former is external to the quiddity of the proposition and the latter internal but they imply each other's modality (57.7–10).

Ḥillī mentions that some of the later logicians (*ba ʿd al-mutaʾakhkhirīn*), by which he must mean Kātibī and perhaps Urmawī, objected to the argument that the nexus of the subject to the predicate by predicate-hood is not the same as that by subject-hood (57.11–19). The objection is the one that Kātibī had offered: the argument is only correct if the original proposition were an expression of the nexus of its subject to its predicate by subject-hood and the converse an expression of the nexus of the original subject to the original predicate by predicate-hood. But this is not the case: the former nexus is external to the quiddity of the proposition, and the second internal. Hence, as it does not follow from the identity of two things one of which is external to a quiddity while the other is internal to it that they be distinct, it also does not follow that the two nexus be distinct. The same can be applied to the predicate and its nexus (57.20–58.3). Ḥillī says:

TEXT 64: IBN AL-MUṬAHHAR AL-ḤILLĪ, *AL-ASRĀR AL-KHAFIYYA FĪ L-ʿULŪM AL-ʿAQLIYYA* (ANONYMOUS, QUM 2000), 58.4–8

I say: The true position here is to say the following. If we say "A [is] B," there are two nexus: one of them is the nexus from A to B by subject-hood, and the second is that from B to A by predicate-hood. And if we say "B [is] A," there are two nexus: one of them is the nexus from B to A by subject-hood, and the second is that from A to B by predicate-hood. If the first and the fourth nexus, and the second and the third, were identical, then what is understood from the proposition and from its converse would imply each other. But this is absurd.

Ḥillī follows Kātibī here, except that he simply denies the identity of any of the four nexus and does not even say, as Kātibī had, that the first and the fourth, as well as the second and the third, nexus are their counterparts in potentiality.[35]

Ḥillī's other major summa, the *Marāṣid al-tadqīq wa maqāṣid al-taḥqīq*, contained the three parts typical of philosophical works—Logic, Metaphysics, and Physics—but only the Logic part has come down to us.[36] We do not know for certain when the work was composed but it is likely later than all his other works discussed earlier, save the *Muḥākamāt*. Its structure is different from that of the Logic of his early philosophical work in the *Asrār* as well as from that of the logic part in Avicenna's *Ishārāt*. The work is divided into four "places of destination" (*maqāṣid*): "Eisagoge" (*Īsāghūjī*), "The Proposition and Its Properties," "The Syllogism," and "Demonstration and Dialectics," each containing a number of "observation points" (*marāṣid*).

It is noteworthy that, in contrast to presentations of logic that follow the *Ishārāt* structure, it includes dialectics, but excludes all other syllogistic arts, like Rhetoric or Poetics, which Ṭūsī had included in the *Tajrīd al-manṭiq* and in the *Asās*.[37] This may be taken to reflect the increasing integration of the new dialectics within logic toward the end of the 7th/13th century.

While it is true that Ḥillī's method consists largely in the synthesis of different emerging Avicennisms—with an evident inclination to the Ṭūsīan line—this does not preclude him from advancing innovations on certain logical issues.[38] Concerning the analysis of simple categorical statements in the *Marāṣid*, Ḥillī here describes predication (*ḥaml*) and subjection (*waḍʿ*) in a Rāzian fashion as secondary intelligibles that accrue to first intelligibles and have no actualization in reality: there is nothing that is a predicate in the extramental world (92.6–7).

At the beginning of the second "Destination" (*maqṣid*) Ḥillī standardly presents the categorical proposition as consisting of three parts: the subject, the predicate, and the copula between them, connecting the subject such that it is the predicate, or that it is not it (134.15–16). Ḥillī is, like Rāzī, a nominalist about the quantifier and a realist about the nexus (136.10–15). With regard to Rāzī's Repetition Argument, he here takes a middle position between Avicenna/Ṭūsī and Rāzī: verbs and derived names in the predicate place do not need a copula in the way non-derived names do, but they still need to signify a determinate subject (which supposedly they do in the context of a sentence). For Ḥillī, as for Avicenna and Ṭūsī, binary propositions are those in which the auxiliary is suppressed. Unlike Avicenna and Ṭūsī, and arguably like Rāzī, he calls those propositions incomplete ternary in which there is no copula expressed as the predicate is a verb or derived name (135.5–10).

The question whether verbs and derived names signify a nexus to a determinate subject—by means of the implied pronoun that refers back to the subject—is here simply dismissed as a purely linguistic (*lughawī*) controversy (135.11–13). In the *Marāṣid* Ḥillī does not talk about the four distinct nexus that he mentions in the *Asrār* and the *Muḥākamāt*. He simply restates Kātibī's tentative position, namely that the nexus of subject to predicate is distinct from the nexus of predicate to subject, but that they are logically related. The reason is this. If the subject is such that, insofar as the predicate subsists for it, it is necessary, then likewise the predicate, insofar as it subsists for the subject, is necessary. Hence it is impossible that the two nexus differ in mode or modality, and one of them is in the potentiality of the other (136.1–5).

Even though Ḥillī made substantial contributions to logical theory—not least in his analysis of the ways in which the subject can be presented in a proposition—with regard to questions the tradition raised about the copula and the nexus signified by it, he by and large sided with the positions of his predecessors, notably including Rāzī and Kātibī. It was however not until the commentaries written by his student Quṭb al-Dīn al-Rāzī that the traditional accounts of the copula were comprehensively challenged.

THE GREAT COMMENTARIES OF QUṬB AL-DĪN AL-RĀZĪ AL-TAḤTĀNĪ: ELIMINATING THE COPULA

Quṭb al-Dīn al-Rāzī al-Taḥtānī was born and raised around the turn of the 8th/14th century in Warāmīn, the new Mongol administrative center in Rayy.[39] He studied with the Twelver Shīʿī Ḥillī (Taḥtānī's own sectarian affiliation remains unclear: he might have always been, or else later in his life become, a Sunnī),[40] and at a relatively young age appears to have received a teaching certificate (*ijāza*) from him. Shihāb al-Dīn al-Shushtarī (d. 1019/1610) reports that on his travels to Syria he read on the back of Ḥillī's copy of the *Qawāʿid [al-jaliyya fī sharḥ al-Risāla al-Shamsiyya?]* in Ḥillī's hand the following *ijāza* dated to 713/1313:[41]

> [Quṭb al-Dīn] al-Rāzī studied intensively with me most of this treatise, researching, verifying, and establishing [the text's] accuracy [. . .] I have authorized him to transmit this treatise and also my other writings and transmissions [. . .] and all of our predecessors' treatises in an uninterrupted chain of transmission through my authority—being [as he is] well qualified to do that.[42]

It is likely that Ḥillī and Taḥtānī both traveled, studied, and taught in the "mobile school" (*madrasa-yi sayyāra*) that was part of the Īlkhān Öljaitu's entourage on his expeditions.[43] If that was indeed the case, it is not unlikely that Quṭb al-Dīn also studied at the Marāgha observatory at some point. It is doubtful that he studied with the other famous Quṭb al-Dīn, the astronomer and scholar al-Shīrāzī (d. 710/1311), as is sometimes claimed in the sources, and the story that Shīrāzī suggested to Taḥtānī to write a *Muḥākamāt* is almost certainly a myth.[44]

The connection with another Sunnī scholar who also traveled with the mobile school and who authored the standard work on *ʿilm al-waḍʿ*, ʿAḍud al-Dīn al-Ījī (d. 756/1355), is more likely: Taḥtānī may have studied with him at Sulṭāniyya, the new Īlkhānid capital near Zanjān when Ījī was supreme judge (*qāḍī l-mamālik*) under the Īlkhān Abū Saʿīd (*reg.* 716–736/1316–1335).[45] Toward the end of his life, Taḥtānī taught at the Ẓāhiriyya madrasa in Damascus and died there in 766/1365.

Quṭb al-Dīn Taḥtānī was arguably the most influential Arabic logician of the 8th/14th century, if measured against the sheer number of super-commentaries and glosses elicited by his two monumental lemmatic commentaries on the new logical *summae*: the *Lawāmiʿ al-asrār fī sharḥ Maṭāliʿ al-anwār* (The Blazing Secrets in Commenting upon the Dawning Lights) on Urmawī's *Maṭāliʿ* (completed 728/1328) and the *Taḥrīr al-qawāʿid al-manṭiqiyya bi-sharḥ al-Risāla al-Shamsiyya* (Redacting the Rules of Logic in Commenting upon the Epistle for Shams al-Dīn) on Kātibī's *Shamsiyya* (completed 729/1329).[46] The former commentary was dedicated to the Īlkhānid vizier Ghiyāth al-Dīn Muḥammad (d. 736/1336), the latter to the vizier's younger brother.

The commentary on Urmawī can be regarded as Taḥtānī's most thorough textual confrontation with the revisionist Avicennans. Overall, in this work as in others, Taḥtānī sought to rehabilitate Avicenna against the revisionists, believing that almost all departures from Avicenna proposed by Khūnajī and his followers were ill considered and based on misunderstandings.[47] Besides these two major commentaries and some shorter treatises on specific topics in logic, Taḥtānī completed in 756/1355 his own *Muḥākamāt* on the *Ishārāt* commentaries. The *Muḥākamāt* was widely glossed in later centuries, but the Logic part seems to have enjoyed less popularity than the Metaphysics and Physics, possibly because it was superseded by the *Lawāmiʿ*.[48]

A Revised View in a Later Addition to the Lawāmiʿ al-asrār

The *Lawāmiʿ* itself contains a later addition transmitted in only two MSS that shows that Taḥtānī was troubled by traditional accounts of the syntax and semantics of atomic propositions. For him, the main problem in these accounts was a confused understanding of the copula. I have discussed in greater detail elsewhere why he might have found traditional accounts so problematic and what might have led him to criticize Avicenna—an otherwise unusual gesture for him—and to revise his own views.[49]

It seems to me that Taḥtānī, after having discussed in a piecemeal fashion the lemmata of Urmawī's entire text, realized that the positions of his predecessors, including Avicenna, on the problem of predication and the role of the copula were incoherent, so that he revisited several of his own comments and then, at a later date, inserted a passage into the finished manuscript in which he summarized his considered opinion.

Among the issues that might have led him to reformulate his views are (1) the classification of utterance types, (2) the semantics of first- and second-person inflected verbs, (3) the account of "*huwa*" as a non-temporal copula, and, perhaps most importantly, the (4) question of the number of parts in a proposition.[50] The result is an account of the proposition according to which every Arabic expression that can appear as a predicate signifies as part of its meaning that it has a nexus to an indeterminate subject, and that it is by mentioning the subject that the judgment is expressed. This account is extended to hyparctic verbs that include in their signification the nexus to both an indeterminate subject and an indeterminate predicate. The copula "*huwa*" is not needed on this account—Arabic is in perfect order with regard to the expression of logical syntax, and the Avicennan distinction between binary and ternary propositions is rendered practically obsolete.

All this is in some respects close to the Fregean analysis, in that Taḥtānī clearly distinguishes between judgment and judgeable content, eliminates the copula from the analysis of (most) propositions, and formulates a unified criterion for the unsaturatedness of 1-place and 2-place predicates, no matter of which utterance type, that become saturated once their empty places are filled by mentioning the missing expressions.

Central to this novel account is Taḥtānī's contention—regarding (4)—that a simple categorical proposition consists of four parts, not three: the meaning of the subject, the meaning of the predicate, the nexus between the two, and additionally the judgment of the obtaining or not of the nexus.[51] Commenting on the passage by Urmawī, Taḥtānī interestingly presents the proposition as a hylomorphic compound as Rāzī did, and then first suggests that the proposition in fact consists of four parts, countering a possible objection:[52]

TEXT 65: QUṬB AL-DĪN AL-RĀZĪ, *LAWĀMIʿ AL-ASRĀR* (RAḤMĀNĪ), II 17.4–19.2

But it might be said: The parts of the proposition, when analyzed, are four, i.e., the subject, the predicate, the nexus between them, and the judgment, that is: the obtaining or not of the nexus. If, then, that which is signified by the copula is the nexus, then inevitably there must be another expression for the judgment, so that the expressions correspond to the meanings. And if [what is signified by the copula] is the judgment, then the words of the author [Urmawī] "the copula is what signifies the nexus" are not correct, and the expression "*huwa*" in "Zayd, he (*huwa*) is not a writer" is not a copula. [. . .]

Then we say: That which signifies the judgment [also] signifies the nexus, and there is no need for signifying it with another expression. As for the expression "*huwa*," it is the affirmative copula, just as they express the negational copula independently of it with a negational particle. Then, the copula leaves a support for the mind to conceive its meaning, and the proposition in its expression is divided into two parts. Because if it is mentioned in it, it is ternary, and if it is not mentioned, but supplied in the mind, then it is binary.

Here, Taḥtānī still seems to embrace the Avicennan idea that "*huwa*" functions as a copula—except that it signifies not only the nexus, but also the judgment—and that hence propositions may be classified into binary and ternary ones, depending on whether or not the copula is made explicit. Shortly after, however, he voices his disagreement with taking "*huwa*" to be a copula.

TEXT 66: QUṬB AL-DĪN AL-RĀZĪ, *LAWĀMI ʿ AL-ASRĀR* (RAḤMĀNĪ), II 20.5–8

There is an issue with what [Avicenna] transmitted about the Arabic language. For the expressions "he," "she," and "they" (*huwa, hiya, humā, hum, hunna*) are just pronouns and they are used when something has been mentioned before, and they do not have the signification of the nexus at all, let alone the judgment-nexus. They only signify that they refer to what came before, and there is nothing signified by "*huwa*" in the sentence "Zayd, he is alive (*Zayd huwa ḥayyun*)" except "Zayd," so how is it supposed to be a copula?

Whatever the copula is, it was supposed to signify the judgment-nexus. But pronouns do not do that. In fact, they do not signify any nexus at all according to Taḥtānī. He then argues:

TEXT 67: QUṬB AL-DĪN AL-RĀZĪ, *LAWĀMI ʿ AL-ASRĀR* (RAḤMĀNĪ), II 20.9–21.7

If you said: What is meant by it [the copula] is the partitive and the copulative pronoun, then we say: the examples in which he adduced ["*huwa*"] are not such, for he expresses this in flawless Arabic [elsewhere] in his book; the partitive pronoun also does not signify for [the grammarians] the judgment-nexus; rather [it signifies] the difference between the attribute and the predicate.

As for the hyparctic verbs, they do in fact signify the nexus, but they do not signify the judgment, as has become clear from the [discussion of] the present-tense third-person inflected verb, because if they did signify the judgment, then they would be susceptible to truth and falsehood, but this is not so. Moreover, considering [hyparctic verbs to be] copulae here contradicts what was said earlier in [the chapter on] expressions about taking [hyparctic verbs to be] different from auxiliaries [i.e., Avicenna had said that auxiliaries and hyparctic verbs were both defective in their meaning, but that auxiliaries behaved to names as hyparctic verbs to proper verbs (I 126.2ff)].[53] It is clear that what [Avicenna] takes to be a copula in Arabic is in fact not a copula. Rather, the copula for them [the grammarians] is the nominative vocalization of the declension and what is analogous to it, because it signifies the meaning of being an agent [grammatical subject], which is [what the grammarians call] nexus of subordination (*isnād*). Thus, if there is a construction of declined [elements], then the proposition is ternary, as when we say "Zayd [is] standing (*Zaydun qāʾimun*)." And if [the elements are] indeclinable then the proposition is binary, as when we say: "This [is] Sibawayhi (*hādhā Sībawayhi*)"; that is why they say that both elements [in the latter example] are in the state of a nominative noun, pointing at the hiddenness of the copula in the soul.

Wondering whether, if the judgment is a distinct part of the proposition, there must be a feature on the level of language signifying it, Taḥtānī comes to question the very idea that partitive pronouns like "*huwa*" should function as a copula. It is in this passage that Taḥtānī reconsiders two issues that he discussed earlier in the commentary (I 128–138), namely, (1) the definitions of different word-classes, and (2) the semantics of inflected verbs. Both issues he discussed with reference to Avicenna's elaborations in *al-ʿIbāra* of the *Shifā'*.[54]

On his account, third-person inflected verbs do signify a nexus (as do derived names) but not the judgment-nexus—until a subject is mentioned. Further, hyparctic verbs are a word-class distinct from names, statement-words, and particles, because they are semantically incomplete like particles but tensed like real verbs and thus likewise signify a nexus but not the judgment—until subject and predicate are mentioned. Based on these observations, Taḥtānī is the first to suggest that "*huwa*" is not a copula at all, for it signifies neither a nexus nor the judgment.

Still, he thinks there must some feature of language signifying the nexus, and that feature simply is the fact that in a declarative sentence subject and predicate are put in the nominative case, signified by the vocalization. Only in the rare cases where grammatical irregularities of indeclinable words come into play is the expression of the proposition binary. Admittedly, the formulation in the passage is not a paradigm of clarity. It seems that Taḥtānī wrestled with these problems for a while until he decided to insert a clarification that is preserved in only two manuscripts:[55]

TEXT 68: QUṬB AL-DĪN AL-RĀZĪ, *LAWĀMIʿ AL-ASRĀR* (RAḤMĀNĪ), II 26.6–27.18

Know that in this investigation there is a confusion (*khabṭ*) that must be pointed out. We say: When the proposition comprises three meanings, the meaning of the subject, the meaning of the predicate, and the meaning of the judgment, in this case the expression is not complete unless there are three signs for the three meanings; then the proposition is tripartite. And if only two meanings are signified, then the proposition is bipartite.

If the predicate is a verb or a derived noun, the meaning of the predicate and of the judgment-nexus are conveyed by a single expression. As for the predicate, this is clear. As for the meaning of the judgment-nexus, this is because the verb contains the nexus of the event to a determinate subject, as set out [earlier] in the investigation of expressions. If the subject is stated, then [the verb] positively conveys that nexus: considering [the verb] inasmuch as it signifies the nexus of a determinate predicate to the subject, it is the copula; considering it inasmuch as it signifies the event, it is the predicate. In this case the proposition is ternary, for what it means for a proposition to be ternary is just for it to have something in it that signifies the judgment-nexus. But the first- or second-person inflected verb, if it conveys [these] three meanings, is a ternary proposition as well.

Let it not be thought that the copula is that which signifies the judgment-nexus alone, because otherwise hyparctic verbs would not be copulae. For just as they signify the nexus, they also signify its time.

The difference between [hyparctic] and real verbs—even if they share the property of containing the nexus of a determinate predicate to a determinate subject—is that the real verb signifies by itself the determinate predicate, unlike the hyparctic verbs, for they do not signify a determinate subject, or a determinate predicate.

Just as the real verb, if its subject is explicitly stated, signifies the judgment-nexus, so does the hyparctic verb, if its subject and predicate are explicitly stated. And here there is no need in the connection of the predicate to the subject for the provision of a pronoun, *as the Shaykh [Avicenna] falsely assumed*. Similarly, if the real verb comes after the subject, then there is no need for a pronoun, for on account of the mere mention of the subject the judgment-nexus is understood from [the verb]. In this case all [three] meanings of the proposition are conveyed. [. . .] There is no difference between the meanings conveyed by the propositions "Got up Zayd" (*qama Zayd*) and "Zayd got up" (*Zayd qama*).[56]

When the predicate is a non-derived name (*ism jāmid*), if there are nominative vocalizations in the proposition, then it is ternary, because [these vowel signs] signify the nexus of subordination (*isnād*), and this is the judgment-nexus; if there are no nominative vocalizations in [the proposition], then nothing at all in [the proposition] signifies a nexus, and it is a binary proposition.

This is what was summarized after careful reconsideration. Think about it and consider!

This passage is remarkable for several reasons. In the first paragraph Taḥtānī reiterates the position that really only rare cases that are due to grammatical irregularities like "*hādhā Sībawayhi*" count as binary or *secundum adiacens* propositions. This is not at all the distinction that Aristotle or Avicenna had intended, but Quṭb al-Dīn's revision of the traditional position shows that he had a keen sense for the fact that the Arabic tradition, including Avicenna, had held on to some Aristotelian doctrines that in fact made little sense in Arabic. The revised *secundum/tertium adiacens* distinction can be seen as an upshot of Taḥtānī's semantic considerations and his criticism of Avicenna's use of the copula "*huwa*" in the following way.

Coming from the semantic analysis of third-person inflected verbs, Taḥtānī develops a unified notion of unsaturatedness for all predicates, including those in nominal sentences. Based on his intuition that simple expressions may co-signify the judgment-nexus once placed in the *context of the sentence* and his position that there are four conceptually distinct parts in atomic propositions, he argues that all possible predicates, that is, real verbs, hyparctic verbs, and derived and non-derived names (even in nominal sentences), contain in themselves and as simple expressions a signification of a nexus to one or more indeterminate syntactical elements that need to be supplied for the signification of the judgment to obtain. Let us say they contain a signification of their unsaturatedness.

In the case of verbs, their unsaturatedness, or, in his words, the nexus to an indeterminate subject, is signified by their augment; in the case of nouns in nominal sentences, their unsaturatedness is signified by their vocalization. Hence, contrary to what Avicenna thought, there is no need to provide "*huwa*" in order to complete an atomic proposition. This not only makes the theory more economical, but it does away with an awkward artificiality of language that was a remnant of the Arabic translation of Aristotle's Greek. It seems that for Quṭb al-Dīn there was no semantic intuition that would qualify "*huwa*" as a copula.

The crucial point for which I take Quṭb al-Dīn to have penned this later addition is that the judgment, which as we have seen is signified by the same sign that signifies the nexus, is expressed when an unsaturated predicate is saturated by a subject expression. In other words, a proposition expresses a judgment once a value is assigned to the variables in the argument places. Remarkable here is that Taḥtānī, based on his argument that hyparctic verbs are a distinct category of simple expressions, because they do not signify by themselves a complete meaning, formulates what in modern terminology would be called the distinction between 1-place and 2-place predicates. While real verbs have one empty argument place, hyparctic verbs are doubly unsaturated: they have two empty argument places. Filling these argument places, or assigning values to the variables, amounts to signifying the judgment-nexus: "Just as the real verb, if its subject is explicitly stated, signifies the judgment-nexus, so does the hyparctic verb, if its subject and predicate are explicitly stated" (II 27.6–8). The same applies to derived names. Even non-derived names in a nominal sentence work the same way: if the empty argument place that is signified by the vocalization is filled, the judgment-nexus is expressed.

Since the copula needed to signify the judgment-nexus is on Taḥtānī's view nothing but the syntactic property intrinsic to the semantic content of predicates when their argument place is filled, it should be clear why he thinks that there is no need to use an awkwardly artificial term like "*huwa*" as a third element in propositions. But then, since most propositions that consist of two simple expressions signify the three (or four, if nexus and judgment are distinguished) meanings needed for a complete atomic proposition, it makes little sense to classify atomic propositions into binary and ternary depending on whether or not a copula is used, or what kind of simple expression functions as a copula. All that remains is to acknowledge that there are certain propositions for which a semantic analysis may not identify these three meanings because of grammatical irregularities. But such cases are for grammarians to sort out, not logicians.

Based on this analysis Taḥtānī has a decidedly distinct take on the question of whether there are two distinct nexus in a proposition to account for modality and conversion. He summarizes (II 40.5–42.5) his lengthy discussion of Urmawī's, Rāzī's, and Khūnajī's (with whom he agrees) arguments (II 31–40), emphasizing his view that the parts of the proposition are four. All of them must be present in the mind for there to be a proposition: and as there are numerous possible nexus for the concept signified by the predicate, there must be present in the mind not only a specific nexus, say the nexus of *writer* to *Zayd*, but also the judgment that this specific nexus in fact obtains. If the former is not present in the mind, there is no way the latter can become present in the mind. If the former is present, but not the latter, there still is no proposition, as is the case with doubts and fictions. Only when a judgment occurs, a property occurs to "Zayd," namely that of being a subject, and another property to "writer," namely that of being a predicate. Hence predicate-hood and subject-hood are only realized once a judgment occurs, so that both nexus—that by subject-hood and that by predicate-hood—are not realized before the judgment is realized. Therefore, neither of them is part of the quiddity of a proposition.

Criticism in the Muḥākamāt

We do not know when Taḥtānī added the passage to the *Lawāmiʿ*. But it seems that he had formed his considered opinion before he wrote his *Muḥākamāt*, because what he says in his comment on the passage that Rāzī had used to advance his Repetition Argument reflects the points made in the later addition quoted earlier. And it also seems he knew Samarqandī's *Bishārāt*, which suggests he might also have known the *Qisṭās*, and gotten the idea of the judgment-nexus from him. The beginnings of their respective comments on the lemma are strikingly similar.

TEXT 69 (SAMARQANDĪ/TAḤTĀNĪ): SHAMS AL-DĪN AL-SAMARQANDĪ, *BISHĀRĀT AL-ISHĀRĀT* (SEE TEXT 60)/QUṬB AL-DĪN AL-RĀZĪ, *AL-MUḤĀKAMĀT BAYNA SHARḤAY L-ISHĀRĀT* (ANONYMOUS, TEHRAN 1965 [1393]), 125 (INFRA)

I say: when he explained that the negational particle is a part of the predicate, then the proposition is metathetic. If not, it is positive. It is necessary to explain this so it is known what the difference is between the negational particle that is part of the predicate and that which is not.

We say: The categorical proposition is composed of three parts. The meaning of the subject, the meaning of the predicate, and the meaning of the connection (*ijtimāʿ*) between them.

If one is to be conspicuous about the correspondence between expressions and meanings, then a third expression signifying the meaning of the connection is needed. This is the copula.

I say: when he explained that the negational particle is a part of the predicate, then the proposition is metathetic. If not, it is positive. It is necessary to explain this so it is known what the difference is between the negational particle that is part of the predicate and that which is not.

We say: The categorical proposition is composed of three parts. The subject, the predicate, and the nexus between them, which connects the predicate to the subject.

Just as it is right to signify the subject and the predicate by an expression, so it is right that the nexus be signified by an expression, so that the expressions correspond to the meanings. This utterance is called the copula.

But Taḥtānī continues to criticize the very exposition that their commentaries share almost verbatim, by using similar wording to that in Samarqandī's *Qisṭās* to argue for the conceptually distinct judgment-nexus as a fourth part of the proposition.

TEXT 70: QUṬB AL-DĪN AL-RĀZĪ AL-TAḤTĀNĪ, *AL-MUḤĀKAMĀT BAYNA SHARḤAY L-ISHĀRĀT* (ANONYMOUS, TEHRAN 1965 [1393]), 125–126 (INFRA)

Thus, we say: The categorical proposition is composed of three parts, the meaning of the subject, the meaning of the predicate, and the meaning of the combination of the two. Since the parallelism extends to utterances and meanings, inevitably there must be a third utterance that signifies the meaning of the combination, and this is the copula. This is the argument that people give, to the effect that the concept of the copula is the nexus between the meaning of the subject and the meaning of the pred-icate—but the verification [of the matter] requires that the concept of [the copula] is the *occurrence* of the nexus if it is an affirmation, or the lack of its occurrence if it is a negation. Hence, we say that the argument here should be to the effect that the concept of the copula is the nexus, which is the place of the occurrence of affirmation and negation, because the combination of two meanings occurs by considering the nexus *simpliciter*, whereas its occurrence or lack thereof is something additional to the meaning of combination. When there is a meaning-connection between the verb and the agent-noun, then the connection between them does not require the men-tioning of a copula. This is evident from the meaning of the verb, as we said. If the nexus to the subject is a part of its concept, then there is no need for a copula when we say "Zayd said," in contrast to "Said Zayd," because here "Zayd" is not an agent-noun, but its agent-noun is the hidden pronoun, and the sentence is predicated of it.

In this comment Taḥtānī first provides an exposition of his revised view on the analysis of propositions, insisting on the distinction between nexus and judgment. Referring to his discussions of the semantics of verbs, he reiterates that the copula is not needed to express the nexus, for verbs and derived names connect to the subject by dint of their semantic structure (*irtibāṭ ma'nawī*). Next, he discusses Rāzī's Repetition Argument, which he thinks contains in fact a twofold objection to Avicenna.

TEXT 71: QUṬB AL-DĪN AL-RĀZĪ AL-TAḤTĀNĪ, *AL-MUḤĀKAMĀT BAYNA SHARḤAY L-ISHĀRĀT* (ANONYMOUS, TEHRAN 1965 [1393]), 126–128 (INFRA)

If you say: Why is it not permissible that the hidden pronoun connects the sen-tence to Zayd, then we say: Because the copula is an auxiliary and the agent-noun is a name, and it is impossible that one utterance be both name and auxiliary, like-wise the derived names, since they fall in the place of the verbs, connect their agent-nouns by a connection in terms (*min jihati*) of the meaning. For example, when you say: "*a-qā'im Zayd* [Standing [is] Zayd?]" this is like when we say "*'a-yaqūmu Zayd* [Stands Zayd?]," in distinction to "*Zayd qā'im* [Zayd [is] standing]," for it requires the copula to prevent that "Zayd" is the agent-noun of "standing." The objection raised by the Imām [al-Rāzī] here contains in fact two aspects of an objection.

The first is that the Shaykh [Avicenna] mentioned in the *Eastern Philosophy* that the proposition is only binary when no copula is mentioned in it, either on account of not needing one, because its predicate is a statement-word or derived name that comprise the mentioned nexus, or on account of the economy [of expression], which is explained by the fact that derived names contain the signification of the nexus and there is thus no need for the copula. But [Avicenna's] words here, "and it really should be said 'Zayd, he [is a] writer,'" outright deny that. Thus, the commentator [Ṭūsī] pointed out that the two accounts converge, in that the independence of statement-words and derived names from the copula only applies with respect to their agent-nouns and the subject here is not an agent-noun.

The second is that "writer" is in fact one of the derived names, and they are connected all by themselves to their subjects on account of them signifying meanings that subsist for indeterminate subjects. For "writer," for example, does not signify writing alone, but it also signifies the subsistence of writing for something, and that is the nexus obtaining between writing and its subject. Since the nexus is internal to the concept of derived names [according to Rāzī], there is no need to mention a simple expression signifying the nexus, exactly as is the case with verbs. The commentator [Ṭūsī] says that this is careless [on the part of Rāzī], because the connection of the verb and the derived name [happens] all by itself only with the agent-noun, and what precedes them is not an agent-noun.

The first objection is that Avicenna contradicts himself by, on the one hand, saying that derived names connect to a subject by themselves, because they contain the signification of a nexus, and, on the other hand, in the *Ishārāt*, urging use of the copula "*huwa*" in sentences like "*Zayd huwa kātib,*" which clearly have a derived name as a predicate. The second is that in such sentences mentioning the copula in fact causes a repetition. Both objections, according to Taḥtānī, were countered by Ṭūsī, who said that verbs and derived names only connect by themselves insofar as they connect to an agent-noun preceding it. But Taḥtānī has a further criticism of Ṭūsī's position:

TEXT 72: QUṬB AL-DĪN AL-RĀZĪ AL-TAḤTĀNĪ, *AL-MUḤĀKAMĀT BAYNA SHARḤAY L-ISHĀRĀT* (ANONYMOUS, TEHRAN 1965 [1393]), 128 (INFRA)

But there is an issue here. For from "Zayd [is] standing" [*Zayd qāʾim*] we understand nothing but the judgment of Zayd's standing, just as we understand that from "Zayd got up" [*qāma Zayd*] as well. In both compounds that about which judgment is passed is Zayd, and that with which judgment is passed is [the act of] standing. As for that with which judgment is passed in the compound, it is the totality of verbs and agent-nouns, and that is a matter that does not attach to the meaning. The grammarians, when they were attempting to preserve their principles, said that it was necessary for the verb to precede the agent-noun [to avoid] confusion and disorder; they made it obligatory to conceal the agent-noun in the verb, which really should succeed the verb, if it is made explicit. But there is no verification for this argument because the Arabs who are not steeped in the science of grammar and the account of

> hidden pronouns still understand from both compounds the intended meaning. If it
> were not for that compound, there would be no need for hidden pronouns for such
> cases. For the Kūfan [grammarians] did not hide the agent-noun, but rather put the
> nominative on what preceded the verb. We concede this, but the nexus of the suc-
> ceeding verb is not to the utterance of a pronoun, but to its meaning, and its meaning
> is nothing but [the meaning of] "Zayd" that precedes it. It may be conceded that the
> verb is connected to what connects to it by itself, and then the succeeding verb is
> connected to Zayd by itself and there is no need for a copula.

Ṭūsī's argument is groundless, Taḥtānī concludes, for it rests on mere grammatical
convention, which could well be otherwise. As proof he adduces the fact that the
man in the street has no trouble understanding what is meant by Ṭūsī's example
sentences, no matter the word order or the lack of grammatical propriety. Hence,
there is no need for a copula.

CONCLUSIONS

If the discussions on the analysis of atomic propositions and the role of the copula
are at all indicative of broader developments in the history of Arabic logic, we may
note the following points. First, it would not seem that the 8th/14th century was
the beginning of ossification in the rational sciences, of which logic is the prime
example. It would seem that the problem was discussed more intensely and more
widely than before. There seems to be little connection between the inventiveness
and originality of a text and the genre it was written in.

While some commentaries on logical works, like those Ḥillī wrote on the handbooks of his teachers, are programmatically geared to explaining difficult texts (as
some of the *Ishārāt* commentaries were, while others were openly problematizing), some of the most inventive contributions to the problem of the copula came
from commentaries, like Taḥtānī's *Lawāmi ʿ*, or even from auto-commentaries, like
Samarqandī's *Sharḥ Qisṭās al-afkār*.

The systematic integration of *ādāb al-baḥth* into the logical canon that began
with Samarqandī is an expression of the cross-pollination between this newly
codified science and research in logic. Merging the Islamic tradition of juridical
eristics with the principles of Aristotelian propositional logic made the formalized rules for dialectics not only a part of the logical canon, but also an integral
part of the logicians' methodology. I suggest that the adoption of the dialectical
style of writing in logical works blurs the boundaries between independent works
and commentaries (as is evidenced by auto-commentaries), so that the deepening
of logical questions and original research may occur in both.

We may think of their intertextuality as an ongoing kind of regulated disputation. If that is indeed the case, the numerous unedited commentaries awaiting
study in manuscript libraries around the globe will further substantiate the idea

that the post-Avicennan logicians discussed here were not a coda to Ibn Khaldūn's four great Arabic philosophers, but represent an overture to a lively tradition of logical research, which was by then thoroughly Arabic, and fully severed from its Greek roots.

The scholars discussed in this last chapter all made, or likely will be shown to have made, contributions to logical theory more important than those they made to the discussions we traced. But Taḥtānī's intervention to do away with the traditional accounts of the analysis of atomic propositions is remarkable. However, it was hardly his own imagination alone that led him to it.

His teacher Ḥillī had already revised the traditional doctrine of binary and ternary propositions. Samarqandī had anticipated the distinction between judgment and judgeable content, and in his auto-commentary on the *Qisṭās* raised the point that the combination of subject and predicate may, in Arabic, simply be signified by the syntax that is marked by the signs of declension (*al-ʿallāmāt al-iʿrābiyya*). Ḥillī and Samarqandī, in turn, relied on the positions of their predecessors, as the discussions on conversion and the distinct nexus in a proposition show.

The increasing focus, beginning with Abharī and especially his student Kātibī, on the modalities of the nexus in conversion betrays a growing concern with the problems inherent in their conception of the proposition. Even though Taḥtānī's analysis rests on a notion that I think it is justified calling "unsaturatedness," there is of course no notion of two fundamentally different types like the Fregean concepts and objects, and there is no resistance to moving about an expression from the predicate-place to the subject-place. Whether Taḥtānī, and all other authors, saw problems with that, and if so, how precisely they accounted for them in their presentation of the syllogistic, is a subject for another study.

8

To Shīrāz and Mughal India

A "Semantic Turn"

Drawing to a close, I would like to give a sense of the intricacy of the operatic plot to which the developments of 7th/13th- and early 8th/14th-century Arabic logic were an overture. With Ḥillī and especially Taḥtānī, the new logic handbooks by Kātibī and Urmawī, containing many of the logical innovations made in the 7th/13th century, found their way into monumental dialectical commentaries that became the staple of advanced logical studies in large parts of the Islamic realm. In some sense, this was the end of an era, because after Taḥtānī Arabic logic became once again largely tied to textual commentary, not least on his own works.[1] But as suggested in the last chapter, this did not mean that original research in logic subsided—quite the contrary. It appears to have become more intense.

More importantly, however, developments in other disciplines—especially in semantics/rhetoric and in the emerging science of imposition (*'ilm al-waḍ'*)—had a palpable influence on theories of the copula and on the development of logic more generally. The late 8th/14th century may be described as a "semantic turn" in the rational sciences, where the most intensely examined philosophical questions became questions in philosophy of language.[2]

Couched in the evermore complex intertextual web of layered commentaries, authors developed their own thoughts in conversation with their predecessors within the discursive framework dictated by the rules of *ādāb al-baḥth* that had been codified by Samarqandī. In the late 8th/14th and throughout the 9th/15th century philosophers both reflected on the earlier tradition and forged something new. It is noteworthy, for example, that scholars rediscovered Fārābī's theory of predication, and that they independently—though much in the spirit of Fārābī's discussions of the semantics of particles—developed a new formal approach to the

156

semantics of the three Arabic word-classes, with a marked focus on explaining the semantics of particles and the copula.

TAFTĀZĀNĪ, *BALĀGHĀ*, AND THE DEVELOPMENT OF *'ILM AL-WAḌ'*

There are several strands along which discussions on the copula continued. Many of the texts containing them have yet to be discovered. But even the available sources are too numerous to be taken into account in any representative manner.[3] So let us pick only one strand of the tradition. Pursuing further the same line of transmission, there was another scholar—reportedly a student of Taḥtānī and Ījī, though the sources are late and there is no internal evidence of a personal relation[4]—by the name of Saʿd al-Dīn al-Taftāzānī (d. 792/1390). He wrote one further enormously influential handbook on logic titled *Tahdhīb al-manṭiq* (The Revision of Logic).[5] Three commentaries on this work were particularly influential as teaching texts well into the 14th/20th century across the Eastern Islamic world: the first in Ottoman Turkey and Mughal India (by Dawānī), the second at the al-Azhar College in Cairo (by ʿUbaydullāh Khabīṣī [*fl.* 950s/1540s?]), and the third in Safavid and Qajar Iran (by Mullā ʿAbdullāh Yazdī [d. 981/1573]).[6] We shall focus on the first strand here, in Shīrāz and then in Mughal India.

Ījī, who is best known for his seminal *kalām* work titled *al-Mawāqif fī ʿilm al-kalām* (Stations in Rational Theology), wrote not only a treatise on *ādāb al-baḥth* that was to replace Samarqandī's *al-Risāla al-Samarqandiyya*. In the new methodological sciences, he also redacted a short epistle on semantics (*al-Risāla al-waḍʿiyya*) of no more than a folio, which inaugurated a new formal discipline called *ʿilm al-waḍ'*.[7] We shall see that this new science provided the tools for a new conceptualization of the semantic role of particles and the copula. It was masterfully employed for that purpose by al-Sayyid al-Sharīf al-Jurjānī.

Taftāzānī and the Influence of balāgha

Before that, however, there was already in Taftāzānī's discussion of the copula a discernible influence from the tradition of Arabic semantics/rhetoric (*ʿilm al-balāgha*). It is perhaps no coincidence that Ījī also wrote two important works in that discipline, namely, *al-Fawāʾid al-ghiyāthiyya* (The Useful Points for Ghiyāth [al-Dīn Muḥammad]) and *al-Madkhal fī ʿilm al-maʿānī wa l-bayān wa l-badāʾiʿ* (Introduction to the Science of Semantics, Clear Exposition, and Stylistic Figures of New Poetry).[8] This discipline had first been codified in Abū Yaʿqūb al-Sakkākī's (d. 626/1229) *Miftāḥ al-ʿulūm* (Key to the Sciences) and was then widely disseminated through Jalāl al-Dīn al-Qazwīnī al-Khaṭīb's (d. 739/1338) more accessible summary of it, the *Talkhīṣ al-Miftāḥ* (Epitome of the Key).[9]

Taftāzānī, a central figure linking Taḥtānī and Ījī to the later tradition, wrote—besides his *Tahdhīb al-manṭiq*—an influential commentary on Kātibī's *Shamsiyya*. Like Ījī, he wrote several influential works in the tradition of *'ilm al-balāgha*, most importantly *al-Sharḥ al-Muṭawwal 'alā Talkhīṣ al-Miftāḥ* (The Long Commentary on [Qazwīnī's] Epitome of the Key).[10] But unlike Ījī, he was at the same time an influential logician. The confluence of the different semantic disciplines—*'ilm al-ma'ānī, 'ilm al-waḍ'*, and logic—can be discerned in Taftāzānī's treatment of the copula.

While Taftāzānī agrees with Taḥtānī that there are four distinct parts of the proposition and that the copula may be employed to signify both the nexus between subject and predicate and the judgment-nexus, he uses the grammatical terminology also typically used in *balāgha* works to explain that the nexus is in fact a single entity that primarily attaches to the predicate. One of the constituting elements of *'ilm al-balāgha* was semantics (*'ilm al-ma'ānī*), and it consisted of discussions on the multiple ways in which a grammatical predicate (*musnad*) may connect to a grammatical subject (*musnad ilayhi*).[11] This is the terminology Taftāzānī employed in his commentary on Kātibī's *Shamsiyya*:

TEXT 73: SA'D AL-DĪN AL-TAFTĀZĀNĪ, *SHARḤ AL-RISĀLA AL-SHAMSIYYA* (ṢĀLIḤ 2011), 204.3–205.02

This is why they limited the utterances to three, for the copula signifying the judgment [also] signifies this nexus. When the judgment obtains, then the property of being a subject applies to the term on which judgment is passed (I mean: because it is being judged and made the grammatical subject [*musnad ilayhi*]), and the property of being a predicate applies to the term by which judgment is passed (I mean: because it is being predicated and made the grammatical predicate [*musnad*]). [. . .] The true answer is that the nexus between two terms is a single entity that exists whenever [they] are joined. When the predicate is considered, it may be called the "ascription" (*isnād*) because it is being ascribed [to something]; when the subject is considered, it may be called the "ascribed-to" (*al-isnād ilayhi*) because [something] is being ascribed to it. The distinction between the "ascription" and the "ascribed-to" is realized by the fact that the former is an expression of the nexus insofar as it attaches to the predicate.

The asymmetry of the subject-predicate relation is here explained in terms of the asymmetry evident in the grammatical terminology of *isnād*. Just like Samarqandī, Taftāzānī argues that being a subject and being a predicate are facts that only obtain once a judgment is made. Picking up on the discussions about whether the nexus that is a property of the subject and the nexus that is a property of the predicate are to be conceptually distinguished, he argues that this is just a pseudo-distinction, because it is simply a matter of perspective parallel to the grammatical distinction between *musnad* and *musnad ilayhi*. Further, he thinks that that was Rāzī's position:

TEXT 74: SAʿD AL-DĪN AL-TAFTĀZĀNĪ, *SHARḤ AL-RISĀLA AL-SHAMSIYYA* (ṢĀLIḤ 2011), 205.3–11

What the Imām [Rāzī] said in the *Mulakhkhaṣ*, namely that the nexus that is part of the proposition is that of the subject being a subject, does not contradict—as most of the later logicians have falsely assumed—what he says in the commentary on the *Ishārāt*, namely that the copula expresses the nexus of the predicate to the subject and hence the modality of the proposition is the same as the quality of that nexus. But it is obvious that the nexus of the predicate is a property of the predicate, i.e., being-a-predicate, that is: an ascription. [What Rāzī said is correct] because the nexus of the predicate to the subject is [also] a property of the subject, that is, its being such that the predicate is connected to it, I mean: an ascribed-to. Just as the predicate may be described by its nexus to the subject, so may the subject be described by the nexus of the predicate to it. If we now make the nexus to the subject part of the property [qualifying the subject], then it is a property of the subject. Otherwise, it will be a property of the predicate. This is just like when there is an image of a thing in the mind; this is a property of the mind, as we said before. Remember this!

Taftāzānī reads Rāzī as claiming what in fact is his own position: the nexus is a relational property. Depending on whether the subject or the predicate is in focus, it will be a relational property of the subject, or of the predicate. The parallel to be drawn from the comparison with a mental image being a property of the mind is presumably this: Suppose you have an image of a red apple before your mind. The relation between the image and your mind is now similar to the relation between subject and predicate. While you may say that it is a property of the image that it is produced by your mind, the more natural way to think about it is to say that the mental image is a property of your mind. Likewise, you may say that it is a property of the subject that the predicate is ascribed to it, but the more natural way to put it is that the predicate's disposition to be ascribable to the subject is a property of the predicate. This idea is however difficult to square with Rāzī's insistence that the nexus that is part of a proposition is a property of the subject.

Raising the question whether the copula is in fact an auxiliary (*adā*) or a pronoun (*ḍamīr*), Taftazānī uses terminology that is otherwise used in ʿ*ilm al waḍʿ*. Instead of calling the meaning of an auxiliary "incomplete" (*ghayr tāmm* or *nāqiṣ*), he uses "dependent" (*ghayr mustaqill*).[12] He objects to both options, and questions the idea that hyparctic verbs are copulae, eventually proposing a version of Taḥtānī's account:

TEXT 75: SAʿD AL-DĪN AL-TAFTĀZĀNĪ, *SHARḤ AL-RISĀLA AL-SHAMSIYYA* (ṢĀLIḤ 2011), 206.1–207.4

The first [objection] is that if what is understood from an utterance determined that such utterance is an auxiliary, then all nouns that signify connections or relations would have to be auxiliaries.

The second is that if the utterance "was" (*kāna*) were a copula, then "Every old man was a youngster" would convert to "Some youngster was an old man" according to the conversion rules. But since the converse of this proposition is "Some of what was young is an old man" we know that the utterance "was" (*kāna*) is part of the predicate and signifies the specification of time.

The third is that the utterance "he" (*huwa*) in "Zayd is knowing" (*Zayd huwa ʿālim*) is a pronoun referring back to Zayd as an expression of him, which is what the grammarians call a subject (*mubtadaʾ*), and as such has no signification of a nexus whatsoever. If I mean by this what they call the partitive or adjuvative pronoun, then why is it not [needed] in "Zayd [is] knowing" (*Zayd ʿālim*)? If it is assumed that it is in there, then [mentioning] it only serves to disambiguate and emphasize.

The true answer is that what comes after it is a report (*khabar*) and not an adjective (*naʿt*), and that it has no signification of the nexus whatsoever. What should be understood from this is that the copula in the Arabic language consists in the vocalizations that mark the declension. But the nominative vocalization must be real or assumed, otherwise it does not work. For if we say "Zayd, knowing" (*Zayd, ʿālim*) in the sense of a list and without case-marking vocalization, no copula is understood from it, or any ascription. But if we say "Zayd is knowing" (*Zaydun ʿālimun*) with nominative markers, then it is understood. Hence, the copula is the case-marker [in Arabic]. [[This is amply clear, and I don't know how this could have escaped the notice of anyone. How could anyone think otherwise?

Based on what we said, if the subject and the predicate are both indeclinable (*mabniyyīn*), then the proposition is binary. If they are both declinable, then it is a complete ternary [proposition], and if only one of them is declinable, then it is a deficient ternary [proposition]. I said: If the copula is expressed as a case-marking vocalization, then the binary proposition is one in which the case-marking vocalization is assumed, not one in which it is realized. The ternary one is [a proposition] in which it is realized. The completeness or deficiency of the ternary [proposition] depends on the completeness of the realization [of the vocalization] or lack thereof. All of this is because what is clearly observable when a proposition is being understood, is the existence of a copula, by which I mean that one cannot say about a proposition that it is true or false except if there exists a copula (and a nexus).]][13] And in general, the utterance "he" (*huwa*) is not employed in the Arabic language as a copula, as can be seen by the fact that none of the serious scholars use it, except the verifying philosophers.

Taftāzānī rejects the use of "*huwa*" as a copula and states that in Arabic the vocalizations play the same role as the copula plays in other languages. From the following remarks it is clear that he was puzzled by the questions concerning the role of the copula and that he set out to do research, both historical and empirical, to find answers to these questions.

TEXT 76: SAʿD AL-DĪN AL-TAFTĀZĀNĪ, *SHARḤ AL-RISĀLA AL-SHAMSIYYA* (ṢĀLIḤ 2011), 207.5–209.2

I was immediately wondering how to solve these problems and began inquiring into the truth of the matter until I found in *The Book of Utterances and Letters*[14] by the verifying philosopher Abū Naṣr al-Fārābī something indicating the following. They [i.e., the philosophers] never meant that the utterance "*huwa*" in Arabic is established for the copula, and they did not use it in this way. Rather, what they meant is that the philosophers translated it (*naqalūhā*) like that. He said that when Aristotle's philosophy was translated into Arabic, the philosophers—who spoke Arabic and forged their own Arabic expressions for the meanings [they found in] Aristotle's philosophy and logic—needed an utterance they could use instead of the Persian *hast* and the Greek *estin*. Those are the words that signify the a-temporal copulation of a predicate-name to a subject. But they did not find any expression in Arabic that was originally coined for that [meaning]—as opposed to the temporal copula. For there are the hyparctic verbs like "was" (*kāna*), "is" (*yakūnu*), and "will be" (*sayakūnu*) signifying that. So they used those instead of the Persian *hast* and the Greek *estin*. But some then preferred the expression "*huwa*" because it had already been in use metonymically (*kināyatan*), as in "This, he's Zayd" (*hadhā huwa Zayd*) or "This, he's the poet" (*hadhā huwa al-shāʿir*). The utterance "*huwa*" is distant enough [in its meaning] to be used here metonymically. So they came to use "*huwa*" in Arabic instead of *hast* in Persian and they [even] formed a *maṣdar* from it, "*huwiyya*," just like "humanity" (*insāniyya*) from "human" (*insān*). Some also chose to exchange "*huwa*" for "*mawjūd*" and they replaced "*huwiyya*" by "*wujūd*" and "*kāna*," "*yakūnu*," and "*sayakūnu*" by "*wujida*," "*yūjadu*," and "*sayūjadu*." These were [Fārābī's] words.

Based on the above: If the utterance "*huwa*" is expressed, as in "Zayd, he's knowing" (*Zayd huwa ʿālim*), then the proposition is called ternary on account of its having three parts on the level of utterances. If it is omitted because the mind perceives its meaning, then it is called binary on account of its being shortened to two [utterances]. The distinction is based on the mind's distinguishing the use of two copulae together, or using only the temporal one, or only the a-temporal one, either [as being] necessary or possible or impossible, so that there are nine (combinations).

It is remarkable that Taftāzānī went back to Fārābī's discussions in the *KH* (and perhaps *AM?*) and studied them in detail. Leaving aside the Andalusian philosophers, no one in the tradition surveyed here showed awareness of Fārābī's linguistic theory to this extent. Noteworthy is also that he uses the term "*kināya*" (roughly, metonymy) for the metonymical use of "*huwa*" that predisposed it to be transferred to a copulative use by the early philosophers: *kināya*, the use of a word to signify something that is logically related to its original meaning, is one of the *balāgha* notions central to ʿilm al-bayān.[15]

Taftāzānī went further:

But [Kātibī] said only "in some languages," for we don't know if it is possible to omit the copula in all languages. Regarding what has been said about the Persian language, namely that it is always required to mention a copula, either as a simple utterance or as part of the vocalization, this is only the case when the predicate is not a verb, as in "Zayd came" or "Zayd comes" (*Zayd mī āmad va āyad*). We thoroughly investigated the matter and found that in all languages that we had access to and that do not require the use of a copula (based on what people explained to me), the predicate statement-word by itself signifies the nexus. Know that it is evident that the rules of logic do not comprise propositions whose predicate is a verb, i.e., sentences that the grammarians call verbal sentences (*jumla fi ʿliyya*), like "Zayd stands" (*qāma Zayd*). But [this sentence] may be reinterpreted as "Zayd is a person to whom 'standing' applies."

In the end, Taftāzānī sees himself corroborated by his historical and empirical research. The discussions on the use of "*huwa*" as a copula all have been misdirected, simply because such use was never meant to be more than a rendering of the Greek. In Arabic, vocalizations are enough for that purpose. Many languages need not express a copula-word, not even Persian when the predicate is a verb. In general, verbal predicates always include the signification of the copula, and even though verbal sentences are not used in syllogistic premises, all verbal sentences can be suitably paraphrased. Some *balāgha* notions central to *ʿilm al-maʿānī* (*isnād*) and *ʿilm al-bayān* (*kināya*) clearly had an influence on Taftāzānī's approach to the question of the semantic role of the copula. Even though he also uses terminology associated with *ʿilm al-waḍʿ* literature (e.g., *mustaqill*), it is difficult to determine how far the influence went here.

The Influence of ʿilm al-waḍʿ

When compared to *balāgha*, which deals with applied semantics, *ʿilm al-waḍʿ* may be said to deal with theoretical or foundational semantics. The discipline of *balāgha* developed out of the long tradition of Arabic literary criticism, out of the tradition of writings on the inimitability of the Qurʾān (*iʿjāz*), and out of legal theory (*uṣūl al-fiqh*), arguably subsuming influences from Aristotelian Poetics, Rhetoric, and Logic. But *ʿilm al-waḍʿ* was entirely new and its genealogical story remains less clear, as, in fact, much else about this strange new science.

Other than an unpublished dissertation and three short articles by Bernhard Weiss, no substantial scholarship on this new science exists in any Western language, and the vast majority of the over forty commentaries on the short foundational and eponymous work for this new science remains unedited.[16] An indication of the significance of this new science, besides the sheer number of commentaries on Ījī's *al-Risāla al-waḍʿiyya*, is the fact that the foundational principles of Ījī's short treatise on semantics came to be included in a number of pivotal works from different disciplines, ranging from jurisprudence (*uṣūl al-fiqh*), morphology (*al-ṣarf*), and theology (*kalām*), to semantics/rhetoric (*balāgha*) and logic (*manṭiq*).[17]

If Taftāzānī was aware of and perhaps influenced by Ījī's *Risāla*, it was al-Sayyid al-Sharīf al-Jurjānī who visibly tied together *balāgha*, *ʿilm al-waḍʿ*, and logic. Before we turn to his works that repeatedly make reference to ideas developed in Ījī's *Risāla*, a brief outline of some general ideas formulated there is in order. Roughly, *ʿilm al-waḍʿ* is the science of the founding of language—except that it does not ask who founded it or how it came into being.[18] The term *waḍ ʿ* is used in the tradition for the imposition or assignment of utterances (*alfāẓ*) to ideas or concepts (*ma ʿānī*). It was widely accepted that it was Allah who made the assignments for all utterances and meanings when he taught Adam the names of all things, as is stated in the Qur'ān (al-Baqara, Q2:31). After some initial discussions about the origin of language that were inherited from the Greek tradition, the Arabic tradition mustered little opposition to the idea that language was conventional (i.e., established by *thesis*), and not natural (i.e., established by *physis*).[19]

Hence, the science of imposition was not out to find answers to the question of the origin of language. Rather, Ījī's *al-Risāla al-waḍ ʿiyya* sought to categorize different types of meaning assignments and thus to lay bare the underlying semantic structure of all the different bits of the Arabic language. The question of the founder of language (*wāḍi ʿ al-lugha*) was eventually irrelevant to *ʿilm al-waḍ ʿ*. Even though it may rightly be called an "Islamic" science, it was a study of the semantics of natural language that could be carried out in any language and cultural context. It was in a sense the study of the constraints on linguistic meaning by asking how the founder of language must have conceived of language so that it could work as well as it does.

Ījī distinguishes three different sets of ways in which the founder of language imposed linguistic items for meanings. The first is a distinction between general (*ʿamm*) and particular (*khāṣṣ*) imposition.[20] He argues that particles and pronouns, even though they can be applied to many referents, always fix a particular referent in a speech-situation. Second, he distinguishes between the imposition of morphological generality and particularity. Structural features of word formations can be understood as a type of morphological generality, in the sense that for example *fā ʿil* structures will always signify an agent under normal conditions, even though the referent can be anything whatsoever. And third, he distinguishes between impositions of linguistic items that need something additional to refer to their metaphorical meaning, and impositions that directly refer to their referents.

One radically novel aspect of Ījī's theory was his description of how the reference of pronouns is determined.[21] Pronouns are established as a general imposition for a specific reference (*waḍ ʿ ʿāmm li-khāṣṣ*). Against the ideas of his predecessors who assumed that meanings were ideas arising in the mind of the founder of language for which utterances were imposed like tags for artifacts in a museum, Ījī noted that this account was inadequate for certain indexical expressions like personal, demonstrative, and relative pronouns—and, by extension, to particles of all kinds.

Take our pronoun "*huwa*," which logicians have been using as a copula. On the old account it is inexplicable how "he" can refer now to Zayd and then to ʿAmr. If "he" referred to a universal or a class, say the class of "absent male persons" (*ghā'ib*), it remains unexplained how it can refer to particulars. So we have to assume, according to Ījī, that the founder of language had this general idea arising in his mind, but then established "*huwa*" as referring not to the class of "absent male persons," but to every single particular member of that class individually. The specific reference is then fixed in any given context or speech-situation (*qarīna muʿayyana*).

For Ījī, particles semantically function in a similar way: they are established as a general imposition for a specific reference (*waḍʿ ʿāmm li-khāṣṣ*). Particles all signify relations. They are established—on the basis of a universal idea—as referring to each particular instance of whatever relation they signify. However, in contrast to pronouns, their reference is fixed for each given context by supplying the *relata* of that relation. This novel semantic theory for indexical pronouns and for particles was taken up by Jurjānī and employed in his discussion of the copula.

AL-SAYYID AL-SHARĪF AL-JURJĀNĪ AND THE "SEMANTIC TURN"

Zayn al-Dīn Abū l-Ḥassān al-Jurjānī (d. 818/1413), who because of his noble lineage is called al-Sayyid al-Sharīf al-Jurjānī in the sources, was an important figure in the development of Arabic logic, linking Taftāzānī to Dawānī.[22] For a while he enjoyed the same patronage as Taftāzānī, who was twenty years older, at Timur's court in Samarqand. In the years between 789/1387 and Taftāzānī's death in 792/1390 the two scholars reportedly became intellectual rivals engaging in public court debates. Earlier in his life, after some time spent in Anatolia, Jurjānī studied with a mysterious Mubārakshāh in Cairo. Mubārakshāh had read the *Mawāqif* under Ījī himself and read it with Jurjānī, who would later write the definitive commentary on it. He likely also redacted his glosses on Taḥtānī's logic under Mubārakshāh's guidance and might have been sent to Cairo for this reason by Taḥtānī himself.[23] Eventually Jurjānī settled as a teacher in Shīrāz, where Dawānī's father was among his students. After his stay in Samarqand, he returned to Shīrāz in 807/1405 and stayed there until his death.[24]

Jurjānī wrote a set of influential glosses on Taḥtānī's commentaries on the *Shamsiyya* and the *Maṭāliʿ* as well as a short ("*Sughrā*") and long ("*Kubrā*") introduction to logic in Persian.[25] The glosses on the *Lawāmiʿ* only cover material from the first part, on the acquisition of concepts, heavily focusing on semantic questions, and never even reach the part on the acquisition of assent, where the parts of the proposition are discussed. Nevertheless, Jurjānī has much to say about the copula and the nexus. For example, he treats at length the question about third-person inflected verbs that Avicenna had raised, which Taḥtānī had discussed extensively.[26]

As El-Rouayheb has pointed out, Jurjānī's logical œuvre exemplifies a larger trend of moving away from the technicalities of the syllogistic and toward a focus on issues pertaining to semantics and what we today call "philosophy of language."[27] For example, in his glosses on the *Lawāmiʿ*, Jurjani spends a good third just on Taḥtānī's proem, raising philosophical questions as he considers the *matn* lemma by lemma. The lemmatic comments, however, do not serve a primarily exegetical purpose. Rather, they are often taken as prompts for independent philosophical arguments.

Jurjānī seems to have also played an instrumental role in the ascendancy of Shīrāz as a major center of philosophy in the 9th/15th and 10th/16th centuries.[28] His glosses came to be read alongside Taḥtānī's commentaries in Shīrāz and far beyond, and his emphasis on semantic matters certainly influenced the later tradition. His immediate influence is reflected in the works of Dawānī, who wrote his own super-glosses on Jurjānī's glosses on the *Lawāmiʿ*.[29]

While the glosses on the *Lawāmiʿ* end before the sections where the parts of the proposition are discussed, Jurjānī's shorter gloss on Taḥtānī's *Shamsiyya* commentary treats the issue, showing awareness of Taftazānī's commentary:

TEXT 78: AL-SAYYID AL-SHARĪF AL-JURJĀNĪ, *ḤĀSHIYA ʿALĀ TAḤRĪR AL-QAWĀʿID AL-MANṬIQIYYA* (BĪDĀRFAR), 233.7 (*INFRA*)–234.13 (*INFRA*)

His words: The utterance that signifies the occurrence of the nexus also signifies the nexus itself. I say: [That is, it has a] clear and regular signification, but also an implicational (*iltizāmiyya*) signification.

His words: And [the nexus] is not distinct from its consisting of that on which and that by which judgment is passed. I say: He means that <u>the nexus which connects that on which judgment is passed with that by which judgment is passed by means of a judgment is conceived insofar as it is a state obtaining between the two, and it is a tool (alā) that helps to understand their state. But this meaning is not distinct [from the two]. This is correct, because [the meaning] is something on which judgment is passed or by which judgment is passed, so the utterance signifying this is an auxiliary (adā)</u>.

His words: But it may be in the form of a noun, like "huwa" in the example mentioned. I say: This issue has been debated. The utterance "*huwa*" in "Zayd, he (*huwa*) is knowing" signifies Zayd, because the suffix pronoun refers back to him and in this case is not a copula. It has been said that in this proposition it is the nominative vocalization (*ʿālim-un*) because it signifies the connection (*irtibāṭ*) and the [grammatical] relation (*isnād*). The proof for this is that when simple [utterances] are spoken and the [vocalized] endings are muted, like with "Zayd," [instead of the nominative Zaydun] then no composition obtains, nor is any [grammatical] relation signified.

Or it is in the form of a statement-word, like the defective "*kāna*" and its conjugations, and then it is called a temporal [copula], because in contrast to "*huwa*" and its sisters it signifies time. For those do not signify time at all. This issue has been debated as well. For what is signified by "*kāna*" is something additional to what is signified by the copula, because "*kāna*" signifies a time that is not part of what the copula signifies.

His words: This points to the fact that languages are different with regard to how the copula is used. I say: It is said that the point is precisely that there are three things to consider. Necessity, impossibility, and possibility, and to multiply those by three further things. These are the joint presence of two copulae together, of the temporal copula alone, and of the non-temporal copula alone, resulting in the obvious number [i.e., nine].

Like Taftāzānī, Jurjānī agrees with Taḥtānī that there are four distinct parts of a proposition. And like Taftāzānī, he explains the nexus, expressed by the vocalization in Arabic, as being the relation of *isnād*. The number of the possible combinations, depending on whether both temporal and atemporal copulae are used together, or each of them separately, for each of the modalities, is the same as Taftāzānī's. But the explanation of why the nexus is a single entity is different.

This explanation (underlined in the text) is based on ideas Jurjānī has elaborated more fully elsewhere, notably in his glosses on Taftāzānī's *Muṭawwal*.[30] Jurjani considered these ideas important enough to redact them as independent short treatises titled *Risāla ʿalā Taḥqīq maʿnā al-ḥarf* (Epistle on the Verification of the Meaning of Particles) and *al-Risāla al-Mirʾātiyya* (Mirror Epistle).[31] A closer look at the *Risāla ʿalā Taḥqīq maʿnā al-ḥarf* will suffice to demonstrate how Jurjānī incorporated developments in *balāgha* and *ʿilm al-waḍʿ* to reconceptualize the semantic role of the copula.

A short treatise of a mere two folios, the mirror epistle is a fascinating testimony that has however not yet received a satisfactory interpretation.[32] To appreciate the text fully, it needs to be read in connection with the discussions on the copula. The treatise consists of four parts: an introductory simile in which a mirror is likened to the object of mental perception, a discussion of the semantics of particles and names, a discussion of the semantics of verbs, and a section containing three objections and replies. The introductory mirror simile is key to understanding the discussion of the semantics of names, particles, and verbs.

Jurjānī explicitly relates the mirror analogy to the predicative nexus in propositions in such a way that the mirror is to eyesight what the nexus is to mental perception:

TEXT 79: AL-SAYYID AL-SHARĪF AL-JURJĀNĪ, *RISĀLA ʿALĀ TAḤQĪQ MAʿNĀ AL-ḤARF* (AKTAŞ 2018), 83.3–18

Know that the relation (*nisba*) between mental perception and its perceptible objects is like the relation between eyesight and its visible objects. If you look into a mirror, you see an image in it. Now there are two possible situations for you. First: You are paying attention to that image, intentionally observing it, and thus turning the mirror into a tool for seeing [the image]. It will not escape your notice that it is a mirror, even if you are seeing it in this way. But it is not [a mirror] inasmuch as you believe that you judge it to be [so] and turn your attention to its properties. Second: You turn your attention to the mirror itself and you intentionally look at it, such that it is appropriate for you to make a judgment concerning it. In this case you observe the image only in a secondary way because your attention is not directed toward it.

It is clear that visible objects are sometimes seen by themselves, and sometimes as a tool to see something else. Now, draw the analogy for these meanings perceived by mental perception—I mean, the internal faculty—and clearly bring it out for the following sentences: "Zayd is standing" (*Zayd qāʾim*), and "The nexus of standing to Zayd" (*nisbat al-qiyām ilā Zayd*). Again, there are two situations for the way in which you perceive the nexus of standing to [Zayd]. But the nexus in the first situation is perceived inasmuch as it is a state of affairs obtaining between Zayd and standing, so it is a tool for getting to know the state of affairs both are involved in. It is as if [the nexus] was a mirror for seeing the two. That is why it is impossible to pass judgment on [the nexus] or use it for passing judgment [on something else]. In the second situation, [the nexus] is regarded by itself and intentionally perceived as such. Now you can pass a judgment on it. Whereas, in the first situation, the nexus is a concept that cannot be independently understood, in the second situation, it is a concept that can be understood independently. Just as there is a need to express concepts that are seen by themselves and that are independently understood, so there is a need to express meanings that are seen for something else, and that cannot be independently understood.

To clarify the nature of the predicative nexus and to give an account of why it is that the nexus can be an object of both conception and assent, Jurjānī distinguishes between two distinct ways in which the nexus as a mental object can be perceived. The first is like a mirror, in that the object is not really perceived in itself, but only as a tool to perceive a state of affairs, like an image seen in the mirror. On this view, the nexus is no more a part of the state of affairs than the mirror is a part of the image it reflects. The analogy stops, presumably, at the point where our minds cannot directly perceive a state of affairs without the tool of the nexus, whereas our eyes can very well see the image that the mirror reflects, directly and without the help of the mirror.

The advantage of this account is that Jurjānī need not postulate more than one nexus, as logicians from Rāzī onward have done, and thus avoids all theoretical complications that come with it. The account also forestalls any regress arguments because the nexus is not a real relation connecting two items to form a state of affairs. It just is the tool necessary for us to be able to conceptualize that state of affairs. As such it is the object of conception, but only accidentally, and it can only be conceptualized once the constituents of that state of affairs are conceptualized with it. It cannot (yet) be the object of assent. It is, as Taftāzānī in the terminology of *'ilm al-waḍ'* had also characterized auxiliaries, semantically dependent (*ghayr mustaqill*) because it cannot be understood independently from its *relata*.

The second way the mind can perceive the nexus is in the way that one can look at a mirror itself, as for example, to use Weiss's formulation, "when cleaning it."[33] On that view the nexus is a concept that can be independently understood and thus can fill the subject or predicate place of a proposition. Presumably you can, for example, judge that the nexus is possible or necessary, or that it is true or false, or even, as Jurjānī does, judge that the nexus is the tool necessary for getting to know a state of affairs.

On this account, the reason that there is only one entity that is the nexus between subject and predicate is not simply that it is the relation of *isnād* that may be considered from the perspective of the *musnad* or the *musnad ilayhi*, as Taftāzānī claimed earlier. Jurjānī here gives more fundamental grounds. What he said in his glosses on Taḥtānī's *Shamsiyya* commentary given earlier has to be understood in the context of the mirror analogy. The nexus is merely the tool, like a mirror, for conceiving a state of affairs *in such a way that eventually it can be judged to be true or false*. It is nothing over and above the constituting elements of the state of affairs itself. But it can be conceptually isolated and made a mental object that can then be judged, just as a mirror can be regarded by itself and judged (to be clean or dirty, or whatever). This does not mean, however, that there is more than one nexus. What logicians have called the judgment-nexus is only distinct in the sense that the nexus needs to be viewed in the second way to pass a judgment.

Based on the mirror analogy, Jurjānī next gives a summary account of the semantics of particles—under which copulae presumably also fall—that is largely lifted out of the ʿilm al-waḍʿ tradition. Particles as essentially relational in meaning semantically behave exactly like the copulae—or whichever signs there are that signify a nexus.

Now that this is settled, we say: "Beginning" (*al-ibtidāʾ*) has the following meaning. It is a state for something other than it, that is however still attached to it. When the mind intentionally regards [this concept] by itself, it is a concept that is independent by itself as long as it is regarded by itself. It is appropriate to be judged or to be used to judge [another concept]. What is attached to it is necessarily perceived in a secondary way and generally speaking accidental. In this sense, it is signified by the utterance "beginning" (*ibtidāʾ*). After regarding it in this way you can supply a specific attachment to it. So we say for example: "The beginning of my trip to Baṣra" and here the independence of the concept is retained.

When, however, the mind regards it insofar as it is a state of affairs obtaining between the trip and Baṣra, [the mind] turns it into a tool to get to know the state of affairs they are involved in, and the concept is no longer independent by itself. It is no longer appropriate to judge it or use it to judge [another concept]. In this sense it is signified by the expression "from" (*min*).

Jurjānī extends the mirror analogy further to the semantics of particles. Just as the nexus may be perceived by itself as a mirror may be seen by itself, so the meaning of particles may be seen in the same way. As such it is independently understood and can fill the subject- or predicate-place of a proposition. When we want to refer to this independent meaning, naturally we cannot use a particle, but must use a noun, just as we have to use a noun ("*nisba*") to refer to what the copula signifies. The isolated meaning of the particle "from" (*min*) is "beginning." That isolated meaning is universal because it is applicable to many things. It can be independently understood, and it can be in the subject- or predicate-place of a proposition.

It is this general idea the founder of language has before the mind when establishing the particular reference to every instance of "beginning" for the particle "from" (*min*), as Ījī laid out in *al-Risāla al-Waḍʿiyya*.[34] Similar to the reference of pronouns, the reference of particles like "from" (*min*) needs to be fixed by context. Since the meaning of particles is like the nexus and the mirror a tool for getting to know a relational state, the meaning becomes fixed only once the *relata* are supplied.

Nouns and particles are counterparts in that nouns express the isolated and independent idea that particles express as a function of the *relata* that fix the specific particular reference. Verbs, which Jurjānī discusses next, combine both aspects in their semantic structure:

TEXT 81: AL-SAYYID AL-SHARĪF AL-JURJĀNĪ, *RISĀLA ʿALĀ TAḤQĪQ MAʿNĀ AL-ḤARF* (AKTAŞ 2018), 85.3–9

Now that you have learned the meaning of "name" and "particle," know that a verb (*fiʿl*), like "hit" (*ḍaraba*), signifies a concept that can be independently understood—which is that of "event"—and a meaning that cannot be independently understood, but that is a tool for seeing something else. I mean the particular judgment-nexus in the earlier example. It is regarded insofar as it is a state of affairs between two terms and a tool for getting to know the state of affairs they are involved in. But one of them is determined by the signification of the utterance, whereas the other—even if it is determined in itself in some way—is regarded in just this way. Otherwise it would not be possible for that nexus to obtain. But the utterance signifies it, even though the nexus that is a part of what the verb signifies does not obtain except when the agent (*fāʿil*) is also considered. Hence, [the agent] inevitably needs to be mentioned, too, just as in the case with what is attached to the particle.

Verbs are mixed creatures for Jurjānī. Their semantic content consists of two elements. One element functions like a name, signifying a concept that can be independently understood, i.e., "hitting" or whatever event a given verb signifies. The other element functions like a particle, signifying a nexus that at first serves as a tool for conceptualizing a state of affairs, just like the mirror image. However, there is a difference:

TEXT 82: AL-SAYYID AL-SHARĪF AL-JURJĀNĪ, *RISĀLA ʿALĀ TAḤQĪQ MAʿNĀ AL-ḤARF* (AKTAŞ 2018), 85.10–86.11

When one considers that the verb includes [the signification] of a concept that is independent in itself, it becomes distinct from the particle. Now, when it is considered further that it includes [the signification of] a complete nexus to the effect that that independent concept [i.e., "event"] is connected to something else by this nexus, then a judgment comes to pass, namely, with regard to this independent concept. And this does not apply to the class of particles, or to the class of names.

In general, then, when a particle is instituted for specific relational (*nisbiyya*) concepts—which are tools for seeing other concepts and for getting to know the states of affairs they are involved in—by a general imposition (*waḍʿan ʿāmman*), then it is impossible that [such a concept] be judged or used to pass judgment. It is inevitable that each of the two concepts [i.e., those signified by the two terms] be regarded by themselves, for it to be possible that the nexus between one and the other can be considered, and what attaches to [the nexus] needs to be mentioned and considered in parallel between the utterances and the mental images.

When a name is instituted for concepts that are regarded by themselves and can be independently understood, then no complete nexus is expressed alongside them, neither in the sense that they are connected to something else, nor in the sense that it is possible to connect to them a judgment or use them for a judgment.

As for the verb, when one considers [the notion of] "event" in it (which is the independent concept), its connection to something else is joined to it as a complete nexus (which is the tool for seeing its two [related] terms); [in that case] it is necessary that it be [also] connected [*musnad*] to the event (for that had been considered part of the concept at [the original] imposition), and that its agent be mentioned so that this nexus obtains. As for the totality of [the verb's] meaning, it is not appropriate to pass judgment on it or use it to pass judgment. This is evident from deliberating on the truth.

Particles signify a particular relation that is only grasped when the *relata* are in view. That relation is not yet amenable to judgment. For example: "my trip from (*min*) Baṣra" signifies a specific relation but it is not a proposition—it becomes one if the whole phrase is put in the subject- or predicate-place of a proposition, as in "My trip from Baṣra was strenuous." In contrast, verbs signify already by default a complete nexus that is amenable to judgment. That is, once the agent is supplied, so that the *relata* and the nexus as a tool for conceptualizing the state of affairs are in view, the nexus can be conceptually isolated and judged.

The point where the perspective switches from the state in which the nexus is considered only as a tool to the state in which it can be considered as an object is precisely when its other *relatum*, the agent (*fā ʿil*), is supplied. This is reminiscent of what Taḥtānī stated. And, as Taḥtānī argued as well, Jurjānī points out—after "deliberating on the truth"—that a verb alone cannot be judged or used to judge something as long as the agent is not made explicit. That implies that third-person inflected verbs by themselves are not propositions. It would, however, also imply that first- and second-person inflected verbs are not propositions. Presumably, Jurjānī would say that this is true so long as they are considered outside of a concrete speech-situation in which the hidden pronouns would have their reference fixed.[35]

Jurjānī's novel account of the semantics of particles, names, and verbs, and of the nature of the predicative nexus, has greater explanatory power than those of his predecessors, because it connects semantic observations with claims about the mind. It is also more economical, because it avoids the multiplication of nexus needed to explain conversion, and the regress arguments that arise from postulating a real relation between the referents of subject and predicate. But the account has its own problems, and Jurjānī anticipates possible objections at the end of the treatise:

TEXT 83: AL-SAYYID AL-SHARĪF AL-JURJĀNĪ, *RISĀLA ʿALĀ TAḤQĪQ MAʿNĀ AL-ḤARF* (AKTAŞ 2018), 86.12–18

If you were to say: Why is the complete nexus made to join the predicate (*mansūb*), and together they are made that which is signified by a [single] utterance, namely, the verb, but it is not joined to the subject (*mansūb ilayhi*) in the same way? And why, even though [this nexus] is the state of affairs between the two, is it specified only in relation to one of them?

Then I would say: Perhaps the reason for this is that the nexus that exists for the predicate is attached to the subject in the same way that fatherhood that exists for the father is attached to the son. Or don't you see that you say: Standing is predicated of Zayd, and don't say: Zayd is predicated of standing? And you say: Standing is connected to Zayd, and Zayd is connected to it. As the attributes [i.e., "standing"] are based on transitivity, I say: Standing is the predicate and Zayd the subject. All this leads you on the right path to what we have already said.

The first objection lies at the heart of the whole issue: What is the difference between subject and predicate, noun and verb, particular reference and general characterization?[36] If, on Jurjānī's account, the verb includes the signification of a complete nexus, it is not only semantically distinct, but also syntactically. Why should this be so? That is just what the nexus is like, Jurjānī counters. It is an asymmetric relation like the relation of fatherhood as it obtains between father and son. The father is a father to the son, but the son is not a father to the father. The reason for this is that attributes are transitive because by definition they always are attributes *of* something. Jurjānī continues:

TEXT 84: AL-SAYYID AL-SHARĪF AL-JURJĀNĪ, *RISĀLA ʿALĀ TAḤQĪQ MAʿNĀ AL-ḤARF* (AKTAŞ 2018), 86.18–87.10

And if you were to say: If, just as the combination of verb and agent as in "Zayd (is) standing" (*qāma Zayd*) prompts you to understand a nexus that is not understood independently, and the two terms become the nexus as a tool for getting to know the state of affairs the two [terms] are involved in, and in the same way the attribute "standing" (*qāʾim*) prompts you to understand a certain thing in itself, namely, *standing* (*al-qiyām*), and the nexus between them, which is the tool for seeing the two [as related]—then why is it possible that the attribute be judged or used to judge something else, but not the verb?

Then I respond: The nexus in the verb is a complete nexus isolated by itself and it does not connect to anything else at all. The primary intention of the expression is to signify that nexus. It is not possible that it is derived from one of the two terms at all. As for the attribute, the nexus that is expressed in it is a specifying nexus that is however not complete, and it does not require the isolation of a concept from another or the lack of its connection to it. Nor is it the nexus primarily intended by the expression. Sometimes it is a description, and then it is turned into something by which judgment is passed. As for the nexus expressed in [the attribute], it is not appropriate for it to be judged or to be used to judge something else, not by itself alone or together with something else, because it is not an independent [concept].

The second objection turns on the question of how, on Jurjānī's account, we are to decide which types of nexus signified by which types of utterances are amenable to judgment. Verbs alone cannot go in the subject-place, and verbs together with their agents can go neither in the subject- nor the predicate-place. This is because verbs contain a complete nexus that relates its independent meaning to a subject. The last objection Jurjānī considers is this:

TEXT 85: AL-SAYYID AL-SHARĪF AL-JURJĀNĪ, *RISĀLA ʿALĀ TAḤQĪQ MAʿNĀ AL-ḤARF* (AKTAŞ 2018), 87.11–88.4

If you were to say: You said that the combination of the verb and its agent is not such that it can be used to make a judgment. But this contradicts what the grammarians said, namely that the *relatum* in "Zayd's father is standing" (*Zayd qāma abūhu*) is the [entire] verbal sentence [i.e., "his father's standing" (*qāma abūhu*)].

Then I respond: What is intended here are in fact two judgments. The first is the judgment that the father of Zayd is standing, and the second is that Zayd [is such] that [his] father is standing. No doubt these two judgments are not clearly and distinctly understood from the sentence. But one of them is the primary intention [of the sentence] and the other is understood by implication. If what is intended is the first, then in this sentence Zayd is considered as a clear and distinct concept and in reality no judgment is made about him or by means of him. But he is a determination that attaches to that on which judgment is passed [i.e., the father as being *his* father]. If what is intended is the second, as is obvious, no distinct judgment is passed between standing and the father, but the father is a determination for a *relatum*, i.e., *standing* (*qiyām*), for with it the attribution to Zayd is completed. Don't you see that if you say "Standing the father of Zayd" (*qāʾim abū Zayd*) and the nexus between them disappears, nothing is being connected to anything at all. If the meaning of "his father is standing" (*qāma abūhu*) is also that, then it does not connect to Zayd, and no declarative sentence (*khabar*) results from it. And then you hear the grammarians say that "his father is standing" (*qāma abūhu*) is a sentence, but not proper discourse, because it is stripped of the occurrence of the nexus between the two terms as the context requires the mention of Zayd and the mention of the pronoun signifying the mentioning of the connection, which is however impossible to exist when it falls apart.

In the third objection Jurjānī turns to an interesting borderline case that is supposed to bring out an important point: the grammarians' example "Zayd, his father is standing" (*Zayd qāma abūhu*). This is a perfectly correct Arabic sentence, with the syntactic peculiarity—which is however ubiquitous in Arabic—that the verbal sentence grammatically acts as the predicate of the overall nominal sentence. Logically, this is not how Jurjānī sees the matter. The problem for him is that there are two nexus, one between *standing* and Zayd's father, which is the one naturally understood from the sentence, and the one between Zayd and *his-father's-standing*, which is the nexus that one would have to understand from the grammarians' parsing. Logically, the latter does however not really connect. It seems that, here, grammar goes against logic. Dawānī should likewise engage the grammarians on the issue.

JALĀL AL-DĪN AL-DAWĀNĪ: THE PROPOSITION AS A PICTURE

Jalāl al-Dīn al-Dawānī was born around 830/1426.[37] He studied with his father and a local scholar of his hometown, Dawān, both of whom were students of Jurjānī. Measured against the number of commentaries and glosses written on his logical works, he was arguably the most influential logician in the Eastern Islamic world of the 9th/15th century. Much of his output remains in manuscript form. An edition or study especially of his two glosses on Jurjānī's gloss on Taḥtānī's *Lawāmiʿ* is a major *desideratum*. One of the glosses is a counter-gloss responding to an earlier counter-gloss by his intellectual rival in Shīrāz, Ṣadr al-Dīn al-Dashtakī (killed in 903/1498). All three glosses discuss issues raised by Jurjānī in the early parts of the *Maṭāliʿ*, again focusing on philosophical issues in semantics.[38]

Dawānī's critical engagement with Taḥtānī's, Taftāzānī's, and Jurjānī's positions on the copula, the nexus, and the parts of the proposition is felt across his works. Dawānī argued against Taḥtānī that the parts of the proposition are really only three, because the nexus can be the object of both conception and assent. This position is closely connected to a number of other novel views defended by Dawānī, like his solution to the liar paradox, or his doctrines on negative existential predication.[39]

In his commentary on Taftāzānī's *Tahdhīb*, Dawānī likens the proposition to a picture. His point is that we only say that a picture is true to what it depicts if the painter actually wants to represent something. This is what the predicative nexus is like. A picture in which the painter does not want to represent anything is like the nexus present in sentences expressing, for example, wishes.[40] A little later in the commentary, when the terms "nexus" and "copula" are introduced, he cites Avicenna's position from *al-ʿIbāra* in the *Shifāʾ* and then comments:

TEXT 86: JALĀL AL-DĪN AL-DAWĀNĪ, *SHARḤ TAHDHĪB AL-MANṬIQ* (AL-MALĪBĀRĪ), 176.6–178.3

These are [Avicenna's] words, and they make clear that the parts of the intelligible proposition are three, and this is what the old [logicians] thought. For them the grasping of the nexus that subsists between the subject and the predicate [simply] was the judgment, and [the judgment] was not preceded by the conception of a nexus that then became the object of the judgment. The subsistence of that [latter] nexus belongs to the subtle [innovations] of the later [logicians]. They believed that in the case of doubt, the nexus is conceived without judgment, since as long as no nexus is conceived, doubt cannot occur either. From the arising of doubt they added to the things [already] grasped another thing, as is attested by introspection, because one thing grasped cedes and another takes its place.

There is room for discussion here. For introspection does not require that the thing grasped in the case of doubt not be the same thing as that which is grasped in the case of a judgment, I mean the actual occurrence or not [of the nexus], and which is considered in the act of grasping. In the first case, the thing grasped is grasped without acknowledging, and in the second it is grasped with acknowledging [its occurrence]. In what preceded you may have called attention to the consideration [in the mind] of the acts of grasping in themselves, and not of the thing grasped, and this is not contradicted by introspection. Think about it!

[Having said] this, you learned from it that there must be something in propositions that is the meaning of the copula, whether it is mentioned by means of an expression or whether it is omitted, or else has its meaning contained in the expression that signifies the predicate, as what has been said about statement-words. [Taftāzānī, by saying] *and for it "huwa" may be used*, indicates that "*huwa*" is a pronoun referring back to the subject, and that it is in reality not a copula, because a copula is an auxiliary, and a pronoun is a noun, as its meaning is the same as that to which it refers back. People came to represent the copula by "*huwa*," because they found that in Arabic speech there was no expression signifying a non-temporal copula like "*ast*" in Persian or "*estin*" in Greek, so they metaphorically used the expression "*huwa*" for this meaning, and their way of representing [the copula] is correct. This is what the author [Taftāzānī] said.

After rejecting the "subtle [innovation] of the later [logicians]" that the proposition has four distinct parts, Dawānī moves on to the copula. That which the copula signifies must no doubt be a part of the proposition if it is to have a truth value. How that meaning is expressed on the level of language and how to classify the linguistic sign doing the job is the question that Dawānī seeks to answer in the remainder of the comment on this lemma. From the quotation given earlier it is clear that Dawānī had read Taftāzānī's elaborations on the Graeco-Arabic history of the copula in the commentary on the *Shamsiyya*. As so often, Dawānī cites the authority of Avicenna stating that the copulative "*huwa*" is an auxiliary, because it has no complete meaning by itself. But even some grammarians considered "*huwa*" a particle and not a noun, which is of course what Jurjānī's mirror analogy was supposed to bring out:

TEXT 87: JALĀL AL-DĪN AL-DAWĀNĪ, *SHARḤ TAHDHĪB AL-MANṬIQ* (AL-MALĪBĀRĪ), 179.1–9

These are his words, even though some of the foremost grammarians considered ["*huwa*"] a particle. Raḍī [al-Dīn Muḥammad b. al-Ḥasan al-Astarābādī (d. 686/1287 or 688/1289)] transmitted this position from some Baṣrian [grammarians] and adopted it, when he said: "Then, since the goal of the partitive pronoun's [*scil.* '*huwa*'] function is as we said, i.e., to prevent the ambiguity of the grammatical predicate that is mentioned after it and an attribute [of the grammatical subject]. And this is the meaning of the particle, I mean: in communicating the meaning in something other than itself [i.e., by disambiguating the word following it], it turned into a particle, and hence was stripped of its cloak of being a noun. But it must have a determinate morphological form, I mean: the form of a nominative pronoun, even if what comes after it changes from nominative to accusative, as we mentioned. This is because particles are indeclinable; but in this case there remains one feature of declension characteristic of nouns, by which I mean its being singular, dual, or plural, masculine or feminine, first-person, or second- or third-, on account of the lack of declinability when it is a particle. This is alike to the second-person marker '*k*,' since it sheds its meaning as a noun and becomes a particle. End of quote."

Dawānī insists that the copulative "*huwa*" is neither a noun nor a partitive pronoun in the grammarians' terminology, because its technical usage established by logicians has nothing to do with the phenomenon of its use in natural language that grammarians are describing. For Dawānī, it is in fact a particle performing the role of a copula, and as such an auxiliary:

TEXT 88: JALĀL AL-DĪN AL-DAWĀNĪ, *SHARḤ TAHDHĪB AL-MANṬIQ* (AL-MALĪBĀRĪ), 179.10–180.12

Now then, even if we suppose all grammarians agree that it is a noun, it does not follow that it is not an auxiliary for all logicians. What the author [Taftāzānī] mentioned apropos its referring back to the subject, this is the same in terms of the meaning only being complete if it is granted that it is a noun. But if we say it is a particle performing the role of a copula, then it is not [a noun], but an auxiliary in the form of a noun, as is the case with the markers for the second- and third-person "*k*" and "*h*" in "*iyyāka*" and "*iyyāha*" [you, beware of . . . ; he, beware of . . .].

It is evident that what the author [Taftāzānī] mentioned, elliptical though it may be, is an allusion to the arguments of the logicians who do not agree with this. They make clear that it is an auxiliary and do not stipulate about its proper role what the grammarians stipulate with regard to the grammatical predicate being disambiguated from adjectives and so forth, but they examine [sentences] like "Zayd, [he] is a writer" where there is no ambiguity [between taking "writer" as a predicate or] as an attribute, as the [grammarians] had laid out.

If you were to say: It is evident that the copula in the language of the Arabs is [represented by] the inflectional signs. For if simple expressions are uttered with no inflectional signs pronounced at the end, they do not signify a connection. But when they are uttered with their inflections, they do signify that. Therefore, the inflectional signs signify the copulation.

I respond: The logicians made clear that the copula is the expression "*huwa*" or "*hiya*" and so forth, and the inflectional signs are not a copula for them, but they signify [a word's] being a subject, or an object, and so forth, just as the Arabic grammarians think, and the meaning of the copula is understood—even if it is omitted—from those signs by way of implication. For those signs signify these conceptualized meanings that are not without a copula.

Dawānī in this passage shows awareness of the earlier discussions as well as familiarity with the opinions of grammarians on the issue. Noteworthy is not only that he argues against the idea that there is a judgment-nexus, but also that he rejects the argument that the meaning of the copula may be expressed by signs of inflection. Both are positions Samarqāndī and Taḥtānī developed. That a comment of this length (further multiplied by super-commentaries) was deemed adequate to explain the phrase "and for it '*huwa*' may be used" suggests that the discussions on the copula became even more extensive. Dawānī's work enjoyed a lively reception not only in his native Persia and the Ottoman Empire, but also, and especially, in Mughal India.

A LOOK AHEAD TO THE INDO-MUSLIM TRADITION

One strand for following the subsequent development of discussions on the copula is the Indo-Muslim tradition of glossing the major commentaries by Taḥtānī and Dawānī, and later that on Muḥibb Allāh al-Bihārī's (d. 1119/1707) 12th/17th-century handbook on logic, titled *Sullam al-ʿulūm*. Up to the 12th/18th century, the study of logic had become a prominent part of madrasa curricula across the Indian subcontinent.[41] One important figure was the logician ʿAbd al-Ḥakīm al-Siyālkūtī (d. 1067/1657), who glossed both of Tahtānī's commentaries. His *Ḥāshiya ʿalā Taḥrīr al-qawāʿid al-manṭiqiyya* (Glosses on Ṭahtānī's *Shamsiyya* Commentary, completed 1053/1643) had such a lasting influence that it was—between 1870 and 1905—lithographed in Delhi and Lakhnaw, and printed in movable type multiple times in Istanbul and Cairo. It perpetuated the Shīrāzī tradition and widely disseminated it in Mughal India and beyond, especially in the Ottoman Empire.[42] Typically, it focused on the earlier parts of the base text centering on semantics, and it engaged with both Jurjānī and Dawānī.[43]

Another central text was Bihārī's *Sullam al-ʿulūm*, whose commentary tradition has now been carefully studied and presented by Asad Ahmed.[44] A late-12th/18th-century commentary by Mullā Mubīn Lakhnawī (d. 1225/1810) titled *Mirʾāt al-shurūḥ sharḥ Sullam al-ʿulūm* (The Mirror of Commentaries Commenting on the Ladder of the Sciences) gives a good impression of the continuity and further stratification of discussions on the problem of predication.[45]

Mubīn's commentary is both exceptionally clear and unusually extensive (over 420 pages in the 1909/1910 Cairo edition), routinely engaging with several of his predecessors.[46] As Mubīn himself states in the proem, this was his express goal in redacting the commentary, and the reason why he gave it the title *Mirror of Commentaries*. He wanted it to be as clear and lucid as a mirror, and he wanted it to be comprehensive and conclusive, in the sense that it reflects like a mirror all the other commentaries on the *Sullam*.[47]

It is tempting to read the title and Mubīn's methodological remarks in light of Jurjānī's mirror simile: Mubīn may have played with the idea that the truth of

Bihārī's impenetrable (*mughlaqan ghāyat al-ighlāq*)[48] base text is only rendered intelligible when his own commentary is first used as a tool—like a mirror—to see all the other commentaries, and to then focus the attention on his commentary as an object of clarity to which the reader is prompted to give her assent. That the mirror simile was well known to both Bihārī and Mubīn is clear from the following passage.

TEXT 89: MULLĀ MUBĪN LAKHNAWĪ, *MIR ʾĀT AL-SHURŪḤSHARḤ SULLAM AL-ʿULŪM* (ANONYMOUS, CAIRO 1910), II 4.18–5.5

The nexus, that is, the complete predicative nexus, *is only part of what attaches to the judgment*, that is, the assent, *in a secondary way*, that is, by means of something else, not by means of itself. The assent attaches primarily and by itself to the subject and predicate, and secondarily and accidentally to the nexus between them. This is the account of what the judgment attaches to. But there are different [opinions] on this. For some it is the same as the meaning of a proposition composed of subject and predicate regarded as being [semantically] independent (*istiqlālī*), whereas the copulative nexus is regarded as not [semantically] independent. Some said that [the judgment] attaches in its general sense primarily to [the nexus?] and what obtains after the analysis [of the proposition]. For others the subject and the predicate *just are* the state of being a copulative nexus. This option is also attributed to the Master [Avicenna]. But the majority position is that the judgment attaches to the copulative nexus, and it is possible [for the judgment] to attach to the nexus [only] after it is regarded independently. He [Bihārī] said in [his auto-]gloss: There is a difference between [the idea that] the judgment attaches to the occurrence or non-occurrence [of the nexus] that is part of the proposition and [the idea that] it attaches to the proposition itself [and as a whole]. The majority position is the first, but the true position is the second, and it is the one chosen by Mīr Bāqir Dāmād [d. 1041/1631–1632] and the Eminent Maḥmūd al-Jawnpūrī [d. 1062/1652]. The author [Bihārī] rejects this, even though it is the majority position, and proves it by saying: *because it*, that is, the nexus, *is one of the concepts* that are semantically dependent particle-meanings, *which are not considered independently*. Inevitably, there must be [such a nexus] for the assent to attach to it. But it attaches not the nexus [alone], *for it*, that is, the nexus, *is only a mirror*, that is, a means, *for seeing the two terms*, that is, the subject and the predicate. This is the proof for the claim that the nexus is not semantically independent.

This passage amounts to less than half a page taken from a discussion that runs over more than seventeen pages. In fact, the first twenty or so pages of the second volume that contains the section on assents (*taṣdīqāt*) are devoted to a thorough discussion of the nature of judgment, the logical form of a proposition, and how the two relate to each other. The way Mubīn structures his commentary is no more pedagogical or doxographic than the great 8th/14th-century commentaries. And it was not the end, either. Such multilayered commentaries in logic continued to be produced in the 13th/19th century.[49]

Concluding Remarks

The story of the problem of predication in the Graeco-Arabic tradition, posed in its specific form as the question of the semantic role of the copula, is also a story of the development of Arabic logic and its emancipation from its Greek roots. I suspect that its sequel up to at least the 13th/19th century would bring to light discussions that—given a discernably growing concern with semantic matters—may help to delineate the further development of the discipline and that would speak even more directly to issues in contemporary philosophy of language. This sequel can now be told. The details of the story followed in the present study already throw new light on the history of Aristotelian logic and they may, I imagine, be fruitfully compared with the medieval Latin developments that Nuchelmans and Geach have studied. The following is a concise summary of the arguments making up this story, with references to the texts cited. An index of those texts is provided at the end of the book.

Aristotle had a theory of inference and a theory of the sentence, but no theory of the copula. While syntactic homogeneity was presupposed by the *APr*, the *DI* presents APs as consisting of a NW and a SW, of which SWs are always predicative, thus presupposing syntactic heterogeneity (Texts 1–2). Aristotle did, however, say several things about the word "is" (Texts 3–6). For example, "is," if said by itself, signifies nothing (Text 2); or when you say "Homer is a poet," you are thereby not saying that Homer is (alive) (Text 6); or in APs "is" may be predicated as a third item—whence the distinction between *secundum adiacens* ("Socrates is") and *tertium adiacens* ("Socrates is wise") (Text 3).

The Greek commentators sensed the tension that Geach pointed out exists between the syntactic presuppositions of the *DI* and the *APr*. Already Alexander suggested that each text had a different perspective on the sentence (Text 7). But as the commentators sought to explain Aristotle by Aristotle, they were forced to engage with the question of the role of the word "is" in predication. Alexander conceptualized the copula as a purely syntactic marker, to be distinguished from "being" when it occurs in the predicate place (Texts 8–12). However, as far as we can tell, none of the Greek commentators gave up heterogeneity in their commentaries on the *DI*. As for its syntactic role, by the end of late antiquity there was among *DI* commentators, broadly speaking, agreement on the following (Texts 13–16). APs dissolve into NWs and SWs. Any SW either has the structure (cop+NW) or else, if the SW is a grammatical verb, it can be paraphrased to have that structure, where the NW is a participial form to which "is" is prefixed.

With Stephanus at the latest, "to be" and other copulative verbs were called "hyparctic verbs" (Text 17). The later commentators also agreed that there are two fundamentally different types of predications (Texts 17–18). Aristotle had distinguished them in the *Cat*, and commentators saw the *DI* as referring to this distinction. A predicate is said synonymously *of* a subject, if the predicate is a universal picking out an essential feature of a particular. A predicate is said paronymously *in* a subject, if the predicate is an accident inhering in a substance. For example, in "Socrates is a man," "is" signifies that Socrates is *an instance* of man (and thereby of animal, and ultimately of substance), whereas in "Socrates is wise" it signifies that Socrates *has* wisdom (which is a quality in the sense of the *Cat*, and thus an accident *in* a substance).

The Arabic translators of the *DI* were, for lack of a natural counterpart to the Greek "*esti*," forced to create neologisms whenever they felt that this little word mattered for logical analysis (Texts 19–22). Particular historical circumstances shaped Fārābī's philosophical project in such a way that he saw himself as constructing within Arabic a new language that would allow Arabs to do Aristotelian logic (and then philosophy) as a shortcut to the ultimate personal and political perfection for the good of Arabo-Muslim civilization. Fārābī thus forged an Arabic Aristotelian logic on the assumption that Greek was superior to Arabic as a language for logic: whatever resisted straightforward translation needed to be instituted as a technical term in the new Arabic logical lexicon.

Two of Fārābī's contributions to logical theory were particularly influential. The first was that he insisted—against any grammatical intuitions from Arabic—that a copula (*rābiṭa*) must be used in categorical statements to signify the predicative relation between subject and predicate (Texts 27–31). The second was that he amalgamized the notion of paronymous predication of the Greek commentators with the theory of etymological word-derivation (*ishtiqāq*) of the Arabic grammarians, introducing a new kind of heterogeneity (Texts 23–26). The idea that an artificial copula must be used to make up for a deficiency of the Arabic language was comprehensively challenged only four centuries later (Texts 63, 68, 70). The core doctrine of derived names (*al-asmā' al-mushtaqqa*) remained an integral part of Arabic logical theory.

The details of Fārābī's contributions, however, even though they continued to be discussed by Avempace and Averroes in the Islamic West, were largely forgotten after Avicenna in the East. These details were nevertheless remarkable. Derived words, among which he counted verbs, are essentially predicables (in Geach's sense) that cannot occur in the subject place and are always predicated paronymously (Texts 24–25). Hence, derived words always signify an attribute, never a substance. There is clear heterogeneity. However, that did not mean for Fārābī that no copula was needed (Text 27). Since scientific statements need to be expressible as timeless and non-paronymous predicative statements, which was otherwise impossible on the doctrine of derived names, Fārābī proposed that the copula "*mawjūd*" be used. Syntactically, "*mawjūd*" bars homogeneity, because you cannot exchange what comes before it with what comes after it without marking that exchange by changing the respective case-endings (Text 28). That "*mawjūd*" is grammatically a derived name is for Fārābī a consequence of the contingent development of the Arabic language, and it is central to his philosophical project to set out the semantics of this philosophical misnomer. Semantically, he treats "*mawjūd*" as a particle. That means that it is neither a predicable nor a name but a syncategorematic marker of a relation (Texts 29–30). This relation is a secondary intelligible, namely, the instantiation of a predicative function. In Fregean terms, Fārābī's account of the role of "*mawjūd*" may be expressed by a function with two arguments whose value is the True, iff the object falls under the concept: $f(F(x))$.

Avicenna represents the cusp between the appropriation of the Greek tradition and the beginning of an emancipation from it. This is reflected by the difference in orientation between his early and late work. The *Shifā'* in a sense looks back to and is determined by Aristotle's method and the structure of the transmitted corpus. The *Easterners* and the *Ishārāt* prefigure the method and structure of later works on logic and philosophy. In the *Shifā'* (Texts 32–37) Avicenna still engaged with Fārābī's doctrine of derived names and scolds Aristotle for not having discussed auxiliaries (*adāt*), a third class of expressions roughly corresponding to Fārābī's particles (*ḥurūf*), which includes hyparctic verbs.

Not only does Avicenna here further develop the doctrine of derived names, he also ruminates on the question whether expressions like "*yamshī*" (a one-word expression in Arabic that however signifies "he walks") should be understood as SWs or as APs. He concludes that such expressions are SWs and not APs, in contrast to *tamshī* (you walk) and *amshī* (I walk), which are APs and not SWs. The reason is that the former signify the nexus to an indeterminate subject, whereas the latter signify the nexus to a determinate subject (namely, the addressee or the speaker, respectively). This feature third-person inflected verbs share with derived names. The idea that these expressions signify the nexus to an indeterminate subject and that an AP requires that the nexus to a determinate subject is signified was important in the later tradition.

While clearly embracing a form of Fārābian heterogeneity, Avicenna did not follow Fārābī in his theory of *mawjūd*. Avicenna merely insists that an AP consists of three parts—subject, predicate, and nexus—that in principle must be signified separately, but in the case of the nexus its signification may be left implicit (Text 34; 35–36 on the unity of the proposition). Accordingly, Avicenna distinguishes between APs that are complete ternary using the copula "*huwa*" ($S+cop_{untensed}+P$), incomplete ternary using a tensed copula like "*yūjad*" ($S+cop_{tensed}+P$), and binary because the copula is left implicit ($S+P$). This classification he takes to represent the Aristotelian *secundum/tertium adiacens* distinction (Text 37). All this detail notwithstanding, Avicenna's late work (Texts 38–39), of which particularly the *Ishārāt* became the point of reference for the later tradition, makes no mention of any of it. He appears to not have thought it relevant for his new presentation of philosophy.

In a spirit critical of Avicenna, Rāzī advanced what I have called the Repetition Argument: If an IM includes the signification of a nexus, mentioning the copula "*huwa*" in sentences in which the predicate is an IM amounts to useless repetition (Texts 40–44). In such cases, Rāzī thinks the copula is redundant. In his *Mulakhkhaṣ*, Rāzī presents APs in terms of hylomorphic compounds whose matter are the terms and whose form is the nexus signified by the copula. Contrary to the quantifier that is only part of the proposition when it is expressed in words but has no distinct expression in reality, the nexus and its modality do have such distinct expressions in reality (Texts 45–46).

Khūnajī dedicated an entire chapter of his *Kashf al-asrār* to the copula. In it he rejects Avicenna's idea that first- and second-person inflected verbs are APs (Text 47) and criticizes Rāzī's Repetition Argument. According to Khūnajī, Rāzī had failed to see that the signification of a nexus contained in the meaning of IMs is not the same as what the copula "*huwa*" signifies: while the former only signifies a nexus to an indeterminate subject, the latter signifies the nexus to a determinate subject, as Avicenna had said, and it is the latter that is needed to form an AP (Text 48–49). Like Rāzī, Khūnajī also remarks that the nexus of the predicate to the subject must be distinct from the nexus of the subject to the predicate, because the two may differ in modality. This issue was extensively discussed in the later tradition, particularly by Kātibī.

Abharī and Ṭūsī critically engaged with Rāzī, just as Rāzī had engaged critically with Avicenna. Both rejected the Repetition Argument along the same lines as Khūnajī (Texts 50–53). Ṭūsī distinguishes between the significations of the copulative and the pronominal "*huwa*." The latter is contained implicitly by inflected verbs and IMs. Hence, they essentially signify a nexus to an indeterminate subject. However, they may also accidentally signify a nexus to a determinate subject in the context of a sentence, as the pronominal "*huwa*" implicitly contained in inflected verbs and IMs can be taken to refer back to the subject and thereby make the nexus to it determinate. "*Zayd yakūnu kātib*" signifies the same proposition as that expressed by "*Zayd huwa kātib*," except that in the former a tense is specified (Text 51).

Kātibī wrote commentaries on both Rāzī and Khūnajī. In the commentary on Khūnajī's *Kashf al-asrār* he presents a possible argument in support of the Repetition Argument. Along the lines of what Ṭūsī had proposed, he points out that if we take inflected verbs and IMs to contain the pronominal "*huwa*," and that "*huwa*" makes the nexus to a subject determinate once it refers back to the subject in the context of a sentence, then there would be no need to state the copula again to make the nexus determinate (Text 54–55). This, however, seems not to have been Kātibī's considered opinion, because in other works he clearly states that he rejects the Repetition Argument. In his commentary on Rāzī's *Mulakhkhaṣ* the bulk of his commentary discusses not the copula but the nexus signified by it. He criticizes Rāzī's arguments for the claim that the nexus is a concept distinct from the concepts of subject and predicate (Texts 56–57), as well as the arguments for the claim that in a proposition there are two distinct nexus (as Khūnajī had pointed out), i.e., that of the predicate to the subject and that of the subject to the predicate. He argues that there are actually four distinct ways to consider a nexus between two terms (Text 58).

Urmawī wrote a non-confrontational commentary on the *Ishārāt*. But in his summa *Bayān al-ḥaqq* he shows detailed knowledge of the history of the discussions on the copula and weighs in on the question of whether there are two distinct nexus in a proposition and how they are to be distinguished, criticizing the Rāzīan argument (Text 59). A digest of these discussions is contained in the influential advanced handbook *Maṭāliʿ al-anwār*.

Samarqandī, who first included formal disputation theory in a major logical work, rejects the Repetition Argument along familiar lines (Text 60). With regard to the question of whether there are two nexus in a proposition, and which should be counted as part of the proposition, Samarqandī presents a new position. According to him, it is the occurrence of the affirmative nexus that is part of the proposition, a position that might have influenced Taḥtānī, who recognized a fourth part of the proposition that he called the judgment-nexus (Text 61; for Taḥtānī 65). Samarqandī also discusses the idea that in Arabic the role of the copula may be played by the vocalization that indicates the syntactic role of words in sentences. While he dismisses the idea, Taḥtānī takes it more seriously (Text 63; for Taḥtānī 68).

Ḥillī's adjudicative commentary on the *Ishārāt*, while showing a clear allegiance with his teacher Ṭūsī in his assessment of Rāzī's Repetition Argument, nevertheless provides a charitable and faithful presentation of Rāzī's claims. Ḥillī closes with some general remarks on issues that had been discussed in connection with the copula, and suggests that in every proposition there are in fact four distinct nexus (not unlike Kātibī's position in Text 58), a point that he had already made in his *al-Asrār al-khafiyya* (Text 64).

Taḥtānī seems to have had major misgivings about traditional accounts of the copula. In his commentary on Urmawī's *Maṭāliʿ al-anwār* he offers a comprehensive re-evaluation. Not only does he insist on distinguishing the judgment ("judgment-nexus") from the judgeable content (Text 65), he also denies that the word "*huwa*" does act as a copula at all (Texts 66–67). In fact, according to Taḥtānī, we do not need a copula in any kind of proposition, for the signification of the nexus is contained in verbs and IMs, and even in nominal sentences, it is expressed by the vocalization. For Taḥtānī, all these expressions—when they are in a form in which they can occur in the predicate-place, that is, when conjugated or declined appropriately—are unsaturated. It is by supplying the subject that they come to signify the nexus to a determinate subject. On this view, the Avicennan distinction between binary and ternary propositions becomes practically obsolete (Texts 68, 70–72). Taḥtānī's intervention was perhaps the most forceful rejection yet of the traditional doctrines on the copula and the nexus. His great dialectical commentaries had an exceptionally far reach for centuries, shaping the formalized disputational praxis first properly introduced by Samarqandī in logical commentary writing.

Taḥtānī's rejection of the Greek remnants in the theory of predication prompted Taftāzānī, who was baffled that anyone could have thought otherwise than Taḥtānī, to research the history of the copula in the Arabic tradition by reading Fārābī (Text 76–77). Even though largely agreeing with Taḥtānī's account of the problem of predication, Taftāzānī insisted that the nexus was a single entity (Text 73). Aligning his account of the nexus with the theories of predication formulated in *balāgha* works, he argued that the nexus was an asymmetric relation, just like the relation of *isnād* between the *musnad* and the *musnad ilayhi* (Text 74).

To explain why the converse of a proposition may have a different modality from the original proposition, he compares the nexus to the relation between the mind and an image in the mind. The fundamental relation is a property of the mind, namely that there is an image of, let's say, a red apple in it. Likewise, the fundamental nexus is a property of the predicate, namely that it is ascribable to subjects. One may say that it is a property of the image of a red apple that it is in the mind, or of a subject that a predicate may be ascribed to it, but that is merely a different perspective. Without a mind, there is no image, and without a predicate, there is no nexus and hence no subject. An example he gives is a rejection of the interchangeability thesis: "Every old man was young" does not convert to "Some young man was old" but rather to "Something that was young is old," because the nexus is precisely not what is signified by "was." Rather, what is signified by "was" is part of the predicate. Like Taḥtānī, Taftāzānī thinks that in Arabic, the nexus is signified by case-markers. But in contrast to Taḥtānī, he classifies propositions in which both or one term is indeclinable as binary and incomplete ternary propositions, respectively. In such propositions, the case-markers signifying the nexus are not, or not fully, realized (Text 75).

While the influence of *balāgha* was already discernible in Taftāzānī's approach to the problem of predication, the influence of *ʿilm al-waḍʿ* becomes fully apparent with Jurjānī's account of the problem of predication in his *Treatise Verifying the Meaning of the Particle* (Texts 79–85). In his commentary on Kātibī's *Shamsiyya* (Text 78), Jurjānī generally agrees with Taftāzānī on the main points. He thinks that the copula may be employed to signify both the predicative nexus and the judgment-nexus, and that the nexus is a single entity. However, his argument for why the nexus is simple is distinct.

What he only summarily expresses in the commentary on the *Shamsiyya* is fully laid out in his *Treatise Verifying the Meaning of the Particle*. Framed in the theory of reference provided by *ʿilm al-waḍʿ*, Jurjānī compares the nexus to a mirror (Text 79). Like a mirror that you can look into to see an image, or look at as an object to inspect, for example, the cleanliness of its surface, the nexus can be looked at to see a state of affairs or it can be looked at as an object in itself. This is similar to particles in that particles signify relations (Text 80). According to the semantic theory for particles developed in *ʿilm al-waḍʿ*, they signify a general relation, like the relation of "beginning," and all the particular instances of relations falling under the general idea. The reference of particles is fixed by the *relata*, for example, "the journey from here to Baghdād." Likewise, the general idea of predication is expressed by the copula, and its reference is fixed once subject and predicate are supplied. Jurjānī extends the semantic theories of *ʿilm al-waḍʿ* to his discussion of the nexus in connection with verbs (Text 81–82). Verbs include the signification of the nexus and hence need a subject to be supplied to determine the predicative relation. Jurjānī's account is remarkable for its novelty, economy, and explanatory power. But it raised new problems, some of which Jurjānī addressed (Text 83–85).

Dawānī would not accept most of the new approaches to the problem of predication. In his commentary on Taftāzānī's *Tahdhīb*, he not only denies that a proposition has four parts, but also rejects the idea that in Arabic the role of the copula is played by case-markers (Text 87–88). His criticism is however not reactionary. He compares the proposition to a painting by a painter who actually wants to depict something (as opposed to an imaginary *sujet*) (Text 86). The nexus between subject and predicate is just like the intention of the painter: it may depict something, or it may just propose something. Dawānī is aware of Taftāzānī's comments on Kātibī's *Shamsiyya* (Text 87), but he himself believes that the disagreement about what kind of expression "*huwa*" is boils down to a terminological misunderstanding between the logicians and the grammarians (Texts 87–88). Citing the grammarians, he argues that the copula is neither a noun nor a partitive pronoun, but a particle performing the role of the copula. Its usage established by logicians has nothing to do with the grammarians' descriptions of natural language.

A glance at a short passage from Mubīn's commentary on Bihārī's *Sullam* (Text 89) shows that the discussions on the problem of predication continued into the

13th/19th century and beyond. In Bihārī and Mubīn the problem of predication is closely linked with the discussion on the nature of judgment. It remains to explore more systematically the rich tradition of philosophy of language contained in the countless commentaries that were written between the 10th/16th and 14th/20th century in the Arabic world.

NOTES

INTRODUCTION

1. For recently revived ideas on the notion of "paraphilosophy," see Gutas, 2018a.

2. Gutas, 2002.

3. An exception is El-Rouayheb, 2010b.

4. Davidson, 2005, pp. 76–77. The review Davidson cites (Rodenbeck, 2000) discusses the novel *A Banquet for Seaweed* (*Walīma li-ʾaʿashāb al-baḥr*) by the Syrian author Ḥaydar Ḥaydar, originally published in 1983. The republication in 2000 as part of the modern Arabic Classics series sponsored by Egypt's Ministry of Culture sparked protests among students of the al-Azhar university in Cairo, leading to a heated public controversy and eventually the banning of the book.

5. Sir Peter Strawson, for example, agreed; see especially the rather neglected Strawson, 1995. Two years after Davidson's passing and only months before his own, he urged in a review of Davidson's book that "perhaps this is not quite the end of the story" (Strawson, 2005). More recent attempts at the problem are Gaskin, 2008 (with a solution quite different from Davidson's and Frege's) and Soames, 2010 (arguing against Davidson's use of Tarski's theory of truth to solve the problem), or more generally Gibson, 2004; King, 2007; Collins, 2011. A new surge in interest in propositions is spearheaded by King, Soames, and Speaks; see, e.g., King, Soames, & Speaks, 2014 and also Tillman, 2021. For a more detailed treatment of the problem of predication in analytic philosophy, see Klinger, 2021, chapter 1.

6. Davidson, 2005, pp. 4–5: "The story of the problem of predication, or of the closely related problem of the unity of the proposition, stretches over more than two millennia; it should be told at much greater length than it is here, and by far more knowledgeable historians than I can pretend to be. [. . .] My excuse for neglecting the great logicians of the Middle Ages is that Aristotle's logic, impressive as it was, was designed to defeat a reasonable semantics of predicates, since terms like 'all men,' 'some horses,' and 'no member' are semantically and logically indigestible. Failure to plug this vast historical hole in my

187

account is mitigated by the existence of Peter Geach's book *Reference and Generality*, which does much to fill the gap." Geach only discusses medieval authors writing in Latin.

7. Davidson, 2005, p. 5.

8. The syntax trees splitting up sentences into NPs and VPs I present are of course those traditionally used by linguists at least since the publications in the 1910s and 1920s by Leonard Bloomfield (1887–1949): Bloomfield, 1914a, 1914b, 1916. Frege, however, would not have known them, and his own notation is different. Early generative grammar (Chomsky, 1965; reprint Chomsky, 2015) paid little attention to the problem of predication. But see especially the work of Piotr Stalmaszczyk for a contextualization of the notion of predication in generative linguistics and its recent minimalist program (Stalmaszczyk, 1999, 2000), and for the relationship between Fregean analysis and linguistics (Stalmaszczyk, 2010, 2014, 2016, 2017). For current controversies regarding the notion of a universal grammar (UG) in linguistics and the philosophy of cognitive science, see Lerner, Cullen, & Leslie, 2020; and for the exposition of UG, see Hornstein & Pietroski, 2020, pp. 13–14. For an attempt to use recent insights in linguistics and formal logic for constructing a sound and complete system for natural logic, see Ludlow & Živanović, 2022.

9. This is the view most forcefully advanced by Geach, 1968. Modern advocates of the homogeneity-view are few, but see for example the work of the Polish mathematician Leśniewski, 1992 (translated into English); or Sommers, 1982; Englebretsen, 1987, 1996.

10. Davidson, 2005, p. 5.

11. Geach, 1972, p. 48: "It is logically impossible for a term to shift about between subject and predicate position without undergoing a change of sense as well as a change of role. Only a name can be a logical subject; and a name cannot retain the role of a name if it becomes a logical predicate." But see Barnes, 2012, p. 165: "It is hard to believe that that is correct. Of course, a term in predicate position plays a different role from a term in subject position: in the one case, its role is to be subject of the sentence and in the other to be predicate. But why should the change of role carry with it a change of sense so that genuine interchange of one and the same term is impossible?"

12. Geach, 1972, pp. 53–57, gives a genealogy of the problem. For a defense of Aristotle and an argument that the underlying grammar of Aristotelian syllogistic did not in principle bar the path to multiple quantification, see Barnes, 1996.

13. Geach, 1968, p. 47.

14. Davidson, 2005, p. 5.

15. For the unlikely role the *DI* played in 17th-century Paris and Oxford, in the Port-Royalistes and Henry Aldrich, see Barnes, 2009a.

16. Davidson, 2005, p. 76.

1. SETTING THE SCENE: THE COPULA, ARISTOTLE, AND THE ANCIENTS

1. See Geach, 1972, p. 47. Geach's view is still mirrored in many histories of logic. A good example is the entry for "history of logic" from the *Oxford Handbook of Philosophy* (King & Shapiro, 2005).

2. This view is put forward most succinctly in Geach, 1968; for a detailed study of the theory of distribution, see Geach, 1962 *viz.* Geach, 1980. "Subject and Predicate" (Geach, 1950) presents a new terminology—largely Fregean, with a few inspirations from Aristotle

and Aquinas—for the analysis of propositions and a set of logical principles that Geach would revert to throughout his career. For a summary, see Kenny, 2015, p. 190. On the doctrine of distribution in Arabic logic, see El-Rouayheb, 2023.

3. These are Geach's examples: Geach, 1972, p. 57.

4. Geach, 1968, p. 57. Geach's point is that without such a rule the example would be formally invalid just as, e.g., "All men are mortal; Cato is a man; therefore: Cato is mortal" would be formally invalid if "Cato" referred first to the Elder, then to the Younger.

5. Geach, 1968, p. 57.

6. Geach, 1968, pp. 54–55.

7. Geach, 1972, p. 61; see also his *Three Philosophers: Aristotle, Aquinas, Frege*, jointly written with his wife, Elizabeth Anscombe, in which he contributed the sections on Aquinas and Frege: Anscombe & Geach, 1961, p. 134f.

8. "Ausführungen über Sinn und Bedeutung," in Frege, 1983, p. 128; English translation in Frege, 1979, p. 118.

9. As further developed in "Funktion und Begriff" (Frege, 1891), "Über Sinn und Bedeutung" (Frege, 1892b), and "Über Begriff und Gegenstand" (Frege, 1892a), all translated in Beaney, 1997.

10. But see, on the "Frege-Russell ambiguity thesis," Vilkko & Hintikka, 2006.

11. See Bradley, 1897, chapters 2 and 3; Russell & Whitehead, 1910–1913, §52, and Ramsey, 1925, p. 403; *cf.* also Gaskin, 1995. The metaphysical charge itself can be dismantled and has been in various ways by both ancient and modern commentators. But any resolution will eventually have to appeal to some form of heterogeneity of the elements of the proposition, ultimately depending on an account of the copula. *Cf.* Barnes, 2012, pp. 154–155. See Gaskin, 2008.

12. First raised in Kerry, 1887. Kerry primarily refers to Frege's distinction of "concept" and "object" in his *Grundlagen der Arithmetik* (Frege, 1884 [translated into English by Austin as *The Foundations of Arithmetic*, Frege, 1980]), where it features as one of the three guiding principles of the work, "never to lose sight of the distinction between concept and object"; Frege, 1884, p. x (= Frege, 1980, p. xxii).

13. As Angelelli, 1967, p. 188 n40 put it: "there is no way out of the paradox, if one wishes to stay within Frege's system." The problem of the ineffability of logical category distinctions later exercised Wittgenstein interpreters. It has been variously argued that the concept *horse* problem inspired Wittgenstein's notion of logical category distinctions and the distinction between saying and showing in the *Tractatus*; see, e.g., Proops, 2013.

14. Frege, 1892a, pp. 204–205; translation in Beaney, 1997, pp. 192–193.

15. As suggested already in Ramsey, 1925 and more recently in Potter, 2000, p. 116. Attempts to amend the Fregean account are Black, 1954, pp. 229–254 (chapter 13, "Frege on Functions," *cf.* the review Church, 1956), Resnik, 1965, Dummett, 1973, p. 204ff. Wiggins, 1984 suggests reintroducing the copula as a running repair. But the widespread sentiment has been that Aristotle and everyone else got it wrong when they thought that a proposition consisted of two homogenous terms and a copula, until Frege in 1879 got it right when he analyzed propositions into a function and an argument. Many have taken Frege's account to be the only correct one. So for example Dummett, 1981, p. 175: "the functional conception of concepts [. . .] provides *the* correct account of their incompleteness," and especially Geach, 1955, pp. 258–259, 1957, p. 39, 1975, pp. 149–150; Anscombe & Geach, 1961, pp. 79–80. See also

Land, 1974, pp. 179–180; Carruthers, 1983, p. 51; Currie, 1984, p. 153; Stevens, 2005, p. 234, Soames, 2019, p. 17; or Potter, 2020, p. 10. An exception is Hintikka's "Twofold (Theoretical and Historiographical) Revolt against Frege"; see Angelelli, 2015. General assessments of the role of Aristotelian analyses of simple sentences are to be found in large-scale histories of logic like Prantl, 1855, pp. 159–165, and Ueberweg, 1857, which are pre-Fregean and were superseded by Bocheński, 1961, Kneale & Kneale, 1962, Dumitriu, 1973 (translated to English from Rumanian in Dumitriu, 1977), and now in the first of the recent multi-volume project *Handbook on the History of Logic*, edited by Gabbay & Woods, 2004.

16. This story has not yet been told in any systematic way. For some punctual studies on theories of the proposition from Plato to Averroes, see the edited volume Büttgen, Diebler, & Rashed, 1999. Since Ibrāhīm Madkūr's seminal but now outdated work (Ibrāhīm Madkūr, 1934) much has happened in the study of Arabic Aristotelian logic, but to date there is no systematic account of the tradition on the linguistic sections of the *DI*; Deborah Black has pioneered the comparative study of Aristotle's *Organon* and especially the *DI* in the medieval Latin and Arabic traditions: Black, 1990, 1991.

17. The development of "Boolean algebra" is often considered the beginning of modern logic, but *The Laws of Thought* (Boole, 1854) is best seen as extending and perfecting Aristotelian syllogistic, and thereby paving the way for some of the more momentous changes to logical theory that were to happen in its wake. For this and a logical comparison between Aristotle's syllogistic and Boolean algebra, see Corcoran, 2003.

18. Barnes, 2007, p. 107.

19. On the peculiarity of the transmission of the *Corpus Aristotelicum*, the bulk of which was never intended for publication but rather should be seen as teaching material for internal use in the Lyceum, see Weidemann, 2014, p. 60; Moraux, 1973–2001, pp. I.3–31; Primavesi, 2007.

20. For the transmission and genesis of the *DI* as part of the *Organon* and the role of Andronicus of Rhodes as the first editor of Aristotelian texts, see Weidemann, 2014, pp. 59–69; Hatzimichali, 2016.

21. Flashar, 2004, pp. 277–278; he writes that the *Cat* and *DI*, with regard to the *Analytica*, are "gewiß nicht als deren Bestandteile systematisch integrierbar." *Cf.* also Weidemann, 2014, p. 68, and note that the *DI*, as Whitaker, 1996 has argued, may be seen as providing the groundwork for the *Top* and *Soph. El.* By offering a systematic account of contradictory sentence pairs used in dialectical argumentation.

22. On the introduction of the title "*Organon*" for those works taken together, see Weidemann, 2014, pp. 68–69. *Cf.* Barnes, 2007, pp. 106–107: "The *de Interpretatione* neither builds on the *Categories* nor lays the foundations for the *Analytics*. The *Analytics* has no use either for the *Categories* or for the *de Interpretatione*. The *Organon* was jerry-built—and jerry-built long after Aristotle's day. It is the ricketiest of constructions. Yet how it lasted."

23. Montanari, 1988. Andronicus of Rhodes even doubted the authenticity of the text, as we learn in detail from Boethius, 1877–1880, pp. 11.13–30; *cf.* Bonelli, 2009.

24. On Latin discussions of the question whether the copula is a *secundum* or *tertium adiacens*, see Nuchelmans, 1992. More generally for the history of theories of the proposition, see Nuchelmans, 1973, 1980, 1983.

25. The title "*Peri hermeneias*," or its Latin translation, "*De interpretatione*," i.e., "On interpretation," was almost certainly not Aristotle's (Weidemann, 2014, pp. 39–42; Maier,

1900, p. 72). The title has confused nearly every scholar of the work, and various suggestions have been made to explain it. Ammonius thinks the title is apt insofar as the treatise deals with affirmative sentences that "interpret" the cognition of the soul (Ammonius, 1897, p. 18f.); *cf.* Weidemann, 2014, p. 40, and similarly Kapp, 1965, p. 57: "Der Titel *De interpretatione* bedeutet 'Über den Ausdruck von Gedanken in der Rede'". Weidemann thinks the *DI* has what he calls "apophantische Logoi," i.e., affirmative sentences, as its subject matter, and can be characterized with Gadamer as a "kind of logical grammar" (Weidemann, 2014, p. 39; Gadamer, 1974, p. 1062). Perhaps, but the purpose of the treatise is to work out a theory of contradictories, as Whitaker, 1996, convincingly argues, and not the analysis of propositions with a logical grammar in mind. That the outcome is something like a logical grammar for atomic propositions, mainly established in chapters 1–4, must have been a corollary for the author. We shall see that the Graeco-Arabic reception history made it into a more central concern.

26. For the two constituent elements of a proposition, Aristotle in the *DI*—likely drawing on a passage from Plato's *Sophist* (261d–263d; *cf.* Kapp, 1965, pp. 63, 70)—uses *onoma* and *rhēma*, which are standardly translated by the cognates of the Latin *nomen* and *verbum* that Boethius had used: "noun" or "name" and "verb." While "name" in our contemporary philosophical usage as a word that *names* something seems to work well enough, "verb" is definitely a misleading translation in the context of the *DI*, for Aristotle seems to consider "white" (*leukon*) a *rhēma* (*DI* 1, 16a15; 10, 20b2 and 20a32). It would appear appropriate to translate *onoma* and *rhēma* as "subject" and "predicate," but Aristotle has his own words for these notions, i.e., *hypokeimenon* and *katēgoroumenon*, and he does not use them in the *DI* (for the relation between these two pairs of terminology, see Barnes, 2007, pp. 106–115). The semantic history of *onoma* and *rhēma* notwithstanding (Ademollo, 2015), I agree with Weidemann that a neutral translation for the *DI* should account for those facts. Unfortunately, it is impossible to render Weidemann's elegant translation (*Nennwort, Aussagewort*) into English; I shall use "name" in the sense of "naming-word" for *onoma* and "statement-word" for *rhēma*; *cf.* Weidemann, 2014, pp. 158–159.

27. Whether or not what Aristotle gives here is a real definition is contested; see Arens, 1984, pp. 25, 36; Montanari, 1988, pp. 89–92; *cf.* Weidemann, 2014, p. 159.

28. Scholars have disagreed on the exact interpretation of the examples given in 16a21–26; so for example Belardi, 1985, pp. 109–120; Montanari, 1988, pp. 113–123; Charles, 1994, pp. 49–51. A key issue here is whether Aristotle uses "Fairsteed" (*Kalippos*) as an example of a simple or of a compound naming-word (and, more generally, whether he is treating proper names on a par with common nouns, *cf.* Barnes, 2012, p. 154; and Geach, 1968, p. 61); Weidemann gives a succinct overview of the debate and argues for the former solution (Weidemann, 2014, pp. 160–163).

29. Kalippos was a common name in 4th-century Athens. We know that the astronomer and mathematician Kalippos of Cyzicus (*ca.* 370–300 BCE) studied with Eudoxus of Cnidus at Plato's Academy and worked with Aristotle at the Lyceum; see Segonds, 1994.

30. "Cutter-ketch" (*epaktrokelēs*) is clearly meant as an example for a compound naming-word—but we do not know what the Greek precisely meant, and that makes it difficult to see what exactly Aristotle's point was in choosing this particular example. We only know that *epaktris* and *kelēs* (literally, runner) were both used for certain types of boats, so that it has to be assumed that the compound is a nautical term for a specific kind of maritime

vessel—easy to maneuver, for we know that it was used by pirates—that combines the properties of both types of boats (see Weidemann, 2014, p. 164, and references). Presumably it was some conventional mid-sized mercantile naval vessel optimized for speed. Hence, I translate "cutter-ketch," the nautical term for a two-mast ketch with additional headsails typical of the cutter. Weidemann translates "Jollenkreuzer" (*cf.* Weidemann, 2014, pp. 164–165) and Montanari "brigantinogoletta" (*cf.* Montanari, 1988, p. 125); Ackrill's translation "pirate-boat" (*cf.* Ackrill, 1963, p. 116) is unfortunate, for it is not even a real compound, but only artificially hyphenated. Moreover, it does not serve to illustrate that the meanings of both elements of the compound contribute to the compound meaning, i.e., a naval vessel with characteristics of both boat types.

31. *Cf.* Weidemann, 2014, pp. 164–166.

32. See especially *Cratylus* 431b1-c2 (Plato, 1995); *cf.* Weidemann, 2014, pp. 166–170.

33. Aristotle does make the distinction between proper names and common nouns in *DI* 7 17a39–14b4, but overall, like Plato had in the *Sophist*, he treats common nouns as naming-words and not, as modern logic would, as some sort of Fregean concept-words; *cf.* Barnes, 2012, p. 154. It is noteworthy that Geach thought Aristotle was actually right about naming in the *DI*, and better off than Frege; see Geach, 1968, p. 61; and Geach, 1950 *passim*.

34. In *DI* 3, 16b6–8, Aristotle defines the verb (*rhēma*) as co-signifying time; "white" (*leukon*) does not do that, and in *Poetica* 20 (1457a16f.), "white" (*leukon*) is, together with "man" (*anthrōpos*), contrasted with verbs. It seems, however, that in the *DI*—both in this passage and in *DI* 10, 20b2 and 20a32—"white" (*leukon*) is used as an example for a verb. Thus Ammonius, 1897, pp. 28.5f., 53.9–16; Ackrill, 1963, p. 119; Kahn, 1973, p. 47, reprinted with new introduction as Kahn, 2003; Arens, 1984, p. 34f.; but not so Montanari, 1988, p. 69f.; *cf.* Weidemann, 2014, p. 155. I translate the definite article *to* before *leukon* against Minio-Paluello (Aristotle, 1956) and with Montanari, 1984, p. 148f., 151, and Weidemann (Aristotle, 2014; Weidemann, 2014, p. 155).

35. "Logical grammar" as per Gadamer, 1974, p. 1062. That Aristotle considered "white" (*leukon*) a verbal phrase (*rhēma*) insofar as it is a possible predicate in a statement once it is supplied with *esti* (and then does co-signify time) is defended by Ammonius, 1897, pp. 28.7–9, 53.5–8, and Stephanus, 1885, pp. 6.26–29; and Weidemann, it seems, who cites Kühner, 1898, p. 40 to point out that the copulative "is" is often omitted in Greek (Weidemann, 2014, p. 155). In my translation "but it is still a sign of something" I follow Weidemann's argument—against the majority (see Ackrill, 1963, p. 43)—and read it as qualifying the words "white" and "man" as signifying something even though they have no truth-value, as opposed to introducing the word "goat-stag" as an example for a compound utterance that however has no truth-value; *cf.* Weidemann, 2014, p. 156.

36. Weidemann, 2014, pp. 175–176. Ammonius, 1897, pp. 50.8–12 reports that Porphyry did not read the words in question, but thinks that they should be kept, based on the supposed reference to *Cat.* 5. Montanari, 1984, pp. 174–179; 1988, pp. 183–199, argues with Ammonius that they should be kept, whereas Minio-Paluello (Aristotle, 1956) excised them, supported by Tugendhat, 1958, pp. 40, note 3; and Weidemann (Aristotle, 2014; Weidemann, 2014, p. 175). See also Zimmermann, 1981, p. 14ff.

37. Weidemann, 2014, p. 176. Note that I translate *hygiainei* and *hygieia*, whose literal translation would be "is healthy" and "health," with "recovers" and "recovery" to account for the fact that in Greek Aristotle uses a full verb and a cognate noun. Translating *hygiainei*

with "is healthy" would introduce a copula where the Greek has none; translating with, e.g., "thrives" would leave no cognate noun to translate *hygieia*.

38. Kahn, 1972, p. 144; for interpretations ancient and medieval, see De Rijk, 2002, pp. 215–247, 2003; and for modern approaches, see Sonderegger, 1989. *Cf.* Weidemann, 2014, pp. 178–187.

39. Abelard uses "copula" in the relevant sense, but he certainly was not the first; for a discussion, see Kahn, 1972. Fārābī (d. 950) uses the Arabic equivalent ("*rābiṭa*") in the relevant sense. More has been written on the verb *einai* than on any other single word in the history of philosophy. One of the central issues has been whether and in what way *einai* was understood to mean a range of different aspects by ancient authors. It has variously been argued that *einai* was understood to multifariously mean "to be x" (copulative function), "to exist" (existential function), and "to be true" (alethic function). On *einai* in Greek philosophy, Kahn, 2003, 2009; Matthen, 1983; De Rijk, 1996, 2002; on the logic of "being," Knuuttila & Hintikka, 1986 present the most comprehensive work on the subject; partly reacting to Kahn, Bäck, 2000 has argued that Aristotle, like Avicenna (according to Bäck), and some of the commentators, understood *einai* to always mean "exists as x." I think that this interpretation lacks sufficient textual evidence but cannot here undertake an argument against it. When I say Aristotle has no and needs no theory of the copula, I do not mean that he does not at length theorize about *einai*, of course. He has a great deal to say in the *Cat* and especially the *Met*, which after all is the science of being *qua* being (*einai ē einai*), and commentators have often attempted to synthesize what Aristotle says there with what he says in the *DI*. But none of this is relevant to the logical analysis of APs in the *DI*. The fact that Aristotle distinguishes ten classes of terms in the *Cat* and ten different senses of "to be" in *Met* Δ 1017a22–29 has no bearing on anything said in the *DI*; for "just as the syllogistic has not the remotest interest in what the *Categories* says about terms, so it is wholly indifferent to what the *Metaphysics* says about the ten senses of 'is'!" (Barnes, 2009b, p. 42).

40. For a detailed study of discussions on the *secundum*/*tertium adiacens* distinction in this passage from Aristotle to the 14th-century Latin scholastics and beyond, see Nuchelmans, 1992.

41. The passage has elicited much discussion among commentators both ancient and modern; five different interpretations are Maier, 1936, p. 115ff.; Oehler, 1962, p. 144ff.; Rapp, 1991; Nuchelmans, 1992, p. 9f.; and Weidemann, 2014, pp. 338–345.

42. Barnes, 2009b, pp. 31–32, thinks that for Aristotle the copulative "is" plainly is a verb. I do not see why this should be plain, unless we have a supporting reading of this sentence. And we do not seem to have one.

43. See Text 2. The main difficulty for any interpretation of the passage in question is that in the preceding clause ("for it is not a sign for the being or not being of the thing [meant], nor is 'being' if you say it in isolation") is supposed to give a reason or explication (*gar*) of why a statement-word in isolation does not yet signify whether that which it signifies holds or not. That there is no such relation in what the clause literally says, i.e., that the being or not-being is not a sign of the thing, is obvious. I follow in my translation Weidemann's arguments at Weidemann, 2014, pp. 180–187, where the main interpretations are all discussed. See also Ax, 1979; Weidemann, 1982b; Sonderegger, 1989.

44. Weidemann discusses a number of unsatisfactory interpretations in Weidemann, 2014, pp. 390–393.

45. Porphyry said that the scholars of his time who wanted to comment on it had to consult the earlier commentaries of Aspasius, Herminus, and Alexander—but would then despair because of their incoherence and decide the *DI* was too tricky to comment upon and too taxing to read. This is reported from Porphyry's lost commentary on the *DI* in Boethius, 1877–1880, pp. II 293.27–294.4 (reprinted as Boethius, 1987). There might be a bit of self-adulation on Porphyry's part, since *he* wrote a commentary after all. But it underlines the historical peculiarity of the text, since as Barnes, 2009a, p. 143, put it, "même un étudiant en logique aristotélicienne a de bonnes raisons pour ne pas se frotter au *De l'interprétation*. Pourquoi se tracasser sur un ouvrage d'une difficulté légendaire et qui—malgré la doctrine officielle—ne contribue en rien à la syllogistique ? Pourquoi labourer un champ rocailleux et infertile ? Laissons-le en friche." And yet, the *DI* continued to be read, studied, commented upon, and stealthily made its way into early modern presentations of logic (*cf.* Barnes, 2009a).

46. Weidemann, 2014, p. 70. We do have a *De interpretatione*, which is not a commentary but a treatise on the *DI* and *Analytics* attributed to Apuleius (d. after 170). Even though the authorship remains contested, it is still our first Latin work on logic, and it remained influential as Apuleian logic well into the 13th century in Europe (Huby, 2007, p. 1; the text is edited in Apuleius, 1991). Galen (d. between 199 and 216) says in his *De libris propriis* that he wrote three commentaries (ὑπομνήματα, which might also indicate the number of books the works consisted of) on the *DI* and six on Theophrastus's *On Affirmation and Denial*, but no such text has come down to us (Galen, 1884, pp. 122.19–123.9; *cf.* Huby, 2007, p. 28).

47. Weidemann, 2014, p. 71.

48. Weidemann, 2014, p. 71.

49. So called by Stephanus, 1885, p. 63.10; *cf.* Zimmermann, 1981, p. lxxxv. As Zimmermann put it, "it must be sound policy to suspect originating from [Alexander] every feature the existing commentaries have in common or attribute to Porphyry, unless there is evidence to the contrary"; Zimmermann, 1981, p. lxxxv. For the exceptional value of Boethius not only for our knowledge of Porhyry's but also Alexander's commentary, see Bonelli, 2009.

50. For Boethius there is a monograph study on both commentaries: Suto, 2012. There is no evidence that Boethius was known to the Arabic philosophers, and their knowledge of Stoic philosophy appears to have mainly been secondhand. For a collection of relevant passages on *lekta*, simple propositions and composite propositions in Stoic logic, see Long & Sedley, 1987, pp. 196–221. There is an intriguing, if somewhat provocative, attempt to prove the direct influence of Stoic logic (through Prantl, 1855 and perhaps Diogenes Laertius) on Frege: Bobzien, 2021.

51. Huby, 2007, p. xv. For a commented collection of Theophrastus's fragments, see Fortenbaugh & al., 1992; Huby, 2007. Theophrastus was known, if only secondhand, in the Arabic tradition through translations of Diogenes Laertius (third century CE), Themistius (d. 388), and especially Galen; see Huby, 2007, p. 2.

52. Eudemus fr. 27, in Wehrli, 1944. Wehrli, 1944, p. 79 thinks that the *On Interpretation* mentioned by Philoponus should be identified with (part of) Eudemus's *Peri lexeōs*—but Theophrastus also wrote a *Peri lexeōs* (Diogenes, 1999–2002, p. V 47): are they the same as well?

53. It is a *desideratum*—impossible within the confines of this project—to compare and contrast the development of grammar as a science alongside the development of

propositional analysis in logic. Great milestones in the development of ancient grammar are the *Technē grammatikē* (Linke, Neitzel, & Haas, 1977) attributed to the Alexandrian Dionysius Thrax (*ca.* 170–90 BCE) and the works of Apollonius Dyscolus (fl. 2nd century in Alexandria; Apollonius, 1878; see also Blank, 1982) and his son Herodian (Herodianus, 1867), both of whom had a substantial influence on Priscian's (*fl.* 500, active in Constantinople) *Institutiones Grammaticae* (Priscianus, 1855–1859), a systematic exposition of Latin grammar used widely during the Middle Ages. Recent work has done much to clarify the early development of Greek grammatical theory; see for example Schironi, 2018; Montanari & Pagani, 2011; Jungen, 2007; and Swiggers & Wouters, 1996, 2002. An important aspect in the coming of age of the grammatical science was of course the classification of parts of speech, their functions, and, especially, syntax—approaches to language very similar to those taken by commentators on the *DI*, yet with distinct results. Grammarians came (like Aristotle in the *Poetics*) to standardly recognize eight parts of speech, and Peripatetic commentators increasingly felt the need to demarcate their technical terminology and approach to language from that of the grammarians (so, e.g., Ammonius, 1897, p. 12.15ff.; Stephanus, 1885, p. 12.9ff.).

54. Galen's writings on the *DI* are lost and we only have *in toto* his introductory *Intstitutio Logicae*. His influence, however, both on the teaching praxis in late antique Alexandria as well as for the Arabic reception of the Greek sciences was enormous; see Gutas, 1999 and Ibn Abī Uṣaybiʿa, 1882–1884 [1299–1301] (reprint Ibn Abī Uṣaybiʿa, 1995), II.134.30–135.24; Ibn Riḍwān, 1986, 66f.; Yaʿqūbī, 1883, I, 148f. Fārābī extensively studied the works of Galen in the translations by Ḥunayn ibn Isḥāq (d. 873). But Fārābī had little esteem for Galen, and the *Institutio* is a text mainly concerned with syllogistic that does not present anything for which I could detect any substantial influence on Fārābī's new conception of the copula.

55. The sentence is obscure, as Volait, 1907, p. 3, and Barnes, Bobzien, & Flannery, 2014, p. 55, noted. I think Volait gives a reasonable interpretation, which I accept. The thought would then be this: two different utterances may state the same thing, but since they are made up of different stuff, they cannot be the same proposition—for propositions are the constituents of syllogisms and as such it matters for inferences how a truth or falsity is expressed in them. But not only is that the case, we can also (*alla kai*) have two true utterances that differ not in what they are made up of, but in one being affirmative and the other negative (e.g., "justice is good" and "justice is not not-good"), yet still express the same statement without therefore being the same proposition.

56. This reading is different from Bäck, 2000, pp. 275–276, who disregards the evidence from the *DI* commentary and claims—hesitantly I admit—that Alexander "seems to favor the aspect theory," yet "in his *Analytics* commentary at least, he keeps close to the tripartite, term logic of the Aristotelian syllogistic." I do not think that Alexander holds either of the two theories of predication that Bäck has on offer. It is clear that he cannot hold what Bäck calls the "copulative theory," simply because Alexander outright denies that "is" is part of the proposition; for him, it is a mere annex to the predicate (and this is in the commentary on the *APr*). Nor can he subscribe to the "aspect theory" because he would not subscribe to the existential import of the equivocal "is." If Boethius is to be believed, Alexander held that the sense of "is" is only determined once a subject is supplied, and if the subject is such that the sense of "is" appropriate for it does not imply existence (like Homer), then it does not have to have existential import (*cf.* his analysis "Socrates is a being").

57. Ammonius, 1899, pp. 23.8–11.

58. For a brief introduction and further references to Ammonius's life and work, see Blank, 2014, pp. 1–7; most of our information comes from Damascius's *Life of Isidore* (Damascius, 1967).

59. Damascius, 1967, p. 110.

60. Ammonius, 1899, pp. 15.30–31.

61. Plato, *Sophist* 261d-e (Plato, 1995). Ammonius later in his commentary states clearly: "It was the doctrine both of Plato and Aristotle, that the parts of speech were two, the noun and the verb; the first denoting substances, the other the properties of substances: and indeed there can nothing exist in nature, but things and their qualities. So whatever more parts of speech we make, they can only be subdivisions of the members of this grand division," Ammonius, 1897, pp. 40.24–30. Ammonius and the later Greek commentators never lost Geach's "Platonic insight" that Aristotle supposedly lost. They all keenly presented Plato's and Aristotle's agreement on the issue. In fact, this was evident enough for the 18th-century linguist Lord Monboddo to approvingly cite Ammonius's passage in his *Of the Origin and Progress of Language* (Monboddo, 1773–1792, pp. II.3 31–32 [repr. Monboddo, 1974]; *cf.* Gaskin, 2008, p. 202).

62. But see Matthen, 1983; De Rijk, 2002, 1996, 2003 (*cf.* Sorabji, 2005, pp. 241–242), who interpret Aristotle somewhat like this. On De Rijk's reading Aristotle does not—as Alexander and Porphyry thought—take "is" to conjoin two parts, say "Socrates" and "wise," but "wise Socrates" is a compound already existing, of which "is" merely predicates that it obtains or is the case. However, Text 16 clearly shows that for Ammonius "is" takes an adjective to a predicate.

63. Translations in Texts 15–16 slightly modified from Blank, 2014, pp. 62–63.

64. Bäck, 2000, p. 278.

65. Ammonius, 1897, pp. 49.25–50.14. There, Ammonius reports an *altera lectio* from Porphyry, according to which a statement-word is not always a sign "of what is said of something else, either of a subject, or *in* a subject," but of "things that exist, e.g., of those said of a subject" that he immediately rejects. Stephanus bluntly says about the *altera lectio* "this is not true" (Stephanus, 1885, pp. 14.29–30), and Anonymous does not even mention it. See also Weidemann, 2014, p. 175f.

66. Charlton, 2014, p. 12, calls the *DI* a "popular text in sixth-century Alexandria." Besides the edited commentaries of Stephanus (Stephanus, 1885 [Charlton, 2014]) and Anonymous and the fragments of Olympiodorus (both edited in Tarán, 1978), Busse in his supplementary preface to his edition of Ammonius mentions another anonymous commentary (MS Coisliniano 160, fols.1–96), apparently later than our Anonymous, but still Alexandrian in style, that remains however unedited (Ammonius, 1897, p. xixff.; *cf.* Charlton, 2014, p. 13). Both Philoponus and Elias seem to have written commentaries that are now lost, and the story of Greek commentaries continues in Constantinople after the Arab conquest of Alexandria (see Busse in Ammonius, 1897, pp. xv–lii; *cf.* Regla Fernández, 1996, p. 319; Charlton, 2014, p. 13).

67. Just as Ammonius had, Stephanus likened NWs and SWs to the planks of a ship, and the remaining eight parts of speech distinguished by grammarians to nails, dowels, and glue; Stephanus, 1885, pp. 3.33–38 *cf.* the similar formulation in Ammonius, 1897, p. 12.25f.

68. Stephanus, 1885, pp. 11.6, 13.33–34, 39.27, 40.36–37, 52.12.

69. In the *DI* Aristotle uses the word four times; one occurrence is doubtful. *Cf.* Zimmermann, 1981, pp. lx, note 1.

70. Frege, 1892a, pp. 99–100; *cf.* Barnes, 2012, p. 163.

2. HISTORICAL PRELUDE: FĀRĀBĪ'S PHILOSOPHICAL PROJECT

1. Gutas, 2014, p. 305, note 74: "A detailed study of all these dimensions to assess the contribution of this 'war of signification' among the various disciplines to the formation of the classical Islamic position is a major desideratum." For a study of "*ma 'nā*" (meaning) in that period, see Frank, 1981. See also Key, 2018, for later developments.

2. Frank, 1978, p. 4; *cf.* Gutas, 2014, p. 304. Especially difficult was the translation and reception of the *Poetics*; see e.g., Adnan, 2020, pp. 75–134.

3. It was, by the 4th/10th century, common to include in works on grammar, theology, Qur'ānic exegesis, or jurisprudence, a substantial element dealing with linguistic and semantic matters. See Versteegh, 1977 for grammar, and Rosenthal, 2007, pp. 208–239, for the religious sciences; *cf.* Gutas, 2014, p. 305.

4. One of the main sources is an account by Fārābī himself, but it is tendentious. Meyerhof, 1930, who had first coined the phrase "Von Alexandrien nach Baghdād" with his study, argued, on the basis of Fārābī's account in the *Fī Ẓuhūr al-falsafa* that there was a single identifiable institution of learning that physically moved from Alexandria via Antioch to Baghdād. Since Strohmeier, 1987 confidence in the veracity of Fārābī's account has been waning until the account seemed no longer tenable (Lameer, 1997 and Gutas, 1999). For recent developments in the study of Syriac philosophy, see especially Fiori & Hugonnard-Roche, 2019; on the Syriac commentary tradition, Lössl & Watt, 2011; and on the *Organon*, Watt, 2009, 2019a, 2019b.

5. Gutas, 1999 reevaluated the historicity of Fārābī's account based on an analytic comparison between the narratives of several sources, saving some of the information as still useful for the historian. The text of Fārābī's account as reported by Ibn Abī Uṣaybiʿa was first edited in Steinschneider's Fārābī, 1869 and then in Ibn Abī Uṣaybiʿa, 1882–1884 [1299–1301] (reprint Ibn Abī Uṣaybiʿa, 1995), II.134.30–135.24.

6. Gutas, 1999, pp. 184–185. This is attested in numerous manuscript sources of translations and commentaries, beginning at least as early as Probus (6th century). See also Hugonnard-Roche, 1991.

7. Watt, 2008, p. 758. There were many Syrian and Armenian students in 6th-century Alexandria (and Athens); see Watt, 2013, p. 28; and Barnes & Calzolari, 2009 for the Armenian tradition. For recent scholarship responding to Gutas, see Hugonnard-Roche, 1999, Hermans, 2018, responding to Gutas, 1983; more recently, and more generally, Watt, 2008, 2010, 2013, 2016, 2017, 2019a.

8. The fact that several Syriac translations and commentaries on the *Organon* lack the latter part of the *APr* and all of the *APo* can thus be explained by practical decisions made for teaching purposes, not necessarily religious reasons. Given that many places of learning, for example, the monastery of Qenneshre (founded 531 by John bar Aphtonia), were clearly diglossic environments, the fact that Syriac manuscripts do not deal with the latter parts of the *Organon* might just be evidence that introductory logic teaching for those members of the community that had no ready grasp of Greek was restricted to the basics of Aristotle's logic. See Watt, 2008, p. 764.

9. Almost all known Syriac manuscripts written before the 7th/13th century come from a single monastic library, that of Dayr al-Suryan in Egypt (now in the British Library and the Vatican); see Brock, 2004; *cf.* Watt, 2013, pp. 29–30, and *passim* for the turn to Aristotle.

10. Sergius commented on the *Cat*, but did not translate them (and it seems that the earliest Syriac translations postdate the commentary; but see also King, 2010), expecting his

readers to be able to read the Greek text; Watt, 2013, pp. 28–29. On Sergius, see Hugonnard-Roche, 1989a and Watt, 2010.

11. Hugonnard-Roche, 2009, p. 154; for a full table of translations, see Hugonnard-Roche, 1989b. A recent study of the transmission and its challenges of the *APr* (and the *Organon* more generally) in the Syriac and Arabic tradition is Vagelpohl, 2010.

12. Hugonnard-Roche, 1999. For Probus's commentary on the *Eisagoge*, see Hugonnard-Roche, 2012.

13. The epitome has recently been edited by Hugonnard-Roche, 2013. Noteworthy about this text is that Paul distinguishes six parts of speech, not two or eight, of which name and verb are only the most important (the name being the most important of all). Paul was the philosophy teacher to Khosrow I and might have come in contact with Damascius and the other last members of the Athenian academy who sought refuge at the Sasanian court in Ctesiphon after the school was closed as a result of Emperor Justinian's anti-pagan legislation in 529; see Agathias's account in Dindorf, 1871, p. 231 (Ag. Hist. II.30).

14. ʿAbd Allah Ibn al-Muqaffaʿ was the famed Persian-born belles-lettrist and translator (from Pahlavi to Arabic) of *Kalīla wa Dimna* (Panchatantra), who served as state secretary first under the Umayyads, and after the ʿAbbāsid revolution under the uncles of the caliph al-Manṣūr, who ultimately ordered his execution. It has been speculated that he was the "Abdala the Saracen" with reference to whom Pico della Mirandola opened his *Oration on the Dignity of Man* (1486); see Arjomand, 1994.

15. Ibn al-Muqaffaʿ's epitome and Ibn al-Bahrīz's *Ḥudūd al-manṭiq* (Definitions of Logic) have been edited by Dānishpazhūh in Ibn al-Muqaffaʿ, 1978 [1357] (reprinted Ibn al-Muqaffaʿ, 2002/2003 [1381]) with a French and Persian introduction. Ibn al-Muqaffaʿ's epitome is relatively short and simplifying, with copious examples and tabular arrangements; he also divides the parts of speech into eight (Ibn al-Muqaffaʿ, 2002/2003 [1381], p. 26). Ibn al-Bahrīz's is a more independent work (he also translated the *Cat* and *DI* for al-Maʾmūn) whose center of gravity is the syllogistic. On Ibn al-Muqaffaʿ and early negotiations between translation, grammar, and logic, see Troupeau, 1981 and Hugonnard-Roche, 1989b, p. 9f.; on Ibn al-Bahrīz, Fiey, 1990; Troupeau, 1997; Rescher, 1964, p. 100.

16. One telling piece of evidence of the difficulties faced in translation and the degree of terminological systematization leading up to the time of Ḥunayn are the Syriac-Arabic glosses compiled in the course of the process. See for example Hoffmann, 1874 (reprint Hoffmann, 2010) and Gottheil, 1908 (reprint Gottheil, 2010); *cf.* Hugonnard-Roche, 1989b, p. 9.

17. On Ḥunayn's workshop, see Overwien, 2012 and Vagelpohl, 2011; see also Connelly, 2020.

18. Sībawayhi, 1991 [1411]; Ibn al-Sarrāj, 2018. The questions of the origin of Arabic grammar and the directions of influence between Arabic grammar and Greek logical and linguistic thought remain contested. Merx, 1889, p. 137ff., first submitted the hypothesis that Arabic grammar had, via Syriac, borrowed from Aristotelian logic, among others, the tripartite division of the parts of speech, the distinction of genres, and the notions of tense and agency. While Fleisch, 1957 entertained the possibility that the early grammarians had borrowed concepts from Greek logic, but noted substantial independencies, M. G. Carter, 1972 entirely dismissed the Merx hypothesis. The question is not resolved: Versteegh, 1977 presented a substantial study arguing for such influence, but Troupeau, 1981 and Larcher, 2007 remain critical regarding the early development of Arabic grammar. For Sībawayhi, see Sībawayhi, 1991 [1411] and the discussions in Baalbaki, 2008; Marogy, 2009; for Ibn

al-Sarrāj, Ibn al-Sarrāj, 2018 and the discussion in Ghersetti, 2017. The sources claiming that Fārābī taught Ibn al-Sarrāj logic and studied grammar with him need to be viewed with some healthy skepticism, for they are relatively late and it is not unlikely that this connection was extrapolated by chroniclers retrospectively; the 7th/13th-century sources are Ibn Khallikān, 1968–1972, V 153.13–154.5; and Ibn Abī Uṣaybiʿa, 1995, II 136, 23–24; Gutas, 1999, urges for skepticism here, but see Vallat, 2004, p. 11.

19. For the conception of language as an intrinsically rational mirror of reality, see Ibn al-Anbārī, 1913, pp. 23.1, 17; 26.20; 35.14; 63.23; 69.8ff.; 103.21; 104.2; 121.22; 227.12; 251.25; and p. 7 of the introduction. It should be noted that the status of the Arabic language as the language in which Allah revealed the Qurʾān substantially shaped the conception of Qurʾānic Arabic as a rational and reliable mirror of reality. The idea that the Baṣrian and Kūfan grammarians were systematically antagonistic "schools," as Flügel, 1862 thought, was already questioned by Weil (Ibn al-Anbārī, 1913); *cf.* Troupeau, 2012. Abū al-Barakāt Ibn al-Anbārī's (d. 577/1181) *Kitāb al-inṣāf fī masāʾil al-khilāf* (Just Treatment of the Points of Divergence [between Baṣrian and Kūfan Grammarians]), discussing 121 grammatical points on which Kūfans and Baṣrians differed, is—albeit late—still our best source on the differences between these two "schools." But see also Furat, 1978 for one additional source.

20. For the characterization of the Baṣrian and Kūfan approaches to grammar as evinced by Ibn al-Anbarī, see Weil's introduction in Ibn al-Anbārī, 1913, pp. 3–116.

21. Whether Fārābī's (and Sibawayhi's) tripartite classification of linguistic items was original or influenced by an Aristotelian proto-grammar is discussed in Gätje, 1971 and Eskenasy, 1988. In any case, it has been the standard division in Arabic grammar from its formative period and it still is today. On *ishtiqāq* more later.

22. This is discussed in question 38 [39], Ibn al-Anbārī, 1913, p. 102ff.

23. Jurjānī, 2003, under the entry for "*ishtiqāq*," defines it as the formation of a word from another (*nazʿ lafẓ min ākhar*). No less than twelve monograph studies written on *ishtiqāq* before the end of the 4th/10th century are listed in al-Suyūṭī's (d. 911/1505) *al-Muzhir* (Suyūṭī, 1907, pp. 351.3–5): they are by al-Mufaḍḍal al-Ḍabbī (d. 170/786), Quṭrub (d. 206/821), al-Aṣmaʿī (d. 216/831), al-Akhfash (d. 215/830), Abū Naṣr al-Bāhilī (d. 231/846), al-Mubarrad (d. 285/898), al-Zajjāj (d. 310/922), Ibn al-Sarrāj (d. 316/929), Ibn Durayd (d. 321/933), Ibn al-Naḥḥās (d. 338/949), Ibn Khālawayh (d. 370/980), al-Rummānī (d. 384/994). Only that by Ibn Durayd is extant (Ibn Durayd, 1991), but it is a mere collection of etymological explanations of proper names. See also Fleisch, 2012.

24. Abū al-Fatḥ ʿUthmān Ibn Jinnī was the student of the great grammarian Abū ʿAlī al-Ḥasan b. ʿAlī al-Fārisī (d. 377/987), who had himself studied with al-Sarrāj and al-Zajjāj in Baghdād. Both spent some time (like Fārābī, but after his death) at the court of Sayf al-Dawla in Aleppo and were on friendly terms with the poet Mutanabbī. Ibn Jinnī was criticized for his formal grammatical approach to Mutanabbī's poetry by Abū Ḥayyān al-Tawḥīdī (on whom more later). In his commentary *al-Munṣif* on Abū ʿUthmān al-Māzīnī's work on *taṣrīf* Ibn Jinnī defines *taṣrīf* as the study of words halfway between linguistics (*lugha*) and grammar (*naḥw*): while linguistics deals with vocables, grammar deals with inflection (*iʿrāb*); the study of *taṣrīf* deals with a specific kind of inflection, namely that of the derived forms of the trilateral root (*awzān*), and not, for example, with inflections for gender, number, or person; *ishtiqāq* deals with the same material, but from the point of view of its historical origin (Ibn Jinnī, 1999, pp. 33–34; *cf.* Fleisch, 2012). On Ibn Jinnī's view on the nature of language: Germann & Rivera Calero, 2020.

25. The non-Arabist may refer to a useful illustration of the Arabic language as relevant to this point in Zimmermann, 1981, pp. xxviii–xxxi.

26. See Ibn al-Anbārī, 1913, p. 34.

27. Zajjājī, 1995, p. 54; 142; 146, note 3; see Fārābī, 1960, pp. 40.1–18; *cf.* Schöck, 2006, p. 146.

28. On the relationship between logic and theology in classical Islam, see Mahdi, 1970 and El-Rouayheb, 2016c.

29. The ʿAbbāsid caliph al-Maʾmūn in 218/833 instituted an inquisition (*miḥna*) requiring all judges (*quḍāt*) to publicly affirm the Muʿtazilī position of the createdness of the Qurʾān; those who refused, like Aḥmad b. Ḥanbal (d. 241/855), eponym of the Ḥanbalī school of law, were imprisoned, leading to public uprisings. On the *miḥna*, see Nawas, 2015; on the doctrine of the createdness of the Qurʾān, van Ess, 1991–1997, pp. III.199–508 (English: van Ess, 2018, pp. 214–550) and Frank, 1978; on the close connections between Muʿtazilite theological doctrine and grammatico-linguistic thinking, see for example Rashed, 2014.

30. Schöck, 2006; on Ibn al-Muqaffaʿ, see chapter 7, and on Fārābī, chapter 14. See also, especially on the notion of derived names (*asmāʾ mushtaqqa*), Schöck, 2008.

31. See Rashed, 2014, and now especially Rashed, 2020 for connections to the algebraic theories of al-Khwarizmī and a likely influence on Fārābī.

32. For a brief overview of the development of *adab* and the roles played by al-Muqaffaʿ and al-Jāḥiẓ, see Gabrieli, 2012; and on *adab* and science Lettinck, 2011. On al-Jāḥiẓ's linguistic foundation of his Muʿtazilī theology, see Montgomery, 2008, 2009a, 2009b, 2009c, and, generally, van Ess, 1991–1997, pp. IV.96–117 and Heinemann, Kropp, Khalidi, & Meloy, 2009. The theory of meaning al-Jāḥiẓ presents in his *Kitāb al-Bayān wa l-tabyīn* (Jāḥiẓ, 1948–1950, pp. I.75–87) has, to my knowledge, not yet been systematically studied (but see Baalbaki, 2009). It shares some traits with the Baṣrian grammatical understanding of language: there are five different carriers of signification (*dalāla*) that make the world intelligible (*bayān*) to us: utterances (*lafẓ*) are only one of them. The others are writing (*khaṭṭ*), gestures (*ishāra*), and two others that are difficult to translate: "ʿaqd," which I take to be the general order of things, like the succession of day and night etc. that makes God's creation intelligible; and the last, "*naṣba*," is what His creation tells us without using any of the other four (Jāḥiẓ, 1948–1950, pp. I.80–81).

33. Edited in Tawḥīdī, 1939–1944, pp. 107–129 (in-text references to this edition, in volume 1), first translated and discussed in Margoliouth, 1905; for discussions, see Mahdi, 1970; Taha, 1978, 1979; Elamrani-Jamal, 1983; Abū Ḥamdah, 1984, Endreß, 1986 (following Endreß, 1977); together with Kühn, 1986; Versteegh, 1997; Ouyang, 2016; chapter 11 of Nusseibeh, 2017; Giolfo & Hodges, 2018; and the dissertation Gunaydin, 2006.

34. Endreß, 1986, pp. 206–211.

35. Abū Saʿīd says: "There is no way that you create a new language within a language that is already established among its speakers. In any case, your [new language] consists only of what you have borrowed from the Arabic language, like cause (*sabab*) and instrument/*organon* (*āla*), negation (*salb*) and affirmation (*ījāb*), subject (*mawḍūʿ*) and predicate (*maḥmūl*), [. . .] and the like, that are nonsense and of no use, mere stutters far from conducing to any real understanding (*ilā al-ʿayy aqrab wa fī l-fahāmati adhhab*)" (Tawḥīdī, 1939–1944, p. I.122.15 f.); note that al-Sīrāfī here includes the technical terms for subject and predicate.

36. The list features the Arabic terms for Porphyry's five praedicabilia (*jins, naw*, *khāṣṣa, faṣl, ʿaraḍ*) and includes "*haliyya*" (if-ness), "*ayniyya*" (ubiquity? Or, per Endreß, 1986, p. 262, "*anniya*": existence; see also Frank, 1956, and Adamson, 2002), "*māhiyya*" (quiddity), "*kayfiyya*" (quality), "*kamiyya*" (quantity), "*dhatiyya*" (essentiality). Like in Latin the suffix "-tas"/English "-ty"; noteworthy are the constructions "*aysiyya*" and "*laysiyya*," probably (as suggested by Endreß, 1986, p. 262) from Syriac "*īth*" (being) and "*lait*" (not-being), translating to "entity" and "non-entity" (?), or rather "is-ness" and "is-not-ness"; Tawḥīdī, 1939–1944, p. I.123.10. Both terms are not common in the later logical tradition.

37. On Fārābī and the formation of abstract nouns, see Abed, 1991, pp. 155–157.

38. There is relatively little we can say with certainty about Fārābī's life: the contemporary or near-contemporary sources are sparse, and the later sources suspiciously rich and tendentious. A comprehensive presentation with bibliography is Rudolph, 2012, pp. 369–377 (English: Rudolph, 2017, pp. 526–544). See also Netton, 2005.

39. Gutas et al., 1999, p. 212; but for a comprehensive list of works, see now section 3 in the chapter on Fārābī in Rudolph, 2012 (= Rudolph, 2017, pp. 545–593).

40. Gutas et al., 1999, p. 213. Among the works dealing with language are notably *Iḥṣā' al-ʿulūm* (Classification of the Sciences: Fārābī, 1949, and recently Fārābī, 2015) and the *Kitāb al-Ḥurūf* (Book of Letters/Particles: Fārābī, 1970).

41. Rudolph, 2017, p. 529. We have (1) the epitomes *Īsāghūjī ay al-Madkhal* (*Eisagoge*, i.e., Introduction), *Qāṭīghūriyās ay al-Maqūlāt* (Categories), *Bārī Arminiyās ay al-ʿIbāra* (On Interpretation, i.e.,The Expression), two epitomizing works on the *APr*, *al-Qiyās/ al-Madkhal ilā al-qiyās* (The Syllogism/Introduction to the Syllogism) and *Mukhtaṣar al-Manṭiq al-saghīr ʿalā ṭarīqat al-mutakallimīn* (Short Summary of Logic as Practiced by the Theologians), as well as *al-Burhān* (The Demonstrative Proof = *APo*), *al-Jadal* (The Dialectics = *Top*), *al-Amkina al-mughliṭa* (The Positions Inducing Error = *Sop. El.*), *al-Khiṭāba* (Rhetoric), *al-Shiʿr* (Poetry = *Poetica*). Of the (2) commentaries we only have that on the *DI*, some Arabic and recently discovered Hebrew fragments of that on the *Cat* (see the critical edition with English translation in Zonta, 2006), and a fragment of that on the *APr*. All except the fragments on the *Cat* have been edited by Dāneshpazhūh in Fārābī, 1987–1990 [1408–1410]. For other editions and translations, as well as other (3) supplementing works on the epitomes of the *Organon*, see Rudolph, 2012 (Rudolph, 2017, pp. 529–531). The introductory works include *al-Tawṭi'a fī l-manṭiq* (Introduction to Logic) with the alternative title *al-Risāla allatī suddira bihā l-manṭiq* (The Treatise with Which Logic Begins), which is intended as a propaedeutic to the *Īsāghūjī* and begins with a preliminary distinction of logic from grammar (see Dunlop, 1956); *Fuṣūl tashtamil ʿalā jamīʿ mā yuḍtarr ilā ma'rifatihi man arāda al-shurūʿ fī ṣinā'at al-Manṭiq [al-Fuṣūl al-Khamsa]* (Chapters Containing Everything a Beginner in the Art of Logic Needs to Know [The Five Chapters]) with chapter 1 making clear that every discipline has its respective technical terminology, chapter 3 introducing essential and accidental connections, and chapter 5 presenting the tripartite division of simple expressions into name (*ism*), statement-word (*kalima*), and particle/auxiliary (*harf/adāt*); and finally *al-Alfāẓ al-musta'mala fī l-manṭiq* (Linguistic Expressions Used in Logic), a more substantial introductory work in which Fārābī, based on the insight that "logic deals not only with (universal) intelligibles but also with those (Greek, Arabic, etc.) words which denote those intelligibles, [. . .] strives to present the basic concepts and assumptions of the *Organon* in clear and comprehensible form, and thus makes a major

contribution to the conceptualization and development of Arabic terminology" (Rudolph, 2017, p. 553); notably, Fārābī begins by the tripartite division of simple utterances and then extensively discusses five different types of particles (*ḥurūf*) (see here also Dunlop, 1955a).

42. See note 4; and Rudolph, 2017, pp. 594–596.

43. Gutas, 1999.

44. "Thus it went until the coming of Christianity. Then teaching came to an end in Rome while it continued in Alexandria until the king of the Christians looked into the matter. The bishops [. . .] formed the opinion that the books on logic were to be taught up to [. . . *APr* I.7] but not what comes after it, since they thought that that would harm Christianity. [. . .] Of public teaching then this much remained, [. . .] until Islam came after a long period. The teaching was transferred from Alexandria to Antioch. There it remained for a long time until only [one] teacher remained" etc.; transl. from Gutas, 1999, pp. 163–165.

45. Gutas, 1999, p. 177.

46. Anti-Byzantine sentiment would have been especially strong at the court of Sayf al-Dawla ("Sword of the Dynasty"), who was awarded his sobriquet for holding out against the armies of Constantine VII—but the Byzantines conquered Cilicia in 356/967 two years before he died; see Robinson, 2010, p. 355.

47. See page 37; another noteworthy feature of the account is that there is no mention of the Neo-Platonist philosopher al-Kindī, which may be understood as programmatic of Fārābī's push for Aristotelianism.

48. See also the telling chapter on religion and philosophy in the *Kitāb al-ḥurūf* (Fārābī, 1970, pp. 154–157).

49. On the myth of Fārābī's alleged awe-inspiring polyglossia, see Rudolph, 2017, p. 540.

50. Zimmermann, 1981, pp. lxviii–xv, remains the most comprehensive overview of Fārābī and the Greek tradition with regard to his commentary on the *DI*; for textual evidence of Fārābī's direct acquaintance with respective parts of the *Organon*, see Zimmermann, 1981, pp. lxviii– lxix and notes. Zimmermann presumes that the texts compiled in the MS Parisinus Ar. 2346 at the Bibliothèque Nationale—a collection of sometimes several translations of the books from the *Organon*, redacted in 418/1027 with numerous notes by Ibn al-Khammār (d. between 407–421/1017–1030)—represent an Arabic "school canon" and thus the state of the Arabic translations, from Syriac and from Greek, available to Fārābī. If that is the case, Fārābī also knew Abū Bishr Mattā's (poor) translation of the *Poetica* (Zimmermann, 1981, lxix).

51. Zimmermann, 1981, p. lxxx.

52. *Cf.* Zimmermann, 1981, p. xcviii; see also Hasnawi & Hodges, 2016, 46.

53. See Zimmermann, 1981, pp. lxviii–xv; Fārābī knew Ammonius, and he likely knew of the Alexandrian-Porphyrean prototype through Syrianus. He also had knowledge of the mysterious Allīnus (on the identification with David, see Rashed, 2005; but see also Hugonnard-Roche, 2009, pp. 168–170). And he knew Galen: see on page 195n54.

54. The *KH* has been edited by Mahdi from a single MS (Fārābī, 1970); Butterworth is preparing a critical edition to come out with Cornell University Press (Hilal, 1997 uses the superior Baku MS for his translation and study). In-text references in this sub-section are to Mahdi's edition, by page and line number, or else to Mahdi's paragraph numbers.

55. I do not use "Linguistic Constructivism" in the sense of Jean Piaget and Lev Vygotsky, or generally in the sense current in developmental psychology. But I do use it to

indicate a theory that is based on the idea that language is not recursive on an innate structure, but rather empirically coordinated over time—and thus that structural similarities between different languages are explained by the similarity of human experience, not by any hard-wired disposition.

56. Scholarship on the *KḤ* has tended to focus on Part II and has on the whole been punctual (e.g., in Vallat, 2004; Abed, 1991; Diebler, 2005; Druart, 2007, 2010), rather than aiming at a holistic reading of the work in its entirety, but see Hilal, 1997, 2001. Menn, 2008, announcing a monograph on the work, has broached an integral reading of the work's overall aims and achievements, focusing on Fārābī's disambiguation of the senses of "being."

57. The beginning of Part I is fragmentary, and Mahdi (pp. 40–43) conjectures that it may have fallen out of an ancestor of the extant MS and been put back in the wrong place, so that the order might have been II–III–I. I think the order is II–I–III, as does Menn, 2008, p. 66, note 9. Perhaps Butterworth's edition will bring clarity on the matter.

58. See Druart, 2010, pp. 4–6.

59. The emergence of art of the knowledge of language Fārābī describes here (§§132–135) is reminiscent of the early Arabic writings on literary criticism, collecting and recording pre-Islamic poetry, and searching for the pure and "correct" Arabic that the Bedouin communities were thought to have preserved—against the influx of loanwords to which the more cosmopolitan city-dwellers were so susceptible. See for example the early anthology of poetry *al-Mufaḍḍaliyyāt* (Ḍabbī, 1942), or al-Aṣmaʿī's *Fuḥūlat al-shuʿarāʾ* (Aṣmaʿī, 1971), or the *Ḥamāsa* by Abū Tammām (Abū Tammām, 1846, with German translation).

60. For the Greek origin of Fārābī's notion of "prototype," see Zimmermann, 1981, p. xxxff. See also Menn, 2008, pp. 65–67, and especially Karimullah, 2017, pp. 257–259.

61. Edited from the unicum MS Tehran: Majlis, Ṭabāṭabāʾī 1376 in Endreß, 1978. For a French translation, see Elamrani-Jamal, 1982; for a commented German translation, see Endreß, 1986, pp. 271–296.

62. Fārābī, 1949; in-text references in this section are to Amīn's edition. Other than in this text and the *KḤ*, it is especially in *al-Tawṭiʾa fī l-manṭiq* (Introduction to Logic) and *al-Alfāẓ al-mustaʿmala fī l-manṭiq* (Linguistic Expressions Used in Logic) that Fārābī discusses the difference between logic and grammar. Since the 1980s, beginning with Endreß's and Elamrani-Jamal's pioneering work, a good deal of research has been done on Fārābī's conception of the relation between language and logic: Endreß, 1977, 1986; Elamrani-Jamal, 1983, 1990; Hasnawi, 1985; Eskenasy, 1988 responding to Gätje, 1971; Abed, 1991; Black, 1991; Schneider, 1994; Lameer, 1994; Schöck, 2006; Türker, 2007; Menn, 2008; Mandosio, 2013; Chatti, 2014; Germann, 2015; Druart, 2007, 2010, 2016.

63. *Cf.* Street, 2008 and Druart, 2016.

64. Fārābī, 1949, p. 18.11ff. Fārābī might have known the contents of the *Ars grammaticae* attributed to Dionysius Thrax (*ca.* 90 BCE) through Syriac and Arabic translations, but probably not systematically. He likely was well acquainted with Sibawayhi's *Kitāb* and Ibn al-Sarrāj's commentary. It has been argued that the early Arabic grammarians were themselves influenced by Aristotle's threefold division, rather than by the Graeco-Syriac grammatical tradition that recognized eight types of linguistic items, in dividing linguistic signs into nouns (*ism*), verbs (*fiʿl*), and particles (*ḥarf*). Aristotle nowhere proposes this division, but in *Poetica* 20, and *Rhet* Γ.2,5,12, he speaks of *sundesmos*, and also mentions *arthron* as a part of speech. Already al-Khalīl b. Aḥmad (d. 169/786?), Sībawayhi's teacher, introduced

the threefold distinction in Arabic. Whether or not there was an influence of Greek grammar on Arabic grammar, the fact that Fārābī makes a conscious decision to use the technical terms from the Arabic translations of Aristotle, i.e., *ism* for noun, *kalima* for verb, and *adā* for particle, suggests that he considered it important to keep apart logical and Arabic grammatical terminology; *cf.* Zimmermann, 1981, pp. 135–137.

65. For Aristotle, name (*onoma*) and verb (*rhema*) matter in logic, while particles (*sundesmos*) and conjunctions (*arthron*) are merely part of the lexis. *Cf.* Gätje, 1971, p. 2.

66. Karimullah, 2017.

3. GREEK LOGIC ARABICIZED AND THE COPULA TRANSFORMED

1. This fact may reflect the relative influence of his commentaries. Fārābī used the Arabic text of Isḥāq b. Ḥunayn, edited by Pollak in Aristoteles Arabus, 1913. The commentary has been edited by Kutsch and Marrow in Fārābī, 1960. An excellent English translation of both the commentary and the epitome, together with a substantial study in the introduction, is Zimmermann, 1981; I have in this chapter freely adapted Zimmermann's translation. In-text citations refer to Kutsch & Marrow and the page number of Zimmermann's translation, e.g., (44.3–4; Z 36). See also Hasnawi, 1985. For the *APr* we have some fragments of the commentary (edited by Dānishpazhūh in Fārābī, 1987–1990 [1408–1410], pp. II.261–553), an introductory text (Fārābī, 1987–1990 [1408–1410], pp. I.115–151), and the epitome (Fārābī, 1987–1990 [1408–1410], pp. I.152–194); see the presentation in English in Hodges & Chatti, 2020.

2. Zimmermann, 1981, pp. xxxviii–xxxvix calls Fārābī's formalism a "*leitmotiv* [running] throughout the work," and a "new departure in the exegesis of the *De interpretatione*."

3. For some examples of how Fārābī interfered with the Arabic text, see Zimmermann, 1981, pp. lxx–lxxvi.

4. Ibn al-Nadīm, 1871–1872, pp. I.248.16–17; *cf.* Zimmermann, 1981, p. lxviii. Hoffmann, 1869 studied the extant Syriac fragments of the *DI* (found, e.g., in Probus) and compared them to the Arabic translation; besides the studies by Hugonnard-Roche I am not aware of more recent philological scholarship on the connection between the Syriac and Arabic *DI*. For this connection regarding the *Cat*, see Georr, 1948. On Ḥunayn and his school, Bergsträßer, 1913 is still a monumental study, but see Gutas, 2018b for the progress made since then.

5. Aristoteles Arabus, 1913; *P*, contrary to descriptions in some MS catalogues (see, e.g., Klamroth, 1887, p. 439, note 1), still appears to be the only witness of the complete Arabic *DI* (for misattributions, see Aristoteles Arabus, 1913, pp. viii–ix), except perhaps MS Istanbul: Topkapı Sarayı Ahmet III 3362, which contains a *DI*, but I have not been able to ascertain whether it is complete (but see Zimmermann, 1981, p. cxlii; the incomplete translation of the *APr* contained in that MS seems to be an earlier redaction than that in *P*; see Lameer, 1994, pp. 5, 8). A fragment of the Arabic *DI* (up to Bekker 17b14) contained in the Syriac codex MS Berlin: Staatsbibliothek Petermann 9 (fols. 68v–72v) is edited in Hoffmann, 1869. Pollak notes the divergences in his edition and the fragment seems to be closer to the Greek original.

6. For a brief description of *P* (now accessible online) in connection with the Arabic *DI*, see Aristoteles Arabus, 1913, pp. xi–xiii; Zimmermann, 1981, pp. vxix–vxxviii; for a more

general discussion: Hugonnard-Roche, 1993. Some of the school notes appear in almost identical form in Fārābī's commentary and are printed by Zimmermann. However, many are not: the relatively high density of marginalia on the first chapters of the *DI* in the hand of the copyist, the Nestorian philosopher, logician, and student of Yaḥyā b. ʿAdī Ibn Suwār (or Ibn al-Khammār, on whom see the entry Endreß, 2012; the suggested date of death is 421/1030, according to Gutas, 2014, p. 62), may provide insights about the precise details that caused problems of understanding in the process of honing the text by "critical translation" (Hugonnard-Roche, 1993, pp. 20–21). Unfortunately, the marginal notes are mostly illegible in the scanned version on gallica.fr, and the pandemic has prevented me from autopsy.

7. Pollak speaks of a "geradezu barbarischen Stil"; see Aristoteles Arabus, 1913, p. vi. The barbarisms of these texts were of course a main reason for the eloquent Sīrāfī and his likes to criticize translators; see page 41.

8. The circumstances under which, and to what extent, Ḥunayn came to master the Greek language is reported by an eye witness named Yūsuf Ibrāhīm, recorded in Ibn Abī Uṣaybiʿa, 1995, p. I.185f.

9. Biesterfeldt, 2015, p. 127; see especially Rosenthal, 1965, pp. 15–23 (English: Rosenthal, 1975, pp. 15–23) for a collection of pertinent texts telling of the rigorous method followed by Ḥunayn and other translators. On Ḥunayn's splendid reputation as a translator, see Olsson, 2016.

10. Isḥāq's eloquence in Arabic was considered superior to that of his father by, e.g., Ibn al-Nadīm or Ibn al-Maṭrān; see Strohmaier, 1978. For evidence that Ibn Suwār in the process of producing *P* collated Greek and Syriac MSS with the text of the Arabic translations of what was likely Ibn ʿAdī's autograph of the *Organon*, see Georr, 1948, p. 369; cf. 358.

11. The 3rd/9th-century historian Aḥmad b. Wāḍiḥ al-Yaʿqūbī still listed the title as *Kitāb al-tafsīr* (Klamroth, 1887, p. 422), and the title *Kitāb al-qaḍāyā* is also attested (see Aristoteles Arabus, 1913, pp. xiv–xv). The Baghdād Peripatetics were aware of the late antique discussions of the meaning of the title, but it seems that by Fārābī's time the title *Kitāb al-ʿIbāra* had achieved widespread acceptance. Ibn al-Nadīm (d. 385/995) explains the Greek title by giving *al-ʿIbāra* as its meaning (Ibn al-Nadīm, 1871–1872, pp. I.248.16–17). Fārābī himself explains the title thus: "Its title is *On interpretation* because 'interpretation' means 'complete phrase.' Generally speaking, a thing that is complete is the most perfect [and the first] of its kind. [Thus a complete phrase] is the most perfect and the first of phrases. Hence, in using the term ['interpretation'], Aristotle specifies the first of complete phrases as the subject of this book. He has thus given it a title which sums up its content"; translation Zimmermann, 1981, pp. 3–4.

12. Translation Zimmermann, 1981, p. 14, note 1.

13. See chapter 1, note 34.

14. Translation Zimmermann, 1981, p. 101, note 5.

15. Jabre, 1973 has produced a substantial study of the ways in which *einai* has been translated in the *Cat*. Since the *Cat* was also translated by Isḥāq, much of what he says has an immediate relevance to the *DI*.

16. Fārābī discourages the use of "*huwa*" and its abstract derivation "*huwiyya*," because he thinks it is not good Arabic (Fārābī, 1970, pp. 114.15–20 [I.86]); and presumably, because using "*huwa*" as a copula has the disadvantage of not having available the tensed cognates

that, for example, can be formed from the passive participle *"mawjūd"* (*cf.* Menn, 2008, p. 76).

17. Fārābī's lemma has here *ḍarbayn* instead of *ḍiddayn*, which, even though it does not strictly translate the Greek *antitheseis*, still preserves the same sense.

18. See page 23.

19. The Arabic here may convey a sense different from the Greek. There are two issues. First, the *mā* may be taken as a *mā maṣdariyya* so that we would have to translate: "The verb is always a sign of being said of something else," i.e., a sign of predication, instead of, when taken as a relative pronoun, "a sign of what is said of something else," i.e., a sign of the predicate. In Greek, only the latter is possible, amounting to the claim that a verb is always a predicate. But Fārābī, as becomes evident in the following paragraph, understood it in the former way, amounting to the claim that the verb always includes in its meaning the copulative function; *cf.* Zimmermann, 1981, p. 22, note 3. Second, there is, as noted by Zimmermann, 1981, p. 22, note 9, the possibility to understand from the Arabic "Always a *verb* is the sign of . . . ," i.e., not only is it the case that a verb always is a predicate, but a predicate is always a verb. It strikes me as a very unnatural reading of the Arabic, but it appears that some have understood it that way, for Fārābī argues immediately afterward, at Fārābī, 1960, p. 33.27f., against the opinion of "others," that this is not the case.

20. At *DI* 3, 16b 9–11: Weidemann brackets the last three words *ē en hypokeimenō*, noting "recte seclusit Minio-Paluello" (Aristotle, 2014, p. 4). The entire sentence was subject to textual criticism already by Ammonius and Stephanus; see pages 22, 32. Isḥāq b. Ḥunayn's text reads: *wa-l-kalimatu dā'iman dalīlu mmā yuqālu ʿalā ghayrihi ka-annaka qulta mā yuqālu ʿalā l-mawḍū ʿi aw mā yuqālu fī l-mawḍu ʿ* (in Pollak's edition, Aristoteles Arabus, 1913, p. 4). *Cf.* Zimmermann, 1981, p. xxivff.; and Schöck, 2006, pp. 146–147, 286.

21. Especially *Cat* 1a12–15, Aristotle, 1956, p. 3; for Isḥāq b. Ḥunayn's Arabic see also Badawī, 1980, pp. 33–34. Compare: Ammonius, 1962, p. 49.24ff., and Stephanus, 1962, pp. 13.15–18; and Ibn al-Muqaffaʿ, 1978 [1357], pp. 28.11–16; *cf.* Zimmermann, 1981, pp. xxiv–xxvi; and Schöck, 2006, p. 144.

22. Stephanus, 1962, pp. 13.15–18; compare Ammonius, 1962, p. 49.24ff.; *cf.* Zimmermann, 1981, pp. xxiv–xxv and Schöck, 2006, pp. 146–147. See page 33.

23. See page 39.

24. *Cat* 2, 1a20–1b9 (Aristotle, 1956). See pages 22, 32; *cf.* Kalbarczyk, 2018, p. 58, and for an exposition of the fourfold division, see Porphyry's commentary on the *Cat* (Porphyry, 1887, pp. 71.20–22); Ammonius, 1962, p. 22; *cf.* Zimmermann, 1981, pp. xxiv–xxv. The difference becomes clear from the following pair of sentences: "Socrates is a man" and "Man is an animal" versus "Socrates is white" and "White is a color." Let all four statements be true. The first pair is a case of homonymous predication, in which "man" has the same definition in both sentences, i.e., "rational animal," and hence we can infer from the pair of sentences that "Socrates is an animal." In the case of the second pair, paronymous predication, "white" does not have the same definition in both sentences: "white" in the sense of being white colored is an accident in Socrates and as such a paronym of "white" in the sense of abstract whiteness, a universal, and hence we are not licensed to infer that "Socrates is a color." The example is from Sinaiti, in Menne & Öffenberger, 1985, 56f.

25. This is likely a calque from Stephanus's Greek; *cf.* page 33.

26. See page 31.

27. Just before, he gives an interesting argument, addressed to those who maintain that all predicates are verbs and that hence verbs can predicate essentially. If verbs were to predicate essentially, we could form, e.g., the verb "anthropize" (*yata'annasa*); if that is considered legitimate, we should like to say that verbs can predicate essentially, but as long as we understand that predication to be of a circumscribed time, we still would have to admit that even though predication may be synonymous, it will not be essential, since by signifying a circumscribed time, that predication could be true at that time even though it was not or will not be at some other time. But essential predication has to be true regardless of time. If we verbalize differentiae (*fuṣūl*), it might look like we are using verbs to predicate differentiae, but they then really express actions, not essences.

28. Fārābī, 1960, pp. 35.5–11; Zimmermann, 1981, pp. 24–25.

29. Compare here the corresponding passage in the *Mukhtaṣar*: "Genera and species of substance are mostly signified by prototypes, such as 'man' (*insān*), 'horse' (*faras*), 'tree' (*shajar*), 'plant' (*nabat*), 'body' (*jism*), 'substance' (*jawhar*). In some languages some of them happen to have the shape of a derived noun, though their meaning is not derivative; for they fall short of what has been stipulated for derivatives, namely that the alteration made in the prototype should signify an inderterminate subject in which it subsists. For no species of substance subsists in a subject. Differentiae, if used as such, are always signified by derived nouns"; Fārābī, 1990, pp. 55–56 (ed. Türker-Küyel); Zimmermann, 1981, pp. 232–233.

30. Ammonius and Ibn al-Muqaffaʿ had classified *maṣādir* and participial forms as signifying an extended time, while followers of Abū Muʿād al-Ṭūmanī had argued against Wāṣil b. ʿAṭāʾ that someone who fornicated can only be described as having fornicated at a certain time, not as a fornicator *tout court*, or essentially. *Cf.* Schöck, 2006.

31. *KḤ* I.83 = Fārābī, 1970, 112.3; *cf.* Menn, 2008, p. 73. For a study of Arabic translations of *einai*, see Jabre, 1973.

32. The Arabic text does not translate the Greek *on*; it only transliterates it (*ʾn*), see Aristoteles Arabus, 1913, pp. 5–6; *cf.* Fārābī, 1960, pp. 43.22–44.1; Zimmermann's English translation reads: For even if we said "was" or "will be," we should not signify a referent, similarly "was not" or "will not be." Nor should we, if we said "*on*" (*ʾn*) alone by itself, signify it. For in itself it is nothing, but it signifies, in addition to what it signifies, a composition. This composition cannot be understood without the components"; Zimmermann, 1981, pp. 34–35.

33. See page 31; and Ammonius, 1962, pp. 55.10–56.13.

34. Chapters 8–11 of Mahdi's first (which I think should be the second) part of the *KḤ* are devoted to an analysis of relations, i.e., *nisba* and *iḍāfa*; see Fārābī, 1970, pp. 82–95. On my reading, the positioning of these discussions matters: Fārābī begins with what I think he considers the two most fundamental notions for any science whatsoever: "that" and "when," expressed by the particles *anna* and *mattā* (§§1–2). The distinction suggested here is, I think, that between tenseless and tensed copulae, which is also spelled out in the *Sharḥ*. Fārābī then goes on to discuss the categories as the most generic names of all possible notions with which one will make statements about particular perceptibles or about what is abstracted from them employing the two fundamental notions of "that" and "when" (§3). Having presented the categories as being intelligibles that are predicated of particular perceptibles, Fārābī now introduces secondary intelligibles to account for the kinds of intelligibles that are not predicated of any particular perceptibles outside the soul (§4). This is the meta-language the logician uses to analyze natural language. He then embarks on the

logician's task to analyze the properties of the categories, i.e., the primary intelligibles (§§5–6). All of this, I think, is in a sense preliminary; for he then explains the relation between expressions and intelligibles, advancing his theory of derivatives and pointing out the traps of natural language (§7), before picking out several notions for which these dangers are pertinent. The discussions of the notions of "relation" (§§8–11) and of "*mawjūd*" (§15) occupy by far the most space. See pages 43–48; see also Menn, 2008, pp. 60–71 and Karimullah, 2017, pp. 261–270.

35. *KH* §101, Fārābī, 1970, pp. 125.13–126.12. Reading in line 12 *alifun mawjūdun bāʾan . . . bāʾun mawjūdun li-alifin* with the MS and Zimmermann, 1981, p. xxxv, note 2; *cf.* Mahdi's footnote *ad loc.*

36. "Correlates are related by a single notion they have in common, which holds of both of them. For example, if the correlates are A and B, rendering the relation as 'A is to B' is to say that A is thus related to B, and rendering it as 'B is to A' is to say that B is thus related to A. [. . .] This single notion is like the way between the roof and the floor of a house: taken as beginning on the roof and ending on the floor it is called descent; taken as beginning on the floor and ending on the roof it is called ascent." *KH* §41, Fārābī, 1970, pp. 85.9–16; Zimmermann, 1981, p. xxxv.

37. Fārābī, 1960, p. 45; Zimmermann, 1981, pp. 36–37. This is for Fārābī a prime example of how language can be misleading if taken to express logical form. Even though grammatically *mawjūd* is a derived name, it would be wrong to assume that it signifies a subject not articulated of which existence is predicated paronymously as being in that subject. This Fārābī spells out most clearly in the *KH*, and we shall return to this discussion later.

38. Fārābī, 1960, pp. 45–46; Zimmermann, 1981, p. 37. Zimmermann thinks that Fārābī's answer to the objection is not satisfactory, because he does not explain why, if two words need a third to connect them, the third does not need a fourth etc. (note 1). However, what is expressed as being related by the copula are not the words, but their meanings. Fārābī's point is that you may well be asked to clarify your use of a secondary intelligible. A secondary intelligible is retrieved from an appraisal of the properties of primary intelligibles, e.g., the property of "being-predicable-of-many" that we find in the primary intelligible signified by "human." The way Fārābī explains it in the *KH* §4 (Fārābī, 1970, pp. 24–26) is that some properties that accrue to primary intelligibles also accrue to secondary intelligibles, so that they can be predicated of themselves, e.g., "nominative" is itself a nominative, "genus" is itself a genus, etc. The example of Antisthenes's worry about definitions perhaps brings this out most clearly: you may be asked to give a definition of "man." You then say that it is "rational animal." If you're then asked what the definition of "definition of 'man'" is, you may say that it is "a phrase signifying the essence of 'man.'" Let this be the "definition of the 'definition of 'man.'" If you're now asked what the definition of this is, you can repeat your answer, and you could do so infinitely. Since you are at no time referring to anything that has extramental existence, there is no harm in repeating your answer. But nothing new is gained from your answer whenever you repeat it, so you might just as well only give it once. This does, I think, respond to the version of Bradley's regress that Fārābī anticipates. Giving a definition for the definition of "man" was still informative, because you were explaining the use of a secondary intelligible. So is saying that the copula expresses the relation between subject and predicate; but to go any further would add nothing. Note the similarities to the infinitistic logical copula in Gaskin, 2008.

39. For Fārābī the ability to express essential, or *per se*, predication, absolutely and without reference to time, is the basis for demonstrative inferences; see Strobino, 2019.

40. *Cf.* Zimmermann, 1981, p. 38, note 6; but *īth* can be used verbally, too: see Nöldeke, 1966, p. §199.

41. *KH* §83; Fārābī, 1970, pp. 112.1–2, and generally 112–113.

42. *KH* §86; Fārābī, 1970, pp. 114.15–20; Menn, 2008, p. 76.

43. *Cf.* the definition of "using a term in the wider and narrower sense" in the *Mukhtaṣar*: "A term is used in the wider and narrower (*bi-ʿumūmi wa khuṣūṣi*) sense if it is the name of a genus and at the same time serves as a label for a species of this genus, *qua* the species it is. Such a term is applied to such a species in two different ways: first, in a wider sense [i.e., *kalima* in the generic sense of 'word'], in that it is common to the other species which are subdivisions of the genus [i.e., *kalima* in the senses of 'copula' and of 'verb'], because the name of a genus applies to all its species; secondly, in a narrower sense [i.e., *kalima* in the sense of 'copula' or in the sense of 'verb'], if it is used as a label signifying the particular species *qua* the species it is." Fārābī, 1990, p. 51 (ed. Türker-Küyel); Zimmermann, 1981, p. 230, and note 1: "At *Isagoge* 2.20, ʿalā jihati l-ʿumūmi— ʿalā jihati l-khuṣūṣi tr. koinōs— idiōs (Badawi, *Manṭiq* Aristū iii. 1025.3f)."

44. *Cf.* chapter 1, note 35.

45. The reference to the *Poetics* and *Rhetoric* are *Poet* 20, 1456b21ff.; and *Rhet* Γ 5f., 1407a20–1513b32.

46. It should be noted that for Aristotle and early Greek grammarians there were in a sense three parts of speech, as reported, e.g., by Dionysios of Halicarnassus (d. *ca.* 7 BCE), but particles (*sundesmoi*, which by them was used more broadly than later by Dionysisios Thrax) were characterized as a *phōnē asēmos*, i.e., precisely as *not* having meaning: *Poet* 20, *Rhet* Γ 2,5,12; *cf.* Gätje, 1971, p. 2 (who falsely gives Dionysios of Halicarnassus's *floruit* as the 3rd century BCE).

47. The closest to a positive definition is perhaps from the introductory *Al-Fuṣūl al-khamsa*: Fārābī, 1987–1990 [1408–1410] (ed. Dāneshpāzhū), I.23; Dunlop, 1955a, pp. 270.10–11 (Arabic), 278 (English translation): "The particle is a simple word (*lafẓatun mufrada*) whose meaning cannot be understood in isolation and by itself, but only in connection with a name or a verb or both, such as the words 'from,' 'on' and the like." In the *Sharḥ* Fārābī nowhere gives a definition of the particle; in the *Mukhtaṣar* he only gives the syntactic criteria implied in the quotation given earlier: "A particle cannot be a predicate or subject by itself; it can only be *part* of a predicate or subject": Fārābī, 1990, p. 44; Zimmermann, 1981, p. 225.

48. On Fārābī's classification of the particles and its relation to Arabic and Greek grammar, see Gätje, 1971; Haddad, 1967; Eskenasy, 1988; Chatti, 2014; Türker, 2007; Versteegh, 1977; Ghersetti, 2017.

49. Eskenasy, 1988. For Sergius, see page 37.

50. Rummānī, 1973.

51. Gätje, 1971, p. 14 and *passim*.

52. Fārābī, 1968, pp. 42.16–17: "Every particle (*ḥarf*) is connected to an expression in one of these ways and it signifies that that which is understood (*al-mafhūm*) from the expression is in a certain state (*bi-ḥālin mina l-aḥwāl*)."

53. Fārābī, 1998, pp. 43.1–8; *cf.* Eskenasy, 1988, p. 60.

54. Menn, 2008; the arguments I am summarizing are found on pp. 60–76.

55. Syncategorematic expressions are something that we are used to from medieval European scholastic logic, e.g., from John Buridan. I think the terminology applies equally well to Fārābī's conception. For a study on Fārābī's and Avicenna's conception of syncategoremata, see Chatti, 2014. Most of these particles signify relations or more broadly connections of some sort. This is why Fārābī inserts a discussion about these two notions. Most, if not all, particles seem to signify a connection (*nisba*), where some signify a relation (*iḍāfa*) proper. (Not all connections are relations, but all relations are connections.) For example, the *wāsiṭāt*, like "in," "on," "to," etc., signify a connection, which is asymmetrical, because not convertible, as in "Zayd is *in the house*" (not convertible to "the house is in Zayd"); others, like hyparctic verbs, and especially the technical term "*mawjūd*," signify a relation, which similarly is not convertible, but which is also internal, in the sense that just as from "father of ʿAmr" we can deduce that ʿAmr is the son of whatever that expression refers to, in predication, that means that we can infer from the predicate, as long as the predication is paronymous, that there is a subject in which the predicate inheres.

56. In what follows I rely on Menn, 2008, pp. 80–82.

57. Fārābī, 1970, pp. 117, 4–5.

58. Menn, 2008, p. 82, note 33.

4. AVICENNA: RADICAL RESHAPING IN THE EAST

1. Klinger, forthcoming a.

2. See Gutas, 2018a, but also Kaukua, 2020.

3. *Madkhal* I.4 = Ibn Sīnā, 1952, pp. 23.5–8. He also says: "[They are] only babbling and showing their stupidity—for they do not really get what the subject-matter of logic is." Ibn Sīnā, 1952, pp. 23.8–9. *Cf.* Black 1991, pp. 54–56.

4. This prompts Avicenna to reject the *Cat* as useless for the study of logic and to eventually exclude it from the logic curriculum of the *Organon*. See especially the recent study in Kalbarczyk, 2018. As has now been amply discussed in the literature, Avicenna responded to the traditional debate about the question whether logic was a mere instrument or an independent part of philosophy by carving out a domain proper to the study of logic, thereby elevating it to a science in its own right. On this, the classic article is Sabra, 1980; see also Germann, 2008; El-Rouayheb, 2012; Karimullah, 2017.

5. As Avicenna also says in *al-Ilāhiyyāt* of *al-Shifāʾ*: Ibn Sīnā, 1960, p. 10; *cf.* the translation and discussion in Sabra, 1980, p. 753. See also Wisnovsky, 2000. Avicenna seems to have no other means to distinguish the subject-matter of logic from that of grammar than to say that the former is second intentions, *qua* useful for proceeding from the known to the unknown, while the latter is second intentions, *qua* relevant to the correctness of speech; *cf.* Karimullah, 2017, p. 292.

6. Sabra, 1980, p. 751, Karimullah, 2017, pp. 289–290; see *Madkhal* I.4: Ibn Sīnā, 1952, pp. 21.15–22.12 and *cf.* Kalbarczyk, 2018, pp. 21–22 and Street, 2015, p. [Text 7].

7. Sabra, 1980, pp. 763–764; Sabra was understandably puzzled by this passage: "In any case, however one interprets his words, and I am not sure I quite understand them, he seems to be making a stronger claim for the role of utterances in logic than I have encountered in any writer before and up to his time" (p. 763). That Avicenna meant to say that there is an influence of linguistic practice on thought itself in some such way is confirmed by a

similar passage in the *Ishārāt*; see Ibn Sīnā, 2002, p. 40, *Ishāra* 3: "Because there is a certain relation between the utterance and the meaning, and [because] some features of utterances often affect some features of meanings, the logician must also pay attention to the aspects of the utterance taken by itself (*al-muṭlaq*) insofar as that is not specific to one language or another, except rarely." My translation is somewhat different from Inati (Ibn Sīnā, 1984, p. 48).

8. Ibn Sīnā, 1970, pp. 17.4–5 (= *DI* 16b6–8); in-text citations in the remainder of this subchapter are to the edition by el-Khodeiri at al.

9. See page 57ff.

10. See page 38f.

11. See page 67.

12. See page 23.

13. The only edition (Logic part only) is rather poor: see Ibn Sīnā, 1910. Even the Logic part is incomplete. But of the extant chapters almost half of those dealing with conception (*taṣawwur*) and a quarter of those dealing with assent (*taṣdīq*) are related to issues to do with the subject-predicate relation.

14. Today, we only have the logic part up to the treatment of the *APr*, and some fragments from the *Physics*. Most likely the work was partially lost during al-Ḥamdūnī's attack on Iṣfahān in 425/1034. In a letter to an anonymous recipient, Avicenna says he stored some quires of the autograph—presumably as a precaution to avoid loss. Whatever he had stored was likely pillaged and taken to Ghazna after the attack. Those parts were however burned in 545/1150–1151 together with the libraries of the Ghaznavid Sultan Masʿūd b. Maḥmūd by Ghūrid troops of the King of Jibāl, al-Ḥusayn. Perhaps Avicenna had hidden most of the work, but not, e.g., the *Logic*, and all of that was later destroyed in Ghazna. Whatever he did not hide in 425/1034, i.e., at least the *Logic* and some of the *Physics*, could have been rediscovered after his death and copied subsequently. For a discussion of the evidence for the circumstances of the work's disappearance, see Gutas, 2014, pp. 130–137, 138.

15. Ibn Sīnā, 1910, pp. 62.7–8.

16. For the problem of singular predication in Aristotle and the Greek commentators, see Barnes, 2007, pp. 154–167; on Avicenna's take multiple predication, see Thom, 2019, pp. 83–84; and on quantified predicates, see Hasnawi, 2008.

17. Kalbarczyk, 2018, pp. 61–67.

18. See the text edited in Kalbarczyk, 2012, pp. 328.6–11; *cf.* Kalbarczyk, 2018, pp. 74–77.

19. Ibn Sīnā, 1959, pp. 23.11–17. For Fārābī's theory, see pages 56–60.

20. Kalbarczyk, 2018, p. 82.

21. Avicenna says: "with regard to 'that which exists in a subject' [they stipulated] that it be 'accidental' (*ʿaraḍī*); for in their view 'accident' (*ʿaraḍ*) and 'accidental' (*ʿaraḍī*) are one and the same thing, even though they differ in many respects. But in this place, the multitude of the differences between these two did not cross their minds." Translation Kalbarzcyk; Ibn Sīnā, 1959, pp. 23.4–6.

22. Kalbarczyk, 2018, p. 113; see also Bäck, 1999.

23. Kalbarczyk, 2018, p. 115 (emphasis in the original). Ackrill had such worries: "Aristotle relies greatly on linguistic facts and tests, but his aim is to discover truths about non–linguistic items"; Ackrill, 1963, p. 71. Or Mann: "Aristotle pays virtually no attention to anything like the use/mention distinction"; Mann, 2000, p. 52.

24. *Ishāra* 3, Ibn Sīnā, 2002, p. 40.

25. Ibn Khaldūn, 1900, p. 481; *cf.* Dunlop, 1957, p. 290. Ibn Khaldūn ranks Fārābī and Avicenna among the greatest philosophers in the East, and Ibn Bajjā and Averroes among the greatest philosophers of al-Andalus.

26. Gutas, 2014, p. 305, note 74.

27. Recent scholarship on Averroes has been seeking to rectify more broadly the idea that Averroes was an entirely unoriginal commentator limiting his work to the explication of Aristotle's text (see for example the study on Averroes's *Physics* by Glasner, 2009, or on his *Metaphysics* by Cerami, 2015; see also Adamson & Di Giovanni, 2019), and more specifically the idea that Averroes's work had no afterlife in the Arabic tradition (for a continuation of his teachings through his immediate students, see the introduction in Ibn Ṭumlūs, 2019; for an Averroist renaissance in 12th/18th-century Safavid Iran, see El-Rouayheb, 2019b, pp. 143–172). These trends in Averroes studies are attempts to better understand Averroes as a thinker in his own right by trying to reach beyond the persona created by the Latin Averroists and returning to his own writings. These developments notwithstanding, it is still true that Avicenna's influence over the Eastern Islamic intellectual tradition was incomparably more significant than that of the Andalusian tradition. Hence, we may, with some justification, abandon this tradition here.

28. We know relatively little about the beginnings of Aristotelian philosophy in Muslim Spain. But a crucial early work is Ibn Ḥazm's *al-Taqrīb li-ḥadd al-manṭiq* (the title contains a pun: it may either be understood as "Bringing [Someone] Close to the Limit of [Aristotelian] Logic," or as "Clarifying the Definition of [Aristotelian] Logic"). A recent edition with facing Turkish translation is Ibn Ḥazm, 2018. On the signification of the pun in the title in connection to the general outlook of the work as both an introduction to Aristotelian logic and an effort to make the strange terminology of logic more palatable to its critics, see Gutas, 2014, pp. 305–307 as well as Chejne, 1984 and Guerrero, 2012. For Ibn Ḥazm's logical pedigree, see Dunlop, 1955b, pp. 105–108 with references to the sources, and more recently, Lameer, 2012, with some revisions based on a second copy of the *Taqrīb* found in Izmir.

29. See especially *Taʿālīq Ibn Bājja li-Manṭiq al-Fārābī*, edited by Fakhry in Ibn Bājja, 1994. Dānishpazhūh's three-volume edition of Fārābī's logic includes Ibn Bājja's annotations in volume 3; see Fārābī, 1987–1990 [1408–1410].

30. See Averroes's *Talkhīṣ Kitāb al-ʿIbāra*, edited by Qāsim, Butterworth, and Harīdī in Ibn Rushd, 1981. Another edition (not critical, but with an accompanying volume on editorial method with an extensive index) of the middle commentaries on *Cat, DI, APr, APo, Top.*, and *Soph. El.*, in seven volumes, is that of Jihāmī in Ibn Rushd, 1982. Especially important is a short treatise titled *Maqāla fī l-kalima wa l-ism al-mushtaqq* found in the MS Madrid: Escorial, Derenbourg 632, which explicitly and critically engages with Fārābī's theory of derived names. The short treatise was first brought to attention by Elamrani-Jamal in a notice with brief discussion, provisional edition, and French translation in Elamrani-Jamal, 1990. For the specific point Averroes is criticizing, see Fārābī, 1960, 33.13–26 = Fārābī, 1987–1990 [1408–1410], II 21.13–22.3, and Zimmermann, 1981, p. 22.

5. THE "NEW LOGICIANS" STIRRING THINGS UP

1. See for example Adamson & Benevich, 2023 and the forthcoming volumes of the *Heirs of Avicenna* project (Adamson, Klinger, & Benevich, 2024).

2. Gutas, 2018a.

3. Gutas, 2018a, p. 66.

4. For a recent study of the formation of post-classical philosophy in Islam, see Griffel, 2021.

5. On now outdated assessments of al-Ghazālī's role, see Griffel, 2009, pp. 3–12.

6. This view was first explicitly expressed in 1844 by Munk in an entry to the *Dictionaire des sciences philosophiques* (Franck, 1844, p. II.512) and then in Munk, 1859, p. 382. Even though challenged by Shlomo Pines already in 1937 (Pines, 1937, p. 80), it was really only from the late 1980s onward (e.g., Sabra, 1987; Frank, 1994) that this view began to be revised in a more systematic manner.

7. See especially Griffel, 2009; and for the impact of al-Ghazālī's thought on the later tradition, see Griffel, 2016. For a revision of the view—put forward most forcefully in Goldziher, 1916—that the study of logic was widely considered as *ḥarām* (forbidden) after the 5th/11th century, see El-Rouayheb, 2004.

8. For the development of post-Avicennan Arabic philosophy in that period, see besides Griffel, 2021, the forthcoming volumes of Peter Adamson's *Heirs of Avicenna* project, especially Adamson, Klinger, & Benevich, 2024.

9. For Abū al-Barakāt's role in shaping a more dialectical scholarly praxis, see Griffel, 2011a. Abū al-Barakāt's *magnum opus, al-Kitāb al-muʿtabar* (Baghdādī, 1995), meaning "the book established by careful consideration, i.e., of the merits of positions of others," presented an attractive *falsafī* alternative to Ibn Sīna; see Shihadeh, 2005, p. 150. For his use of Avicenna's logic of *al-Ḥikma al-Arūḍiyya*, see Janssen, 2016.

10. Suhrawardī's *Ḥikmat al-ishrāq* (Shihāb al-Dīn Yaḥyā b. Ḥabash al-Suhrawardī, 1945) and his *Talwīḥāt (Intimations)*, the logic part of which has been edited in Yaḥyā b. Ḥabash al- Suhrawardī, 1955, were subject to numerous commentaries, of which more influential ones were by Ibn Kammūna and Qutb al-Dīn al-Shīrāzī.

11. See the study Bonadeo, 2013.

12. Shihadeh, 2016c, pp. 8–11.

13. Wisnovsky, 2013b, 2014.

14. Labeling strands of Avicennism is still controversial at this stage. One way is to distinguish by gradation of willingness to reject Avicennan positions. Following Tony Street, I use "school Avicennism" for the conservative side of the spectrum.

15. Shihadeh, 2016c, pp. 7–8, with further references.

16. Shihadeh, 2016c, p. 8, with further references.

17. Shihadeh, 2005, p. 151. For Balkhī and the contested nature of Avicennan logic in that period, see Klinger, forthcoming b.

18. Shihadeh, 2005, pp. 151–153. Ibn Ghaylān wrote logical treatises responding to Rashīd al-Dīn Waṭwaṭ's (d. 578/1182) *Epistle on reductio ad absurdum Arguments* and to Sharaf al-Dīn al-Masʿūdī's (d. *ca.* 585/1189–590/1194) *Epistle on Mixed Modal Categorical Syllogisms*; see Dadkhah & Fallāḥī, 2016.

19. *Munāẓarāt Fakhr al-Dīn al-Rāzī fī bilād mā warāʾa al-nahr*, in: Kholeif, 1966, p. 31 (55 of Kholeif's translation); see Shihadeh, 2005, p. 153.

20. Ibn Ghaylān, 1998, pp. 11–12 [= Michot, 1993, pp. 340–341]; see Shihadeh, 2005, p. 154. For a critical edition and analysis of al-Masʿūdī's polemical commentary, see Shihadeh, 2016c. Rāzī composed, at the very beginning of his career as an author of philosophical

works and over a decade before his own commentary on the *Ishārāt*, a detailed set of responses to al-Masʿūdī's commentary titled *Jawābat al-masāʾil al-bukhāriyya* (Responses to the Bukhārian [Philosophical] Problems; al-Masʿūdī was at the time in Avicenna's hometown Bukhāra); see Shihadeh, 2016c, p. 2 and for the *Jawābāt* itself, Shihadeh, 2014b.

21. For the dialectical middle-ground between exegesis and aporetics that informed Rāzī's methodology, see Shihadeh, 2016a.

22. For such depictions in modern scholarship, see for example Schmidtke, 2000, pp. 5–6; see Wisnovsky, 2014, pp. 326–328, for a Qajar-era source praising Ṭūsī as the savior of Avicennism, and *passim* for a criticism of this depiction.

23. Wisnovsky, 2014, p. 324.

24. El-Rouayheb, 2019b, p. 38; see also Wisnovsky, 2014; Shihadeh, 2016a.

25. Rescher, 1964, p. 185; *cf.* El-Rouayheb, 2019b, p. 37.

26. Rescher, 1964. Similar views are found in Maróth, 1989, p. 216ff. and Inati, 1996. For a revised historical presentation of the development of Arabic logic in the 7th/13th century, see El-Rouayheb, 2016a, 2019b, pp. 29–36.

27. El-Rouayheb, 2019b, p. 38.

28. El-Rouayheb, 2019b, p. 38.

29. See the introduction to Khūnajī, 2010.

30. On the lead-up to and the emergence of Marāgha Avicennism, see Wisnovsky, 2013b, 2014, 2018.

31. Street, 2005b. Street corrected (*per litteras*) that he now tends to think of the revisionists as first taking over from the school Avicennans and subsequently splitting up into "purists" and "Rāzians." This seems to me to be borne out by the authors studied here.

32. El-Rouayheb, 2019b, p. 36.

33. Ibn Khaldūn, 1900, pp. 491.21–492.9; translation slightly adapted from Rosenthal, in Ibn Khaldūn, 1958, pp. 142–143. See also Street, 2005b, pp. 251–252. Compare Saʿd ad-Dīn at- Taftāzānī, 2011, pp. 92.1–3.

34. Ṭūsī did include all books of the *Organon* in his Persian summa on logic titled *Asās al-iqtibās* (Foundation of [Knowledge-]Aquisition). Later, there were some scholars, for example Ibn Turkā (d. 835/1432), who felt that the many-layered intertextual web of dialectical objections and counter-objections was mere eristics, and wished to return to the pristine clarity of the "older logicians"; El-Rouayheb, 2019b, p. 92. This foreshadows a broader tendency among Safavid scholars, like Mīr Damād (d. 1041/1631), Mulla Ṣadrā (d. 1045/1635), and Muḥammad Yūsuf Tehrānī (*fl.* 1104/1692), to disapprove of the dialectical approach, a seemingly pedantic back-and-forth over minor points, and likewise to seek to return to the clarity of the "older logicians"; El-Rouayheb, 2019b, pp. 145–146.

35. See here especially El-Rouayheb, 2019b, pp. 29–74 with further references.

36. On Fakhr al-Dīn's life, intellectual influences, and patronage: Griffel, 2007; Shihadeh, 2014c, 2016a; Ömer Türker & Demir, 2013. On the intellectual/dialectical environment more generally: Shihadeh, 2005, 2014a, 2014b, 2016c with references. See also Rescher, 1964, p. 185; Street, 2004, 2005a; El-Rouayheb, 2010b, pp. 39–48.

37. See the recently edited Makkī, 2013, pp. 41–43.

38. Shihadeh, 2016b; *cf.* Shihadeh, 2016a, p. 297.

39. See Griffel, 2011b.

40. A partial and tentative relative chronology is given in Griffel, 2007, p. 344. See also Shihadeh, 2014b, p. 308 and Ḥājjī Khalīfa (Kātib Çelebī), 1835–1858, p. I.94; for the dating of the *Sharḥ ʿuyūn al-ḥikma*, see Shihadeh, 2006, p. 11.

41. The commentary titled *Ghāyat al-Āyāt* (The Aims of the Signs) is preserved in a manuscript in the Alexandria Municipal Library in Egypt (MS 1957D, fols. 1–77, copied in 679/1280); see El-Rouayheb, 2019b, p. 61.

42. El-Rouayheb, 2019b, p. 40.

43. I hope to treat this issue elsewhere. The MS contains no readily accessible data for a secure ascription to any author. Knobel, 2015 argued for Rāzī's authorship, but her evidence rests on stylistic grounds and remains slight. I am grateful to Dr Akyüz for providing me with a copy of his dissertation, which includes an edition and discussion in Turkish (Akyüz, 2017). Fallahi, 2023 has recently argued that its author is Burhān al-Dīn al-Nasafī.

44. Di Vincenzo, 2018, pp. 31–32. Only two partial commentaries on the *Shifāʾ* are attested before the 10th/16th century, one by Ibn Zayla (d. 439/1048) and another by al-ʿAllama al-Ḥillī (d. 726/1325), of which the latter (preserved in a unicum manuscript: MS Dublin: Chester Beatty Library, Arabic 5151, 102 folios) however only covers material up to the *Cat* (*al-Maqūlāt*); see Wisnovsky, 2013a, p. 194.

45. Rāzī's marginal notes on the linguistic section of *al-ʿIbāra* include two that explain Avicenna's treatment of third-person inflected verbs. The first is this: "If you judge about something in the world that it walks, and you predicate that proposition [i.e., ∃x(Mx)] according to its definition inasmuch as truth and falsehood are included in it, then predicating [such proposition] of Zayd is not valid. Like when you say 'ʿAmr walks,' and predicated that proposition according to its definition, then it would not be possible for you to predicate this proposition of Zayd, since you do not say: 'ʿAmr walks [is] Zayd'; since the latter is not valid, neither is the former. From the pen of the Imām, may God have mercy on him." And the second: "[Avicenna] said so because, when you say 'the thing in the world described as having 'walking' and then stop, the soul looks for the completion of this phrase, since this phrase by itself is not understandable, nor can it stand all by itself; rather, it is a subject requiring a predicate in order to be true or false. Therefore, he said that the utterance 'in fact' (*inna*) cannot be used with this description, i.e., cannot be used in such a way that, when used, the phrase can stand on its own and either truth or falsity follow from it. Yet when we judge about something in the world that it walks, in this case it is possible for us to say 'something walking in the world walks' and to stop, as this is a complete statement susceptible of truth and falsity. From the pen of the Imām, may God have mercy on him"; Di Vincenzo, 2018, pp. 61–62 (texts nr. 1 and nr. 2).

46. Rāzī, 1986, p. 34.

47. On Khūnajī's life and environment: Khūnajī, 2010, pp. i–xxv; El-Rouayheb, 2019b, pp. 41–43.

48. See Bar Hebraeus, 1663, p. 485 (ed. Pococke) = Bar Hebraeus, 1890, p. 445 (ed. Ṣāliḥānī); *cf.* Khūnajī, 2010, p. xii; El-Rouayheb, 2019b, p. 41.

49. Ibn Abī Uṣaybiʿa, 1882–1884 [1299–1301], reprint Ibn Abī Uṣaybiʿa, 1995.

50. See above on page 93. It has been edited, though unsatisfactorily, in Ghurāb, 1980, pp. 29–39; *cf.* El-Rouayheb, 2019b, pp. 44–45. For Ibn Wāṣil's (d. 697/1298) commentary, see El-Rouayheb's recent edition with introduction: Ibn Wāṣil, 2022.

51. Ghurāb, 1980, p. 31.

52. Ghurāb, 1980, p. 32.

53. Ghurāb, 1980, p. 32. On the quantification of predicates in Avicenna and Ibn Zurʿa, see Hasnawi, 2008.

54. Two relatively early manuscripts of the work are MS Cambridge: University Library: Ll. 6.24, fols. 3b–43b (copied in 750/1349) and MS Tehran: Majlis Library 1984, fols. 4–92 (copied in 687/1288); see El-Rouayheb, 2019b, p. 45.

55. El-Rouayheb, 2019b, p. 45.

56. Edited by El-Rouayheb in Khūnajī, 2010. Some of the still relatively few contributions to scholarship are Rescher, 1964, pp. 194–195; El-Rouayheb, 2009 and especially the introduction to Khūnajī, 2010; El-Rouayheb, 2010a; Fallāḥī, 2013; Street, 2014; and recently El-Rouayheb, 2019b, pp. 44–47. See also Ibn Wāṣil, 2022.

57. See Khūnajī, 2010, pp. iii–iv; El-Rouayheb, 2012, p. 70, 2019b, p. 44. Ibn Khaldūn, who himself studied logic using *al-Jumal*, states that Khūnajī's influence was such that Eastern scholars relied (*muʿtamad*) on his logical works until Ibn Khaldūn's day (late 8th/14th century); see Ibn Khaldūn, 1900, p. 492.

58. On the relative dating and related problems of Khūnajī's works, see Khūnajī, 2010, pp. xxi–xxii.

59. Quoted from El-Rouayheb, 2019b, p. 46, translation by El-Rouayheb.

60. For example, Khūnajī's discussion of immediate implications of conditional and disjunctive propositions, recognizing De Morgan's Laws, i.e., $\neg(P \wedge Q) \equiv (\neg P) \vee (\neg Q)$ and $\neg(P \vee Q) \equiv (\neg P) \wedge (\neg Q)$; his claim that possibility propositions do not convert; his claim that first figure syllogisms with possibility minors cannot be shown to be productive; his rejection of Aristotle's thesis (no proposition is implied by its own negation) by claiming that two contradictory propositions may be implied by one and the same impossible antecedent. See El-Rouayheb, 2012, p. 70; for more detail, see also Khūnajī, 2010, pp. xxiv–xlviii. For the discussion of impossible antecedents, see El-Rouayheb, 2009.

61. See El-Rouayheb, 2012, p. 71 and Khūnajī, 2010, pp. xxvi–xxviii. The way Kātibī understood Khūnajī's position, i.e., that the subject-matter of logic is more general (*aʿamm*) than secondary intelligibles, is preferable, according to Kātibī, because "[t]he logician may investigate matters that do not accrue to second intentions at all . . . but rather to single notions (*maʿānī*) that occur in the mind. For he investigates the concept of "essential," "accidental," "species," "genus," "differentia," "subject," and "predicate" and other things that accrue to single notions that we intellect"; Kātibī, *Jāmiʿ al-daqāʾiq*, fol. 12v, translation from El-Rouayheb, 2012, p. 73.

62. In what follows I summarize; in-text references to the *Kashf al-asrār* in this section are to Khūnajī, 2010.

63. Samarqandī, *Sharḥ al-Qistās*, MS Yale: University Library (Beinecke), Arabic 11, fol. 14r; see Khūnajī, 2010, p. xxvii. On conception and assent as the subject-matter of logic and the ramifications of this fundamental epistemological distinction, see Klinger, forthcoming c.

64. *Cf.* Ibn Sīnā, 1970, p. 7.

65. *Cf.* Ibn Sīnā, 1970, p. 24.

66. See chapter 4 on page 73. *Cf.* Ibn Sīnā, 1970, pp. 18–19.

67. *Cf.* Ibn Sīnā, 1970, pp. 76–77.

68. Ibn Sīnā, 2002, p. 79. See Rāzī's criticism on page 96f.

69. The statement in question is made in *Manṭiq al-mashriqiyyīn*, Ibn Sīnā, 1910, p. 67.

70. Rāzī, 2005–2006 [1384], pp. 154.12–155.6.

71. See page 97; Rāzī, 1381/2002–2003, p. 130.

6. THE MARĀGHA GENERATION OF LOGICIANS

1. Or, less likely, he was from the small town (*qarya*) of Abhar near Iṣfahān: see Al-Rahim, 2018, p. 95, with notes. On Abharī's life and environment, see Şeşen, 1997, 2008;

Eichner, 2014; on his life and work, see, for sources, Al-Rahim, 2018, pp. 95–105, and, for a brief sketch and his logical work, El-Rouayheb, 2019b, pp. 47–53.

2. Bar Hebraeus, 1663, p. 485; 1890, p. 445; *cf.* El-Rouayheb, 2019b, p. 59. For his studies with al-Miṣrī in Nīshāpūr, see Shihadeh, 2005, pp. 153–154; Endreß, 2006, pp. 410–415; El-Rouayheb, 2019b, p. 47.

3. Qazwīnī, 1960, p. 536, *cf.* Hees, 2002, p. 58.

4. Ibn Khallikān, 1968–1972, p. V.313.

5. See Hasse, 2000, pp. 146–147 and *passim*; for a collection (in German translation) of biographical material on Kamāl al-Dīn Ibn Yūnus, see Suter, 1922.

6. Ibn Khallikān, 1968–1972, p. V.313.

7. The colophon is described in Şeşen, 1997, pp. 270–271; 2008; see also El-Rouayheb, 2019b, p. 48.

8. See Khūnajī, 2010, pp. xxiii–xxv; El-Rouayheb, 2019b, p. 48.

9. Eichner, 2014; see Eichner, 2009, pp. 104–126 for Abharī's hybrid presentation of philosophy, incorporating structural elements from both Avicenna's *Ishārāt* and from Rāzī's *Mulakhkhaṣ*.

10. On Abharī's relation to Khūnajī (and Urmawī), see El-Rouayheb, 2019b, pp. 48–49. The edition of Abharī's *Muntahā* is Abharī, 2016–2017 [1395]-b.

11. Street, 2016b, p. 350, suggests—without citing a source, but likely relying on Sayili, 1956—that "[s]ometime after its foundation, Abharī also worked at the observatory, though it seems he left before his death." The Marāgha observatory was founded in 657/1259, and if Abharī had indeed passed away by the time Ṭūsī finished his *Taʿdīl* in 656/1258, that would be impossible. However, he probably did die in Shabistar near Marāgha, and thus might still have been involved with the planning in the last year or so of his life before the institute was officially opened.

12. Eichner, 2014. For his connections to Frederick II, see for example Hasse, 2000.

13. For a list of Abharī's works, see the introduction to Abharī, 2016–2017 [1395]-b, pp. 20–25; and Al-Rahim, 2018, pp. 102–105. For a survey of MSS in Turkish libraries, see Şeşen, 1997, pp. 266–272, together with ʿAbdallah Nūrānī's introduction to the *Taʿdīl al-miʿyār* in Muḥaqqiq & Izutsu, 1974, pp. 34–48 and Muwaḥḥid, 1988 [1367]; additional important MSS include MS Istanbul: Ayasofya 2319, containing the *Kitāb al-shukūk*, a polemic semi-commentary on Rāzī's *Mulakhkhaṣ*; MS Istanbul: Murat Molla Kütüphanesi 1416 (copied from the ill-preserved MS Istanbul: Köprülü Kütüphanesi 1618, which contains the *Bayān al-asrār, Talkhīṣ al-ḥaqāʾiq, Kitāb al-Maṭāliʿ*, and *Zubdat al-ḥaqāʾiq* together with reading certificates for Kātibī, signed by Abharī, with whom Kātibī read them in 628–629/1228–1229); and MS Qum: Kitābkhāna-yi Ayatollah Marʿashī Najafī 4060 containing the *Zubdat al-asrār* on fols. 2–38; see Eichner, 2014; and Eichner, 2012, p. 130.

14. Kātib Çelebī remarked, in the mid-11th/17th century, that the *Īsāghūjī* was the standard logic textbook in his time, and that its title was metonymycal for the entire subject; Ḥājjī Khalīfa (Kātib Çelebī), 1835–1858, p. I.502; *cf.* Calverly, 1933, p. 76. See also Al-Rahim, 2018, pp. 98–99, and note 307 for an extensive list of the numerous editions that contain the text; an English translation is Calverly, 1933, and another more recent is by Feriyal Salem (Abharī, 2022). For the reception of Porphyry's *Eisagoge* in Arabic, see D'Ancona, 2011, and for the Arabic and Latin reception Lagerlund, 2008; and Atademir, 1948.

15. The *Īsāghūjī* is not in any straightforward sense "a short digest of the nine Aristotelian books of the *Organon*" (Al-Rahim, 2018, p. 89), but clearly evinces structural innovations

attributable to the "later logicians (*al-muta'akhkhirūn*)." For example, in the text dialectical (*jadal*), rhetorical (*khitāba*), poetic (*shi'r*), and sophistical (*safasata*) syllogisms are but mentioned in passing at the end, whereas Abharī earlier introduces four syllogistic figures and discusses in some detail the "combinatorial-hypothetical" (*sharṭī iqtirānī*) syllogism—both post-Avicennan features of Arabic logic.

16. As suggested by their respective titles, Abharī in these works strove to point out the mistakes of previous scholars—including Avicenna, Rāzī, and perhaps to a lesser extent Khūnajī—and to provide superior solutions to philosophical problems. In the proem to the *Tanzīl* he states that based on his own critical scrutiny (*mā addā ilayhi afkāruna*, Şeşen, 1997, p. 267; see also El-Rouayheb, 2019b, p. 50) he wished to "recalibrate" (*ta'dīl*) a philosophical tradition that he judged to contain "weak arguments" (*ḥujaj wāhiyya*), as he puts it in the proem to the *Kashf al-ḥaqā'iq* (ed. by Sarıoğlu: Abharī, 1998, p. 4.16).

17. There is no edition of Abharī's *Tanzīl*, but lemmata from this work are reproduced in the edition of Tūsī's *Ta'dīl* in Muḥaqqiq & Izutsu, 1974, pp. 139–248.

18. Even though we have no exact dates for the completion of the two recensions (sometime between 634/1237 and 642/1244), we can tentatively group the following logical works relative to this turning point. While the logic parts of the *Hidāyat al-ḥikma*, the *Talkhīṣ al-ḥaqā'iq* (Epitome of Truths) and the *Zubdat al-asrār* (The Cream of Secrets), appear to be early works, the *Kashf al-ḥaqā'iq* and the *Tanzīl*, as well as the *Khulāṣat al-afkār wa-naqāwat al-asrār* (The Synopsis of Thoughts and the Choice of Secrets), a substantial summa exclusively dealing with logic, were most probably written after the *Muntahā* recensions. See the introduction to Abharī, 2016–2017 [1395]-b and El-Rouayheb, 2019b, pp. 47–52. The logic of the *Hidāya* has been edited in Dānishpazhūh, 1961 [1340] and that of the *Talkhīṣ al-ḥaqā'iq* in 'Azīmī, 2016–2017 [1395]; the *Khulāṣat al-afkār* has recently been edited by 'Azīmī and Qurbānī in Abharī, 2018. The *Zubdat al-asrār* remains unedited. Three extant MSS of the work are Ayatollah Mar'ashī Najafī Library, Qum 4060, fols. 2–38; Millet Library, Istanbul: Feyzullah 1210, fols. 100–168; Burdur İl Halk Library, Burdur: 1180, fols. 1–51; see El-Rouayheb, 2019b, p. 51. I only have access to the MS Istanbul: Feyzullah 1210, and it does not contain the Logic part. The present state of research does not allow for a confident dating of another important text, the *Kitāb al-shukūk* (Book of Doubts) in which Abharī picks lemmata from Rāzī's *Mulakhkhaṣ* in order to refute specific claims or arguments. It survives in the unicum MS Istanbul: Ayasofya 2319, which is incomplete, has no colophon, and to my knowledge has never been systematically studied. But see Eichner, 2011, pp. 146–147, for a partial English translation from the part on Metaphysics, and pp. 129–130 for a brief discussion. The *Kitāb al-Shukūk* is however important evidence that Abharī was by no means uncritical of Rāzī. Evidence from this MS as well as from the *Khulāṣat al-afkār* suggests that some of Tūsī's proverbial intellectual enmity toward Rāzī may have found supporting arguments in Abharī's work. All these works seem to have been among the more influential ones, but it should be borne in mind that they represent less than half of Abharī's known works on logic.

19. The first presentation of formalized disputation theory (in the sense of a topic-neutral science, *ādāb al-baḥth*) appeared much later and is usually credited to Shams al-Dīn al-Samarqandī (d. 722/1322) with his *al-Risāla al-Samarqandiyya fī ādāb al-baḥth* (The Samarqandian Epistle on Disputation Theory), see Miller, 2019, and the revised version of his 1984 dissertation: Miller, 2020; see also page 133.

20. Ibn Khallikān, 1968–1972, p. V.313. Both these texts seem not to be extant. But we do have other writings on dialectics by Abharī, including *al-Qawā'id al-jadaliyya* (Dialectical Confutations), edited by al-Ḥawshānī in Abharī, 2004; *Tahdhīb al-Nukat* (Emendations to the Impressions), a revision of a work titled *Impressions* by Abū Isḥāq al-Shīrāzī (d. 476/1083) (for MSS, see Al-Rahim, 2018, p. 104); *al-Risāla al-Zāhira fī bayan fasād al-muqaddimāt al-jadaliyya* (The Luminous Epistle on the Explanation of the Falsity of Dialectical Premises), edited in ʿAzīmī & Qurbānī, 2011–2012 [1390].

21. On Ṭūsī's life and environment, see Raḍawī, 1975–1976 [1354], and El-Rouayheb, 2019b, pp. 54–56.

22. Al-Rahim, 2003, p. 223.

23. According to an *isnad* reported by al-Ṣafadī, Ṭūsī read the *Ishārāt* with Abharī, Abharī with al-Miṣrī, who in turn read it with Rāzī, who read it with al-Masʿūdī, who read it with Ibn al-Khayyāmī, who read it with Bahmanyār, who read it with Avicenna himself; see Endreß, 2006, pp. 411–412, but *cf.* Al-Rahim, 2018, pp. 23–25 for doubts.

24. For a study of Ṭūsī's life, his patronage, and the question of whether and how far he was involved in the Īlkhānid conquests, see Joráti, 2014. For a general study, see Meisami, 2019. A recent general historical presentation of the Mongols in the Islamic world during that period is Jackson, 2018.

25. See Al-Rahim, 2003, p. 227. An edition of the *Tajrīd al-manṭiq* is Ṭūsī, 1988, and the *Tajrīd al-iʿtiqād* is printed with the commentary by Ḥillī. The commentaries by Ḥillī are *al-Jawhar al-naḍīd fī sharḥ kitāb al-Tajrīd* (The Tiered Jewel in Commenting upon the Book of Extracted Points), edited by Bīdārfar in Ḥillī, 1992–1993 [1413], and *Kashf al-murād fī sharḥ Tajrīd al-iʿtiqād* (The Disclosure of Intention in Commenting upon the Extracted Points of the Creed), edited by al-Āmulī in Ḥillī, 2011–2012 [1433].

26. See page 93. The *Asās al-iqtibās* has been edited by Mudarris Raḍawī in Ṭūsī, 1368/1990; it was translated into Arabic by the Ottoman scholar Mullā Ḥüsrev (d. 885/1480) and dedicated to Sultan Mehmed II—an "unsatisfactory and incomplete edition" (according to El-Rouayheb, 2019b, p. 55) is Ṭūsī, 1999.

27. A recent study of Ṭūsī's propositional logic (in Turkish) is Kuşlu, 2016.

28. The *Kitāb al-shukūk*, a largely but unduly neglected text in scholarship, unfortunately has nothing to say on Rāzī's Repetition Argument. Abharī does, however, criticize Rāzī on a number of points to do with the analysis of simple categorical statements. For example, where Rāzī says that the quiddity of a proposition is only realized when the predicate subsists for the subject, Abharī objects that in modalized propositions where the predicate is said to possibly subsist for the subject this cannot be true (MS Istanbul: Ayasofya 2319, fol. 14v6ff.; for the relevant passage in the *Mulakhkhaṣ*, see Rāzī, 1381/2002–2003, p. 160). He further distinguishes the nexus-quality from the subsistence-quality, and argues that in a proposition, they need not be the same (MS Istanbul: Ayasofya 2319, fol. 15r9ff., *cf.* Rāzī, 1381/2002–2003, p. 169). The proem, in which Abharī states that the work was requested from him by "some of the most eminent learned men and verifying scholars," provides a glimpse of both the reverential attitude toward Rāzī and the desire among his disciples to engage critically with his arguments point for point. Also noteworthy is that Abharī, who did not write a commentary on the *Ishārāt*, emphasizes that it is his intention to critique Rāzī at his best, as he thinks, and not in relation to his reading of Avicenna. The fact that Abharī, upon encouragement by his peers, chose to write an eclectic and aporetic

commentary more in the style of al-Masʿūdī and not a lemmatic running commentary as Rāzī himself and others did may be an indication of an early inclination to conceive of logic as both a school and a research science, a trend that found its first concrete expression, or so I argue, in the second half of the 7th/13th century.

29. The *Ḥall al-mushkilāt* is printed in many (insufficient) editions together with the *Ishārāt*; I use Fayḍī's edition: Ṭūsī, 1383/2004–2005.

30. There are, for example, the commentaries by Najm al-Dīn Nakhjuwānī (fl. 626/1229), *Sharḥ al-Ishārat*, also known as *Zubdat al-naqs wa-lubāb al-kashf* (MS Istanbul: Ahmet III 3264), and by Sayf al-Dīn al-Āmidī (d. 641/1243), *Kashf al-tamwīhāt fī Sharḥ al-Ishārāt wa-l-tanbīhāt* (MS Istanbul: Laleli 2519; MS Berlin: Petermann II 596) and some others; see Wisnovsky, 2013b, pp. 352–353, 2014. After Ṭūsī, however, the *Ḥall* became the crucial text mediating most engagements with Avicenna's *Ishārāt*. Noteworthy examples of such *Muḥākamāt* commentaries are Ḥillī's *al-Muḥākamāt bayna shurrāḥ al-Ishārāt* (MS Istanbul: Damat Ibrahim Paşa 817, MS Istanbul: Ahmet III, A3400) and Quṭb al-Dīn al-Rāzī's *al-Muḥākamāt bayna Sharḥay al-Ishārāt* (MS Istanbul: Şehit Ali Paşa 1750; there is an anonymous edition [not critical] published in Tehran 1393 [1965] that contains Quṭb al-Dīn's text at the bottom of the page), both of which will be discussed in the next chapter.

31. As Kātibī is going to explain in his commentary on the *Mulakhkhaṣ*, Rāzī divides his discussion of categorical propositions (Rāzī, 1381/2002–2003, p. 121ff.) into issues to do with the intrinsic properties (*arkān*) and immediate implications (*aḥkām*) of propositions. The intrinsic properties of propositions are those that make up their essence, i.e., their form and matter. The form of a proposition is its nexus while its matter are subject and predicate; see page 121. Ṭūsī's criticism of the Repetition Argument remains on the level of the semantics of specific word-classes in Arabic. Both agree that the nexus is a third concept, and that it is formal, not material. They only differ about how this formal concept may be signified.

32. Ṭūsī, 1988, p. 17.

33. On Kātibī's life and work, see El-Rouayheb, 2020a. See also Street, 2016a, 2016b; Kātibī, 2007; Āl Yāsīn, 1956; Karimullah, 2015; Arıcı, 2015; İhsan, 2016.

34. Ḥājjī Khalīfa (Kātib Çelebī), 1835–1858, p. III.103 (nr. 4586).

35. Ibn al-Fuwaṭī, 1995, pp. 54–55 (nr. 2175).

36. El-Rouayheb, 2020a.

37. We have, for example, an extensive series of exchanges between Kātibī and Ṭūsī on proofs for the Necessary Existent, as well as an exchange on the nature of hot and cold (for editions, translations, and MSS, see Al-Rahim, 2018, pp. 115–116); the exchange about logical matters (*Muṭāraḥāt manṭiqiyya bayna Najm al-Dīn Dabīrān al-Kātibī al-Qazwīnī wa-Naṣīr al-Dīn al-Ṭūsī*—Logical Exchanges between Kātibī and Ṭūsī) has been edited by Nūrānī and is printed in Muḥaqqiq & Izutsu, 1974, pp. 279–286. The first question on the parts of the proposition is, however, in contrast to the other issues, a mere exposition that does not add much to our understanding of the respective positions of the authors. Other extant exchanges on logical issues are, for example, that with Ibn Kammūna (*Ajwibat masāʾil Ibn Kammūna* [Replies to Ibn Kammūna's *Quaestiones*]: Kātibī, 2007).

38. Ibn al-Fuwaṭī, 1995, p. III.123 (nr. 2320); Al-Rahim, 2018, pp. 108–109.

39. Ibn al-Fuwaṭī, 1995, p. III.533. (nr. 3137); Al-Rahim, 2018, p. 109.

40. Ibn al-Fuwaṭī, 1995, p. V.107f. (nr. 4733); Al-Rahim, 2018, p. 109.

41. Ibn al-Fuwaṭī, 1995, p. III.440f. (nr. 2927); Al-Rahim, 2018, p. 109.

42. Schmidtke, 1991, p. 18f.; Al-Rahim, 2003.

43. See Street, 2016b, p. 350.

44. El-Rouayheb, 2019b, p. 57.

45. For the text of Kātibī's commentary on the *Kashf al-asrār* I collated two early manuscripts that virtually agree throughout this passage (the main divergences are minor scribal errors). MS Istanbul: Süleymaniye Carullah 1417 comprises 226 folios with thirty-one lines to a page and was written by two anonymous hands. The first copied Kātibī's commentary on *Kashf al-asrār* and the second added Kātibī's completion of the work, including the sections that he believed Khūnajī intended to write but never did. The second part was completed in 678/1280. The former, and major, part must have been copied at an earlier date—perhaps in Kātibī's own lifetime. The second manuscript, MS Istanbul: Süleymaniye Carullah 1418, was copied by a certain ʿAbd al-Wahhāb b. Aḥmad b. ʿAbd al-Wahhāb in 687/1288 and comprises 278 folios with thirty-five lines to a page; see El-Rouayheb's introduction in Khūnajī, 2010, p. liii. The section on the copula is found at MS Istanbul: Süleymaniye Carullah 1417 fols. 57v2–59v21; in-text citations in this subsection refer to this manuscript. It has now come to my attention that in 2019 Anūr Shāhīn has edited the entire commentary in thirteen hundred pages. To my knowledge, it remains unpublished.

46. El-Rouayheb, 2019b, pp. 57–58.

47. Abharī has a long section on conversion of categorical and hypothetical propositions in his *Kashf al-haqāʾiq* (Abharī, 2016–2017 [1395]-a, pp. 89–116), where he takes on and refutes positions by Avicenna, Rāzī, and Kashhshī.

48. For the text of this section, "On Categorical Propositions," of Najm al-Dīn al-Kātibī's (d. 1276) commentary (*sharḥ*) on Rāzī's *Mulakhkhaṣ*, I collated two manuscripts, one of which was copied during the author's lifetime, the other some fifteen years after his death. Overall, the manuscripts do not differ greatly, but we sometimes find omissions and mistakes in the older copy to be remedied in the later one. Both manuscripts agree throughout in their rubrications. The first manuscript is MS Mashhad: Kitābkhāna-yi Markazī-yi Āstān-i Quds-i Raḍawī 1201, comprising 337 folios with thirty-three lines to a page, written in an orderly *naskh* hand in black ink with rubrications marking the *matn*. It was copied on 18 Ramaḍān 671/April 8, 1273, with the comments (*taʿliqa*) added in Jumādā II 693/May 1294. The second manuscript is MS Leiden: University Library Or. 36, comprising 345 folios with thirty-seven lines to a page, written in free-standing *naskh* with black ink and rubrications marking the *matn*. It was copied by Naṣīr Muḥammad b. Asʿad b. Muḥammad al-Tamanī (?) in Rabīʿ II 692/March 1293. The section on the categorical propositions is found at MS Mashhad: Kitābkhāna-yi Markazī-yi Āstān-i Quds-i Raḍawī 1201, fols. 30v30–35r2 = MS Leiden: University Library Or. 36, fols. 24r31–26v31; in-text citations in this subsection refer to the Mashhad MS.

49. If that were indeed so, it would follow what Rāzī said (*lazima mā dhakartumūhu*), fol. 32r32; see Rāzī, 1381/2002–2003, pp. 130.5–6.

50. For sources on Urmawī's life and work, see Al-Rahim, 2018, pp. 118–125. A survey of biographical and bio-bibliographical sources reconstructing the personal and professional trajectory is Marlow, 2010; a brief biographical sketch is El-Rouayheb, 2019b, pp. 59–63.

51. Bar Hebraeus, 1663, p. 485; 1890, p. 445; *cf.* El-Rouayheb, 2019b, p. 59.

52. Marlow, 2010, pp. 283–285.

53. El-Rouayheb, 2019b, p. 59.

54. See Marlow, 2010, pp. 290–297.

55. In his *Laṭāʾif al-Ḥikma, cf.* Marlow, 2010, p. 297.

56. For a brief discussion of the circumstantial evidence of this view, see El-Rouayheb, 2019b, pp. 59–60. For the view that Urmawī influenced Khūnajī, see Lameer, 2014.

57. El-Rouayheb, 2019b, p. 61.

58. Ṭāshkubrīzādah, 2010, pp. 471–477. A good sense of what the standard works on logic were in the Ottoman world in the late 9th/15th century is ʿAṭūfī's inventory of Bayezid II's Palace Library from 1502/1503–1503/1504; see the facsimile of MS Török F.59 (Magyar Tudományos Akadémia Könyvtára Keleti Gyűjtemény) in volume 2, pp. 339–363 of Necipoğlu, Kafadar, & Fleischer, 2019 (transliteration pp. 222–239), and El-Rouayheb's description in volume 1 at pp. 891–906.

59. He wrote a commentary on Khūnajī's short logic primer *al-Mūjaz* (*terminus post quem* likely 646/1248), and commentaries on Rāzī's logical work *al-Āyāt al-bayyināt* (The Evident Signs)—titled *Ghāyāt al-Āyāt* (The Aims of the Signs)—as well as on the juridical work *al-Maḥṣūl* (The Yield) and the *kalām* work *al-Arbaʿīn* (The Forty). See El-Rouayheb, 2019b, p. 60; I did not have access to the text of *Sharḥ al-Mūjaz*, of which a manuscript is extant in the Qarawiyyīn library in Fes (Fāsī 1979–89, III, 334, nr. 1278), or to the *Ghāyāt al-Āyāt*, of which a manuscript is extant in the Alexandria Municipal Library in Egypt (MS 1957D, fols. 1–77, copied in 679/1280); see El-Rouayheb, 2019b, pp. 61–62. He also wrote a commentary on the *Ishārāt* (completed 659/1261), an intermediate length handbook on logic titled *al-Manāhij* (The Trails) with an auto-commentary by the title of *al-Mabāhij* (The Joys), and a summa on logic and metaphysics titled *Bayān al-ḥaqq wa lisān al-ṣidq* (The Exposition of Truth and the Language of Verity), which he completed late in his life (675/1276). Urmawī's *Sharḥ al-Ishārāt* (MS Istanbul: Topkapı Sarayı Müzesi Ahmet III Kitaplığı A 3269) is currently being edited by al-Tamīmī. For *al-Mabāhij*, there is an autograph copy from Konya in Turkey (Konya Karatay Yusufağa Kütüphanesi, MS 5482, fols. 75–229, dated 671/1273); for the *Bayān al-ḥaqq* I refer to the MS Istanbul: Süleymaniye Library, Atıf Efendi 1567 (143 folios, copied in 676/1278); for a list of some of Urmawī's logical works, see El-Rouayheb, 2019b, pp. 60–61; and more generally Al-Rahim, 2018, pp. 124–125.

60. Medieval Persian used a final short vowel for what became the colloquial ending ە– ("he/she is") in modern Persian.

61. This is most likely a reference to Kātibī's argument; see page 124.

62. The text has been edited in a Turkish dissertation; for the passage in question, see Akkanat, 2006, pp. 27.3–28.20.

7. THE GREAT DIALECTIC COMMENTARIES

1. El-Rouayheb, 2019b, p. 66. For Samarqandī and the origins and history of *ādāb al-baḥth*, see the pioneering dissertation in Miller, 1984, now reworked as Miller, 2020; as well as Belhaj, 2016; Miller, 2019; and Young, 2016, 2017, 2018. For an explosion of interest in *ādāb al-baḥth* in the Ottoman empire, see El-Rouayheb, 2015, pp. 60–96.

2. Kātibī may of course not have read Samarqandī's work on the formal theory of disputation, for he died when Samarqandī could hardly have been older than in his twenties. But the formal dialectics developed by Samarqandī contained nothing new: rather, the novelty lay in systematically integrating the rules of juridical eristics previously laid out by, e.g., ʿAmīdī and Nasafī, within the framework of Aristotelian/Avicennan propositional logic.

And the formulaic turns of phrase, a systematic study of which in Kātibī's commentaries would likely confirm this first impression, reflect the argumentative strategies of juridical eristics. In that tradition, for example, it was required to (1) first state, prior to the disputation, the objects of the investigation (*taḥrīr al-mabāḥith*) and establish the relevant opinions and beliefs (*taqrīr al-madhāhib*); then (2) the Questioner may demand a verification of the opinions and beliefs (*taṣḥīḥ al-naql*), before (3) the Questioner may object to the claimant's proposal in several ways, for example, by not conceding that the conclusion is implied by the premises (*lā nusallim al-lāzima*); for a brief summary, see Miller, 2019, pp. 135–137. In the six folios from Kātibī's commentaries that I edited (*Sharḥ Kashf al-asrār*, MS Istanbul: Süleymaniye Carullah 1417 fols. 57v2–59v21; *al-Munaṣṣaṣ fī Sharḥ al-Mulakhkhaṣ*, MS Mashhad: Kitābkhāna-yi Markazī-yi Āstān-i Quds-i Raḍawī 1201, fols. 30v30–35r2), he uses (1) "*taqrīr*" to establish the opinion of the author six times. While (2) is rare, the formulaic markers for objections abound: For example, the specific objection (3) denying the implication (*lā nusallim al-luzūm*) occurs nine times in the *Munaṣṣaṣ*, while other forms of objections introduced by *lā nusallim*, for example, questioning the premises of the argument (*munāqaḍa*), e.g., not conceding an antecedent, occur once in the *Kashf* commentary and six times in the *Munaṣṣaṣ*; "*fīhi naẓr*" occurs once in the *Kashf* commentary and ten times in the *Munaṣṣaṣ*; "*li-qā'il . . .* " occurs four times in the *Munaṣṣaṣ*.

3. On Samarqandī's life and work, see El-Rouayheb, 2019b, pp. 65–68; Miller, 2012, 2020; see also Şeşen, 2008; Eichner, 2009.

4. Miller, 2012; El-Rouayheb, 2019b, p. 65.

5. See Ṣafadī, 1931, p. 282; and Ḥājjī Khalīfa (Kātib Çelebī), 1835–1858, p. nr. 1803.

6. El-Rouayheb, 2019b; *cf.* Miller, 2012.

7. Miller, 2012. For the *Ṣaḥā'if* we have a date on the MS Istanbul: Laleli 2432, fol. 33b; it has been edited by Aḥmed ʿAbd al-Raḥmān al-Sharīf in Muḥammad b. Ashraf al- Samarqandī, 1985.

8. He wrote an esteemed treatise on thirty-five fundamental postulates in Euclid's Elements, titled *Ashkāl al-ta'sīs* (Foundational Forms), edited by Suwaysī in Samarqandī, 1984 (on the content, see also Dilgan, 1960); as well as several works on astronomy, including, probably, the anonymous commentary on Ṭūsī's *sharḥ* on Ptolemy's *Almagest*. For a lists of his works, see Brockelmann, 1898–1902, pp. I.468; Supp. I.840–841, or, now in English, Brockelmann, 2016, pp. 537–538, and Sezgin, 1967–2015, p. V.99; VI.94.

9. The date for the *Qisṭās* is given on MS Istanbul: Fatih 3360; it has been edited by Pehlivan first as a dissertation (Pehlivan, 2010), then in Samarqandī, 2014. The *Sharḥ al-qisṭās* remains unedited, but early extant manuscripts are MS Berlin: Staatsbibliothek Landberg 1035 (completed 693/1294) and MS Yale: University Library Beinecke Arabic 11, copied in Iṣfahān and dated to 705/1305 (both available online).

10. See page 151. The *Bishārāt* is being edited by Awjabī; it survives in numerous manuscripts, some early ones of which are MS Tehran: Kitābkhāni-yi Dānishgāh-i Tehrān 2792, copied 688/1289; MS Istanbul: Carullah 1308; MS Istanbul: Fātiḥ 3195; MS Istanbul: Ayasofya 2418; MS Istanbul: Köprülü 879.

11. Recently edited, together with the commentary by Zakariyyā al-Anṣārī (d. 926/1519), by ʿArafa ʿAbd al-Raḥmān al-Nādī in Anṣārī, 2014. See also Young, forthcoming, for a critical edition of the *Grundtext* and of Quṭb al-Dīn al-Kīlānī's (*fl. ca.* 830/1427) commentary. For a list of the numerous commentaries on the work, see Wisnovsky, 2004, pp. 169–170.

12. For a summary, see Miller, 2020, pp. 120–123.

13. Miller, 2019, p. 131. Other works on dialectics include the commentary on his teacher Nasafī's *Fuṣūl* (for extant MSS, see Samarqandī, 2014, pp. 46–47), the dialectic parts of *al-Anwār al-ilāhiyya* (The Divine Lights), a handbook on rational theology, and the *ʿAyn al-naẓar* (The Quintessence of Ratiocination); for MSS, see El-Rouayheb, 2019b, pp. 76–77.

14. I thank Tony Street for bringing to my attention the recent edition of the *Qisṭās* by Fallāḥī; unfortunately, it was too late to be fully taken into account here. With regard to the passage cited, Fallāḥī points out (Samarqandī, 2019–2020 [1399], p. 229, note 5) that Samarqandī is misrepresenting Rāzī, because in his *Sharḥ al-Ishārāt* Rāzī does not talk about the question of what kind of nexus is a part of the proposition, and that, there, Rāzī clearly takes both nexus he distinguishes as being by predicate-hood, which does not, however, contradict what he says in the *Mulakhkhaṣ*: there, it is the essence of the subject being described *by the predicate* that is part of the proposition.

15. Other MSS of the *Bīsharat* are MS Tehran: Kitābkhāni-yi Dānishgāh-i Tehrān (?) 2792; MS Istanbul: Fātiḥ 3195; MS Istanbul: Ayasofya 2418; MS Istanbul: Köprülü 879. The pagination of this last MS seems to be mis-ordered.

16. See MS Berlin: Staatsbibliothek Landberg 1035, fols. 43r12–32 = MS Yale: Beinecke Arabic 11, fols. 30v21–27.

17. On Ḥillī's life and work, see now Terrier, 2020; and El-Rouayheb, 2019b, pp. 68–70; Schmidtke, 1991, 2001–2003; Street, 2016a.

18. Schmidtke, 1991, pp. 9–11.

19. The evidence is however circumstantial; see Schmidtke, 1991, p. 17.

20. Schmidtke, 1991, pp. 23–27.

21. See Wisnovsky, 2014, for Ḥillī's role in securing the dominance of Ṭūsīan Avicennism. For his lasting influence, see, e.g., El-Rouayheb, 2019b, p. 68; and the introduction in Schmidtke, 1991. The high esteem in which Ḥillī is still being held in certain Shiʿī circles today may be gauged from the publishers' preface in Ḥillī, 2017, pp. 7–9.

22. El-Rouayheb, 2019b, pp. 68–69. On Ḥillī's possibly Twelver-Shiʿī agenda in appropriating the Ṭūsīan line of Avicennism into mainstream Shiʿī theology, see Wisnovsky, 2018.

23. Schmidtke, 1991, p. 61, mentions a *Qawāʿid* MS dated to 679/1280. A relatively early date for its completion is suggested by Street, 2016a, p. 271, given the fact that nowhere in the work does Ḥillī pay pious respects to his teacher Kātibī, which would be odd if Kātibī had died just a few years earlier.

24. The *Qawāʿid* has been edited in Ḥillī, 1992 [1412], the *Jawhar* in Ḥillī, 1992–1993 [1413]. Ḥillī likely also wrote a commentary on Khūnajī's *Kashf*, and certainly on Suhrawardī's *Talwīḥāt*, but neither seems to be extant; see Street, 2016a, p. 272. The *Ishārāt* commentary was thought to be lost by Schmidtke, 1991, pp. 58–59; but see Wisnovsky, 2014, p. 349, note 28; early MSS containing the work are MS Istanbul: Damat Ibrahim Paşa 817 and MS Istanbul: Ahmet III, A3400. For the context of Ḥillī's *Muḥākamāt*, see Wisnovsky, 2014, 2018, 2013b. The commentary on the *Shifāʾ* titled *Kashf al-khifāʾ min Kitāb al-Shifāʾ* (Unveiling the Secrets of the Book of the Cure) was likely never completed and the unicum MS Dublin: Chester Beatty Arabic 5151 only preserves about two-thirds of the commentary on the *Categories* (*al-Maqūlāt*). For a discussion, see Wisnovsky, 2018. The *Asrār* has been edited and appears in Ḥillī, 2000, and the *Marāṣid* has been edited and appears in Ḥillī, 2017.

25. So for example Schmidtke, 1991, p. 60: "The reason why most of al-Ḥillī's philosophical works are lost was presumably that they were of little originality. Since he was a theologian rather than a philosopher, it is most likely that he composed most of his philosophical works as books of instruction for his students. This impression is confirmed by the titles of some of the lost works."

26. See Street, 2016a, pp. 270–276.

27. Ḥillī, 1992 [1412], pp. 179.7–180.2, and 415.7–9: "This is the end of what we wanted to set out in commentary on the epistle, having only intended to elucidate it; we have not turned to mention what we hold to be the truth, except in a few places. We have left that task to the *Asrār*" (translation Street, 2016a, p. 237).

28. Ḥillī, 1992 [1412], pp. 246–247; 247.14–15.

29. Street, 2016a, p. 271f.

30. Ḥillī, 1992–1993 [1413], pp. 73.5–75.17.

31. For the text of the relevant passage from the *Muḥākamāt* I have compared MS Istanbul: Topkapı Aḥmad III 3400, fols. 96v2–98v2 and MS Istanbul: Süleymaniye Damād Ibrahīm Pashā 817, fols. 44v18– 45v13. In-text references in this subsection refer to the Topkapı manuscript.

32. The point is somewhat lost in English, because what Ṭūsī points out here, namely that a verb succeeding its grammatical subject is in Arabic not understood as indicating a connection between the two (as is the case with "Writes Zayd" in English—the expectation is that whatever Zayd writes should precede in quotation marks), is in Arabic parallel in word order to the nominal sentence *Zayd kātib*, which is grammatically perfectly fine, and considered by Rāzī to also be logically fine. Now, Ṭūsī's point is that if Rāzī thinks that grammatical propriety is enough to consider the nominal sentence to be logically complete, then he would have to admit that the perfectly parallel case (as verbs and derived names are treated on a par by Rāzī) lacks grammatical propriety and would need a copula to express a logically complete proposition, which in turn would invalidate the claim that verbs and derived names connect by themselves to a subject.

33. See page 139; *cf.* Street, 2016a, p. 271.

34. Ḥillī, 2000, pp. 55–58; in-text references in this subsection are to this edition.

35. See page 124.

36. Schmidtke, 1991, p. 58.

37. On the division of the two works, see also Ghafūrī-Nazhād's remarks in his introduction: Ḥillī, 2017, pp. 21–22. In-text references in the remainder of this subsection refer to this edition.

38. In the *Marāṣid* he is, for example, the first to distinguish five different ways of presenting the subject in a proposition. The issue of the reference of the subject term became highly contested, already with Quṭb al-Dīn al-Rāzī; see Ahmed, 2010. In addition to the Aristotelian three—universal-quantified, particular-quantified, and unquantified—and the later addition of a fourth way (called a "natural" subject, e.g., in the proposition "human is a species," which not only is not quantified, but cannot even take a quantifier), Ḥillī added a fifth distinction. He relabels the fourth distinction a "general subject" and calls the new distinction a "natural subject," referring to an unquantified quiddity with a property that is true of all its individual instances. A subject of a proposition can thus have one of five distinct references: it can refer to (i) a particular (e.g., this individual human), (ii)

to a particular-quantified extension (some individual humans), (iii) to a universal-quantified extension (all individual humans), (iv) to an unquantified quiddity as a general concept inasmuch as it is what it is (as in "human is a species"), or (v) to an unquantified quiddity inasmuch as what is true of it is true of all individuals (as in "[A] human has a soul"); Ḥillī, 1992–1993 [1413], pp. 35, 55; 1992 [1412], pp. 103, 203. See also Ghafūrī-Nazhād's introduction: Ḥillī, 2017, pp. 19–20. This innovation is tied to Ḥillī's rejection of Rāzī's distinction between *ḥaqīqī* and *khārijī* propositions. For a brief account of this distinction in Rāzī and the tradition, see El-Rouayheb, 2011; and Ahmed, 2011, pp. 352–362.

39. For sources on Quṭb al-Dīn's life and work, see Al-Rahim, 2018, pp. 130–143; El-Rouayheb, 2019b, pp. 72–74.

40. Al-Rahim, 2018, pp. 137–138; El-Rouayheb, 2019b, pp. 72–73.

41. It is unclear which of the three *Qawāʿid* that Ḥillī wrote this refers to, but likely it was the commentary on the *Shamsiyya* discussed earlier; see Al-Rahim, 2018, pp. 131, note 493.

42. Shushtarī, 1986 [1365], p. 227; Shushtarī, 2011 [1433], p. 195; translation adapted from Al-Rahim, 2018, p. 132.

43. Al-Rahim, 2018, p. 131; and Schmidtke, 1991, pp. 30, 39; Melville, 1990, pp. 55–70.

44. See the arguments in Al-Rahim, 2018, pp. 132–134.

45. See van Ess, 1978, pp. 270–283; and Al-Rahim, 2018, p. 132. For the science of *ʿilm al-waḍ*ʿ, see Weiss, 1966, 1987, 1976, 1985. This rather "new" science came to be codified around Quṭb al-Dīn's time, mainly by Ījī's short *al-Risāla al-waḍʿiyya al-Aḍudiyya*, recently reprinted with commentaries in Dusūqī, 2012, pp. 11–13.

46. For a list of super-commentaries and glosses on these works, see Wisnovsky, 2004, p. 165f.; *cf.* also El-Rouayheb, 2019b, p. 72. There are several editions of the *Lawāmiʿ*, the most recent being those by the Iranian scholars ʿAlī Aṣghar Jaʿfarī Valanī and Abū al-Qāsim Raḥmānī, respectively Taḥtānī, 2014b and Taḥtānī, 2014a. Raḥmānī's is the first edition with a thorough introduction and a good critical apparatus; it is also the only edition I have seen that includes Quṭb al-Dīn's later addition on atomic propositions, which we shall discuss later. A recent edition of the *Taḥrīr* is Taḥtānī, 2014c.

47. El-Rouayheb, 2019b, p. 73.

48. For a list of Taḥtānī's philosophical/logical works, see Al-Rahim, 2018, pp. 141–143; and El-Rouayheb, 2019b, pp. 73–74. The shorter epistles on specific logical topics include a treatise on conception and assent (*taṣawwur wa taṣdīq*), edited in Sharīʿatī, 2004, pp. 93–135, and discussed in Türker, 2019 (cf. also Lameer, 2006) and, in a way relevant to the present topic, in Klinger, forthcoming c; a treatise titled *Risāla fī taḥqīq al-kulliyāt*, where he lays out his anti-realist position regarding universals, edited in Taḥtānī, 2013; and a treatise on quantified propositions (*maḥṣūrāt*), which remains unedited. The *Muḥākamāt* glosses are published in numerous editions; I here use the text printed at the bottom of Ṭūsī, 1383/2004–2005.

49. Klinger, 2019.

50. For more detail on how (1) and (2) may have influenced Taḥtānī's revision, see Klinger, 2019, pp. 67–70 and *passim*.

51. For a more in-depth discussion of Taḥtānī's quadripartite analysis, its success, and Jalāl al-Dīn al-Dawānī's (d. 908/1502) criticism of it, see El-Rouayheb, 2016b, pp. 303–309 and 312–318. However, Quṭb al-Dīn was arguably not the first to distinguish between

judgment and judgeable content: Samarqandī seems to have done this as well, and he died about six years before the *Lawāmiʿ* was written.

52. Taḥtānī spends almost thirty pages in Raḥmānī's edition on that passage (II 15–42); in-text references in this section are to that edition by volume, page, and line.

53. *Cf.* Ibn Sīnā, 1970, pp. 28–29.

54. See page 72ff.

55. MS Arbāstān: Dānishgāh-i Arbāstān 7980 and MS Tehran: Kitābkhāna-yi Mellī 5–000242; see also Raḥmānī's note, Taḥtānī, 2014a, p. II.26, note 8.

56. This is impossible to render in English: contrary to English, the natural way to express a verbal sentence in Arabic is to start with the verb. When a sentence begins with a noun in Arabic, the rule is that what follows is a nominal sentence. "*Zayd qama*" is perhaps similarly disturbing to a native speaker's sense of grammatical propriety as is "Got up Zayd." Quṭb al-Dīn's point hinges on the specificity of such grammatical propriety in Arabic, for no one would have suggested to use an artificial copula like "*huwa*" in verbal sentences— "*qāma Zayd*" is perfectly fine, and "*qāma huwa Zayd*" perfectly absurd. Quṭb al-Dīn rightly points out that there should be no difference, or at any rate no difference to be made up for by an artificial copula, in the logical syntax of the two sentences.

8. TO SHĪRĀZ AND MUGHAL INDIA: A "SEMANTIC TURN"

1. See El-Rouayheb, 2019b, pp. 75–79.

2. Versteegh, 2021, in an unpublished paper has recently described the period as a "semantic turn." El-Rouayheb, 2019b, pp. 78–80, noted a tendency beginning with logic commentaries in the late 8th/14th century to focus on semantic questions at the expense of the technicalities of syllogistic; for a rise of semantics beginning with Taftāzānī, see also El-Rouayheb, 2015, pp. 117–118. Scholarly interest in Arabic/Islamic philosophy of language, in both the classical and post-classical period, is only beginning to emerge; see for example Germann & Najafi, 2020.

3. One main strand were the commentaries and super-commentaries on Avicenna's *Ishārāt*. After Taḥtānī, commentaries continued to be written at least until the 12th/18th century, and Taḥtānī's *Muḥākamāt* itself elicited at least three super-commentaries, by Jalāl al-Dīn al-Dawānī (d. 907/1501), Ibn Kamālpāshā (d. 940/1533), and Mīrzājān Ḥabīballāh al-Bāghnawī al-Shīrāzī (d. 994/1586). Another main strand was the tradition on Taḥtānī's commentary *Lawāmiʿ al-asrār*, on Urmawī's *Maṭāliʿ al-anwār*, surveyed in the last chapter. Particularly the gloss by al-Sayyid al-Sharīf al-Jurjānī (d. 816/1413) elicited numerous—at least fourteen—super-glosses (two by the Dawānī given earlier; see Pourjavady, 2011, p. 81), and that in addition to the other direct super-commentaries on the *Lawāmiʿ* by, among others, Abū al-Thanāʾ Maḥmūd b. ʿAbd al-Raḥmān al-Iṣfahānī (d. 749/1348), Jalāl al-Dīn Khiḍr b. ʿAlī b. al-Khaṭṭāb Ḥājjī Pāshā Aydīnī (d. 816/1413), and Ḥusayn al-Ardabīlī al-Abharī (d. 950/1543); see Wisnovsky, 2004, pp. 165–166. There are more places in which questions about the copula and the problem of predication were being raised and from which such discussions evolved. I believe that it is likely, for example, that even though not treated at length in Ḥillī's and Taḥtānī's commentaries on it, such discussions are to be found in the further commentary tradition on Kātibī's *Shamsiyya*, for which Wisnovsky lists twenty-five direct commentaries, thirteen super-commentaries and no less than a combined thirty-two

commentaries on the super-commentaries by al-Sayyid al-Sharīf al-Jurjānī and Mīr Zāhid al-Harawī (d. 1101/1689) alone; see Wisnovsky, 2004, pp. 163–165. Moreover, we find similar discussions in the commentary traditions on specific passages from the early parts (*al-ʿumūr al-ʿāmma*) of creedal or *kalām* works. An example is the tradition on Ṭūsī's *Tajrīd al-ʿitiqād*, with which Dawānī and his intellectual opponent Ṣadr al-Dīn al-Dashtakī (d. 903/1498) engaged by each writing three glosses on ʿAlāʾ al-Dīn al-Qūshjī's (d. 879/1474) commentary of the work. See the debates on existential predication and the role of the copula in Qūshjī, 2014, p. 199ff.; *cf.* Pourjavady, 2016 and El-Rouayheb, 2019a.

4. El-Rouayheb, 2019b, p. 80. But see van Ess, 2013, p. 35 who has no reservations.

5. In various editions, for example, together with the commentaries by Dawānī and Yazdī, in Saʿd al-Dīn Taftāzānī, 2014 [1435].

6. El-Rouayheb, 2019b, pp. 82–83, with references to lithographs and editions.

7. On Ījī and his works, see now van Ess, 2020; and van Ess, 1966. On *ʿilm al-waḍʿ*, see Weiss, 1987.

8. van Ess, 2020.

9. Sakkākī, 1937; and Qazwīnī, 2007. See also Qazwīnī, 1964; Saʿd al-Dīn Taftāzānī, 1960, 2013; Jurjānī, 2007.

10. Taftāzānī, 2013; Jurjānī wrote a gloss on that work (Jurjānī, 2007), as well as his own commentary on Qazwīnī's *Talkhīṣ* (Çelik, 2009).

11. On the history of *ʿilm al-balāgha* and its roots in literary criticism and the inimitability of the Qurʾān, see especially the *Asrār al-balāgha* (Jurjānī, 1954, 1959) and *Dalāʾil al-iʿjāz* (Jurjānī, 1984) by ʿAbd al-Qāhir al-Jurjānī (d. 471/1078); and Noy, 2018.

12. The term occurs more than once in Ījī's *al-Risāla al-Waḍʿiyya*. For a (relatively rare) print of the text without commentary, see Īdrīs, 2016.

13. The double-bracketed text appears in an Indian lithograph, but not in Ṣāliḥ's manuscript.

14. It is unclear whether Taftāzānī refers to the *KH* (Fārābī, 1970, pp. 111–113) and got the title wrong, or whether he in fact refers to both the *KH* and the *Kitāb al-Alfāẓ al-mustʿamala fī l-manṭiq*. In any case, it is remarkable that he read Fārābī.

15. For a discussion of *kināya*, see Sakkākī, 1937, pp. 189–196; and Pellat, 2012.

16. Weiss, 1966, 1976, 1985, 1987. There is some recent scholarship in Turkish, for example, Sürücü, 2019. Giovanni Carrera has just defended (early 2024) a PhD thesis at McGill titled *The Development of ʿilm al-waḍʿ (8th/14th–15th/20th Century): Origins, Contexts and Canons of a Semantic Theory*, which I have not yet had the chance to read.

17. Theoretical discussions of linguistic meaning had been part of propaedeutics in works of Qurʾānic exegesis (*tafsīr*) already in the 5th/11th century; see for example Iṣfahānī, 1984, pp. 27–109. In jurisprudence (*uṣul al-fiqh*), a good third of Fakhr al-Dīn al-Rāzī's *al-Maḥṣūl fī uṣūl al-fiqh* deals with semantic matters (Rāzī, 1999). Or there is Rāzī's *Nihāyat al-Ījāz fī dirāyat al-iʿjāz*, where the first fifth is concerned with the relation between simple utterances and simple meanings (Rāzī, 1985). But by the 9th/15th century, linguistic propaedeutics in works across the Islamic sciences often include introductions to the semantic theory of *ʿilm al-waḍʿ*. For example, in morphology (*al-ṣarf*) there is ʿAlāʾ al-Dīn al-Qūshjī's *ʿUnqūd al-zawāhir fī al-ṣarf*, a grammatical work from the 9th/15th century, where a significant portion of the first part on the principles of the linguistic sciences is concerned with semantics in the sense of *ʿilm al-waḍʿ* (Qūshjī, 2001). For later *uṣūlī* works, see especially al-Maḥallī's commentary on Subkī's *Jamʿ al-Jamāʿa*, printed with ʿAṭṭār's glosses in ʿAṭṭār, 2016, where there is an entire section on *ʿilm al-waḍʿ* in the first book of the first tome, in

the "First Part on Logic and Concept." For *kalām* works, see Jurjānī's commentary on the *Mawāqif*: Jurjānī, 1998 [1419]. For *balāgha*, his gloss on the *Muṭawwal* (Jurjānī, 2007, p. 100) and *waḍ'ī* terminology (passim) in the part on *'ilm al-ma'ānī*.

18. For a more detailed account of what *'ilm al-waḍ'* is about, see Weiss, 1987. Ījī's *Risāla* has been printed, for example, in Īdrīs, 2016, and several times along with the main commentaries: see for example Samarqandī, 1911 [1329]; Dusūqī, 2012. Qūshjī's commentary has been printed at the end of Sayyid Ḥāfiẓ's gloss on it: Shukr, 1851 [1267]. Jāmī's commentary was edited as a master's thesis in Turkey by Can, 2015.

19. On various exegetical positions regarding the verse and the debates surrounding the origin of language, see Loucel, 1964; and Kister, 1988, as well as Carter, 2004. Fārābī was exceptional in that he did not accept the mainstream account, see Roman, 2001; and Druart, 2010. On the place of linguistic sciences, see Hasnawi, 1988.

20. The terminology *'amm* and *khāṣṣ* in connection with linguistic reference had been forged by logicians, especially Khūnajī, who was perhaps the first to systematically analyze the ways in which two propositions—or two terms—can be related to each other: they can be coextensive (*musāwāt*) or disjoined (*mubāyana*), or else one is more specific (*akhaṣṣ*) while the other is more general (*a'amm*); see El-Rouayheb's discussion in Khūnajī 2010, pp. xxix–xxx, and now Street, 2024, especially §§26–27 of Kātibī's *Shamsiyya* with the commentary *ad loc.* and with Fallāḥī, 2019. For the summary account of the theory of reference in Ījī's *Risāla*, I in what follows rely on the presentation in Weiss, 1966, pp. 90–118.

21. See the summary account in Weiss, 1966, pp. 104–106.

22. On Jurjānī, see van Ess, 2013 which is a revised, expanded, and corrected version of his *Encyclopaedia Iranica* entry. See also El-Rouayheb, 2019b, pp. 84–90.

23. On the identity of Mubārakshāh and the connection to Ījī, see van Ess, 2013, p. 24. On the question whether and where Jurjānī met Taḥtānī, see van Ess, 2013, pp. 12–16.

24. El-Rouayheb, 2019b, p. 101; *cf.* Pourjavady, 2011, 2016.

25. For a brief description, see El-Rouayheb, 2019b, pp. 87–90.

26. Jurjānī, 1860, pp. 114–115.

27. El-Rouayheb, 2019b, pp. 75–80, 85.

28. 'Aḍūd al-Dīn al-Ījī was active in Shīrāz between 736/1335 and 754/1353, but even though the Ash'arī theologian was also an accomplished philosopher, it does not seem that philosophy was being taught as an independent subject; see Pourjavady, 2011, p. 1. Jurjānī, who moved to Shīrāz in 779/1377–1378, taught at the Dār al-Shifā' madrasa until 789/1387, when Tīmūr (r. 771/1369–807/1405) called him to his court in Samarqand, returning to Shīrāz for the last years of his life; see Pourjavady, 2011, pp. 1–2.

29. Pourjavady, 2011, p. 81. One of the glosses was written as a response to a gloss by Dashtakī, but none of them has been edited. For extant MSS, see El-Rouayheb, 2019b, p. 103. I have not had the chance to see any MSS of this exchange, but I suspect that it might contain much relevant material.

30. Jurjānī, 2007, p. 88ff.; see also van Ess, 2013, p. 67.

31. Manuscripts of *Risāla 'alā Taḥqīq ma'nā al-ḥarf* are MS Princeton: Garrett 448 H and the three MSS that Aktaş, 2018 used for his edition: MS Istanbul: Süleymaniye 911; MS Istanbul: Laleli 2221; and MS Istanbul: 4468. For *al-Risāla al-Mir'ātiyya*, MS Princeton: Yehuda 5423, fol. 42r. See also Mach & Ormsby, 1987; and van Ess, 2013, p. 67.

32. Besides a short description in Weiss, 1966, p. 112; 1976, p. 28; and van Ess, 2013, p. 67, together with the edition and rather superficial study in Arabic by Aktaş, 2018, I am

not aware of any other attempts to interpret and contextualize the material that bring out its significance.

33. Weiss, 1976, p. 28.

34. See for example in Jāmī's commentary, Can, 2015, p. 65ff.; compare with Weiss, 1966, pp. 110–114.

35. Compare Jurjānī, 2007, p. 89.

36. *Cf.* the introduction and the beginning of chapter 1. The question is discussed in Ramsey, 1925.

37. For Dawānī's life and his works, see El-Rouayheb, 2019b, pp. 101–104; and Pourjavady, 2011, pp. 4–16; 2016.

38. Unfortunately, I have not had access to most of the following MSS containing these glosses: For an early manuscript of Dawānī's first gloss, see Mach & Ormsby, 2017, nr. 694; for his second gloss, titled *Tanwīr al-Maṭāliʿ* (Casting Light on the Dawning), see Khuda Bakhsh Oriental Public Library, 1970—, XXI, nr. 2261 (153 folios, nineteen lines per page, copied in Shiraz in 1049/1639); *cf.* El-Rouayheb, 2019b, p. 100. For Dashtakī's gloss: MS Tehran: Kitābkhāni-yi Mellī: 2717 ح, 117 fols.; MS Qum: Kitābkhāni-yi Marʿashī Najafī, 7312, fols. 61–138; *cf.* El-Rouayheb, 2019b, p. 103.

39. On the question of how many parts a proposition has, see El-Rouayheb, 2016b; on the liar paradox, see Rezakhany, 2018 and El-Rouayheb, 2020b; and on existential predication, see El-Rouayheb, 2019a.

40. Saʿd al-Dīn Taftāzānī, 2014 [1435], pp. 173.9–12.

41. El-Rouayheb, 2019b, pp. 147, 173–176; see also, on the widespread *Ders-i Niżāmī* curriculum, Ḥasanī, 1958, p. 16; and Ahmed, 2015.

42. Ḥasanī, 1955, p. V.210.

43. For Siyālkūtī and his works, see El-Rouayheb, 2019b, pp. 176–178.

44. Ahmed, 2022.

45. There are several prints of the work. Here I refer to the 1909/1910 Cairo edition in two volumes: Mullā Mubīn Lakhnawī, 1909 [1327], 1910 [1328].

46. On Mubīn and his commentarial method, see Ahmed, 2022, pp. 107–110.

47. Mullā Mubīn Lakhnawī, 1909 [1327], p. 3; *cf.* Ahmed, 2022, pp. 108–109.

48. Mullā Mubīn Lakhnawī, 1909 [1327], p. 2.

49. See for example the works listed in El-Rouayheb, 2019b, pp. 193–198, 233–236.

BIBLIOGRAPHY

UNPUBLISHED PRIMARY SOURCES: MANUSCRIPTS

Abharī, Athīr al-Dīn al-. *Bayān al-asrār*. [1] MS Istanbul: Köprülü Kütüphanesi 1618; [2] MS Istanbul: Murat Molla Kütüphanesi 1406, fols. 1–57.

———. *Kitāb al-Maṭāli ʿ*. [1] MS Istanbul: Köprülü Kütüphanesi 1618; [2] MS Istanbul: Murat Molla Kütüphanesi 1406, fols. 98–135.

———. *Kitāb al-Shukūk*. MS Istanbul: Ayasofya 2319.

———. *Talkhīṣ al-ḥaqā ʾiq*. [1] MS Istanbul: Köprülü Kütüphanesi 1618; [2] MS Istanbul: Murat Molla Kütüphanesi 1406, fols. 58–97.

———. *Zubdat al-asrār*. [1] MS Qum: Kitābkhāna-yi Ayatollah Marʿashī Najafī 4060, fols. 2–38; [2] MS Istanbul: Millet Kütüphanesi, Feyzullah 1210, fols. 100–168; [3] MS Burdur: Burdur İl Halk Library 1180, fols. 1–51.

———. *Zubdat al-ḥaqāʾiq*. [1] MS Istanbul: Köprülü Kütüphanesi 1618; [2] MS Istanbul: Murat Molla Kütüphanesi 1406, 136–185.

Āmidī, Sayf al-Dīn al-. *Kashf al-tamwīhāt fī Sharḥ al-Ishārāt wa-l-tanbīhāt*. [1] MS Istanbul: Laleli 2519; [2] MS Berlin: Staatsbibliothek, Petermann II 596.

Fārābī, Abū Naṣr al-. *Kitāb fī l-manṭiq*, MS Bratislava: University Library TE 41.

Hillī, Ibn al-Muṭahhar al-. *Kitāb Kashf al-khifā ʾ min Kitāb al-Shifāʾ*. MS Dublin: Chester Beatty Library, Arabic 5151.

———. *al-Muḥākamāt bayna shurrāḥ al-Ishārāt*. [1] MS Istanbul: Süleymaniye Kütüphanesi, Damat Ibrahim Paşa 817; [2] MS Istanbul: Topkapı Sarayı Müzesi, Ahmet III A3400.

Ibn ʿAdī, Yaḥyā. *Maqāla fī tabyīn al-faṣl bayna ṣināʿtay al-manṭiq al-falsafī wa-n-aḥw al-ʿarabī*. MS Tehran: Kitābkhāni-yi Majlis Ṭabāṭabāʾī 1376.

Ibn Rushd. *al-Kalima wa l-ism al-mushtaqq ʿinda l-Fārābī*. MS Madrid: Escorial, Derenbourg 632, fols. 88v–89r.

Ibn Sawār, Ḥassan. *Organon* (Arabic). MS Paris: Bibliothèque Nationale, Arabe 2346.

Ibn Sīna. *al-Ḥikma al-mashriqiyya.* MS Cairo: Dār al-Kutub, Ḥikma 6 M[uṣṭafā Fāḍil], fols. 116v–138r.

Kātibī, Najm al-Dīn al-. *Baḥr al-fawā'id.* MS Leiden: University Library, Golius Or. 210/2, fols. 72–159, copied 673/1275.

———. *Jāmi' al-daqā'iq fī kashf al-ḥaqā'iq.* MS Istanbul: Topkapı Sarayı Müzesi, Ahmet III 3372.

———. *al-Munaṣṣaṣ fī Sharḥ al-Mulakhkhaṣ.* [1] MS Mashhad: Kitābkhāna-yi Markazī-yi Āstān-i Quds-i Raḍawī 1201, copied 18 Ramaḍān 671/April 8, 1273; [2] MS Leiden: University Library, Golius Or. 36, copied in Rabī' II 692/March 1293.

———. *Sharḥ Kashf al-asrār.* [1] MS Istanbul: Süleymaniye Kütüphanesi, Carullah 1417, first part copied before 678/1280; [2] MS Istanbul: Süleymaniye Kütüphanesi, Carullah 1417, copied 687/1288.

Khūnajī, Afḍal al-Dīn al-. *al-Mūjaz.* [1] MS Cambridge: University Library Ll. 6.24, fols. 3b–43b, copied in 750/1349; [2] MS Tehran: Kitābkhāni-yi Majlis 1984, fols. 4–92, copied in 687/1288.

Nakhjuwānī, Najm al-Dīn al-. *Zubdat al-naqs wa-lubāb al-kashf.* MS Istanbul: Topkapı Sarayı Müzesi, Ahmet III 3264.

Rāzī (ps.), Fakhr al-Dīn. *al-Manṭiq al-kabīr.* MS Istanbul: Topkapı Sarayı Müzesi, Ahmet III 3401, copied in 667/1268.

Rāzī, Fakhr al-Dīn. *Ghāyāt al-Āyāt.* MS Alexandria: Municipal Library 1957D, fols. 1–77, copied in 679/1280.

Samarqandī, Shams al-Dīn. *Bishārāt al-Ishārāt.* [1] MS Tehran: Kitābkhāni-yi Dānishgāh-i Tehrān 2792, copied 688/1289; [2] MS Istanbul: Süleymaniye Kütüphanesi, Carullah 1308; [3] MS Istanbul: Fātiḥ 3195; [4] MS Istanbul: Ayasofya 2418; [5] MS Istanbul: Köprülü 879.

———. *Qisṭās al-afkār.* MS Istanbul: Fātiḥ 3360.

———. *Ṣaḥā'if al-Ilāhiyya.* MS Istanbul: Laleli 2432.

———. *Sharḥ al-qisṭās.* [1] MS Berlin: Staatsbibliothek, Landberg 1035, completed 693/1294; [2] MS Yale: Beinecke Arabic 11, copied in Iṣfahān and dated to 705/1305.

Taḥtānī, Quṭb al-Dīn al-Rāzī al-. *Lawāmi' al-asrār fī Maṭāli' al-anwār.* [1] MS Arbastan: Dānishgāh-i Arbastān 7980; [2] MS Tehran: Kitābkhāni-yi Mellī 5–000242.

———. *al-Muḥākamāt bayna Sharḥay al-Ishārāt.* MS Istanbul: Şehit Ali Paşa 1750.

Urmawī, Sirāj al-Dīn al-. *Bayān al-ḥaqq wa lisān al-ṣidq.* MS Istanbul: Süleymaniye Kütüphanesi, Atıf Efendi 1567, copied in 676/1278.

———. *Mabāhij fī l-Manāhij.* MS Konya: Karatay Yusufağa Kütüphanesi 5482, fols. 75–229, copied in 671/1273.

———. *Sharḥ al-Ishārāt.* MS Istanbul: Topkapı Sarayı Müzesi, Ahmet III Kitaplığı A 3269.

PUBLISHED PRIMARY SOURCES (GREEK, LATIN, ARABIC, PERSIAN)

Abharī, Athīr al-Dīn al-. (1998). *Kashf al-ḥaqā'iq fī taḥrīr al-daqā'iq* (H. Sarıoğlu Ed.). Istanbul: n.p.

———. (2004). *al-Qawādiḥ al-jadaliyya* (S. Ḥawshānī Ed.). Beirut; Riyadh; Damascus: Tawzī' Dār al-Warrāq.

———. (2016–2017 [1395]-a). *Kashf al-ḥaqā'iq fī taḥrīr al-daqā'iq* (M. 'Abbāsī Ed.). Zanjān: Nikān Kitāb.

———. (2016–2017 [1395]-b). *Muntahā l-afkār fī ibānat al-asrār: taḥrīr-hā-yi yakum va duvvum-i manṭiq* (M. ʿAẓīmī & H. Qurbānī Eds.). Tehran: Intishārāt-i Ḥikmat.

———. (2018). *Khulāṣat al-afkār wa-naqāwat al-asrār* (M. ʿAẓīmī & H. Qurbānī Eds.). Tehran: Iranian Institute of Philosophy.

———. (2022). *Isagoge: a classical primer on logic*. Translation and Explanatory Notes by Feryal Salem. Chicago: Blue Mountain Press.

Abū Ḥamdah, Muḥammad ʿAlī. (1984). *Fī l-tadhawwuq al-jamālī: li-munāẓarat Abī Saʿīd al-Sīrāfī wa-Abī Bishr Mattā ibn Yūnus al-Qunnāʾī fī majlis al-wazīr Abī l-Fatḥ al-Faḍl ibn Jaʿfar ibn al-Furāt sanat 326H*. Beirut; Amman: Dār al-Jīl; Maktabat al-Muḥtasib.

Abū Tammām, Ḥabīb b. Aws al-Ṭāʾī. (1846). *Ḥamâsa, oder, Die ältesten arabischen Volkslie-der* (F. Rückert Ed.). Stuttgart: S. G. Liesching.

Aktaş, Sahip. (2018). Seyyid Şerîf el-Cürcânî'nin Risâle fî tahkīk-i ma'ne'l-harf Başlıklı Risâlesinin Tahkikli Neşri. *İslâm Araştırmaları Dergisi, 40,* 69–93.

Akyüz, Turgut. (2017). *Fahreddîn er-Râzî'nin el-Mantıku'l-Kebîr'inin tahkik ve incelemesi.* (PhD), Marmara Üniversitesi, unpublished.

Āl Yāsīn, Muḥammad Ḥasan. (1956). *Muṭāraḥāt falsafiyya bayna Naṣīr al-Dīn al-Ṭūsī wa-Najm al-Dīn al-Kātibī*. Baghdad: Dār al-Maʿārif.

Ammonius. (1897). *Ammonius in Aristotelis de interpretatione commentarius (CAG IV.5)* (A. Busse Ed.). Berolini: Typis et impensis Georgii Reimeri.

———. (1899). *In Aristotelis Analyticorum priorum librum I commentarium (CAG IV.6)* (M. Wallies Ed.). Berolini: Typis et impensis Georgii Reimeri.

———. (1962). *CAG Volumen IV/IV-VI. Pars I: Ammonius in Aristotelis Categorias commentarium. Pars II: Ammonius in Aristotelis de interpretatione commentarius. Pars III: Ammonii in Aristotelis analyticorum priorum librum I commentarium: Editio consilio et auctoritate academiae litterarum regiae Borussicae* (A. Busse & M. Wallies Eds.). Berlin; Boston: De Gruyter.

Anṣārī, Zakarīyā ibn Muḥammad. (2014). *Fatḥ al-wahhāb bi-sharḥ al-Ādāb : lil-Imām Muḥammad ibn Ashraf al-Samarqandī* (A. A. Nādī Ed.). Ḥawallī, al-Kuwayt: Dār al-Ḍiyāʾ lil-Nashr wa-al-Tawzīʿ.

Apollonius. (1878). *Apollonii Dyscoli Quae supersunt* (R. Schneider Ed.). Lipsiae: In aedibus B. G. Teubneri.

Apuleius. (1991). *De philosophia libri* (C. Moreschini Ed.). Stutgardiae; Lipsiae: In aedibus B. G. Teubneri.

Aristoteles Arabus. (1913). *Die Hermeneutik des Aristoteles: in der arabischen Übersetzung des Isḥāḳ ibn Ḥonain* (I. Pollak Ed.). Leipzig: In Kommission bei F. A. Brockhaus.

Aristotle. (1956). *Aristotelis Categoriae et liber De interpretatione* (L. Minio-Paluello Ed. Repr. from corr. sheets of the 1st ed.). Oxonii: E Typographeo Clarendoniano.

———. (2014). *De interpretatione = Peri hemēneias* (H. Weidemann Ed.). Berlin; Boston: De Gruyter.

Aṣmaʿī, ʿAbd al-Malik b. Qurayb. (1971). *Kitāb fuḥūlat al-shuʿarāʾ* (C. Torrey Ed.). Beirut: Dār al-Kitāb al-Jadīd.

ʿAṭṭār, Ḥasan ibn Muḥammad. (2016). *Ḥāshiyat al-ʿAṭṭār ʿalā Sharḥ al-Jalāl al-Maḥalli ʿalā Jamʿ al-jawāmiʿ fī Uṣūl al-fiqh al-Shāfiʿī li-l-Imām Tāj al-Dīn ʿAbd al-Wahāb ibn ʿAlī al-Subkī*. Beirut: Dār al-Kutub al-ʿIlmiyya.

ʿAẓīmī, Mahdī. (2016–2017 [1395]). Manṭiq-i Abharī dar Talkhīṣ al-ḥaqāʾiq. *Jāvidān-i khirad, 30,* 101–132.

'Azīmī, Mahdī, & Qurbānī, Hāshim. (2011–2012 [1390]). "Al-Risāla al-Zāhira" neveshte-ye Athir al-Dīn al-Abharī: nuskheshenāsī, matnshenāsī, taṣḥīḥ, ve-taḥlīl. *Majalla Felsefe ve-Kelām Eslāmī, 44,* 129–163.

Badawī, 'Abd al-Raḥmān. (1980). *Manṭiq Aristū.* Beirut; Kuwait: Wikālat al-Maṭbū'āt; Dār al-Qalam (1st edition Dār al-Kutub al-Miṣriyya, Cairo 1948–1952).

Baghdādī, Abū al-Barakāt al-. (1995). *Kitāb al-Mu'tabar* (reprint of Hayderabad 1357 AH anonymous, 2nd ed.). Isfahan: Isfahan Press.

Bar Hebraeus. (1663). *Tārīkh mukhtaṣar al-duwal = Historia compendiosa dynastiarum* (E. Pococke Ed.). Oxoniae: Excudebat H. Hall . . . impensis Ric. Davis.

———. (1890). *Tārīkh mukhtaṣar al-duwal* (A. Ṣāliḥānī Ed.). Beirut: al-Maṭba'a al-Kāthūlīkiyya li-l-Ābā' al-Yasū'iyyīn.

Boethius, Anicius Manlius Severinus. (1877–1880). *Anicii Manlii Severini Boetii Commentarii in librum Aristotelis Peri hermēneias* (K. Meiser Ed.). Lipsiae: In aedibus B. G. Teubneri.

———. (1987). *Commentaries on Aristotle's De interpretatione: Anicii Manlii Severini Boetii commentarii in librum Peri hermeneias.* New York: Garland.

Can, Ayhan. (2015). *Abdurrahman el-Câmî'nin Şerhu'r-Risâleti'l-Vaz'iyye Adlı Eserinin Edisyon Kritiği.* (Yüksek Lisans Tezi), Hitit Üniversitesi, Çorum.

Çelik, Yüksel. (2009). *al-Miṣbāḥ fī sharḥ al-Miftāḥ.* (PhD), Marmara University, Istanbul.

Ḍabbī, Mufaḍḍal b. Muḥammad al-. (1942). *Mufaḍḍaliyyāt* (A. Shākir & A. Hārūn Eds.). Cairo: Dār al-Ma'ārif.

Dadkhah, Gholamreza, & Fallāḥī, Asad Allāh (Eds.). (2016). *Manṭiq dar Īrān-i sadah-'i shishum = Logic in 6th/12th century Iran.* Tehran: Mu'assasah-i Pizhūhishī-i Ḥikmat va Falsafah-i Īrān.

Damascius. (1967). *Damascii Vitae Isidori reliquiae* (C. Zintzen Ed.). Hildesheim: G. Olms.

Dānishpazhūh, Muḥammad Taqī. (1961 [1340]). Manṭiq Hidāyat al-ḥikma. *Majalla-yi Dānishkāda-yi adabiyyāt va-'ulūm-i insānī 17,* 484–494.

Dindorf, Ludwig August (Ed.) (1871). *Historici Graeci minores* (Vol. 2). Lipsiae: In aedibus B. G. Teubneri.

Diogenes, Laertius. (1999–2002). *Diogenis Laertii Vitae philosophorum* (M. Marcovich & H. Gärtner Eds.). Stutgardiae: In aedibus B. G. Teubneri.

Dusūqī, Muḥammad b. Aḥmad al-. (2012). *Ḥāshiat al-Dusūqī 'alā al-Waḍ'iyya. Sharḥ al-Risāla al-'aḍudiyya.* Beirut: Dār Nūr al-Ṣabāḥ.

Endreß, Gerhard. (1978). Maqālat Yaḥyā ibn 'Adī ibn Ḥamīd ibn Zakariyyā fī Tabyīn al-faṣl bayna ṣina'atay al-naḥw al-'arabī wa-l-manṭiq al-falsafī. *Majallat Tārīḥ al-'Ulūm al-'Arabiyya, 2,* 38–50.

Fārābī, Abū Naṣr al-. (1869). *Kitāb fī Ẓuhūr al-falsafa, aw: kitāb fī ism al-falsafa wa-sabab ẓuhūrihā* (M. Steinschneider Ed.). St. Petersburg: Académie Impériale des Sciences.

———. (1949). *Iḥṣā' al-'ulūm. Statistique des sciences* (U. Amīn Ed.). Cairo: Dār al-Fikr al-'Arabī.

———. (1960). *Alfarabi's commentary on Aristotle's Περὶ ἑρμενείας (De interpretatione) = Sharḥ al-Fārābī li-kitāb Arisṭūtālīs fī l-'Ibāra* (W. Kutsch & S. Marrow Eds.). Beirut: Imprimerie Catholique.

———. (1968). *Kitāb al-Alfāẓ al-musta'mala fī l-manṭiq* (M. Mahdi Ed.). Beirut: Dār al-Mashriq.

———. (1970). *Kitāb al-ḥurūf* (M. Mahdi Ed.). Beirut: Dār al-Mashriq.

———. (1987–1990 [1408–1410]). *al-Manṭiqiyyāt li l-Fārābī* (M. T. Dānishpazhūh Ed.). Qom: Maktabat Āyat Allāh al-ʿUẓma al-Marʿashī al-Najafī.

———. (1990). *Farabi'nin Peri hermeneias muhtasarı* (M. Türker-Küyel Ed.). Ankara: Atatürk Kültür Merkezi.

———. (1998). *al-Alfāẓ al-mustaʿmala fī l-manṭiq* (Ḥ. Malikshāhī Ed.). Tehran: Surūsh.

———. (2015). *Iḥṣāʾ al-ʿulūm. Le recensement des sciences* (A. Cherni Ed.). Beirut: Dar Albouraq.

Galen. (1884). *Claudii Galeni Pergameni scripta minora* (J. Marquardt, I. v. Müller, & G. Helmreich Eds.). Lipsiae: In aedibus B. G. Teubneri.

Ghurāb, Saʿd (Ed.). (1980). *Risālatān fī l-manṭiq*. Tunis: al-Jāmiʿa al-Tūnisiyya; Markaz al-Dirāsāt wa-al-Abḥāth al-Iqtiṣādiyya wa-al-Ijtimāʿiyya.

Ḥājjī Khalīfa (Kātib Çelebī). (1835–1858). *Kashf al-ẓunūn* (G. Flügel Ed.). London: Printed for the Oriental Translation Fund.

Herodianus, Aelius. (1867). *Herodiani Technici reliquiae II* (A. Lentz Ed.). Lipsiae: In aedibus B. G. Teubneri.

Ḥillī, Ḥasan b. Yūsuf ibn al-Muṭahhar al-. (1992 [1412]). *al-Qawāʿid al-jaliyya fī sharḥ al-Risāla al-shamsiyya* (F. Ḥ. Tabrīziyān Ed.). Qom: Muʾassasat al-Nashr al-Islāmī al-tābiʿa bi-Jamāʿat al-Mudarrisīn.

———. (1992–1993 [1413]). *al-Jawhar al-naḍīd fī sharḥ Manṭiq al-tajrīd* (M. Bīdārfar Ed.). Qom: Intishārāt-i Bīdār.

———. (2000). *al-Asrār al-khafīya fī al-ʿulūm al-ʿaqliyya*. Qom: Markaz al-Abḥāth wa-l-Dirāsāt al-Islāmiyya.

———. (2011–2012 [1433]). *Kashf al-murād fī sharḥ Tajrīd al-iʿtiqād* (H. al-Āmulī Ed.). Qom: Muʾassasat al-Nashr al-Islāmī.

———. (2017). *Marāṣid al al-tadqīq wa maqāṣid al-taḥqīq* (M. G. Nijad Ed.). Karbala: al-ʿAtaba al-ʿAbbāsiyya al-Muqaddasa; Qism Shuʾūn al-Maʿārif al-Islāmiyya wa-l-Insāniyya.

Ibn Abī Uṣaybiʿa, Aḥmad b. al-Qāsim. (1882–1884 [1299–1301]). *ʿUyūn al-anbāʾ fī ṭabaqāt al-aṭibbāʾ* (A. Müller Ed.). Cairo; Königsberg i. Pr.: al-Maṭbaʿa al-Wahbiyya.

———. (1995). *Kitāb ʿUyūn al-anbāʾ fī ṭabaqāt al-aṭibbāʾ* (A. Müller Ed. Reprint of the Cairo ed.). Frankfurt am Main: Institute for the History of Arabic-Islamic Science at Johann Wolfgang Goethe University.

Ibn al-Anbārī, ʿAbd al-Raḥmān b. Muḥammad. (1913). *Die grammatischen Streitfragen der Basrer und Kufer, [von] Abuʾl-Barakāt ibn al-Anbāri. Hrsg., erklärt und eingeleitet von Gotthold Weil*. Leiden: Brill.

Ibn al-Fuwaṭī, ʿAbd al-Razzāq b. Aḥmad. (1995). *Majmaʿ al-ādāb fī muʿjam al-alqāb*. Tehran: Muʾassasat al-Ṭibāʿa wa-l-Nashr; Wizārat al-Thaqāfa wa-l-Irshād al-Islāmī.

Ibn al-Muqaffaʿ, Abū Muhammad ʿAbd Allāh Rūzbih b. Dādūya. (1978 [1357]). *al-Manṭiq* (M. T. Dānishpazhūh Ed.). Tehran: Anjuman-i Shāhanshāhī-i Falsafah-i Īrān.

———. (2002/2003 [1381]). *al-Manṭiq* (M. T. Dānishpazhūh Ed.). Tehran: Muʾassasah-i Pizhūhishī-i Ḥikmat va Falsafah-i Īrān.

Ibn al-Nadīm, Abū al-Faraj Muḥammad b. Isḥāq. (1871–1872). *Kitāb al-Fihrist* (G. Flügel, J. Roediger, & A. Müller Eds.). Leipzig: F. C. W. Vogel.

Ibn al-Sarrāj, Muḥammad b. al-Sarī. (2018). *al-Uṣūl fī l-naḥw* (M. Tarrās Ed.). Cairo: Dār al-Salām li-l-Ṭibāʿa wa-l-Nashr wa-al-Tawzīʿ wa-l-Tarjama.

Ibn Bājja, Abū Bakr Muḥammad b. Yaḥyā. (1994). *Taʿlīq Ibn Bājja ʿalā Manṭiq al-Fārābī* (M. Fakhry Ed.). Beirut: Dār al-Mashriq.

Ibn Durayd, Muḥammad b. al-Ḥasan. (1991). *al-Ishtiqāq* (A. M. Hārūn Ed.). Beirut: Dār al-Jīl.

Ibn Ghaylān, Afḍal al-Dīn ʿUmar b. ʿAlī. (1998). *Ḥudūth al-ʿālam* (M. Muḥaqqiq Ed.). Tehran: Muʾassasah-i Muṭālaʿāt-i Islāmī.

Ibn Ḥazm, ʿAlī b. Aḥmad. (2018). *Et-takrib li-haddi'l-mantık: Mantık ve dini ilimler (inceleme—metin—çeviri)* (İ. Çapak & Y. Arıkaner Eds.). İstanbul: Türkiye Yazma Eserler Kurumu Başkanlığı Yayınları.

Ibn Jinnī, Abū al-Fatḥ ʿUthmān. (1999). *al-Munṣif: Sharḥ li-Kitāb al-taṣrīf* (M. ʿAṭā & B. Māzinī Eds.). Beirut: Dār al-Kutub al-ʿilmiyya.

Ibn Khaldūn, Abū Zayd ʿAbd ar-Raḥmān. (1900). *Muqaddimat Ibn Khaldūn*: al-Maṭbaʿa al-adabiyya.

———. (1958). *The Muqaddima: an introduction to history* (F. Rosenthal, Trans.). New York: Pantheon.

Ibn Khallikān, Abū al-ʿAbbās Shams al-Dīn Aḥmad b. Muḥammad. (1968–1972). *Wafayāt al-aʿyān wa-anbāʾ abnāʾ al-zamān* (I. ʿAbbās Ed.). Beirut: Dār Ṣādir.

Ibn Riḍwān, Abū al-Ḥassan ʿAlī. (1986). *al-Kitāb al-Nāfiʿ fī kayfiyyāt taʿlīm ṣināʿat al-ṭibb* (K. al-Sāmarrāʾī Ed.). Baghdad: Maṭbaʿat Jāmiʿat Baghdād.

Ibn Rushd, Abū al-Walīd. (1981). *Talkhīṣ kitāb al-ʿIbāra* (C. Butterworth, A. Harīdī, & M. Qāsim Eds.). Cairo: al-Hayʾa al-Miṣriyya al-ʿĀmma li-l-Kitāb; Markaz al-Buḥūth al-Amrīkī bi-Miṣr.

———. (1982). *Talkhīṣ Manṭiq Arisṭū* (J. Jihāmī Ed.). Beirut: al-Maktaba al-Sharqiyya; al-Jāmiʿa al-Lubnāniyya.

Ibn Sīnā, Abū ʿAlī al-Ḥusayn. (1910). *Manṭiq al-mashriqiyyīn wa-l-Qaṣīda al-muzdawaja fī l-manṭiq* (M. al-Khaṭīb & ʿA. al-Qatlān Eds.). Cairo: al-Maktaba al-Salafiyya.

———. (1952). *Kitāb al-Shifāʾ, al-Manṭiq, al-Madkhal* (I. Madkūr Ed.). Cairo: al-Hayʾa al-ʿĀmma li-Shuʾūn al-Maṭābiʿ al-Amīriyya.

———. (1959). *Kitāb al-Shifāʾ, al-Manṭiq, al-Maqūlāt* (I. Madkūr Ed.). Cairo: al-Hayʾa al-ʿĀmma li-Shuʾūn al-Maṭābiʿ al-Amīriyya.

———. (1960). *Kitāb al-Shifāʾ, al-Ilāhiyyāt* (G. Anawātī & S. Zāyid Eds.). Cairo: al-Hayʾa al-ʿĀmma li-Shuʾūn al-Maṭābiʿ al-Amīriyya.

———. (1970). *Kitāb al-Shifāʾ, al-Manṭiq, al-ʿIbāra* (M. El-Khodeiri & S. Zāyid Eds.). Cairo: Dār al-Kātib al-ʿArabī.

———. (2002). *al-Ishārāt wa l-tanbīhāt* (M. al-Zārʿī Ed.). Qom: Bustān-ī Kitāb.

Ibn Ṭumlūs, Abū al-Ḥajjāj Yūsuf b. Muḥammad. (2019). *Ibn Ṭumlūs (Alhagiag Bin Thalmus d. 620/1223), Compendium on Logic = al-Muḫtaṣar fī al-manṭiq* (F. Ben Ahmed Ed.). Leiden: Brill.

Ibn Wāṣil, Muḥammad ibn Sālim. (2022). *Commentary on the Jumal on Logic by Khūnajī* (K. El-Rouayheb Ed.). Leiden; Boston: Brill.

Īdrīs, Muḥammad Yūsuf (Ed.) (2016). *al-Majmūʿ al-waḍʿī*. Amman, Jordan: Dār al-Nūr al-Mubīn li-l-Nashr wa-l-Tawzīʿ.

Iṣfahānī, Abū al-Qāsim al-Ḥusayn b. Muḥammad al-Raghib al-. (1984). *Muqaddimat Jāmiʿ at-Tafāsīr maʿ Tafsīr al-Fātiḥah wa Maṭāliʿ al-Baqarah*. Kuwait: Dār ad-Daʿwa.

Jāḥiẓ, Abū ʿUthmān ʿAmr b. Baḥr al-. (1948–1950). *Kitāb al-Bayān wa l-tabyīn* (A. M. Hārūn Ed.). Cairo: Maṭbaʿat Muṣṭafā al-Bābī al-Ḥalabī wa-Awlādi-hi.

Jurjānī, ʿAbd-al-Qāhir ibn ʿAbd al-Raḥmān al-. (1954). *Kitāb Asrār al-balāgha* (H. Ritter Ed.). Istanbul: Government Press.

———. (1984). *Kitāb dalā'il al-i'jāz*. Cairo: Maktabat al-Khānjī.

Jurjānī, 'Alī b. Muḥammad al- [al-Sayyid al-Sharīf]. (1860). *al-Sayyid 'alā Sharḥ al-Maṭāli'*. Istanbul: Dār al-Ṭibā'a al-'Āmira.

———. (1998 [1419]). *Sharḥ al-Mawāqif*. Beirut: Dār al-Kutub al-'Ilmiyya.

———. (2003). *Kitāb al-ta'rīfāt* (M. A. al-Mar'ashlī Ed.). Beirut: Dār al-Nafā'is.

———. (2007). *al-Ḥāshiya 'alā al-Muṭawwal*. Beirut: Dār al-Kutub al-'Ilmiyya.

Kātibī, Najm al-Dīn 'Alī b. 'Umar al-. (2007). *As'ilat Najm al-Dīn al-Kātibī 'an al-Ma'ālim li-Fakhr al-Dīn al-Rāzī ma'a ta'ālīq 'Izz al-Dawla Ibn Kammūna [Critical remarks by Najm al-Dīn al-Kātibī on the Kitāb al-Ma'ālim by Fakhr al-Dīn al-Rāzī]* (S. Schmidtke & R. Pourjavady Eds.). Tehran: Mu'assasah-i Pizhūhishī-i Ḥikmat va Falsafah-i Īrān.

Khūnajī, Afḍal al-Dīn al-. (2010). *Kashf al-asrār 'an ghawāmiḍ al-afkār* (K. El-Rouayheb Ed.). Tehran; Berlin: Mu'assasah-'i Pizhūhishī-i Ḥikmat va Falsafah-'i Īrān; Mu'assasah-'i Muṭala'āt-i Islāmī-i Dānishgāh-i Āzād-i Birlīn.

Makkī, Ḍiyā' al-Dīn al-. (2013). *Nihāyat al-marām fī dirāyat al-kalām: facsimile of the autograph manuscript of vol. II* (A. Shihadeh Ed.). Tehran: Freie Universität Berlin; Mīrāth-i Maktūb.

Mullā Mubīn Lakhnawī, Muḥammad ibn Muḥammad. (1909 [1327]). *Kitāb Mir'āt al-shurūḥ* (Vol. 1). Cairo: Maṭba'at al-Sa'āda.

———. (1910 [1328]). *Kitāb Mir'āt al-shurūḥ* (Vol. 2). Cairo: Maṭba'at al-'Āmira al-Sharafiyya.

Pehlivan, Necmettin. (2010). *Şemsu'd-Dīn Muḥammed b. Eşref es-Semerkandī'nin Kisṭāsu'l-efkār fī tahkīki'l-esrār adlı eserinin tahkiki, tercümesi ve değerlendirmesi*. (PhD), Ankara Üniversitesi, Ankara.

Plato. (1995). *Platonis opera. Tetralogiae I-II* (E. A. Duke, W. F. Hicken, W. S. M. Nicoll, D. B. Robinson, & J. C. G. Strachan Eds.). Oxonii: E Typographeo Clarendoniano.

Porphyry. (1887). *Porphyrii Isagoge et in Aristotelis Categorias commentarium (CAG IV.1)* (A. Busse Ed.). Berolini: Typis et impensis Georgii Reimeri.

Priscianus. (1855–1859). *Prisciani grammatici Caesariensis Institutionum grammaticarum libri XVIII, I-II* (M. Hertz Ed.). Lipsiae: In aedibus B. G. Teubneri.

Qazwīnī, Jalāl al-Dīn Muḥammad ibn 'Abd al-Raḥmān al-. (1964). *al-Īḍāḥ fī 'ulūm al-balāghah: al-ma'ānī wa-al-bayān wa-al-badī' :mukhtaṣar talkhīṣ al-miftāḥ*. Cairo: Maktabat wa-Maṭbū'āt M. 'A. Ṣubayḥ.

———. (2007). *Talkhīṣ al-Miftāḥ*. Al-Qāhirah: Publisher not identified.

Qazwīnī, Zakarīyā b. Muḥammad al-. (1960). *Āthār al-bilād wa-akhbār al-'ibād*. Beirut: Dār Ṣādir.

Qūshjī, 'Alā' al-Dīn 'Alī ibn Muḥammad al-. (2001). *'Unqūd al-zawāhir fī al-ṣarf*. Cairo: Maṭba'at Dār al-Kutub al-Miṣrīya bi-l-Qāhira.

———. (2014). *Sharḥ Tajrīd al-'Aqā'id. Tab'a muḥaqqaqa mudhayyala bi-l-ḥawāshī* (M. Ḥ. al-Reẓā'ī Ed.). Qom: Rā'id.

Rāzī, Fakhr al-Dīn Muḥammad b. 'Umar al-. (1381/2002–2003). *Manṭiq al-mulakhkhaṣ* (A. F. Qarāmalikī Ed.). Tehran: Dānishgāh-i Imām Ṣādiq.

———. (1985). *Nihāyat al-ījāz fī dirāyat al-i'jāz*. Bayrūt: Dār al-'Ilm lil-Malāyīn.

———. (1986). *Lubāb al-Ishārāt* (A. al-Saqqā Ed.). Cairo: Maṭba'at Nefertiti.

———. (1999). *al-Maḥṣūl fī 'ilm al-uṣūl*. Bayrūt: Manshūrāt Muḥammad 'Alī Baydūn, Dār al-Kutub al-'Ilmīyah.

———. (2005–2006 [1384]). *Sharḥ al-Ishārāt wa l-tanbīhāt* (A. Najafzāde Ed.). Tehran: Anjumān-i thār-i va Mafākhir-i Farhangī.

Rummānī, ʿAlī b. ʿĪsā al-. (1973). *Kitāb maʿānī al-ḥurūf* (ʿA. Shalabī Ed.). Cairo: Dār Nahḍat Miṣr.

Ṣafadī, Ṣalāḥ al-Dīn al-. (1931). *al-Wāfī bi-l wāfiyyāt* (H. Ritter Ed.). Leipzig: Deutsche Morgenländische Gesellschaft, in Kommission bei F. A. Brockhaus.

Sakkākī, Yūsuf Ibn-Abī-Bakr al-. (1937). *Miftāḥ al-ʿulūm*. Cairo: N. N.

Samarqandī, Abū al-Layth al-. (1911 [1329]). *Sharḥ al-ʿAllāma Abī al-Layth al-Samarqandī ʿalā al-Risāla al ʿAḍudiyya fī ʿilm al-waḍʿ li-Aḍūd al-Dīn ʿAbd al-Raḥman al-Ījī maʿ Hāshiyat al-ʿAllāma al-Shaykh Muḥammad al-Dusūqī*. Cairo: al-Maṭbaʿ al-Jamāliyya.

Samarqandī, Shams al-Dīn al-. (1984). *Ashkāl al-taʾsīs* (M. Suwaysī Ed.). Tunis: al-Dār al-Tūnisiyyah li-l-Nashr; al-Muʾassasa al-Waṭaniyya li-l-Tarjama wa-l-Taḥqīq wa-l-Dirāsāt Bayt al-Ḥikmah.

———. (1985). *al-Ṣaḥāʾif al-ilāhiyya* (A. al-Sharīf Ed.). Kuwait: Maktabat al-Falāḥ.

———. (2014). *Kıstâsu'l-Efkâr = Düşüncenin kıstası: eleştirmeli metin—çeviri* (N. Pehlivan & F. Özpilavcı Eds.). İstanbul: Türkiye Yazma Eserler Kurumu Başkanlığı.

———. (2019–2020 [1399]). *Qisṭās al-afkār fī l-manṭiq: taṣḥīḥ, taqdīm wa taḥqīq Asad Allah Fallāḥī* (A. Fallāḥī Ed.). Tehran: Muʾassasah-i Pizhūhishī-i Ḥikmat va falsafa-i Irān.

Sharīʿatī, Mahdī (Ed.). (2004). *Risālatān fī l-taṣawwur wa-l-taṣdīq*. Beirut: Dār al-Kutub al-ʿilmiyya.

Shukr, Sayyid Ḥāfiẓ. (1851 [1267]). *al-Ḥāshiya al-jadīda ʿalā ʿAlī Qūshjī*. Istanbul: Dār al-Ṭibāʿa al-ʿĀmira.

Shushtarī, Nūr Allāh b. ʿAbd Allāh al-. (1986 [1365]). *Kitāb-i Muṣtaṣb-i Majālis al-muʾminīn*. Tehran: Ketābfurūshī-yi Islāmiyya.

———. (2011 [1433]). *Majālis al-muʾminīn* (M. S. Fākhir, Trans.). Qom: Intishārāt al-Maktaba al-Ḥaydariyya.

Sībawayhi ʿAmr b. ʿUthmān. (1991 [1411]). *Kitāb* (M. Hārūn Ed.). Beirut: Dār al-Jīl.

Stephanus. (1885). *In librum Aristotelis De interpretatione commentarium (CAG XVIII.3)* (M. Hayduck Ed.). Berolini: Typis et impensis Georgii Reimeri.

———. (1962). *CAG Volumen XVIII.I-III. Pars I: Eliae in Porphyrii Isagogen et Aristotelis Categorias commentaria. Pars II: Davidis Prolegomena et in Porphyrii Isagogen commentarium. Pars III: Stephani in librum Aristotelis De interpretatione commentarium*. Berlin; Boston: De Gruyter.

Suhrawardī, Shihāb al-Dīn Yaḥyā b. Ḥabash al-. (1945). *Opera metaphysica et mystica* (H. Corbin Ed.). İstanbul: Maarif Matbaası.

Suhrawardī, Yaḥyā b. Ḥabash al-. (1955). *Manṭiq al-talwīḥāt* (A. Fayyāḍ Ed.). Tehran: Jāmiʿat Tihrān.

Suyūṭī, Abū al-Faḍl ʿAbd al-Raḥmān b. Abī Bakr al-. (1907). *al-Muzhir fī ʿulūm al-lugha wa-anwāʿihā*. Cairo: al-Maktaba al-Azhariyya.

Taftāzānī, Saʿd ad-Dīn al-. (2011). *Šarḥ aš-Šamsiyya* (J. B. Ṣāliḥ Ed.). Jordan: Dār an-Nūr.

———. (1960). *Sharḥ al-Mukhtaṣar ʿalā Talkhīṣ al-Miftāḥ lil-Khaṭīb al-Qazwīnī fī al-maʿānī wa-al-bayān wa-al-badīʿ*. Qum: Kitābfurūshī-i Katabī Najafi.

———. (2013). *al-Muṭawwal: Sharḥ talkhīṣ miftāḥ al-ʿulūm*. Beirut: Dār al-Kutub al-ʿIlmiyya.

———. (2014 [1435]). *Sharḥā l-Muḥaqqiq al-Dawānī wa l-Mullā ʿAbdullāh al-Yazdī ʿalā Tahdhīb al-manṭiq* (A. al-Malībārī Ed.). Kuwait: Dār al-Ḍiyāʾ.

Taḥtānī, Quṭb al-Dīn al-Rāzī al-. (2013). *Risâle fî tahkîki'l-külliyyât = Tümeller risâlesi ve şerhleri: eleştirmeli metin—çeviri—tıpkıbasım* (Ö. Türker Ed.). İstanbul: Türkiye Yazma Eserler Kurumu Başkanlığı.

———. (2014a). *Lawāmiʿ al-asrār fī sharḥ Maṭāliʿ al-anwār* (A. Raḥmānī ed.). 3 vols. Tehran: Muʾassasah-i Pizhūhishī-i Ḥikmat va Falsafah-i Īrān.

———. (2014b). *Lawāmiʿ al-asrār fī sharḥ maṭāliʿ al-anwār* (J. Valānī Ed.). Tihrān: Dānishgāh-i Tihrān.

———. (2014c). *Taḥrīr al-qawāʿid al-manṭiqiyya bi-sharḥ al-Risāla al-Shamsiyya* (E. Qablān Ed.). Beirut: Dār al-Kutub al-ʿilmiyya.

Tarán, Leonardo. (1978). *Anonymous commentary on Aristotle's De interpretatione: Codex Parisinus Graecus 2064.* Meisenheim am Glan: A. Hein.

Ṭāshkubrīzādah, Aḥmad b. Muṣṭafā. (2010). *al-Shaqāʾiq al-Nuʿmāniyya fī ʿulamāʾ al-dawlat al-ʿUthmāniyya* (M. Ṭabāṭabāʾī Ed.). Tehran: Kitābkhāneh-i Mūzih va Markaz-i Asnād; Majlis-i Shūrā-yi Islāmī.

Tawḥīdī, ʿAlī b. Muḥammad Abū Ḥayyān al-. (1939–1944). *Kitāb al-Imtāʿ wa l-muʾānasa* (A. Amīn & A. Zayn Eds.). Cairo: Lajnat al-taʾlīf wa l-tarjama wa l-nashr.

Ṭūsī, Naṣīr ad-Dīn al-. (1368/1990). *Kitāb Asās al-iqtibās* (M. Raḍawī Ed.). Tehran: Intishārāt-i Dānishgāh-i Tihrān.

———. (1383/2004–2005). *al-Išārāt wa t-tanbīhāt bā Šarḥ ḫwāja Naṣīr ad-Dīn aṭ-Ṭūsī wa Quṭb ad-Din ar-Rāzī* (K. Fayḍī Ed. Vol. 1). Qom: Maṭbūʿāt Dīnī.

———. (1988). *Tajrīd al-manṭiq.* Beirut: Muʾassasat al-ʿAlamī.

———. (1999). *Asās al-iqtibās fī l-manṭiq. Tarjamahu ilā l-ʿarabiyya Mullā Khusreh* (Ḥ. al-Shāfiʿī & M. al-Saʿīd Eds.). Cairo: al-Majlis al-aʿlā li-l-Thaqāfa.

Wehrli, Fritz. (1944). *Die Schule des Aristoteles: Texte und Kommentare. Heft VIII: Eudemos von Rhodos* (1969 2nd revised ed.). Basel: Benno Schwabe.

Yaʿqūbī, Aḥmad b. Abī Yaʿqūb al-. (1883). *Tārīkh* (M. Houtsma Ed.). Leiden: Brill.

Zajjājī, ʿAbd al-Raḥmān b. Isḥāq al-. (1995). *The explanation of linguistic causes. az-Zaǧǧāǧī's theory of grammar: introduction, translation, commentary* (C. H. M. Versteegh Ed.). Amsterdam; Philadelphia: J. Benjamins.

SECONDARY SOURCES

Abed, Shukri. (1991). *Aristotelian logic and the Arabic language in Alfārābī.* Albany, N.Y.: State University of New York Press.

Ackrill, John Lloyd. (1963). *Aristotle's Categories and De interpretatione.* Translated with notes. Oxford: Clarendon.

Adamson, Peter. (2002). Before Essence and Existence: al-Kindi's Conception of Being. *Journal of the History of Philosophy, 40*(3), 297–312. DOI: https://doi.org/10.1353/hph.2002.0043.

Adamson, Peter & Benevich, Fedor. (2023). *The heirs of Avicenna: philosophy in the Islamic East from the 12th to the 13th century. Metaphysics and theology.* Leiden; Boston: Brill.

Adamson, Peter, & Di Giovanni, Matteo (Eds.). (2019). *Interpreting Averroes: critical essays.* Cambridge; New York: Cambridge University Press.

Adamson, Peter, Klinger, Dustin, & Benevich, Fedor. (2024). *The heirs of Avicenna: philosophy in the Islamic East from the 12th to the 13th century. Language, logic and epistemology.* Leiden; Boston: Brill.

Ademollo, Francesco. (2015). Names, Verbs, and Sentences in Ancient Greek Philosophy. In M. Cameron & R. J. Stainton (Eds.), *Linguistic content: new essays on the history of philosophy of language.* Oxford; New York: Oxford University Press.

Adnan, K. Abdulla. (2020). *Translation in the Arab world: the Abbasid golden age*. Milton: Taylor and Francis.

Ahmed, Asad Q. (2010). Interpreting Avicenna: Urmawī/Taḥtānī and the Later Logical Tradition on Propositions. *Documenti e studi sulla tradizione filosofica medievale, xxi*, 313–342.

———. (2011). Systematic Growth in Sustained Error: A Case Study in The Dynamism Of Post-Classical Islamic Scholasticism. In A. Q. Ahmed, M. Bonner, & B. Sadeghi (Eds.), *The Islamic scholarly tradition studies in history, law, and thought in honor of Professor Michael Allan Cook* (pp. 343–378). Leiden: Brill.

———. (2015). "Dars-i Niẓāmī." In *Encyclopaedia of Islam, THREE*, online ed., 2015– . Edited by Kate Fleet, Gudrun Krämer, Denis Matringe, John Nawas, and Everett Rowson.

———. (2022). *Palimpsests of Themselves : Logic and Commentary in Postclassical Muslim South Asia*. Oakland: University of California Press.

Akkanat, Hasan. (2006). *Kadı Sıraceddin el-Urmevî ve Metâli'u'l-Envâr: Tahkik, Çeviri, !nceleme*. (PhD), Ankara Üniversitesi, Ankara.

Al-Rahim, Ahmed H. (2003). The Twelver-Shīʿī Reception of Avicenna in the Mongol Period. In D. C. Reisman (Ed.), *Before and after Avicenna.* (pp. 219–232). Leiden: Brill.

———. (2018). *The creation of philosophical tradition: biography and the reception of Avicenna's philosophy from the eleventh to the fourteenth century A.D.* Wiesbaden: Harrassowitz.

Angelelli, Ignacio. (1967). *Studies on Gottlob Frege and traditional philosophy*. Dordrecht: D. Reidel.

Anscombe, Elizabeth, & Geach, Peter Thomas. (1961). *Three philosophers*. Oxford: Blackwell.

Arens, Hans. (1984). *Aristotle's theory of language and its tradition: texts from 500 to 1750, sel., transl. and commentary by Hans Arens*. Philadelphia: John Benjamins.

Arıcı, Mustakim. (2015). *Fahreddin Râzî sonrası: metafizik düşünce, kâtibî örneği*. İstanbul: Klasık.

Arjomand, Said Amir. (1994). ʿAbd Allah Ibn al-Muqaffaʿ and the ʿAbbasid revolution. *Iranian studies, 27*(1–4), 9–36. DOI: https://doi.org/10.1080/00210869408701818.

Atademir, Ragıp Hamdi. (1948). Porphyrios ve Ebherî'nin Isagoci'leri. *Ankara Üniversitesi Dil ve Tarih-Coğrafya Fakültesi dergisi*, 461–468. DOI: https://doi.org/10.1501/Dtcfder _0000000283.

Ax, Wolfram. (1979). Zum isolierten ῥῆμα in Aristoteles' *De interpretatione* 16b19–25. *Archiv für Geschichte der Philosophie 61*(3), 271–279. DOI: https://doi.org/10.1515/agph .1979.61.3.271.

———. (1986). *Laut, Stimme und Sprache: Studien zu drei Grundbegriffen der antiken Sprachtheorie*. Göttingen: Vandenhoeck & Ruprecht.

Baalbaki, Ramzi. (2008). *The legacy of the Kitab: Sibawayhi's analytical methods within the context of the Arabic grammatical theory*. Boston: Brill.

———. (2009). The Place of al-Jāḥiẓ in the Arabic Philological Tradition. In A. Heinemann, M. Kropp, T. Khalidi, & J. L. Meloy (Eds.), *Al-Jāḥiẓ: a Muslim humanist for our time*. Würzburg; Beirut: Ergon Verlag in Kommission; Orient-Institut.

Bäck, Allan. (1999). The Ontological Pentagon of Avicenna. *Journal of Neoplatonic Studies, 7*, 87–109.

———. (2000). *Aristotle's theory of predication*. Leiden; Boston: Brill.

Barnes, Jonathan. (1996). Grammar on Aristotle's Terms. In M. Frede & G. Striker (Eds.), *Rationality in Greek thought*. New York; Oxford: Oxford University Press.

———. (2007). *Truth, etc.: six lectures on ancient logic*. Oxford: Oxford University Press.

———. (2009a). Le *De interpretatione* dans la philosophie moderne. In S. Husson (Ed.), *Interpréter le de interpretatione* (pp. 141–161). Paris: Vrin.

———. (2009b). Notes on the Copula. *Dianoia: annali di storia della filosofia, 14*, 27–62.

———. (2012). *Logical matters*. Oxford: Clarendon.

Barnes, Jonathan, Bobzien, Susanne, & Flannery, Kevin. (2014). *Alexander of Aphrodisias: On Aristotle Prior Analytics 1.1–7*. London: Bloomsbury.

Barnes, Jonathan, & Calzolari, Valentina (Eds.). (2009). *L'Oeuvre de David l'Invincible et la transmission de la pensée grecque dans la tradition arménienne et syriaque: Commentaria in Aristotelem Armeniaca—Davidis Opera Vol. 1*. Boston: Brill.

Beaney, Michael (Ed.). (1997). *The Frege reader*. Oxford; Malden, Mass.: Blackwell.

Belardi, Walter. (1985). *Filosofia, grammatica e retorica nel pensiero antico*. Roma: Edizioni dell'Ateneo.

Belhaj, Abdessamad. (2016). *Ādāb al-baḥth wa-l-munāẓara*: The Neglected Art of Disputation in Later Medieval Islam. *Arabic Sciences and Philosophy, 26*(2), 291–307. DOI: https://doi.org/10.1017/S0957423916000059.

Bergsträßer, Gotthelf. (1913). *Ḥunain ibn Isḥāḳ und seine Schule: Sprach- und literargeschichtliche Untersuchungen zu den arabischen Hippokrates- und Galen-Übersetzungen*. Leiden: Buchhandlung und Druckerei vormals E. J. Brill.

Biesterfeldt, Hinrich. (2015). Secular Graeco-Arabica—Fifty years after Franz Rosenthal's *Fortleben der Antike im Islam*. *Intellectual History of the Islamicate World, 3*(1–2), 125–157. DOI: https://doi.org/10.1163/2212943X-00301006.

Black, Deborah L. (1990). *Logic and Aristotle's Rhetoric and Poetics in medieval Arabic philosophy*. Leiden; New York: Brill.

———. (1991). Aristotle's "Peri hermeneias" in Medieval Latin and Arabic Philosophy: Logic and the Linguistic Arts. *Canadian Journal of Philosophy, 17*, 25–83.

Black, Max. (1954). *Problems of analysis: philosophical essays*. Ithaca, N.Y.: Cornell University Press.

Blank, David L. (1982). *Ancient philosophy and grammar: the Syntax of Apollonius Dyscolus*. Chico, CA: Scholars Press.

———. (2014). *Ammonius: On Aristotle On Interpretation 1–8*. London: Bloomsbury.

Bloomfield, Leonard. (1914a). *An introduction to the study of language*. New York: H. Holt.

———. (1914b). Sentence and Word. *Transactions and Proceedings of the American Philological Association, 45*, 65–75. DOI: https://doi.org/10.2307/282688.

———. (1916). Subject and Predicate. *Transactions and Proceedings of the American Philological Association, 47*, 13–22. DOI: https://doi.org/10.2307/282823.

Bobzien, Susanne. (2021). Frege Plagiarized the Stoics. In F. Leigh (Ed.), *Themes in Plato, Aristotle, and Hellenistic philosophy: Keeling Lectures, 2011–18*. London: University of London School of Advanced Studies, Institute of Classical Studies.

Bocheński, Innocentius Marie. (1961). *A history of formal logic*. Notre Dame, Ind.: University of Notre Dame Press.

Bonadeo, Cecilia Martini. (2013). *ʿAbd al-Laṭīf al-Baghdādī's philosophical journey: from Aristotle's Metaphysics to the "Metaphysical Science."* Leiden; Boston: Brill.

Bonelli, Maddalena. (2009). Alexandre d'Aphrodise et le *De interpretatione*. In S. Husson (Ed.), *Interpréter le De interpretatione* (pp. 51–68). Paris: Vrin.

Boole, George. (1854). *An investigation of the laws of thought, on which are founded the mathematical theories of logic and probabilities*. London: Walton and Maberly.

Bradley, Francis Herbert. (1897). *Appearance and reality: a metaphysical essay* (2nd revised ed.). London; New York: S. Sonnenschein Macmillan.

Brock, Sebastian. (2004). Without Mushê of Nisibis, Where Would We Be? *Journal of Eastern Christian Studies, 56*(1), 15–24. DOI: https://doi.org/10.2143/JECS.56.1.578692.

Brockelmann, Carl. (1898–1902). *Geschichte der Arabischen Litteratur*. Weimar: E. Felber.

———. (2016). *History of the Arabic written tradition*. Leiden; Boston: Brill.

Büttgen, Philippe, Diebler, Stéphane, & Rashed, Marwan (Eds.). (1999). *Théories de la phrase etde la proposition de Platon à Averroès*. Paris: Éditions Rue d'Ulm.

Calverly, Edwin E. (1933). al-Abharī's 'Īsāghūjī fī l-manṭiq'. In W. Shellabear, E. Calverly, E. Lane, & R. Mackensen (Eds.), *The Macdonald presentation volume : a tribute to Duncan Black Macdonald, consisting of articles by former students, presented to him on his seventieth birthday, April 9, 1933* (pp. 75–85). Princeton, N.J.: Princeton University Press.

Carruthers, Peter. (1983). On Concept and Object. *Theoria, 49*(2), 49–86. DOI: https://doi.org /10.1111/j.1755-2567.1983.tb00208.x.

Carter, Michael G. (1972). Les origines de la grammaire arabe. *Revue des Études Islamiques, 40*(1), 69–97.

———. (2004). Adam and the Technical Terms of Medieval Islam. In J. Thielmann, G. Endress, & R. Arnzen (Eds.), *Words, Texts and concepts cruising the Mediterranean Sea. Studies on the sources, contents and influences of Islamic civilization and Arabic philosophy and science dedicated to Gerhard Endress on his sixty-fifth birthday* (pp. 439–454). Leuven: Peeters.

Cerami, Cristina. (2015). *Génération et substance: Aristote et Averroès entre physique et métaphysique*. Berlin: De Gruyter.

Charles, David. (1994). Aristotle on Names and Their Signification. In S. Everson (Ed.), *Companions to ancient thought 3: Language* (pp. 37–73). Cambridge; New York: Cambridge University Press.

Charlton, William. (2014). *On Aristotle On the Soul 3.9–13 with Stephanus: On Aristotle On Interpretation*. London: Bloomsbury.

Chatti, Saloua. (2014). Syncategoremata in Arabic Logic, al-Fārābī and Avicenna. *History and Philosophy of Logic, 35*(2), 1–31. DOI: https://doi.org/10.1080/01445340.201 4.891372.

Chejne, Anwar G. (1984). Ibn Hazm of Cordova on Logic. *Journal of the American Oriental Society, 104*(1), 57–72. DOI: https://doi.org/10.2307/602642.

Chomsky, Noam. (1965). *Aspects of the theory of syntax*. Cambridge, Mass.: MIT Press.

———. (2015). *Aspects of the theory of syntax* (50th anniversary ed.). Cambridge, Mass.: MIT Press.

Church, Alonzo. (1956). Max Black. Frege on Functions. Problems of Analysis, Philosophical Essays, by Max Black, Cornell University Press, Ithaca 1954, pp. 229–254, 297–298. *Journal of Symbolic Logic, 21*(2), 201–202. DOI: https://doi.org/10.2307/2268773.

Collins, John. (2011). *The unity of linguistic meaning*. Oxford: Oxford University Press.

Connelly, Coleman. (2020). Ḥunayn ibn Isḥāq's Conception of His Reading Public according to a Previously Unpublished Letter. *Arabic Sciences and Philosophy, 30*(2), 159–189. DOI: https://doi.org/10.1017/S0957423920000016.

Corcoran, John. (2003). Aristotle's Prior Analytics and Boole's Laws of Thought. *History and Philosophy of Logic, 24*(4), 261–288. DOI: https://doi.org/10.1080/01445340310001 604707.

Currie, Gregory. (1984). Frege's Metaphysical Argument. In C. Wright (Ed.), *Frege, traditionand influence* (pp. 144–157). Oxford; New York: Blackwell.

D'Ancona, Cristina. (2011). Porphyry, Arabic. In H. Lagerlund (Ed.), *Encyclopedia of Medieval Philosophy* (pp. 1056–1062). Dordrecht: Springer Netherlands.

Davidson, Donald. (2005). *Truth and predication.* Cambridge, Mass.: Harvard University Press.

De Rijk, Lambertus Marie. (1996). On Aristotle's Semantics in *De Interpretatione* 1–4. In K. Algra, P. Van der Horst, & D. Runia (Eds.), *Polyhistor. Studies in the history and historiography of ancient philosophy presented to Jaap Mansfeld on his sixtieth birthday* (pp. 114–134). Leiden: Brill.

———. (2002). *Aristotle: semantics and ontology.* Leiden; Boston: Brill.

———. (2003). Boethius on *De interpretatione* (ch. 3): Is He a Reliable Guide? In A. Galonnier (Ed.), *Boèce ou la chaîne des savoirs (Actes du Colloque international de la Fondation Singer-Polignac, présidée par Edouard Bonnefous, Paris, 8–12 juin 1999)* (pp. 202–227). Louvain-la-Neuve: Éditions de l'Institut supérieur de philosophie.

Diebler, Stéphane. (2005). Catégories, conversation et philosophie chez al-Fārābī. In O. Bruun & L. Corti (Eds.), *Les catégories et leur histoire* (pp. 275–305). Paris: Vrin.

Dilgan, Hâmid. (1960). Démonstration du Ve Postulat d'Euclide par Schams-ed-Din Samarkandi. Traduction de l'ouvrage Aschkâl-ùt-teessis de Samarkandi. *Revue d'histoire des sciences et de leurs applications, 13*(3), 191–196. DOI: https://doi.org/10.3406/rhs.1960.3853.

Di Vincenzo, Silvia. (2018). Early Exegetical Practice on Avicenna's Shifāʾ: Fakhr al-Dīn al-Rāzī's Marginalia to Logic. *Arabic Sciences and Philosophy, 28*(1), 31–66. DOI: https://doi.org/10.1017/S095742391700008X.

Druart, Thérèse-Anne. (2007). Al-Fārābī, the Categories, Metaphysics, and *The Book of Letters. Medioevo, 32,* 15–37.

———. (2010). Al-Fārābī: an Arabic Account of the Origin of Language and of Philosophical Vocabulary. *Proceedings of the American Catholic Philosophical Association, 84,* 1–17.

———. (2016). Logic and Language. In R. Taylor & L. López-Farjeat (Eds.), *The Routledge companion to Islamic philosophy* (pp. 69–81). London; New York: Routledge.

Dumitriu, Anton. (1973). *Teoria logicii.* Bucharest: Editura Academie Republicii Socialiste Romania.

———. (1977). *History of logic.* Tunbridge Wells: Abacus Press.

Dummett, Michael A. E. (1973). *Frege. Philosophy of language.* London: Duckworth.

———. (1981). *The interpretation of Frege's philosophy.* Cambridge, Mass.: Harvard University Press.

Dunlop, Douglas. (1955a). Al-Fārābī's Introductory Sections on Logic. *Islamic Quarterly, 2*(4), 264.

———. (1955b). Philosophical Predecessors and Contemporaries of Ibn Bajjah. *Islamic Quarterly, 2*(2), 100.

———. (1956). Al-Fārābī's Introductory *Risāla* on Logic. *Islamic Quarterly, 3,* 224–235.

———. (1957). Remarks on the Life and Works of Ibn Bājja (Avempace). In Z. Togan (Ed.), *Proceedings of the twenty-second congress of orientalists* (pp. 188–196). Leiden: Brill.

Eichner, Heidrun. (2009). *The post-Avicennian philosophical tradition and Islamic orthodoxy: philosophical and theological summae in context,* Martin Luther University of Halle-Wittenberg, Unpublished Habilitation Dissertation.

———. (2012). Essence and Existence. Thirteenth-Century Perspectives in Arabic-Islamic Philosophy and Theology. In A. Bertolacci & D. N. Hasse (Eds.), *The Arabic, Hebrew and Latin reception of Avicenna's Metaphysics* (pp. 123–152). Berlin; Boston: De Gruyter.

———. (2014). al-Abharī, Athīr al-Dīn. In *Encyclopaedia of Islam, THREE*, online ed., 2015–. Edited by Kate Fleet, Gudrun Krämer, Denis Matringe, John Nawas, and Everett Rowson.

Elamrani-Jamal, Abdelali. (1982). Grammaire et logique d'après le philosophe arabe chrétien Yahya Ibn Adi (280–364 H/893–974). *Arabica, 29*(1), 1–15.

———. (1983). *Logique aristotélicienne et grammaire arabe: étude et documents.* Paris: Vrin.

———. (1990). Verbe, copule, nom dérivé (*fi'l, kalima,* ism *muštaqq*) dans les commentaires arabes du *Peri Hermeneias* d'Aristote: Avec un texte inédit d'Ibn Rušd. In K. Versteegh & M. G. Carter (Eds.), *Studies in the history of Arabic grammar II : proceedings of the 2nd Symposium on the History of Arabic Grammar, Nijmegen, 27 April-1 May 1987* (pp. 151–164). Amsterdam; Philadelphia: J. Benjamins.

El-Rouayheb, Khaled. (2004). Sunni Muslim Scholars on the Status of Logic, 1500–1800. *Islamic Law and Society, 11*(2), 213–232.

———. (2009). Impossible Antecedents and Their Consequences: Some Thirteenth-Century Arabic Discussions. *History and Philosophy of Logic, 30(3),* 209–225. DOI: https://doi.org/10.1080/01445340802447905.

———. (2010a). al-Khūnajī, Afḍal al-Dīn. In *Encyclopaedia of Islam, THREE*, online ed., 2015– . Edited by Kate Fleet, Gudrun Krämer, Denis Matringe, John Nawas, and Everett Rowson.

———. (2010b). *Relational syllogisms and the history of Arabic logic, 900–1900.* Leiden; Boston: Brill.

———. (2011). Logic in the Arabic and Islamic World. In H. Lagerlund (Ed.), *Encyclopedia of Medieval Philosophy* (pp. 686–692). Dordrecht: Springer Netherlands.

———. (2012). Post-Avicennan Logicians on the Subject Matter of Logic: Some Thirteenth- and Fourteenth-Century Discussions. *Arabic Sciences and Philosophy, 22*(1), 69–90. DOI: https://doi.org/10.1017/S0957423911000105.

———. (2015). *Islamic intellectual history in the seventeenth century: scholarly currents in the Ottoman Empire and the Maghreb.* New York: Cambridge University Press.

———. (2016a). Arabic Logic after Avicenna. In C. D. Novaes & S. Read (Eds.), *The Cambridge companion to medieval logic* (pp. 67–93). Cambridge: Cambridge University Press.

———. (2016b). Does a Proposition Have Three Parts or Four? A Debate in Later Arabic Logic. *Oriens, 44*(3–4), 301–331. DOI: https://doi.org/10.1163/18778372-04403001.

———. (2016c). Theology and Logic. In S. Schmidtke (Ed.), *The Oxford handbook of Islamic theology.* Oxford: Oxford University Press.

———. (2019a). Dashtakī (d. 1498) and Dawānī (d. 1502) on the Analysis of Existential Propositions. *Oriens, 2019*(3–4), 365–388. DOI: https://doi.org/10.1163/18778372-04800300.

———. (2019b). *The development of Arabic logic (1200–1800).* Basel; Berlin: Schwabe Verlag.

———. (2020a). al-Kātibī al-Qazwīnī. In *Encyclopaedia of Islam, THREE*, online ed., 2015–. Edited by Kate Fleet, Gudrun Krämer, Denis Matringe, John Nawas, and Everett Rowson.

———. (2020b). The Liar Paradox in Fifteenth-Century Shiraz: The Exchange between Ṣadr al-Dīn al-Dashtakī and Jalāl al-Dīn al-Dawānī. *British Journal for the History of Philosophy, 28*(2), 251–275. DOI: https://doi.org/10.1080/09608788.2019.1616156.

———. (2023). "Subject Generality" and Distribution in Medieval Arabic Syllogistic. *Arabic Sciences and Philosophy: A Historical Journal, 33*(2), 141–161. DOI: https://doi.org/10.1017/S0957423923000012.

Endreß, Gerhard. (1977). La controverse entre la logique philosophique et la grammaire arabe à l'époque des *khulafāʾ. Journal for the History of Arabic Sciences, 1*(2), 339–350.

———. (1986). Grammatik und Logik. Arabische Philologie und griechische Philosophie im Widerstreit. In B. Mojsisch (Ed.), *Sprachphilosophie in Antike und Mittelalter. Bochumer Kolloquium, 2.–4. Juni 1982: Bochumer Studien zur Philosophie Bd. 3* (pp. 163–299). Amsterdam: John Benjamins.

———. (2006). Reading Avicenna in the Madrasa: Intellectual Genealogies and Chains of Transmission of Philosophy and the Sciences in the Islamic East. In J. Montgomery (Ed.), *Arabic theology, Arabic philosophy: From the many to the one: essays in celebration of Richard M. Frank* (pp. 371–422). Leuven; Paris: Peeters.

———. (2012). Ibn al-Ḥammār. In U. Rudolph & R. Würsch (Eds.), *Philosophie in der islamischen Welt, 8–10. Jahrhundert* (Vol. 1, pp. 333–341). Basel: Schwabe Verlag.

Englebretsen, George. (1987). *The new syllogistic.* New York: P. Lang.

———. (1996). *Something to reckon with: the logic of terms.* Ottawa, Ont.: University of Ottawa Press.

Eskenasy, Pauline. (1988). Al-Fārābī's Classification of the Parts of Speech. *Jerusalem Studies in Arabic and Islam, 11,* 55–82.

Fallāḥī, Asad Allāh. (2013). *Manṭiq Khūnajī.* Tehran: Muʾassasah-i Pizhūhishī-i Ḥikmat va Falsafah-i Īrān.

———. (2019). Fārābī and Avicenna on Contraposition. *History and Philosophy of Logic, 40*(1), 22–41.

———. (2021). An Inquiry on Fakhr Al-Dīn Rāzī's Authorship of *Al-Manṭiq Al-Kabīr* (MS Aḥmad III, No. 3401). *History and Philosophy of Logic 42*(3), 224–46.

———. (2023). Burhān Al-Dīn Nasafī as the Author of *Al-Manṭiq Al-Kabīr* (MS Aḥmad III, No. 3401). *History and Philosophy of Logic,* ahead of print: 1–16. DOI: https://doi.org/10.1080/01445340.2022.2162320.

Fiey, Jean-Maurice. (1990). Ibn Bahriz et son portrait. *Parole de l'Orient, 16,* 133–138.

Fiori, Emiliano, & Hugonnard-Roche, Henri (Eds.). (2019). *La philosophie en syriaque.* Paris: Geuthner.

Flashar, Hellmut. (2004). Aristoteles. In H. Flashar (Ed.), *Ältere Akademie: Aristoteles-Peripatos. Grundriss der Geschichte der Philosophie / begründet von Friedrich Ueberweg. Die Philosophie der Antike* (2., durchgesehene und erw. ed., Vol. 3). Basel: Schwabe.

Fleisch, Henri. (1957). Esquisse d'un historique de la grammaire arabe. *Arabica, 4*(1), 1–20. DOI: https://doi.org/10.1163/157005857x00165.

———. (2012). Ishtikāk. In P. Bearman, T. Bianquis, C. E. Bosworth, E. v. Donzel, & W. P. Heinrichs (Eds.), *Encyclopaedia of Islam,* Second Edition. Leiden: Brill.

Flügel, Gustav. (1862). *Die grammatischen Schulen der Araber: nach den Quellen bearbeitet.* Leipzig: Brockhaus.

Fortenbaugh, William W., & al. (Eds.). (1992). *Theophrastus of Eresus: Sources for his life, writings, thought and influence.* Leiden: Brill.

Franck, Adolphe (Ed.). (1844). *Dictionnaire des sciences philosophiques, par une société de professeurs de philosophie.* Paris: Hachette.

Frank, Richard. (1956). The Origin of the Arabic Philosophical Term Anniyya. *Cahiers de Byrsa, 6*, 181–201.

———. (1978). *Beings and their attributes: the teaching of the Basrian School of the Muʿtazila in the classical period.* Albany, NY: State University of New York Press.

———. (1981). Meanings Are Spoken of in Many Ways: The Earlier Arab Grammarians. *Le Muséon, 94*, 259.

———. (1994). *Al-Ghazālī and the Ashʿarite School.* Durham, N.C.: Duke University Press.

Frege, Gottlob. (1884). *Die Grundlagen der Arithmetik: Eine logisch mathematische Untersuchung über den Begriff der Zahl.* Breslau: W. Koebner.

———. (1891). *Function und Begriff. Vortrag gehalten in der Sitzung vom 9. Januar, 1891 der Jenaischen Gesellschaft für Medicin und Naturwissenschaft.* Jena: H. Pohle.

———. (1892a). Über Begriff und Gegenstand. *Vierteljahrsschrift für wissenschaftliche Philosophie, 16*(2), 192–205.

———. (1892b). Über Sinn und Bedeutung. *Zeitschrift für Philosophie und philosophische Kritik, 100*(1), 25–50.

———. (1979). *Posthumous Writings* (P. Long & R. White, Trans.). Oxford: Blackwell.

———. (1980). *The foundations of arithmetic: a logico-mathematical enquiry into the concept of number* (2nd revised ed.). Oxford: Blackwell.

———. (1983). *Nachgelassene Schriften und Wissenschaftlicher Briefwechsel: Nachgelassene Schriften. Erweitert um einen Anhang: Nachschrift einer Vorlesung und Protokolle mathematischer Vorträge Freges.* Hamburg: Felix Meiner Verlag.

Furat, Ayşe Zişan. (1978). Ein bisher unbekanntes Werk über die grammatischen Streitfragen der Kufer und Basrer (MS ŞEHID ALI PAŞA BIBL NR. 2348). *Zeitschrift für Arabische Linguistik, 1*, 8–23.

Gabbay, Dov M., & Woods, John (Eds.). (2004). *Greek, Indian and Arabic logic* (Vol. 1). Boston; Amsterdam: Elsevier North Holland.

Gabrieli, Francesco. (2012). Adab. In P. Bearman, T. Bianquis, C. E. Bosworth, E. v. Donzel, & W. P. Heinrichs (Eds.), *Encyclopaedia of Islam*, Second Edition. Leiden: Brill.

Gadamer, Hans-Georg. (1974). Hermeneutik. In J. Ritter, K. Gründer, & G. Gabriel (Eds.), *Historisches Wörterbuch der Philosophie* (pp. 1061–1073). Basel: Schwabe.

Gaskin, Richard. (1995). Bradley's Regress, the Copula and the Unity of the Proposition. *Philosophical Quarterly, 45*(179), 161–180.

———. (2008). *The unity of the proposition.* Oxford; New York: Oxford University Press.

Gätje, Helmut. (1971). Die Gliederung der sprachlichen Zeichen nach al-Farabi. *Der Islam, 47*, 1.

Geach, Peter Thomas. (1950). Subject and Predicate. *Mind, 59*, 461–482.

———. (1957). *Mental acts: their content and their objects.* London; New York: Routledge & Kegan Paul Humanities Press.

———. (1962). *Reference and generality.* Ithaca, N.Y.: Cornell University Press.

———. (1968). *A history of the corruptions of logic: an inaugural lecture.* Leeds: Leeds University Press.

———. (1972). *Logic matters.* Berkeley: University of California Press.

———. (1975). Names and Identity. In S. D. Guttenplan (Ed.), *Mind and language* (pp. 139–158). Oxford: Clarendon.

———. (1980). *Reference and generality: an examination of some medieval and modern theories* (3rd ed.). Ithaca, N.Y.: Cornell University Press.

Georr, Khalil. (1948). *Les Catégories d'Aristote dans leurs versions syro-arabes: édition de textes précédée d'une étude historique et critique et suivie d'un vocabulaire technique.* Beirut: Institut français de Damas.

Germann, Nadja. (2008). Logik zwischen "Kunst" und "Wissenschaft": Avicenna zum Status der Logik in seiner Isagoge. *Recherches de Théologie et Philosophie Médiévales, 75*(1), 1–32.

———. (2015). Logic as the Path to Happiness: Al-Fārābī and the Divisions of the Sciences. *Quaestio, 15,* 15–30. DOI: https://doi.org/10.1484/J.QUAESTIO.5.108587.

Germann, Nadja, & Najafi, Mostafa (Eds.). (2020). *Philosophy in the Islamic World in Context.* Vol. 2, *Philosophy and Language in the Islamic World.* Berlin; Boston: De Gruyter.

Germann, Nadja, & Rivera Calero, Noel A. (2020). The Causes of Grammar: Ibn Jinnī on the Nature of Language. In N. Germann & M. Najafi (Eds.), *Philosophy and language in the Islamic world* (pp. 49–76). Berlin; Boston: De Gruyter.

Ghersetti, Antonella. (2017). Systematizing the Description of Arabic: The Case of Ibn al-Sarrāj. *Asiatische Studien/Etudes Asiatiques: Zeitschrift der Schweizerischen Asiengesellschaft/Revue de la Société Suisse-Asie, 71*(3), 879–906. DOI: https://doi.org/10.1515/asia-2017-0020.

Gibson, Martha I. (2004). *From naming to saying: the unity of the proposition.* Malden, Mass.: Blackwell.

Giolfo, Manuela, & Hodges, Wilfrid. (2018). Syntax, Semantics, and Pragmatics in al-Sīrāfī and Ibn Sīnā. In G. Ayoub & K. Versteegh (Eds.), *The Foundations of Arabic linguistics III* (pp. 115–145). Boston: Brill.

Glasner, Ruth. (2009). *Averroes' physics: a turning point in medieval natural philosophy.* Oxford: Oxford University Press.

Goldziher, Ignác. (1916). *Stellung der alten islamischen Orthodoxie zu den antiken Wissenschaften.* Berlin: Verlag der Königl. Akademie der Wissenschaften, in Kommission bei G. Reimer.

Gottheil, Richard (Ed.) (1908). *Bar ʿAlī (Ishoʾ): the Syriac-Arabic Glosses.* Rome: Reale Accademia Nazionale dei Lincei.

——— (Ed.) (2010). *The Syriac-Arabic Glosses of Isho bar Ali.* Piscataway, N.J.: Gorgias Press.

Griffel, Frank. (2007). On Fakhr al-Dīn al-Rāzī's Life and the Patronage He Received. *Journal of Islamic Studies, 18*(3), 313–344. DOI: https://doi.org/10.1093/jis/etm029.

———. (2009). *Al-Ghazālī's philosophical theology.* New York; Oxford: Oxford University Press.

———. (2011a). Between al-Ghazali and Abu l-Barakat al-Baghdadi: The Dialectical Turn in the Philosophy of Iraq and Iran during the Sixth/Twelfth Century. In P. Adamson (Ed.), *In the age of Averroes: Arabic philosophy in the sixth/twelfth century* (pp. 45–75). London; Savigliano: Warburg Institute, School of Advanced Study, University of London; Nino Aragno.

———. (2011b). Fakhr al-Dīn al-Rāzī. In H. Lagerlund (Ed.), *Encyclopedia of medieval philosophy* (pp. 341–345). Dordrecht: Springer Netherlands.

———(Ed.) (2016). *Islam and rationality. Volume 2. The impact of al-Ghazali: papers collected on his 900th anniversary.* Leiden: Brill.

———. (2021). *The formation of post-classical philosophy in Islam.* New York: Oxford University Press.

Guerrero, Rafael Ramón. (2012). Aristotle and Ibn Ḥazm: On the Logic of the *Taqrīb.* In C. Adang, M. Fierro, & S. Schmidtke (Eds.), *Ibn Ḥazm of Cordoba: the life and works of a controversial thinker* (pp. 403–416). Leiden: Brill.

Gunaydin, Muhammet. (2006). *Al-Sirafi's theory of "lingua-logical" grammar: An analytical study of the grammatical work of al-Sirafi (Sharh Kitab Sibawayhi) within the context of a discussion on language and logic in medieval Islam*. (PhD), University of Pennsylvania, ProQuest Dissertation Publishing.

Gutas, Dimitri. (1983). Paul the Persian on the Classification of the Parts of Aristotle's Philosophy: A Milestone between Alexandria and Baġdâd. *Der Islam, 60*(2), 231–267. DOI: https://doi.org/10.1515/islm.1983.60.2.231.

———. (1999). The "Alexandria to Baghdad" Complex of Narratives: A Contribution to the Study of Philosophical and Medical Historiography among the Arabs. *Documenti e studi sulla tradizione filosofica medievale, 10*, 155–193.

———. (2002). The Study of Arabic Philosophy in the Twentieth Century: An Essay on the Historiography of Arabic Philosophy. *British Journal of Middle Eastern Studies, 29*(1), 5–25.

———. (2014). *Avicenna and the Aristotelian tradition: introduction to reading Avicenna's philosophical works*. Boston: Brill.

———. (2018a). Avicenna and After: The Development of Paraphilosophy. A History of Science Approach. In A. Al Ghouz (Ed.), *Islamic Philosophy from the 12th to the 14th Century* (pp. 19–72). Göttingen: V&R Unipress.

———. (2018b). A New "Edition" of Ḥunayn's Risāla. *Arabic Sciences and Philosophy, 28*(2), 279–284. DOI: https://doi.org/10.1017/S095742391800005X.

Gutas, Dimitri, Black, Deborah, Druart, Thérèse-Anne, Sawa, George, & Mahdi, Muhsin. (1999). Abū Naṣr Fārābī. In E. Yar-shater (Ed.), *Encyclopaedia Iranica* (Vol. 9, fascicle 2, pp. 208–229). London; Boston: Routledge & Kegan Paul.

Haddad, Fuad. (1967). Alfarabi's Theory of Language. In *American University of Beirut festival book (Festschrift)* (pp. 327–351). Beirut: American University of Beirut.

Ḥasanī, ʿAbd al-Hayy. (1955). *Nuzhat al-khawāṭir wa-bahjat al-masāmiʿ wa-l-nawāẓir*. Hyderabad, Deccan: Majlis Dāʾirat al-Maʿārif al-ʿUthmāniyya.

———. (1958). *Al-Thaqāfa al-Islāmiyya fī al-Hind*. Damascus: al-Majmaʿ al-ʿIlmī al-ʿArabī.

Hasnawi, Ahmad. (1985). Farabi et la pratique de l'exégèse philosophique (Remarques sur son "Commentaire au De Interpretatione" d'Aristote). *Revue de Synthèse, 106*(117), 27–59.

———. (1988). Les théories du langage dans la pensée arabo-musulmane. In M.-A. Sinaceur & P. Aubenque (Eds.), *Aristote aujourd'hui* (pp. 218–240). Toulouse; Paris: Unesco.

———. (2008). Avicenna on the Quantification of the Predicate (with an Appendix on [Ibn Zurʿa]). In S. Rahman, T. Street, & H. Tahiri (Eds.), *The unity of science in the Arabic tradition* (pp. 295–328). Dordrecht: Springer Netherlands.

Hasnawi, Ahmad, & Hodges, Wilfrid. (2016). Arabic Logic up to Avicenna. In C. D. Novaes & S. Read (Eds.), *The Cambridge companion to medieval logic*. Cambridge: Cambridge University Press.

Hasse, Dag Nikolaus. (2000). Mosul and Frederick II Hohenstaufen: Notes on Aṯīraddīn al-Abharī and Sirāǧaddīn al-Urmawī. In B. v. d. Abeele, A. Tihon, & I. Draelants (Eds.), *Occident et Proche-Orient: contacts scientifiques au temps des Croisades. Actes du colloque de Louvain-la-Neuve, 24 et 25 mars 1997* (pp. 145–163). Turnhout: Brepols.

Hatzimichali, Myrto. (2016). *Andronicus of Rhodes and the construction of the Aristotelian Corpus*. Leiden; Boston: Brill.

Hees, Syrinx von. (2002). *Enzyklopädie als Spiegel des Weltbildes. Qazwīnīs Wunder der Schöpfung: eine Naturkunde des 13. Jahrhunderts.* Wiesbaden: Harrassowitz.

Heinemann, Arnim, Kropp, Manfred, Khalidi, Tarif, & Meloy, John Lash (Eds.). (2009). *Al-Jāhiz: a Muslim humanist for our time.* Würzburg; Beirut: Ergon Verlag in Kommission; Orient-Institut.

Hermans, Erik. (2018). A Persian Origin of the Arabic Aristotle? The Debate on the Circumstantial Evidence of the Manteq Revisited. *Journal of Persianate Studies, 11*(1), 72–88. DOI: https://doi.org/10.1163/18747167–12341317.

Hilal, Aziz. (1997). *Le livre des lettres de Farabi (Kitāb al-Ḥurūf) introduction, traduction et commentaires.* (PhD), Université Michel De Montaigne-Bordeaux, III, Bordeaux.

———. (2001). Fārābī et le problème de l'homonymie accidentelle. *Studia Islamica*(92), 155–164.

Hodges, Wilfrid, & Chatti, Saloua. (2020). *Al-Farabi, Syllogism: an abridgement of Aristotle's Prior Analytics.* London; New York: Bloomsbury Academic.

Hoffmann, Georg. (1869). *De Hermeneuticis apud Syros Aristoteleis adiectis textibus et glossario.* Lipsiae: I. C. Hinrichs.

———. (1874). *Syrisch-arabische Glossen.* Kiel: Schwers.

———. (2010). *Syrisch-arabische Glossen. Erster Band: Autographie einer Gothaischen Handschrift enthaltend Bar Ali's Lexikon von Alif bis Mim.* Piscataway, N.J.: Gorgias Press.

Hornstein, Norbert, & Pietroski, Paul. (2020). Universal Grammar. In A. Lerner, S. Cullen, & S. Leslie (Eds.), *Current controversies in cognitive science.* New York: Routledge.

Huby, Pamela M. (2007). *Theophrastus of Eresus: sources for his life, writings, thought and influence. Commentary Volume 2. Logic. With contributions on the Arabic material by Dimitri Gutas.* Leiden: Brill.

Hugonnard-Roche, Henri. (1989a). Aux origines de l'exérgèse oriental de la logique d'Aristote: Sergius de Res'aina, médecin et philosophe. *Journal asiatique, 277*(1–2), 1.

———. (1989b). Sur la tradition syro-arabe de la logique péripatéticienne. In G. Contamine (Ed.), *Traduction et traducteurs au Moyen Age. Actes du colloque international du CNRS organisé à Paris, Institut de recherche et d'histoire des textes, les 26–28 mai 1986* (pp. 3–14). Paris: Éditions du CNRS.

———. (1991). L'intermediaire syriaque dans la transmission de la philosophie grecque à l'arabe: le cas de l' Organon d'Aristote. *Arabic Sciences and Philosophy, 1*(2), 187–209. DOI: https://doi.org/10.1017/S095742390000148X.

———. (1993). Remarques sur la tradition arabe de l'*Organon* d'après le manuscrit Paris, Bibliothèque nationale. In C. Burnett (Ed.), *Glosses and commentaries on Aristotelian logical texts: the Syriac, Arabic and medieval Latin traditions* (pp. 19–28). London: Warburg Institute, University of London.

———. (1999). La théorie de la proposition selon Proba, un témoin syriaque de la tradition grecque (VIe siècle). In P. Büttgen, S. Diebler, & M. Rashed (Eds.), *Théories de la phrase et de la proposition de Platon à Averroès* (pp. 191–208). Paris: Éditions Rue d'Ulm, École normale supérieure.

———. (2009). La tradition gréco-syriaque des commentaires d'Aristote. In J. Barnes & V. Calzolari (Eds.), *L'oeuvre de David l'Invincible et la transmission de la pensée grecque dans la tradition Arménienne et Syriaque,* (pp. 151–173). Leiden: Brill. DOI: https://doi.org/10.1163/ej.9789004160477.i-238.44.

————. (2012). Le commentaire syriaque de Probus sur l'Isagoge de Porphyre. Une étude préliminaire. *Studia Graeco-Arabica, 2*, 118–143.

————. (2013). Sur la lecture tardo-antique du *Peri Hermeneias* d'Aristote: Paul le Perse et la tradition d'Ammonius. Édition du texte syriaque, traduction française et commentaire de l'Élucidation du *Peri Hermeneias* de Paul le Perse. *Studia Graeco-Arabica, 3*, 37–104.

Ibn Sīnā, Abū ʿAlī al-Ḥusayn. (1984). *Remarks and admonitions* (S. C. Inati, Trans.). Toronto, Ont.: Pontifical Institute of Mediaeval Studies.

İhsan, Fazlıoğlu. (2016). Metaphysical Thought in the Post-Rāzī Period: The Case of al-Kātibī, Mustakim Arıcı. *Nazariyat: Journal for the History of Islamic Philosophy and Sciences, 2*(4), 141–144. DOI: https://doi.org/10.12658/Nazariyat.2.4.D0029.

Inati, Shams Constantine. (1996). Logic. In S. Nasr & O. Leaman (Eds.), *A history of Islamic philosophy*. London: Routledge.

Jabre, Farid. (1973). Eἶναι et ses dérivés dans la traduction, en arabe, des *Catégories* d'Aristote. *Mélanges de l'Université Saint-Joseph*, 243–268.

Jackson, Peter. (2018). *The Mongols and the Islamic world: from conquest to conversion*. New Haven: Yale University Press.

Janssen, Jules. (2016). Abū al-Barakāt al-Baghdādī and His Use of Ibn Sīnā's *al-Ḥikma al-ʿArūḍiyya* (or Another Work Closely Related to It) in the Logical Part of His *Kitāb al-Muʿtabar*. *Nazariyat: Journal for the History of Islamic Philosophy and Sciences, 3*(1), 1–22. DOI: https://doi.org/10.12658/Nazariyat.3.1.M0035.

Joráti, Hadi. (2014). *Science and society in medieval Islam: Nasir al-Din Tusi and the politics of patronage*. (PhD), Yale University, New Haven.

Jungen, Oliver. (2007). *Geschichte der Grammatiktheorie: von Dionysios Thrax bis Noam Chomsky*. München: Wilhelm Fink.

Jurjānī, ʿAbd-al-Qāhir ibn ʿAbd al-Raḥmān. (1959). *Die Geheimnisse der Wortkunst* (H. Ritter, Trans.). Wiesbaden: In Kommission bei F. Steiner.

Kahn, Charles. (1972). On the Terminology for Copula and Existence. In A. Hourani, S. Stern, & V. Brown (Eds.), *Islamic philosophy and the classical tradition: essays presented by his friends and pupils to Richard Walzer on his seventieth birthday* (pp. 141–158). Columbia: University of South Carolina Press.

————. (1973). *The verb "be" in ancient Greek*. Dordrecht; Boston: D. Reidel.

————. (2003). *The verb "be" in ancient Greek*. Indianapolis, IN: Hackett.

————. (2009). *Essays on Being*. Oxford; New York: Oxford University Press.

Kalbarczyk, Alexander. (2012). The *Kitāb al-Maqūlāt* of the *Mukhtaṣar al-awsaṭ fī l-manṭiq*: A Hitherto Unknown Source for Studying Ibn Sīnā's Reception of Aristotle's *Categories*. *Oriens, 40*(2), 305–354. DOI: https://doi.org/10.1163/18778372-00402006.

————. (2018). *Predication and ontology: studies and texts on Avicennian and post-Avicennian readings of Aristotle's Categories*. Berlin; Boston: De Gruyter.

Kapp, Ernst. (1965). *Der Ursprung der Logik bei den Griechen*. Göttingen: Vandenhoeck & Ruprecht.

Karimullah, Kamran. (2015). Unusual Syllogisms: Avicenna and Najm al-Dīn al-Kātibī on *Per Impossibile* Syllogisms and Implication (*Luzūm*). *Oriens, 43*(1–2), 223–271. DOI: https://doi.org/10.1163/18778372-04301007.

————. (2017). Influence of Late-Antique (ca. 200–800 A.D.) Prolegomena to Aristotle's *Categories* on Arabic Doctrines of the Subject Matter of Logic: Alfarabi (d. ca. 950 A.D.),

Baghdad Peripatetics, Avicenna (d. 1037 A.D.). *Archiv für Geschichte der Philosophie,* 99(3), 237–299. DOI: https://doi.org/10.1515/agph-2017–0013.

Kaukua, Jari. (2020). Post-Classical Islamic Philosophy A Contradiction in Terms? *Nazariyat: Journal for the History of Islamic Philosophy and Sciences, 6*(2), 1–21. DOI: https://doi.org/10.12658/Nazariyat.6.2.M0110en.

Kenny, Anthony. (2015). Peter Geach. *Biographical Memoirs of Fellows of the British Academy,* XIV, 185–203.

Kerry, Benno. (1887). Über Anschauung und ihre psychische Verarbeitung. *Vierteljahrsschrift für wissenschaftliche Philosophie, 11,* 249–307.

Key, Alexander. (2018). *Language between God and the poets.* Oakland: University of California Press.

Kholeif, Fathalla. (1966). *A study on Fakhr al-Dīn al-Rāzī and his controversies in Transoxiana.* Beirut: Dar al-Mashriq.

Khuda Bakhsh Oriental Public Library. (1970–). *Catalogue of the Arabic and Persian Manuscripts in the Khuda Bakhsh Oriental Library.* Volume 21: *Encyclopaedias, Philosophy, Logic and Dialectics.* Patna: Khuda Bakhsh Oriental Public Library.

King, Daniel. (2010). *The earliest Syriac translation of Aristotle's Categories: text, translation and commentary.* Leiden: Brill.

King, Jeffrey. (2007). *The nature and structure of content.* Oxford; New York: Oxford University Press.

King, Jeffrey, Soames, Scott, & Speaks, Jeff. (2014). *New thinking about propositions.* Oxford: Oxford University Press.

King, Peter, & Shapiro, Stewart. (2005). History of Logic. In T. Honderich (Ed.), *Oxford companion to philosophy* (2nd ed.). Oxford: Oxford University Press.

Kister, Meir J. (1988). Legends in Tafsîr and Hadîth Literature: The Creation of Adam and Related Stories. In A. Rippin (Ed.), *Approaches to the history of the interpretation of the Qur'ān* (pp. 82–114). Oxford; New York: Oxford University Press.

Klamroth, Martin. (1887). Über die Auszüge aus griechischen Schriftstellern bei al-Jaʿqūbī. *Zeitschrift der Deutschen Morgenländischen Gesellschaft, 41*(3), 415–442.

Klinger, Dustin. (2019). A New Take on Semantics, Syntax, and the Copula: Note on Qutb al-Din al-Razi al-Tahtani's Analysis of Atomic Propositions in the Lawami' al-asrar. *Nazariyat: Journal for the History of Islamic Philosophy and Sciences, 5*(2), 59–80. DOI: https://doi.org/10.12658/Nazariyat.5.2.M0073en.

———. (2021). *Language and Logic in the Graeco-Arabic Tradition: A History of Propositional Analysis from the Hellenic Commentators on Aristotle to Theories of the Proposition in Arabic Philosophy, 900–1350.* (PhD), Harvard University Graduate School of Arts and Sciences. https://dash.harvard.edu/handle/1/37368232.

———. (2023). Forms of Carroll's Paradox in Post-classical Arabic Logic. *History and Philosophy of Logic, 44,* 1–16. DOI: https://doi.org/10.1080/01445340.2022.2162781.

———. (forthcoming a). The Analysis of Propositions across Avicenna's Main Works: *al-Šifā', Ḥikmat al-mašriqiyyīn, al-Išārāt wa-l-tanbīhāt.* In A. Lammer (Ed.), *Surveying the Summae: Proceedings of the Third Conference of the Avicenna Study Group.* Leiden, Boston: Brill.

———. (forthcoming b). A 6th/12th Century Arabic Attack on Peripatetic Logic: Rašīd ad-Dīn al-Waṭwāṭ's Treatise "A Doubt about *Reductio ad Absurdum*" and Its Aftermath.

In A. Ahmed, R. Strobino, & M. Zarepour (Eds.), *Logic, Soul, and World: Studies in Honor of Tony Street*. Leiden: Brill.

———. (forthcoming c). "All Knowledge Is Either Conception or Assertion": On the History and Significance of a Fundamental Distinction in Islamic Philosophy. *British Journal for the History of Philosophy*.

Kneale, Martha, & Kneale, William. (1962). *The development of logic*. Oxford: Clarendon Press.

Knobel, Franziska. (2015). Fahraddin ar-Razi, Al-Mantiq al-kabir (MS Ahmad III, no. 3401, Year 1268 A.D.): About the Uses of the Dialectics. *Oriens, 43*(3–4), 414–432. DOI: https://doi.org/10.1163/18778372–04303005.

Knuuttila, Simo, & Hintikka, Jaakko (Eds.). (1986). *The logic of being: historical studies*. Dordrecht: Springer Netherlands.

Kühn, Wilfried. (1986). Die Rehabilitierung der Sprache durch den arabischen Philologen as-Sirafi. In B. Mojsisch (Ed.), *Sprachphilosophie in Antike und Mittelalter. Bochumer Kolloquium, 2.–4. Juni 1982.: Bochumer Studien zur Philosophie Bd. 3*. Amsterdam: John Benjamins.

Kühner, Raphael. (1898). *Ausführliche Grammatik der griechischen Sprache. Zweiter Teil, Satzlehre. 3. Aufl. / in neuer Bearbeitung besorgt von Bernhard Gerth*. Hannover; Leipzig: Hahnsche Buchhandlung.

Kuşlu, Harun. (2016). *Nasîruddîn Tûsî'de önermeler mantığı*. İstanbul: Klasik.

Lagerlund, Henrik. (2008). The Assimilation of Aristotelian and Arabic Logic up to the Thirteenth Century. In D. M. Gabbay & J. Woods, Jr. (Eds.), *Handbook of the history of logic: mediaeval and Renaissance logic* (Vol. 2, pp. 281–346). Amsterdam: Elsevier Science & Technology.

Lameer, Joep. (1994). *Al-Fārābī and Aristotelian syllogistics: Greek theory and Islamic practice*. Leiden; New York: Brill.

———. (1997). From Alexandria to Baghdad. In G. Endress & R. Kruk (Eds.), *The ancient tradition in Christian and Islamic Hellenism*. Leiden: Research School CNWS.

———. (2006). *Conception and belief in Ṣadr al-Dīn Shīrāzī: al-Risāla fī al-taṣawwur wa-al-taṣdīq*. Tehran: Iranian Institute of Philosophy,

———. (2012). Ibn Ḥazm's Logical Pedigree. In C. Adang, M. Ferro, & S. Schnidtke (Eds.), *Ibn Ḥazm of Cordoba: the life and works of a controversial thinker* (pp. 417–428). Leiden: Brill.

———. (2014). غير المعلوم يمتنع الحكم عليه (*Ghayr al-maʿlūm yamtaniʿ al-ḥukm ʿalayhi*). *Oriens, 42*(3–4), 397–453. DOI: https://doi.org/10.1163/18778372–04203005.

Land, Stephen. (1974). *From signs to propositions: the concept of form in eighteenth-century semantic theory*. London: Longman.

Larcher, Pierre. (2007). Les origines de la grammaire arabe, selon la tradition: Description, interprétation, discussion. In H. Motzki & E. Ditters (Eds.), *Approaches to Arabic linguistics* (pp. 113–134). Leiden: Brill.

Lerner, Adam, Cullen, Simon, & Leslie, Sarah-Jane. (2020). *Current controversies in philosophy of cognitive science*. Milton: Routledge.

Leśniewski, Stanisław. (1992). *Collected works* (S. Surma, J. Srzednicki, & D. Barnett Eds.). Boston; Warsaw: Kluwer Academic; PWN-Polish Scientific Publishers.

Lettinck, Paul. (2011). Science in Adab Literature. *Arabic Sciences and Philosophy, 21*(1), 149–163. DOI: https://doi.org/10.1017/S0957423910000159.

Linke, Konstanze, Neitzel, Susanne, & Haas, Walter. (1977). *Die Fragmente des Grammatikers Dionysios Thrax. Die Fragmente der Grammatiker Tyrannion und Diokles. Apions Glossai Homerikai.* Berlin: De Gruyter.

Long, A. A., & Sedley, D. N. (Eds.). (1987). *The Hellenistic philosophers* (Vol. 2). Cambridge; New York: Cambridge University Press.

Lössl, Josef, & Watt, John W. (Eds.). (2011). *Interpreting the Bible and Aristotle in Late Antiquity: the Alexandrian Commentary Tradition between Rome and Baghdad.* Farnham, Surrey, UK; Burlington, VT: Ashgate.

Loucel, H. (1964). L'origine du langage d'après les grammairiens arabes. *Arabica, 11,* 57.

Ludlow, Peter, & Živanović, Sašo. (2022). *Language, form, and logic: in pursuit of natural logic's Holy Grail* (First edition. ed.). Oxford: Oxford University Press.

Mach, Rudolf, & Ormsby, Eric L. (1987). *Handlist of Arabic manuscripts (new series) in the Princeton University Library.* Princeton, N.J.: Princeton University Press.

———. (2017). *Handlist of Arabic Manuscripts (New Series) in the Princeton University Library.* Princeton, N.J.: Princeton University Press.

Madkūr, Ibrāhīm. (1934). *L'organon d'Aristote dans le monde arabe.* Paris: Vrin. [first edition].

———. (1969). *L'Organon d'Aristote dans le monde arabe: ses traductions, son étude et ses applications.* Paris: Vrin.

Mahdi, Muhsin. (1970). Language and Logic in Classical Islam. In G. E. v. Grunebaum (Ed.), *Logic in classical Islamic culture* (pp. 51–83). Wiesbaden: Otto Harrassowitz.

Maier, Heinrich. (1900). Die Echtheit der Aristotelischen Hermeneutik. *Archiv für Geschichte der Philosophie, 13,* 23.

———. (1936). *Die Syllogistik des Aristoteles.* Leipzig: K. F. Koehler.

Mandosio, Jean Marc. (2013). Logique et langage: la critique d'al-Fârâbî par Ibn Sînâ (avec des remarques sur les conceptions des stoïciens et des Frères de la Pureté). In J. Brumberg Chaumont (Ed.), *Ad notitiam ignoti: l'Organon dans la translatio studiorum à l'époque d'Albert le Grand* (pp. 311–334). Turnhout: Brepols.

Mann, Wolfgang-Rainer. (2000). *The discovery of things: Aristotle's Categories and their context.* Princeton: Princeton University Press.

Margoliouth, D. (1905). The Discussion between Abu Bishr Matta and Abu Sa'id al-Sirafi on the Merits of Logic and Grammar. *Journal of the Royal Asiatic Society of Great Britain and Ireland,* 79–129.

Marlow, Louise. (2010). A Thirteenth-Century Scholar in the Eastern Mediterranean: Sirāj al-Dīn Urmavī, Jurist, Logician, Diplomat. *Al-Masāq,* 22(3), 279–313. DOI: https://doi.org/10.1080/09503110.2010.522386.

Marogy, Amal. (2009). *Kitāb Sībawayhi: syntax and pragmatics.* Leiden: Brill.

Maróth, Miklós. (1989). *Ibn Sīnā und die peripatetische "Aussagenlogik."* Leiden; New York: Brill.

Matthen, Mohan. (1983). Greek Ontology and the "Is" of Truth. *Phronesis, 28,* 113.

Meisami, Sayeh. (2019). *Naṣīr al-Dīn Ṭūsī: a philosopher for all seasons.* Cambridge: Islamic Texts Society.

Melville, Charles. (1990). The Itineraries of Sultan Öljeitü, 1304–16. *Journal of the British Institute of Persian Studies,* 28, 55–70. DOI: https://doi.org/10.2307/4299835.

Menn, Stephen. (2008). al-Fārābī's *Kitāb al-ḥurūf* and His Analysis of the Senses of Being. *Arabic Sciences and Philosophy,* 18(1), 59–97. DOI: https://doi.org/10.1017/S0957423908000477.

Menne, Albert, & Öffenberger, Niels. (1985). *Formale und nicht-formale Logik bei Aristoteles*. Hildesheim; New York: G. Olms.

Merx, Adalbert. (1889). *Historia artis grammaticae apud Syros*. Leipzig: Brockhaus.

Meyerhof, Max. (1930). *Von Alexandrien nach Bagdad: Ein beitrag zur Geschichte des Philosophischen und Medizinischen Unterrichts bei den Arabern*. Berlin: Verlag der Akademie der Wissenschaften in Kommission bei Walter de Gruyter.

Michot, J. (1993). La pandémie avicennienne au VIe/XIIe siècle: présentation, editio princeps et traduction de l'introduction du Livre de l'advenue du monde (*Kitāb ḥudūth al-ʿālam*) d'Ibn Ghaylān al-Balkhī. *Arabica, 40*, 287–344.

Miller, Larry Benjamin. (1984). *Islamic disputation theory: a study of the development of dialectic in Islam from the tenth through the fourteenth centuries*. (PhD), Princeton University, unpublished.

———. (2012). al-Samarqandī, Shams al-Dīn. In P. Bearman, T. Bianquis, C. E. Bosworth, E. v. Donzel, & W. P. Heinrichs (Eds.), *Encyclopaedia of Islam*, Second Edition. Leiden: Brill.

———. (2019). Shams al-Dīn al-Samarqandī and the Origins of *Ādāb al-baḥth*. In M. Larkin & J. Sharlet (Eds.), *Tradition and reception in Arabic literature: essays dedicated to Andras Hamori* (pp. 129–152). Wiesbaden: Harrassowitz.

———. (2020). *Islamic Disputation Theory: The Uses & Rules of Argument in Medieval Islam*. Cham, CH: Springer.

Monboddo, James Burnett Lord. (1773–1792). *Of the origin and progress of language*. Edinburgh: Kincaid & Creech.

———. (1974). *Of the origin and progress of language*. Hildesheim: Olms.

Montanari, Elio. (1984). *La sezione linguistica del Peri hermeneias di Aristotele*. Florence: Università degli Studi di Firenze, Dipartimento di Scienze dell'Antichità "Giorgio Pasquali."

———. (1988). *La sezione linguistica del Peri Hermeneias di Aristotele*. Florence: Università degli Studi di Firenze, Dipartimento di Scienze dell'Antichità "Giorgio Pasquali."

Montanari, Franco, & Pagani, Lara (Eds.). (2011). *From scholars to scholia: chapters in the history of Ancient Greek scholarship*. Berlin; Boston: De Gruyter.

Montgomery, James. (2008). Speech and Nature: al-Jahiz, *Kitāb al-Bayān wa-l-tabyīn*, 2.175–207, Part 1. *Middle Eastern literatures, 11*(2), 169–191. DOI: https://doi.org/10.1080/14752620802223764.

———. (2009a). Speech and Nature: al-Jāhiz, *Kitāb al-Bayān wa-al-tabyīn*, 2.175–207, Part 3. *Middle Eastern literatures, 12*(2), 107–125. DOI: https://doi.org/10.1080/14752620902951124.

———. (2009b). Speech and Nature: al-Jāḥiẓ, *Kitāb al-Bayān wa-l-tabyīn* , 2.175–207, Part 2. *Middle Eastern literatures, 12*(1), 1–25.

———. (2009c). Speech and Nature: al-Jāḥiẓ, *Kitāb al-Bayān wa-l-tabyīn*, 2.175–207, Part 4.1. *Middle Eastern literatures, 12*(3), 213–232. DOI: https://doi.org/10.1080/14752620903302178.

Moraux, Paul. (1973–2001). *Der Aristotelismus bei den Griechen: von Andronikos bis Alexander von Aphrodisias*. Berlin; New York: De Gruyter.

Muḥaqqiq, Mahdī, & Izutsu, Toshihiko (Eds.). (1974). *Manṭiq wa-mabāḥith alfāẓ: majmūʿah-i mutūn va maqālāt-i taḥqīqī*. Tehran: Tehran University Publications.

Munk, Salomon. (1859). *Mélanges de philosophie Juive et Arabe*. Paris: A. Franck.

Muwaḥḥid, Ṣamad. (1988 [1367]). Athīr al-Dīn al-Abharī. In K. M. Bujnūrdī (Ed.), *Dā'irat al-ma'ārif-i buzurg-i Islāmī* (pp. 6:586–90). Tehran: Markaz-i Dā'irat al-Ma'ārif-i Buzurg-i Islāmī.

Nawas, John Abdallah. (2015). *Al-Ma'mūn, the inquisition, and the quest for caliphal authority*. Atlanta, Ga.: Lockwood Press.

Necipoğlu, Gülru, Kafadar, Cemal, & Fleischer, Cornell H. (Eds.). (2019). *Treasures of knowledge: an inventory of the Ottoman Palace Library (1502/3–1503/4)*. Leiden; Boston: Brill.

Netton, Ian Richard. (2005). *Al-Farabi and his school* (2nd ed.). London: Routledge.

Nöldeke, Theodor. (1966). *Kurzgefasste syrische Grammatik: Mit Anhang: Die handschriftlichen Ergänzungen in dem Handexemplar Theodor Nöldekes und Register der Belegstellen.* Darmstadt: Wissenschaftliche Buchgesellschaft.

Noy, Avigail. (2018). The Legacy of 'Abd al-Qāhir al-Jurjānī in the Arabic East before al-Qazwīnī's Talkhīṣ al-Miftāḥ. *Journal of Abbasid studies, 5*(1–2), 11–57. DOI: https://doi.org/10.1163/22142371–12340036.

Nuchelmans, Gabriël. (1973). *Theories of the proposition: ancient and medieval conceptions of the bearers of truth and falsity.* Amsterdam: North-Holland.

———. (1980). *Late-scholastic and humanist theories of the proposition.* Amsterdam; New York: North Holland.

———. (1983). *Judgment and proposition: from Descartes to Kant.* Amsterdam; New York: North-Holland.

———. (1992). *Secundum/tertium adiacens: vicissitudes of a logical distinction.* Amsterdam; New York: North Holland.

Nusseibeh, Sari. (2017). *The story of reason in Islam.* Stanford: Stanford University Press.

Oehler, Klaus. (1962). *Die Lehre vom noetischen und dianoetischen Denken bei Platon und Aristoteles. Ein Beitrag zur Erforschung der Geschichte des Bewusstseinsproblems in der Antike* (Hamburg: Meiner, 1985 = 2nd ed.). Munich: Beck.

Olsson, Joshua. (2016). The Reputation of Ḥunayn b. Isḥāq in Contemporaneous and Later Sources. *Journal of Abbasid studies, 3*(1), 29–55. DOI: https://doi.org/10.1163/22142371–12340021.

Ouyang, Wen-chin. (2016). Literature and Thought: Re-Reading al-Tawḥīdī's Transcription of the Debate between Logic and Grammar. In M. Pomerantz & A. Shahin (Eds.), *The heritage of Arabo-Islamic learning* (Vol. 122, pp. 444–460). Leiden; Boston: Brill.

Overwien, Oliver. (2012). The Art of the Translator, or: How did Ḥunayn ibn Isḥāq and His School Translate? In P. Pormann (Ed.), *The epidemics in context: Greek commentaries on Hippocrates in the Arabic tradition* (pp. 151–170). Berlin; Boston: De Gruyter.

Pellat, Charles. (2012). KINAYA. In *Encyclopaedia Islamica TWO*: Leiden: Brill.

Pines, Salomon. (1937). Some Problems of Islamic Philosophy. *Islamic Culture, 11*(1), 66–80.

Potter, Michael. (2000). *Reason's nearest kin: philosophies of arithmetic from Kant to Carnap.* Oxford; New York: Oxford University Press.

———. (2008). *Wittgenstein's notes on logic.* Oxford: Oxford University Press.

———. (2020). *The rise of analytic philosophy 1879–1930: from Frege to Ramsey.* New York: Routledge.

Pourjavady, Reza. (2011). *Philosophy in early Safavid Iran: Najm al-Dīn Maḥmūd al-Nayrīzī and his writings.* Leiden; Boston: Brill.

————. (2016). Jalāl al-Dīn al-Dawānī (d. 908/1502), Glosses on ʿAlāʾ al-Dīn al-Qūshjī's Commentary on Naṣīr al-Dīn al-Ṭūsī's *Tajrīd al-iʿtiqād*. In K. El-Rouayheb & S. Schmidtke (Eds.), *The Oxford handbook of Islamic philosophy* (pp. 415–437). Oxford: Oxford University Press.

Prantl, Carl. (1855). *Geschichte der Logik im Abendlande*. Leipzig: Verlag von S. Hirzel.

Primavesi, Oliver. (2007). Ein Blick in den Stollen von Skepsis: Vier Kapitel zur frühen Überlieferung des Corpus Aristotelicum. *Philologus, 151*(1), 51–77. DOI: https://doi.org/10.1515/phil-2007-0105.

Proops, Ian. (2013). What Is Frege's "Concept Horse Problem"? In P. Sullivan & M. Potter (Eds.), *Wittgenstein's Tractatus: history and interpretation* (pp. 76–96). Oxford: Oxford University Press.

Raḍawī, Mudarris. (1975–1976 [1354]). *Aḥvāl va ās̱ār-i qudvah-ʾi muḥaqqiqīn va sulṭān-i ḥukamā va mutakallimīn, ustād-i bashar va ʿaql-i hādī-i ʿashr, Abū Jaʿfar Muḥammad ibn Muḥammad ibn al-Ḥasan al-Ṭūsī, mulaqqab bih Naṣīr al-Dīn*. Tehran: Bunyād-i Farhang-i Īrān.

Ramsey, Frank. (1925). Universals. *Mind, 34*, 401–417.

Rapp, Christof. (1991). *Esti triton*—Aristotle 'De interpretatione' 10, 19b21–22. *Archiv für Geschichte der Philosophie, 73*(2), 125–128.

Rashed, Marwan. (2005). Les marginalia d'Aréthas, Ibn al-Ṭayyib et les dernières gloses alexandrines à l'Organon. In D. Jacquart & C. Burnett (Eds.), *Scientia in margine: Études sur les Marginalia dans les manuscrits scientifiques du Moyen Âge à la Renaissance (École Pratique des Hautes Études 5, Hautes études médiévales et modernes 88)* (pp. 57–73). Geneva: Droz.

————. (2014). Abū Hāshim al-Ǧubbāʾī sur le langage de l'art. *Histoire, épistémologie, langage, 36*(2), 85–96.

————. (2020). Abū Hāšim al-Ǧubbāʾī, Algèbre et inférence. *Arabic Sciences and Philosophy, 30*(2), 191–228. DOI: https://doi.org/10.1017/S0957423920000028.

Regla Fernández, Garrido. (1996). Los comentarios griegos y latinos al *De Interpretatione* aristotélico hasta Tomás de Aquino. *Emerita, 64*(2), 307–323. DOI: https://doi.org/10.3989/emerita.1996.v64.i2.233.

Rescher, Nicholas. (1964). *The development of Arabic logic*. Pittsburgh: University of Pittsburgh Press.

Resnik, Michael David. (1965). Frege's Theory of Incomplete Entities. *Philosophy of science, 32*(3/4), 329–341. DOI: https://doi.org/10.1086/288057.

Rezakhany, Hassan John. (2018). Jalāl ad-Dīn ad-Dawānī's Solution to the Liar Paradox and Its Reception in Qāḍī Mubārak and Mullā Mubīn. *Journal of South Asian Intellectual History, 1*(2), 183–220. DOI: https://doi.org/10.1163/25425552-12340007.

Robinson, Chase F. (Ed.) (2010). *New Cambridge history of Islam: the formation of the Islamic world, sixth to eleventh centuries* (Vol. 1). Cambridge: Cambridge University Press.

Rodenbeck, Max. (2000). Witch Hunt in Egypt. *New York Review of Books* (November 16), pp. 39–42.

Roman, André. (2001). Aperçus sur la naissance de la langue a partir du "Kitāb Al-Ḥuruf" d'al-Fārābī. *Studia Islamica*(92), 127–154. DOI: https://doi.org/10.2307/1596194.

Rosenthal, Franz. (1965). *Das Fortleben der Antike im Islam*. Zürich: Artemis Verlag.

————. (1975). *The classical heritage in Islam*. Berkeley: University of California Press.

———. (2007). *Knowledge triumphant: the concept of knowledge in medieval Islam*. Boston; Leiden: Brill.

Rudolph, Ulrich. (Ed.). (2012). *Philosophie in der islamischen Welt. 8.-10. Jahrhundert* (Vol. 1). Basel: Schwabe Verlag.

———. (2017). *Philosophy in the Islamic world* (R. Hansberger, Trans.). Leiden; Boston: Brill.

Russell, Bertrand, & Whitehead, Alfred North. (1910–1913). *Principia mathematica*. Cambridge: Cambridge University Press.

Sabra, Abdelhamid. (1980). Avicenna on the Subject Matter of Logic. *Journal of Philosophy*, 77(11), 746–764.

———. (1987). The Appropriation and Subsequent Naturalization of Greek Science in Medieval Islam: A Preliminary Statement. *History of Science, 25*(3), 223–243. DOI: https://doi.org/10.1177/007327538702500301.

Sayili, Aydın. (1956). Nasir-ud-Din-i-Tüsi ve Meraga Rasathanesi. *Ankara Üniversitesi Dil ve Tarih-Coğrafya Fakültesi dergisi*, 1–13. DOI: https://doi.org/10.1501/Dtcfder_0000001215.

Schironi, Francesca. (2018). *The best of the grammarians: Aristarchus of Samothrace on the Iliad*. Ann Arbor: University of Michigan Press.

Schmidtke, Sabine. (1991). *The theology of al-ʿAllāma al-Hillī (d. 726/1325)*. Berlin: K. Schwarz.

———. (2000). *Theologie, Philosophie und Mystik im zwölferschiitischen Islam des 9./15. Jahrhundrets: die Gedankenwelten des Ibn Abī Ğumhūr al-Aḥsāʾī (um 838/1434–35-nach 905/1501)*. Boston: Brill.

———. (2001–2003). Ḥellī, Ḥasan b. Yusof. In E. Yarshater (Ed.), *Encyclopaedia Iranica* (pp. XII, 164–169). New York: Bibliotheca Persica Press.

Schneider, Jakob Hans Josef. (1994). Al-Farabis Kommentar zu "De interpretatione" des Aristoteles: Ein Beitrag zur Entwicklung der Sprachphilosophie im Mittelalter. In I. Craemer-Ruegenberg & A. Speer (Eds.), *Scientia und Ars im Hoch- und Spätmittelalter: Albert Zimmermann zum 65. Geburtstag*. Berlin; New York: De Gruyter.

Schöck, Cornelia. (2006). *Koranexegese, Grammatik und Logik: zum Verhältnis von arabischer und aristotelischer Urteils-, Konsequenz- und Schlusslehre*. Leiden; Boston: Brill.

———. (2008). Name (ism), Derived Name (ism mushtaqq) and Description (waṣf) in Arabic Grammar, Muslim Dialectical Theology and Arabic Logic. In S. Rahman (Ed.), *The unity of science in the Arabic tradition* (pp. 329–360). Dordrecht: Springer.

Segonds, Alain. (1994). Calippe de Cyzique. In R. Goulet (Ed.), *Dictionnaire des philosophes antiques* (pp. 179–182). Paris: Éditions du CNRS.

Şeşen, Ramazan. (1997). *Mukhtārāt min al-makhṭūṭāt al-ʿarabiyya al-nādira fī maktabāt Turkiya*. Istanbul: Waqf al-Abḥāth li-l-Tārīkh wa-al-Funūn wa-al-Thaqāfah al-Islāmīyya.

———. (2008). Tawqīʿāt Athīr al-Dīn al-Abharī wa Shams al-Dīn al-Samarqandī. In Y. Zaydān (Ed.), *al-Makhṭūṭāt al-muwaqqaʿa* (pp. 141–147). Alexandria: al-Maktaba al-Iskandariyya.

Sezgin, Fuat. (1967–2015). *Geschichte des arabischen Schrifttums*. Leiden: Brill.

Shihadeh, Ayman. (2005). From al-Ghazālī to al-Rāzī: 6th/12th Century Developments in Muslim Philosophical Theology. *Arabic Sciences and Philosophy, 15*(1), 141–179.

———. (2006). *The teleological ethics of Fakhr al-Dīn al-Rāzī*. Leiden; Boston: Brill.

———. (2014a). Avicenna's Corporeal Form and Proof of Prime Matter in Twelfth-Century Critical Philosophy: Abū l-Barakāt, al-Masʿūdī and al-Rāzī. *Oriens, 42*(3–4), 364–396. DOI: https://doi.org/10.1163/18778372-04203004.

———. (2014b). Fakhr al-Dīn al-Rāzī's Response to Sharaf al-Dīn al-Mas ʿūdī's Critical Commentary on Avicenna's *Ishārāt*. *The Muslim World, 104*, 1–61.

———. (2014c). Rāzī, Fakhr al-Dīn al-. In I. Kalin (Ed.), *The Oxford encyclopedia of philosophy, science, and technology in Islam*. Oxford: Oxford University Press.

———. (2016a). Al-Rāzī's (d. 1210) Commentary on Avicenna's Pointers: The Confluence of Exegesis and Aporetics. In K. El-Rouayheb & S. Schmidtke (Eds.), *The Oxford handbook of Islamic philosophy* (pp. 296–325). New York: Oxford University Press.

———. (2016b). Al-Rāzī's Earliest Kalām Work. In G. Schwarb, L. Muehlethaler, & S. Schmidtke (Eds.), *Theological rationalism in medieval Islam: new sources and perspectives*. Leuven: Peeters.

———. (2016c). *Doubts on Avicenna: a study and edition of Sharaf al-Dīn al-Mas ʿūdī's commentary on the Ishārāt*. Leiden; Boston: Brill.

Soames, Scott. (2010). *What is meaning?* Princeton, N.J.: Princeton University Press.

———. (2019). Analytic Philosophy of Language. From First Philosophy to Foundations of Linguistic Science. In K. Becker & I. Thomson (Eds.), *The Cambridge history of philosophy, 1945–2015* (pp. 17–31). Cambridge; New York: Cambridge University Press.

Sommers, Frederic Tamler. (1982). *The logic of natural language*. Oxford; New York: Oxford University Press.

Sonderegger, Erwin. (1989). " . . . denn das Sein oder Nichtsein ist kein Merkmal der Sache . . . ": Bemerkungen zu Aristoteles, *De interpretatione* 3, 16 b 22f. *Zeitschrift für philosophische Forschung, 43*(3), 489–508.

Sorabji, Richard. (2005). *The philosophy of the commentators, 200–600 AD: a sourcebook* (Vol. 3). Ithaca, N.Y.: Cornell Univesity Press.

Stalmaszczyk, Piotr. (1999). *Structural predication in generative grammar*. Łódź: Wydawnictwo Uniwersytetu Łódzkiego.

———. (2000). The Notion of Syntactic Predication in Generative Grammar. *Polonica, 20*, 23–35.

———. (2010). *Philosophy of language and linguistics*. Volume 1, *The formal turn*. Volume 2, *The philosophical turn*. Berlin; Boston: De Gruyter.

———. (2014). *Philosophy of language and linguistics: the legacy of Frege, Russell, and Wittgenstein*. Berlin; Boston: De Gruyter.

———. (2016). *Philosophy and logic of predication*. Frankfurt am Main: Peter Lang.

———. (2017). *Understanding predication*. Frankfurt am Main: Peter Lang.

Stevens, Graham. (2003). The Truth and Nothing but the Truth, Yet Never the Whole Truth: Frege, Russell and the Analysis of Unities. *History and Philosophy of Logic, 24*(3), 221–240. DOI: https://doi.org/10.1080/0144534031000139237.

———. (2004). From Russell's Paradox to the Theory of Judgement: Wittgenstein and Russell on the Unity of the Proposition. *Theoria, 70*(1), 28–61. DOI: https://doi.org/10.1111/j.1755-2567.2004.tb00979.x.

———. (2005). *The Russellian origins of analytical philosophy: Bertrand Russell and the unity of the proposition*. London; New York: Routledge.

———. (2010). The Unity of the Proposition—Richard Gaskin: Book Review. *The Philosophical Quarterly, 60*(241), 869–871. DOI: https://doi.org/10.1111/j.1467-9213.2010.673_6.x.

Strawson, Peter Frederick. (1995). *The philosophy of P. F. Strawson* (P. Sen & R. Verma Eds.). New Delhi; Bombay: Indian Council of Philosophical Research.

————. (2005). Truth and predication, by Donald Davidson: review. *Times literary supplement, 5348*(September 30), 4.

Street, Tony. (2004). Arabic Logic. In *Greek, Indian and Arabic logic: handbook of the history of logic* (Vol. 1). Amsterdam; Boston: Elsevier North Holland.

————. (2005a). Faḫraddīn ar-Rāzī's critique of Avicennan logic. In D. Perler & U. Rudolph (Eds.), *Logik und Theologie: das Organon im arabischen und im lateinischen Mittelalter* (pp. 99–116). Leiden; Boston.

————. (2005b). Logic. In R. Taylor & P. Adamson (Eds.), *The Cambridge companion to Arabic philosophy* (pp. 247–265). Cambridge; New York: Cambridge University Press.

————. (2008). Arabic and Islamic Philosophy of Language and Logic. In E. N. Zalta (Ed.), *The Stanford Encyclopedia of Philosophy*.

————. (2014). Afḍal al-Dīn al-Khūnajī (d. 1248) on the Conversion of Modal Propositions. *Oriens, 42*(3–4), 454–513. DOI: https://doi.org/10.1163/18778372–04203006.

————. (2015). Arabic and Islamic Philosophy of Language and Logic. In E. N. Zalta (Ed.), *The Stanford Encyclopedia of Philosophy*. URL = <https://plato.stanford.edu/archives /spr2015/entries/arabic-islamic-language/>: Metaphysics Research Lab, Stanford University.

————. (2016a). Al-ʿAllāma al-Ḥillī (d. 1325) and the Early Reception of Kātibī's Shamsīya: Notes towards a Study of the Dynamics of Post-Avicennan Logical Commentary. *Oriens, 44*(3–4), 267–300. DOI: https://doi.org/10.1163/18778372-04403004.

————. (2016b). Kātibī (d. 1277), Taḥtānī (d. 1365), and the Shamsiyya. In K. El-Rouayheb & S. Schmidtke (Eds.), *The Oxford handbook of Islamic philosophy* (pp. 348–374). New York: Oxford University Press.

————. (2024). *The Epistle for Shams al-Dīn. Translation and Commentary of al-Kātibī's al-Risāla al-Shamsiyya*. New York: NYU Press.

Strobino, Riccardo. (2019). Varieties of Demonstration in Alfarabi. *History and Philosophy of Logic, 40*(1), 42–62. DOI: https://doi.org/10.1080/01445340.2018.1514572.

Strohmaier, Gotthard. (1978). Isḥāḳ b. Ḥunayn. In P. Bearman, T. Bianquis, C. E. Bosworth, E. v. Donzel, & W. P. Heinrichs (Eds.), *Encyclopœdia of Islam*, Second Edition (Vol. 4). Leiden: Brill.

Strohmeier, Gotthard. (1987). Von Alexandrien nach Bagdad—eine fiktive Schultradition. In J. Wiesner (Ed.), *Aristoteles: Werk und Wirkung. Paul Moreaux gewidmet* (Vol. 2). Berlin: De Gruyter.

Sürücü, Muhammed Salih. (2019). The Science of *wadʿ* and *"el-'Ucâletü'r-Rahmiyye"* (Study and Review). *Amasya İlahiyat Dergisi*(13), 557–590.

Suter, Heinrich. (1922). Beiträge zu den Beziehungen Kaiser Friedrichs II. zu zeitgenössischen Gelehrten des Ostens und Westens, insbesondere zu dem arabischen Enzyklopädisten Kemâl ed-Dîn ibn Jûnis. In J. Frank (Ed.), *Beiträge zur Geschichte der Mathematik bei den Griechen und Arabern* (pp. 1–9). Erlangen: M. Mencke.

Suto, Taki. (2012). *Boethius on mind, grammar, and logic: a study of Boethius' Commentaries on Peri hermeneias*. Leiden; Boston: Brill.

Swiggers, Pierre, & Wouters, Alfons (Eds.). (1996). *Ancient grammar: content and context.* Leuven; Paris: Peeters.

———— (Eds.). (2002). *Grammatical theory and philosophy of language in antiquity.* Leuven; Sterling, VA: Peeters.

Taha, Abderrahmane. (1978). Discussion entre Abū Saʿīd al-Sīrāfī, le grammairien et Mattā b. Yūnus, le philosophe. *Arabica, 25*(3), 310–323.

———. (1979). *Langage et philosophie essai sur les structures linguistiques de l'ontologie: Avec la traduction de la discussion rapporté par Abû Ḥayyân al-Tawḥîdî entre le logicien Mattâ Ibn Yûnus et le grammairien Abû Saʿid as-Sîrâfî et de deux autres textes.* Rabat: Faculté des lettres et des sciences humaines.

Terrier, Mathieu. (2020). ʿAllama al-Ḥillī. In H. Lagerlund (Ed.), *Encyclopedia of medieval philosophy: philosophy between 500 and 1500* (pp. 129–139). Dordrecht: Springer Netherlands.

Thom, Paul. (2019). Averroes' Logic. In P. Adamson & M. Di Giovanni (Eds.), *Interpreting Averroes: critical essays* (pp. 81–95). Cambridge; New York: Cambridge University Press.

Tillman, Chris (Ed.) (2021). *The Routledge handbook of propositions.* New York: Routledge.

Troupeau, Gérard. (1981). La Logique d'Ibn al-Muqaffaʿ et les origines de la grammaire arabe. *Arabica, 28*(2), 242–250. DOI: https://doi.org/10.1163/157005881x00249.

———. (1997). Abdīsūʿ Ibn Bahrīz et son livre sur les définitions de la logique (*Kitāb ḥudūd al-manṭiq*). In D. Jacquart (Ed.), *Les voies de la science grecque: études sur la transmission des textes de l'Antiquité au dix-neuvième siècle.* Geneva; Paris: Droz; Champion.

———. (2012). Naḥw. In T. B. P. Bearman, C. E. Bosworth, E. van Donzel, W. P. Heinrichs (Ed.), *Encyclopaedia of Islam*, Second Edition (Vol. 7). Leiden: Brill.

Tugendhat, Ernst. (1958). *Tì κατὰ τινός: Eine Untersuchung zu Struktur und Ursprung aristotelicher Grundbegriffe.* Freiburg: K. Alber.

Türker, Ömer. (2019). "Qutb al-Din al-Razi on the Notion of Assent and Its Philosophical Implications." *Nazariyat: Journal for the History of Islamic Philosophy and Sciences 5*(2), 1–23.

Türker, Ömer, & Demir, Osman (Eds.). (2013). *İslam düşüncesinin dönüşüm çağında Fahreddin er-Razi.* İstanbul: İslâm Araştırmaları Merkezi Yayınları.

Türker, Sadik. (2007). The Arabico-Islamic Background of Al-Fārābī's Logic. *History and Philosophy of Logic, 28*(3), 183–255. DOI: https://doi.org/10.1080/01445340701223423.

Ueberweg, Friedrich. (1857). *System der Logik und Geschichte der logischen Lehren.* Bonn: A. Marcus.

Vagelpohl, Uwe. (2010). The *Prior Analytics* in the Syriac and Arabic Tradition. *Vivarium, 48*(1–2), 134–158. DOI: https://doi.org/10.1163/156853410X489745.

———. (2011). In the Translator's Workshop. *Arabic Sciences and Philosophy, 21*(2), 249–288. DOI: https://doi.org/10.1017/S0957423911000038.

Vallat, Philippe. (2004). *Farabi et l'école d'Alexandrie: des prémisses de la connaissance à la philosophie politique.* Paris: Vrin.

van Ess, Josef. (1966). *Die Erkenntnislehre des ʿAdudaddin al-Ici: Übersetzung und Kommentar des 1. Buches seiner Mawaqif.* Wiesbaden: Franz Steiner Verlag.

———. (1978). Notizen zur Islamischen Theologie. *Welt des Islams, 2*(9), 255–289.

———. (1991–1997). *Theologie und Gesellschaft im 2. und 3. Jahrhundert Hidschra: eine Geschichte des religiösen Denkens im frühen Islam.* Berlin; New York: De Gruyter.

———. (2013). *Die Träume der Schulweisheit : Leben und Werk des ʿAlī b. Muḥammad al-Ǧurǧānī (gest. 816/1413).* Wiesbaden: Harrassowitz Verlag.

———. (2018). *Theology and society in the second and third centuries of the Hijra: a history of religious thought in early Islam.* Leiden; Boston: Brill.

———. (2020). ʿAŻOD-AL-DĪN ĪJĪ. In *Encyclopaedia Iranica Online*. Leiden: Brill.

Versteegh, Kees. (1977). *Greek elements in Arabic linguistic thinking*. Leiden: Brill.

———. (1997). The Debate between Logic and Grammar. In *Landmarks in linguistic thought III: the Arabic linguistic tradition* (pp. 39–47). London; New York: Routledge.

———. (2021). The Semantic Turn in the Arabic Linguistic Tradition. Unpublished paper.

Vilkko, Risto, & Hintikka, Jaakko. (2006). Existence and Predication from Aristotle to Frege. *Philosophy and phenomenological research, 73*(2), 359–377. DOI: https://doi .org/10.1111/j.1933–1592.2006.tb00622.x.

Volait, Georges. (1907). *Die Stellung des Alexander von Aphrodisias zur aristotelischen Schlusslehre*. Halle: Druck von E. Karras.

Watt, John W. (2008). Al-Fārābī and the History of the Syriac Organon. In S. Brock & G. Kiraz (Eds.), *Malphono w-Rabo d-Malphone: studies in honor of Sebastian P. Brock* (pp. 751–778). Piscataway, N.J.: Gorgias Press.

———. (2009). Al-Fārābī and the History of the Syriac Organon. *Analecta Gorgiana, 129*, 751–778. DOI: https://doi.org/10.31826/9781463214814–035.

———. (2010). Commentary and Translation in Syriac Aristotelian Scholarship: Sergius to Baghdad. *Journal for Late Antique Religion and Culture, 4*, 28–42. DOI: https://doi .org/10.18573/j.2010.10302.

———. (2013). The Syriac Aristotle between Alexandria and Baghdad. *Journal for Late Antique Religion and Culture, 7*, 26–50. DOI: https://doi.org/10.18573/j.2013.10316.

———. (2016). The Syriac Aristotelian Tradition and the Syro-Arabic Baghdad Philosophers. In D. Janos (Ed.), *Ideas in motion in Baghdad and beyond: philosophical and theological exchanges between Christians and Muslims in the third/ninth and fourth/tenth centuries* (pp. 7–43). Leiden; Boston: Brill.

———. (2017). The Curriculum of Aristotelian Philosophy among the Syrians. *Studia Graeco-Arabica, 7*, 171–192.

———. (2019a). *The Aristotelian tradition in Syriac*. Milton: Routledge.

———. (2019b). Syriac Translators and Greek Philosophy in Early Abbasid Iraq. *Journal of the Canadian Society for Syriac Studies, 4*, 15–26. DOI: https://doi.org/10 .31826/9781463216184–003.

Weidemann, Hermann. (1982a). Ansätze zu einer semantischen Theorie bei Aristoteles. *Zeitschrift für Semiotik, 4*(3), 241–257.

———. (1982b). Aristoteles über das isolierte Aussagewort: De int. 3, 16 b 19–25. *Archiv für Geschichte der Philosophie, 64*(3), 239–256. DOI: https://doi.org/10.1515/agph .1982.64.3.239.

———. (2014). *Peri Hermeneias. Übersetzt und erläutert von Hermann Weidemann* (3rd ed., vol. 1, part 2). Berlin: Akademie-Verlag.

Weiss, Bernard G. (1966). Language in orthodox Muslim thought: a study of "waḍʿ al-lugha" and its development. (PhD), Princeton University, unpublished.

———. (1976). A Theory of the Parts of Speech in Arabic (Noun, Verb and Particle): A Study in ʿilm al-waḍʿ. *Arabica, 23*(1), 23–36.

———. (1985). Subject and Predicate in the Thinking of the Arabic Philologists. *Journal of the American Oriental Society, 105*(4), 605–622. DOI: https://doi.org/10.2307/602723.

———. (1987). ʿilm al-waḍʿ: An Introductory Account of a Later Muslim Philological Science. *Arabica, 34*(3), 339–356.

Whitaker, C. W. A. (1996). *Aristotle's De interpretatione: contradiction and dialectic*. Oxford; New York: Oxford University Press.

Wiggins, David. (1984). The Sense and Reference of Predicates: A Running Repair to Frege's Doctrine and a Plea for the Copula. *The Philosophical Quarterly, 34*(136), 311–328. DOI: https://doi.org/10.2307/2218763.

Wisnovsky, Robert. (2000). Notes on Avicenna's Concept of Thingness (*šay'iyya*). *Arabic Sciences and Philosophy, 10*(2), 181–221. DOI: https://doi.org/10.1017/S0957423900000084.

———. (2004). The Nature and Scope of Arabic Philosophical Commentary in Post-Classical (ca. 1100–1900) Islamic Intellectual History: Some Preliminary Observations. *Bulletin of the Institute of Classical Studies, 47*, 149–191.

———. (2013a). Avicenna's Islamic reception. In P. Adamson (Ed.), *Interpreting Avicenna: critical essays* (pp. 190–213). Cambridge; New York: Cambridge University Press.

———. (2013b). Avicennism and Exegetical Practice in the Early Commentaries on the *Ishārāt*. *Oriens, 41*(3–4), 349–378. DOI: https://doi.org/10.1163/18778372–13413406.

———. (2014). Towards a Genealogy of Avicennism. *Oriens, 42*(3–4), 323–363. DOI: https://doi.org/10.1163/18778372–04203003.

———. (2018). On the Emergence of Maragha Avicennism. *Oriens, 46*(3–4), 263–331. DOI: https://doi.org/10.1163/18778372–04603002.

Young, Walter Edward. (2016). *Mulāzama* in Action in the Early *Ādāb al-Baḥth. Oriens, 44*(3–4), 332–385. DOI: https://doi.org/10.1163/18778372–04403003.

———. (2017). *The dialectical forge: juridical disputation and the evolution of Islamic law*. Cham, CH: Springer.

———. (2018). Al-Samarqandī's Third *Mas'ala*: Juridical Dialectic Governed by the *Ādāb al-Baḥth. Oriens, 46*(1–2), 62–128. DOI: https://doi.org/10.1163/18778372–04601003.

———. (forthcoming). *On the Protocol for Dialectical Inquiry (Ādāb al-Baḥth): A Critical Edition and Parallel Translation of the Sharḥ al-Risāla al-Samarqandiyya by Quṭb al-Dīn al-Kīlānī (fl. ca. 830/1427), Prefaced by a Critical Edition and Parallel Translation of its Grundtext: the Risāla fī Ādāb al-Baḥth by Shams al-Dīn al-Samarqandī (d.722/1322).*

Zimmermann, Fritz W. (1981). *Al-Farabi's commentary and short treatise on Aristotle's De interpretatione*. London: Published for the British Academy by Oxford University Press.

Zonta, Mauro. (2006). Al-Fārābī's Long Commentary on Aristotle's *Categoriae* in Hebrew and Arabic: A Critical Edition and English Translation of the Newly-Found Extant Fragments. In B. Abrahamov (Ed.), *Studies in Arabic and Islamic Culture (Meḥkarim be-'Arvit uve-tarbut ha-Islam)* (pp. 185–254). Ramat-Gan: Keterpress.

Founded in 1893,
UNIVERSITY OF CALIFORNIA PRESS
publishes bold, progressive books and journals
on topics in the arts, humanities, social sciences,
and natural sciences—with a focus on social
justice issues—that inspire thought and action
among readers worldwide.

The UC PRESS FOUNDATION
raises funds to uphold the press's vital role
as an independent, nonprofit publisher, and
receives philanthropic support from a wide
range of individuals and institutions—and from
committed readers like you. To learn more, visit
ucpress.edu/supportus.